C000292210

RESERVE STOCK

ARBROATH

This book is to be returned on or before the last date stamped below.

14 MAR 1987   21 MAY 1988   1 0 AUG 1994
                 25 NOV 1988   1 9 NOV 1994
1 4 APR 1987   2 3 DEC 1988
                 2 8 MAR 1989
1 9 MAY 1987
9 JUN 1987   - 2 MAR 1994   2 3 DEC 1994

30 JUN 1987   05 JUN 19
- 1 AUG 1987   3 0 MAR 1994   2 0 JUL 20
                 2 7 APR 1994
                 ANGUSalive
10 AUG 1987   1 7 AUG 2001
              Withdrawn from stock 9 NOV 2001
                                  17 JUL 2003
26 SEP 1987   - 7 NOV 2008
24 OCT 1987   2 2 JUN 1994   2 1 NOV 2014
                 21 July 94   1 3 JUL 2019
- 2 APR 1988

angus

district

libraries

28 JAN 1987

ANGUS LIBRARIES AND MUSEUMS

3 8046 00453 7790

VW BEETLE

& TRANSPORTER

GUIDE TO PURCHASE & D.I.Y. RESTORATION

LINDSAY PORTER

Foulis

Haynes

A FOULIS Motoring Book

First published 1986

©Lindsay Porter and Haynes
Publishing Group.
All rights reserved. No part of this
book may be reproduced or
transmitted in any form or by any
means, electronic or mechanical,
including photocopying, recording or
by any information storage or retrieval
system, without permission of the
publisher.

Published by:
Haynes Publishing Group
Sparkford, Nr. Yeovil,
Somerset BA22 7JJ, England

Haynes Publications Inc.
861 Lawrence Drive, Newbury Park,
California 91320 USA

**British Library Cataloguing in
Publication Data**
Porter, Lindsay
    VW Beetle & transporter : guide to
    purchase & DIY restoration.
    1. Volkswagen automobile
    I. Title
    629.28'722   TL215.V6
    ISBN 0-85429-474-0 (Hardback)

**Library of Congress Catalog Card
No.**
86-82409
ISBN 0 85429 603 4 (Softback)

Editor: Robert Iles
Page layout: Tim Rose
Printed in England by: J.H. Haynes &
Co. Ltd

**Other Haynes Publishing Group
titles of interest to the VW Beetle
and Transporter enthusiast:**

*VW Beetle 1200 Owners Workshop
Manual* (036)
*VW Beetle 1300 and 1500 Owners
Workshop Manual* (039)
*VW Beetle 1302 and 1302S Owners
Workshop Manual* (110)
*VW Beetle 1303, 1303S and GT
Owners Workshop Manual* (159)
*VW Transporter 1600 Owners
Workshop Manual* (082)
*VW Transporter 1700, 1800 and 2000
Owners Workshop Manual* (226)
VW Beetle ('54 to '77) Handbook
(439)

All of the above should be available
from good bookshops. In case of
difficulty please write to the publisher.

Dedication

I would like to dedicate this book to
two people.

One is Robert Persig, the author
of 'Zen and the Art of Motorcycle
Maintenance' because I have found so
much of what he said there quite
profoundly influential.

The other is Ivan Hirst, the man
primarily responsible for injecting
dignity and success into the all but
ruined Volkswagen factory after World
War Two.

Contents

Foreword by Ivan Hirst

(the British military government's top man at the VW factory from 1945-49 and, in the view of this book's author, the man most centrally responsible for the emergence of the Beetle in series production)

When Lindsay Porter asked me to write this foreword he referred to my "involvement with Beetles". It began in an army workshop in Normandy during 1944 when out of curiosity someone took a captured VW Kübelwagen to pieces. We had read about Hitler's people's car before the war and here it was, the open military version but in the metal. "What a strange animal", we thought, but I was impressed by some of its advanced features; it reminded me of the Lancia Aprilia, which had outstanding roadholding for its time.

My involvement became much closer in the summer of 1945 when I was seconded to military government and sent to "take charge of" the VW factory. Both the new town of Wolfsburg and the factory itself had been designed as a great showpiece of Hitler's new Germany; they had been owned by the German Labour Front, a wing of the Nazi party now abolished by Allied decree. The factory, completed just as the war had started, was built solely to produce the people's car as part of the Strength-through-Joy movement. It had repaired aircraft and built military versions of the VW during the war, but in 1944 it was heavily damaged by air attack. When I arrived the wartime foreign workers had gone, but remnants of the German management and a few key personnel were already back at work in one section of the plant, repairing all kinds of German vehicles under British army supervision. This was part of an emergency programme set up to get transport moving and controlled by one Colonel M.A. McEvoy at army headquarters.

Michael McEvoy had seen and driven one of the preproduction Beetles at a motor show in Berlin before the war, and he realised that the VW was just the light vehicle that the British needed for the occupation role, at no cost to the Treasury at home. An early Beetle was serviced and sprayed khaki green. After it had been demonstrated at headquarters, a "mandatory" order was placed on the VW company to produce cars for the British authorities. This was our signal to go ahead at Wolfsburg. By 1947 some 20,000 had been supplied to the British, US and French and for essential German services. This figure doesn't seem a high one in the light of later production levels, but it was unique in Germany at the time, when the difficulties were enormous — buildings and machine tools had to be repaired, suppliers' factories had to be brought back into production, a workforce had to be built up and housed and fed, all at a time of utter desolation, low morale and acute shortages of everything.

In 1947, the political climate was changing. Much improved cars were beginning to go to the German economy, and also for export after it had been decided that German manufacturers must export in order to offset the cost of food imports. The company had a future. The fact that it had been working for the Allies had saved Wolfsburg from closure and dismantling, to provide machines that would have gone to any of the Allied countries as "war reparations". In January 1948 an ex-Opel man, Heinz Nordhoff, started as chief executive, and in the autumn of 1949 the British military government "trusteeship" came to an end when the company was handed over as a prosperous commercial undertaking to the State government of Lower Saxony.

Looking back, my main recollections are the team spirit that developed in Wolfsburg, not only between the different British interests involved, but also with our German opposite numbers; and our growing enthusiasm for the Beetle and later its Transporter sister, which could cope with both motorways and the atrocious

secondary roads. The Beetle was fun to drive, although the nasty oversteer displayed by the early versions, with their swing axles and the tyres of the time, did lead to accidents when pushed too hard on a slippery bend! We laid great emphasis on aftersales service and parts. Many people asked whether we were not damaging exports from Britain, but we had a job to do in helping Germany back on to its feet, and our personal view was that VW exports might prompt British industry to do better.

Beetle production expanded rapidly from mid-1948 and in 1986 the car is still being built, although outside Europe. Its production run has by far exceeded that of the previous record holder, Ford's Model T — two cars entirely different, but each represented a design concept that branched off from the mainstream of motor car development!

Interest in the original VW is growing and there are many Beetle clubs in various countries, while replacement parts are available from many sources.

What attitude of mind and skills are necessary to restore a Beetle or a Transporter? I'd say first of all enthusiasm and a measure of dedication — plus an understanding spouse. Of course, some basic skills and tackle will be needed, but for the VW know-how you can turn to this book by Lindsay Porter. He has done the job himself. He is not a professional from the motor industry or repair trade but a real enthusiast with a wealth of knowledge, an amateur in the true sense of the word — who better to describe tasks step by step for other enthusiasts?

Find your car and get on with its restoration; you won't regret it. And good fortune!

Ivan Hirst
Marsden
West Yorkshire

Using this book

The layout of this book has been designed to be both attractive and easy to follow during practical work on your car. However, to obtain maximum benefit from the book, it is important to note the following points:

1) Apart from the introductory pages, this book is split into two parts: chapters 1 to 6 dealing with history, buying and practical procedures; appendices 1 to 7 providing supplementary information. Each chapter/appendix may be sub-divided into sections and even sub-sections. Section headings are in italic type between horizontal lines and sub-section headings are similar, but without horizontal lines.

2) Step-by-step photograph and line drawing captions are an integral part of the text (except those in chapters 1 and 2) — therefore the photographs/drawings and their captions are arranged to "read" in exactly the same way as the normal text. In other words they run down each column and the columns run from left to right of the page.

Each photograph caption carries an alpha-numeric identity, relating it to a specific section. The letters before the caption number are simply the initial letters of key words in the relevant section heading, whilst the caption number shows the position of the particular photograph in the section's picture sequence. Thus photograph/caption 'DR22' is the 22nd photograph in the section headed "Door Repairs".

3) Figures — line illustrations follow consecutively with the photo numbering sequence.

4) All references to the left or right of the vehicle are from the point of view of somebody standing behind the car looking forwards.

5) The bodywork repair chapter of this book deals with problems particular to the Volkswagen Beetle or Transporter. In concentrating on these aspects the depth of treatment of body repair techniques in general is necessarily limited. For more detailed information covering all aspects of body repair it is recommended that reference be made to the Haynes 'The Car Bodywork Repair Manual' also by Lindsay Porter.

6) Because this book concentrates upon restoration, regular maintenance procedures and normal mechanical repairs of all the car's components, are beyond its scope. It is therefore strongly recommended that the relevant Haynes *Beetle* or *Transporter Owners Workshop Manual* should be used as a companion volume. (There are 7 different manuals covering most models.)

7) We know it's a boring subject, especially when you really want to get on with a job — but your safety, through the use of correct workshop procedures, must ALWAYS be your foremost consideration. It is essential that you read, and UNDERSTAND, appendix 1 before undertaking any of the practical tasks detailed in this book and check with the suppliers of equipment and materials so that you have in your possesion any health and safety information relating to the work you intend carrying out. Make sure you read it!

8) Before starting any particular job it is important that you read the introduction to the relevant Chapter or Section, taking note of the 'tool box' and 'safety' notes. It is recommended that you read through the section from start to finish before getting into the job.

9) Whilst great care is taken to ensure that the information in this book is as accurate as possible, the author, editor or publisher cannot accept any liability for loss, damage or injury caused by errors in, or omissions from, the information given.

Introduction and Acknowledgements

So many good things have been said about the Volkswagen over the years that now there's almost nothing left to say, except that most compliments have been written about the Beetle and the Transporter when they were new or nearly new. This book is, at the time of writing, the only one of its type; the only one to show how to bring back to life a tired, old Volkswagen and how to repair its bodywork, mechanics and interior in ways that will last, perhaps even longer than they did originally. So what has the Beetle and its derivative, the Transporter (including campers, panel vans, personnel carriers and pick-ups) got to offer from that angle?

From the restorer's point of view, the Volkswagen has an advantage shared by no other car on earth — there are just so many of them! Around 25 million Beetles and Transporters were built, which means that, especially with Volkswagen's spares policy, there are an awful lot of Volkswagen-built spares around and there are even an awful lot of non-Volkswagen spares because it is economic for specialist manufacturers to make parts for vehicles which are still around in such prolific numbers. This is good for the owner, because there is virtually nothing that cannot be bought for most Volkswagens, and it is good for the buyer because

there are large numbers to choose from. What is more it is good for the owner in another way too: The Volkswagen sold in such large numbers simply because it was so good, and it's possible for the present day Volkswagen enthusiast to enjoy a truly great, well-engineered motor car, confident in the knowledge that it was one of the best small cars ever built and that its inherent reliability lingers on.

Of course, the reliability that was built into these vehicles when new depends upon the determination of the owner and those who work on the car to keep it there. I hope that this book shows how to keep the reliability there and how to restore it when it is diminished. If it does that, then thanks are due to a large number of people who have contributed their expertise on Volkswagens. First, I must mention Volkswagen themselves because Audi-Volkswagen in the UK, and through them Volkswagen AG in Germany, have been more helpful than any other manufacturer I have encountered as a motoring writer. They have given this book their blessing and have provided original research and other material in large quantities. In particular, Laura Warren, Suzanne, Beverley and Terry O'Donahue have been magnificent in the assistance they have given.

One of the great things about this business is the number of friends you make and Barry Haselock, proprietor of House of Haselock where virtually all of the pictures were taken for this book, has become a firm friend. I quickly came to realise why Barry is so well known throughout the UK and beyond; it's because of the friendly, enthusiastic way he handles everyone's repair, restoration or servicing problems and the vast range of repairs to Beetles and Transporters, illustrated throughout this book, are a fine testament to the work carried out by House of Haselock. On top of that, his encyclopaedic knowledge of Volkswagens was a tremendous asset. There is an awful lot of House of Haselock in this book and thanks are due to 'Baz', 'young' Barry, 'little' Barry, 'big' Stuart, 'little' Stuart, John, John (can you imagine the complications when one of them is wanted on the 'phone?), and Albert, to say nothing of Baz's missus, Angie who spoiled me something rotten when I stayed with the family.

ICI Autocolor, one of the suppliers of paint to Volkswagen themselves helped enormously with data and paint information through 'Tech Rep' Colin Pattinson. ICI also recommended Graham Maurice Cars of Leicester for carrying out some of the

7

respray sequences shown here, while a firm local to myself called Autoprep of Martley, Worcestershire, carried out the rest of the respray sequences to their usual remarkably high standards. Thanks are due to all.

Many of the parts used in this book were produced by Volkswagen but most were sold by the UK's largest independent supplier of Volkswagen parts, Uro Autospares Ltd. Their range of Volkswagen parts is vast and the quality excellent. They have been really most helpful in connection with the production of this book, and it is a pleasure to have been associated with them. Volkswagen enthusiasts are well served by a magazine known as 'VW Motoring' whose Editor and Publisher, Robin Wager (an ex-Haynes director, as it happens) produced most of the incredibly comprehensive 'Buying' section to this book. If you want any evidence of how much Robin knows about Beetles and how much 'VW Motoring' has to offer Volkswagen owners, just take a look at this section! Also contributing their special knowledge to this area of the book are Jennifer Pedler, Richard Cotton and Ronan Sill who kindly provided 'Buying' information on the Transporter, 'split-screen' Beetle and Karmann Cabriolet respectively. I mustn't forget Yvonne Berkeley, newsletter editor of the Beetle Cabriolet Club who sold me her beloved Cabrio (its restoration is featured in this book) and roped me in to the excellent and friendly owners' club. Thanks Yvonne!

The 'Tuning' section of this book was prepared by foremost Beetle tuning expert, Alan Arnold, MD of UVA Ltd of Newbury and thanks are due to him for the tremendous amount of work he put into this. Thanks are also due to Robin Wager of 'VW Motoring' magazine for allowing me to reprint this section, which first appeared in that magazine and to sub-editor Peter Dickinson for 'sorting' it all for me.

From the 'States, where most Beetles were exported, Rich Kimball, of 'Bugs for You', has ensured that there is a deal of information relevant to American owners. 'Bugs for You' specialises in parts and restorations for early Bugs and Rich has given advice, information and a whole load of 'parts' photographs. He wrote a few lines of encouragement which are repeated here on the back cover. Then, back in the UK, thanks are due to Brian Screaton of VW Books for supplying some of the pictures used in the 'Heritage' section.

Then last of all; but not least because in a very fundamental way, his contribution has been the greatest, comes Ivan Hirst (once Major Ivan Hirst) who did me the great honour of writing the Foreword to this book. Ivan Hirst is modest, self-effacing but in my view a truly exceptional man. From what I know of him, he may even be annoyed to read this eulogy, but how else other than through having such exceptional qualities could a young man, as he was then, with six years of the conflict and hatred of war behind him, with the running of an enormous but badly damaged factory and thousands of 'prisoner of war' workers in front of him, with no brief from the authorities who had put him in charge of Volkswagenwerk in 1945, for that is what I'm talking about; how else could he have turned such abject, miserable failure into an operation which was to go on to become the best of its type in the world? Ivan Hirst's qualities are to combine a mixture of wisdom and compassion such as few people

have. His wisdom led him to see what needed to be done at Wolfsberg and to consult and liaise with those best placed to advise and assist. His compassion (which is an advanced form of wisdom, after all) led him to realise that the physical needs, the dignity and the self-respect of those with whom he dealt came before the requirements of successful Volkswagen production. That ethos was to remain and the hundreds of thousands of people who have earned their living directly or indirectly through Volkswagen, and the countless millions who have enjoyed driving them, can be thankful that a man like Ivan Hirst turned up at Wolfsberg when he did.

Frankly, I'm proud to now have this association with Volkswagens. Writing this book has 'sold' me on the cars to such an extent that my wife and I own the Beetle Cabriolet which Shan proudly drives, and an Audi Coupé, made by the same company, of course. I hope some of my newly discovered enthusiasm comes over on these pages and that the reader enjoys his or her Volkswagen to the full!

Lindsay Porter
Herefordshire

1 Heritage

The First 'World Car'

All the talk among the big car makers these days is of the 'World Car', the mythical beast that will appeal to Americans, Europeans, Asians and Africans alike, a car that can be made in such huge quantities that development costs can be spread widely, making it as inexpensive as possible. Trouble is, they've been beaten to it! When Volkswagen emerged as a car manufacturer from war-torn Germany, Hitler's dream of a 'People's Car' was made reality but, thank goodness, it came from a democratic country and with a willing, highly motivated workforce.

Part of the story behind the car belongs to Hitler, because it was he who wanted to see the car built in the face of those who said it couldn't be done. But most of all, the story belongs to one of the greatest names in motoring history: Ferdinand Porsche. Porsche was a largely self-made engineer who never started from the premise that conventional was best, but was a man who was prepared to try solutions that others had not even considered. He was, of course, the source and inspiration behind the great Porsche marque, but he also designed the Volkswagen and for that achievement alone, he is

respected as one of the motoring 'greats'. The Volkswagen 'Beetle' (if you're British), 'Bug' (if you're American) or 'Kafer' (if you're German) is so much the product of one man and, to a lesser extent, his son 'Ferry' Porsche, that it's well worth taking a look at the background to this great name.

Porsche — The Founding Family

Although the word 'genius' is frequently over-worked in the case of Ferdinand Porsche no other will do! Ferdinand Porsche had a background that was humble and unremarkable. His family were artisans but his father, a stern and typically autocratic head-of-family of the day, had begun to build a small family business of tinsmiths. Ferdinand was expected to carry on the tradition, but inside the boy there was something that had its roots beyond the workaday and routine world of the tinsmith's shop.

Born in Northern Bohemia in what is now East Germany in the year of 1875, Ferdinand was an extraordinarily inventive and gifted boy for someone born into such primitive peasant surroundings. By the age of 15, and already an apprentice to his father, he was

spending his spare time experimenting with electricity, a commodity which was almost unheard of in his village near Reichenberg. His father was infuriated by his son's interest and at first did his best to stamp it out but eventually, so the story goes, he was won over when he returned home one dark evening to find his house lit brightly by electric light, the whole generator-based system having been designed and built by his son. In the days when there was no electricity to be commonly seen in use, and before the era of magazines and easy access to information, young Master Porsche's achievement must have seemed almost incredible. So, at the age of 18, he left home for Vienna where he was employed as a student-employee at the firm of Bela Egger while attending the Technical University on a part-time basis, the only formal education he was to receive.

By 1900 Porsche had left for employment with Jacob Lohner with whom he built Lohner-Porsche cars with battery powered electric motors in the front hubs. One of his designs was for a record-breaking electrically powered car which he drove himself at a mean speed of over 40 kph over an uphill 10 km course. His next technical feat was the design of a 'mixed' car, using

a petrol engine to generate electric current which drove motors mounted in each front wheel hub, thus pre-dating the front-wheel-drive trend by over half a century and the 'mixed' experiment by even longer. This system had some spectacular and, nowadays, half forgotten uses. In the First World War, Porsche's 'mixed' system was used to power a line of wagons, each with its own electrically powered hubs, the power generated by the traction engine in the lead. Porsche's ingenious steering system which enabled each successive wagon to follow the line of the wagon in front instead of cutting the corner was coupled to a brilliantly simple way of getting the whole heavy assembly over bridges built to take only light loads: First, the traction engine would be uncoupled and driven over the bridge then each wagon would be connected by lengthy electric cable and driven over under its own power one at a time until the whole wagon train could be re-formed.

Military projects always featured large in Porsche's designs. He helped to make Austria one of the world's leading aero-powers of the day, in spite of having been cut down to a small country in the wake of the First World War. One of his aero engines was actually an air cooled, overhead valve flat four – a configuration which was to be very significant in the Porsche story in years to come.

After spending some time with Austro-Daimler (he left acrimoniously), Ferdinand Porsche eventually joined Daimler in the early 1920s as Technical Director with a seat on the board. There his most famous designs included the SS, SSK and SSKL seven-litre models. But in 1928, Porsche returned to Austria to join Steyr in an apparent attempt to take on Austro-Daimler on their own terms. The move was to prove significant because Steyr collapsed in 1929 and were taken over, in effect, by a merchant bank – one which was allied to Austro-

Daimler. Needless to say, Ferdinand Porsche was out of a job!

With typical energy, Porsche embarked upon the next stage of his life with hardly a pause. He returned to Stuttgart in Germany, the home of Daimler and set up an independent design house with an all-Austrian team of design engineers including men who were to have a decisive impact on the shape of Porsche designs to come. The team included Porsche's 21-year-old son (who was also called Ferdinand but who, perhaps mercifully, went by the familiar name of Ferry).

Historically speaking, the most important contract in those early days was that from the Zundapp motorcycle factory for a 'Volksauto' as it was called. Back in 1931, the Porsche concern had filled time by developing a purely speculative design of car which they felt was right for the climate of the day. It was to be small but robust and cheap to run and when Zundapp came along in 1932, they felt that the new Porsche project was the sort of thing they were looking for. Although a five-cylinder radial engine was favoured by Zundapp, some of the other specifications now look more familiar: It was to be of 1192 cc (97.5 cu. in.) with beetle-backed streamlined styling featured on two of the prototypes and all round independent suspension. The wheelbase was 2500 mm (97.5 in.). Although three prototypes were built, the car never went into production but in 1931, Porsche had patented the torsion bar independent front suspension with trailing arms and transverse torsion bars enclosed in a tube and that was later to find favour in the Volkswagen and beyond.

Also in 1932, Porsche visited Russia and was there offered the position of State Designer in charge of all vehicle production but it was doubtful whether his free-ranging talents would have found sufficient scope under the Soviet system and he declined the

offer. However, when the chairman of the motorcycle company NSU approached Porsche with a request for the design of another small car, Porsche took the opportunity to refine the Zundapp concept. This time a further link in the Beetle's evolutionary chain was forged when an air-cooled flat-four engine was placed in the rear position in combination with swing axles. The newly patented torsion bar suspension was also featured but once again, the project was cancelled.

In the meantime, a development was taking place which was central to the evolution of another story (See Porsche 911: Guide to Purchase & DIY Restoration by the same author) as Porsche started the design of his own racing car, but that is a tale quite incidental to the development of the Volkswagen Beetle. In 1933 a Nazi (or 'National Socialist') Government came to Germany. Everyone knows of the brutal, inhuman features of the Nazis, but it is worth remembering that their popularity was founded in part on a kind of 'socialism' that promised both glory and material gain to the common man – or at least those who were considered racially suitable. Part of the 'glory' was to be found in proving that the Aryans were superior in every sphere and that included motor racing. Large sums of government money were split between Mercedes and Auto-Union to develop all-conquering racing and speed record cars and Porsche was approached by the latter company to design them such cars.

So much for the glory. Hitler appealed to the motorist-in-the-street directly by planning to abolish car taxes and licences and by building newer, straighter, faster Autobahnen across Germany's large stretches of land. Moreover, the motor car was to be within the reach of everyone who wanted one and Hitler met Ferdinand Porsche in late 1933 to discuss the possibility of

designing a car cheap enough and robust enough to do the job.

On 17 January 1934, Porsche submitted a proposal in words and drawings setting out his plan. The new car was essentially what we would now recognise as a Volkswagen except that alongside the drawing of a flat-four engine was an alternative suggestion, stemming no doubt from the Zundapp prototype and Porsche's aero-engine experience, of a three-cylinder, two-stroke radial engine. (Interestingly, part of the flat-four engine development had been carried out by an Englishman, Walter Moore who, as NSU's Technical Director in the early '30s, worked with Ferdinand Porsche on the design for the still-born NSU: He had previously been involved with the 1904 Fairy motor cycle, the first ever motor cycle with a flat-twin engine. The layout of the Porsche engine was basically Porsche's own, however). The tubular chassis was different from the car that was eventually to follow, but the body styling was eminently recognisable as a 'Beetle'. The car was to be capable of prolonged high-speed work on the new roads, its suspension had to be capable of soaking up the worst bumps of the primitive subsidiary roads and the body had to be capable of carrying a full German family, whilst, being sufficiently aerodynamic so as to be reasonably frugal on fuel. Above all, the car had to be built to a price — although in practice, government subsidy would see that it was met — and that price was to be RM990 or about £86 ($345). Hitler developed an imaginative way of paying for the car which would encourage saving and bring in government revenues at the same time: Buyers were to participate in Hire Purchase in reverse by saving a set amount each month until the car was paid for and then saving a further RM200 in compulsory insurance before taking delivery. Porsche negotiated with the Government so that, should the car see production, he would receive a

royalty on each one and in June 1934, the go-ahead was given to produce prototypes of the Type 60, as it was known on Porsche's books, but only after Hitler himself had examined and slightly modified the planned shape of the car, reportedly commenting that, "It should look like a Beetle".

The first two prototypes, a saloon and a cabriolet, were produced, it is said, in Porsche's own double garage at his home and were tested and running in the Black Forest area by the end of 1935. A variety of air-cooled engines were tried but none of these early motors were to find favour. Finally, another Austrian engineer named Reimspeiss joined Porsche and quickly designed a four-cylinder air-cooled boxer engine which was actually cheaper to produce than the inadequate two- and four-cylinder units previously considered and found wanting. The engine, known as the E-motor, had a capacity of 985 cc and was an amazing blend of simplicity in concept, and efficiency in use. It went on to power 25 million Volkswagens over the next half-century. Incidentally, Reimspeiss received RM100, or £8.59 ($34.50) as a financial reward for his inventiveness!

In October 1936, three fully running Volkswagens, or 'people's cars' known as 'VW3' were handed over for testing. A punishing test routine found weaknesses in the cars' cranks, fuel pumps, front suspension and cable brakes, but all the problems were resolved or deemed resolvable: All that is, except the price, which it was found could not be met. As a total dictator, Hitler had the power to over-ride even that objection and a complex system of funding was set up, using the funds confiscated from the abolished trade unions and by docking the labour force's wages by 1½% — which was in effect an extra tax.

At the next stage of prototype production, headlamps were placed in the wings and the

continued lack of a rear window, supplanted by the use of cooling louvres gave the car an even more beetle-like appearance. The thirty examples were tested to an extraordinary degree, mostly by members of Hitler's notorious SS, with over 2 million kilometres being covered. No wonder that, mechanically, they got it right!

In 1938, a further 44 cars were built with split rear screens and bumpers and in the same year the foundation stone was ceremoniously laid by Hitler at a site about 50 miles East of Hanover in Northern Germany for the factory to build the new car which, it was decided, was to be called the Kdf-Wagen; Kdf standing for Kraft durch Freude or 'Strength through Joy', a strange piece of sloganeering to modern ears, but which was in fact also the name of the 'leisure' section of the state-run substitute for the trade unions. Then, on 1 January 1939, the savings scheme method of buying the Kdf-Wagen was announced but by then, aggression, expansion and world war were inevitable and the money was to be earmarked for other things.

The German invasion of Poland and the British declaration of war in September 1939 did not deter the Germans from producing 630 Volkswagens in order to 'prove' the production equipment but demands on space in the newly-built factory came primarily from the German air-force whose airframes were repaired there, and from the munitions side of the things and so the 'Beetle's' production machinery was mothballed. However, the efficiency of the basic design and Porsche's flair for turning his genius to anything mechanical meant that the Volkswagen was destined to be adapted for the uses of the German armed forces.

In 1938, the inventive Reimspeiss had begun work on a cross-country VW known as the Type 62. This developed into the Kubelwagen, or bucket car which was refined by Porsche's son,

Ferry, into the Type 82. This was itself refined and adapted as the war progressed, including versions for different operating conditions such as mud or desert and even a model with half-tracks for arctic conditions. In 1940, a pinnacle of ingenuity was reached when the Schwimmwagen was introduced. This had optional two- or four-wheel drive and a rear propeller that could be lowered into position when the vehicle, which was sealed all round, was in the water. This made it a true go-anywhere, amphibious vehicle capable of carrying four soldiers. It was fitted with an enlarged 1131 cc (up from 985 cc) version of the engine while the smaller engine was also used in some applications as a stationary engine.

Porsche was also responsible for the design of the most powerful of all World War Two tanks, the Tiger, and the Maustank which used his mixed drive petrol-electric system once again. He also designed a version of the V1 jet-propelled missile which was produced at Volkswagenwerk. After the war, Porsche was condemned by some for his involvement with the Nazis and was arrested and detained for two years by the French during which time, it is said, he actually contributed to the design of the new post-war Renault 2CV; a further indication that his approach was one of an engineer who did not trouble himself with politics or nationalism. In fact, from this distance in time and comprehension it is impossible to judge the man, but it is perhaps worth making two observations: The first is that, just as any engineer or scientist who works on weaponry, he knew what the results of his actions would be and as such he was one of the 'universal soldiers' of Donovan's '60's anti-war song. But the second is that involvement in war destroys judgement, as we have seen time and again in all countries and, what is more, Porsche did not have our historical

perspective of knowing the evil effects of Fascism and of rascism. Let's be charitable and leave it at that. What is certain is that he left a unique car, something which is in itself free of any such value judgements and which actually contributed in no small way to the peace and relative unanimity of modern Europe by helping the German economy to recover its strength and the German workforce to recover its pride and its place among fellow Europeans after the close of the War.

Although Hitler's KdF-Wagen never saw production as the 'People's Car', it certainly saw production as the soldier's car! The air cooling meant that the military versions were as suitable for the boiling heat of Libya as they were for the freezing temperatures of the Russian front – simply because there was no water to boil or to freeze. The incredible mechanical sturdiness of the vehicle, its impressive traction from rear-engine, rear-wheel-drive and the ease with which engine and transmission could be removed and serviced made the Volkswagen military vehicle an asset to the German Army. Its sister vehicle, the Schwimmwagen, was then an amphibious four-wheel-drive military vehicle which, unlike the Jeep, floated without the aid of ballast tanks, used little fuel and carried out its duties in typically admirable Porsche style. Interestingly enough, the concept of the Kubelwagen (which means 'bucket car') was resurrected in August 1979 when it was known as the Type 181. Produced at Hanover, the 'Kubelwagen' as it is still known, started with a 1500 cc engine, but a 1600 cc soon followed. It also started with genuine Kubel-style swing axles and Transporter-type reduction gears in the rear hubs to increase ground clearance but the Beetles semi-trailing-arm layout with double-jointed drive shafts were soon substituted. The post-war 'Kubelwagen', produced only in Mexico from 1973, was a strange

but effective mixture of parts from other air-cooled cars in the Volkswagen range. It was used as an austere transporter for field or battle and farmer's field alike and also by those who just have to drive something that is completely 'different'.

But by 1945, no actual production of the 'People's Car' had taken place, the 600-odd vehicles produced early in the War having been to 'prove' the production equipment which was then mothballed and, as the fighting closed in on Wolfsberg, spread around 'dispersal sites' in the surrounding countryside to save some of it from bomb damage.

At the close of the War, Germany was split up between the Allies who each governed a sector. The British, in whose sector Wolfsberg lay, appointed a Military Government to run the area, one such officer being a 29 year old Major by the name of Ivan Hirst. Hirst had been trained in optical and instrument engineering, he had dealt with Germans through his father's business before the War and had run a tank repair workshop during the hostilities. He must have seemed perfect for the job at Wolfsberg!

When he arrived there in August 1945, he found a partly devastated factory, a demoralised war-time German labour force, or what was left of it. The Nazi's slave labourers had, of course, been repatriated, but not before extracting a terrible revenge on some of the buildings and people of the town, (some of whom had to be dismissed because of Nazi party connections), and a detachment of British Army's REME mending trucks and putting together a few Keubelwagens. And even more importantly, the Army were keeping out those who wanted to ship out the plant as reparations to Allied countries (it was never, as popular myth has it, offered formally to any country or car manufacturer) and those who wanted to destroy the place,

considering it to be capable of armaments production — which of course it was, the factory and town not having existed prior to 1939.

In Ivan Hirst, Volkswagen the company, Wolfsberg the town and even Germany the Country were incredibly fortunate. By little more than chance, a strong-willed individual of considerable determination, foresight and, unusually in such a man, compassion had been chosen for the job. Among his first acts were to have Army sappers repair the bomb damaged sewerage systems because hygiene was a problem in the August heat. Another was to re-activate the three farms owned by the factory and to bring even the frontage before the Administrative Block into food production because Germany was then a starving nation. He considered producing the Keubelwagen in order to put the factory back to work but the body supplier, Ambi-Budd in Russian controlled Germany had been totally destroyed. But the Beetle plant was still largely intact! He took one of the 1942 Beetles which had been returned to the factory for repairs and had languished there when the Allies moved in, sprayed it khaki and had it driven to British Army HQ. They immediately ordered 5,000 and Volkswagen were in business. Orders from all of the other Allies followed and in late 1945, using the most incredibly ingenious means to obtain supplies, materials and even coal to drive the plant's electricity generators, production was painfully restarted. Ivan Hirst maintains to this day that what was done then and subsequently was the result of a team effort, English and Germans together, and that must be true but consider the following:

Assemblies of Germans were banned, but Hirst obtained special permission to have the workers elect their own Works Council to decide on working practices, holidays, hours and the like. It exists to this day and was the benchmark of the co-operative process that has marked Volkswagen. When exports finally started, it was Hirst who insisted that dealers took a full complement of spares as well as the cars, leaning on his wartime experiences of keeping equipment maintained and running. This also became one of Volkswagen's hallmarks. He established the 'exchange' reconditioned unit system to Volkswagen and initiated the writing of comprehensive manuals, the like of which had not been seen there before.

During Hirst's entire time there, there was a continuous search for the right management team, and this was gradually built up to form the basis of the management team that was to see Volkswagen prosper. In 1947, Hirst interviewed Heinz Nordhoff, ex-Opel General Manager who was banned from working for Opel because they were in the US sector and the American authorities refused to allow anyone who had been a Nazi party member — which Nordhoff had been, although as a formality for someone in his position, it is said, — to work at high level. Hirst was looking for a Deputy Manager but after a two-day interview, Hirst was so impressed by his background and technical ability ("We were having problems with the differential gear cutting tools — Nordhoff was one of the very few who understood how the thing worked," said Hirst) that he offered him the post of General Manager. From that point on, Hirst allowed Nordhoff more and more to be his own man, "waiting to catch him if he fell, as so many had done before" but in 1949, Hirst left Wolfsberg to become Director of a German State until national autonomy was reinstated in the mid-50s. He had turned a potential disaster into a company with a future and whose features were already established. Much of what Volkswagen represented thereafter was due to Ivan Hirst, although as a highly modest man, he would be the last to claim it.

It is interesting to wonder what would have happened had Hirst been able to have put the Keubelwagen into production and not the Beetle. As it was, the Beetles mechanical components had been well tested in the military vehicle.

The Porsche story, indicentally, really begins to take on a life of its own from this point on as the Volkswagen royalties enabled Ferry Porsche, son of the brilliant founder, to develop his own variant on the Volkswagen mechanical theme; a story that is just as remarkable in its own, entirely different way. Ferdinand Porsche died in January 1951, but his son's company has developed a product and a name that is every bit as famous all over the world as that of Volkswagen itself. But in the meantime, Nordhoff had stamped his own personality on the Volkswagen, although in an altogether more prosaic way. He found that the Volkswagen as it stood and as it was being produced under the management of the British Armed Forces was too unreliable. The Army were after all doing a job with the sort of social and economic implications that no Army would normally expect to have to control while technological advances in the hothouse atmosphere of armed struggle had made some of the car's specifications obsolete. Nordhoff had every single aspect of the car examined and redesigned so that every single component was altered from the original. The result was the superb reliability for which the Volkswagen name became a by-word and without which the car would surely never have prospered.

In 1950, the Kubelwagen's stepped-down transmission which had given it extra ground clearance was used with the standard 'Beetle' engine in a new model, the VW Transporter. It was initially built at Wolfsberg, but demand was high and after a while, production had to be

transferred to a new factory built at Hanover which began production in 1956. The stepped-down transmission lasted on the Transporter right up until 1968.

Other Volkswagen production facilities also became necessary to supplement the Wolfsberg facility. Front axles were produced at the Brunswick plant, which had actually first opened in 1938. In 1958 a new works opened at Kassel for the production of transmission parts, new components arriving at, and completed cars departing from Volkswagen's own massive railway terminal inside the factory complex.

Once Volkswagen exports got under way, the Beetle was received with very great interest in both Britain and America, but attitudes to the Volkswagen were rarely merely neutral: Folk either loved it or hated it! Stick-in-the-mud types scoffed at the rough sounding air cooled engine, the relatively low power output and what were often described as 'flimsy' body panels (we'd think of them as heavy gauge today!) but they ignored the engineering excellence, good fuel economy on poor grades of petrol and the intelligent weight-saving qualities of the car. 'Beetle' fanatics however, saw nothing but good in their cars, one American road tester going so far as to say, "the Volkswagen just seemed to glide, engine noise and vibration was negligible" and "the car proved itself as comfortable as most American cars". Hmmm!

By 1952, demand for the car had grown at a giddy rate, its unburstable qualities coupled with the fact that it was so 'different' from anything that the neighbours might have, made the car a top seller on two continents; in fact by 1953, the Volkswagenwerk production line was already one mile long! In the same year, the 'Beetle', still with its split rear screen, gained synchromesh on the gears and the process of continuous improvement inside a body shell with more or less fixed

appearance was well under way.

Early Beetles compared well with other small cars of the era. In 1982 the author helped to organise 'back-to-back' road test between an immaculate and original 1952 Beetle and its nearest British competitor, an equally immaculate 1952 Morris Minor. In terms of creature comfort, the Beetle came off worst and it was also the noisier of the two cars. Its roadholding was comparable with that of the Minor even though its ride was a little softer, although it is well known that at the limits, the Beetle's tail is liable to come round and bite the driver, especially when the car is being driven in the wet. Surprisingly, in view of the widespread criticism of the Beetle's power output, it was the faster of the two cars while both had adequate brakes. On the face of it, the Minor may have appeared the better bet, but it departed the motoring scene in 1971 with just over 1½ million having been built, while the Beetle lasted a further ten years or so and 15 times more were built! It's qualities were to be found other than in a road test!

The first two Volkswagens were imported into the United States in 1949 and although they were at first regarded as little more than curiosities when standing alongside their relatively monstrous American counterparts, they were the forefathers of a line that was to become the cornerstone of the company. Nordhoff had to search high and low for dealers to handle his car at first and the earliest was an existing car importer called Hoffman. Sales to the U.S. through the Hoffman franchise reached the figures from 1950 through to 1954 of: 390; 601; 980; 6343 per annum, but after Volkswagen introduced their own dealer bases in 1955, sales immediately jumped to over 36,000 Beetles plus 3000 Transporters in the same year. By 1964, sales were at ¼ million and were an amazing 70% of the total number of cars imported into the U.S. (In fact in 1968, the peak

year for the Beetle in the 'States, almost half-a-million Beetles and Transporters were imported into the country.) So, it was not long before dealership became a privilege to be guarded and when that happened, Nordhoff could dictate the terms under which he allowed dealerships to continue. Following the policy intiated by Ivan Hirst, he insisted that very large quantities of spares were carried and in fact mythology had it that for every car imported, another car's worth of spares had to be carried by the dealerships.

The very existence of stories like that were indicative of the wider sweep of Volkswagen's policies in the area of Marketing. The company's advertising policies turned conventional ad-man wisdom upon its head: Instead of claiming that their cars were bigger, faster, showier than those of the opposition, which of course they were not, Beetle ads pointed out the virtues of a body style that didn't change from year to year, an engine that could be run all day at its maximum speed without ever blowing itself up and all the other non-aggressive, non-materialistic reasons for buying a motor car that you could think of! Neither did they hesitate to poke fun at themselves in their adverts. Who ever heard of a car company doing such a thing? Well, evidently no-one had because the advertisements, the cars' endurance feats in cross-continental type rallies, the reliability and, in U.S. terms, the low running costs made their own mark on the buying public's mind and, quite simply, they went out and bought the car in vast numbers.

The 100,000th Beetle was produced in March 1954 and from then it took only until April 1955 before the millionth car was produced. Production changes were made to the car, in spite of its fairly constant appearance and in fact they were made in very great numbers. Most of them took place at the introduction of a 'model year' which was the start of

a 'new' year for the company every August, after the annual holidays. Early in 1953, the first major change was made to the appearance of the car when the split rear screen, first used in 1938, was dropped in favour of a one-piece screen. Then in 1954 the engine's capacity was raised from 1131 to 1192 cc.

In 1956, Volkswagen made a radical departure from tradition. They were undoubtedly worried by their 'one-model' line-up and introduced a more sporty looking car based on standard Beetle chassis, engine and running gear. Produced by Karmann and called the Karmann Ghia, after the Italian styling house, Ghia, who had styled it, the car's looks were in direct contrast to its performance and somehow, the sound it emitted never quite matched its visual appeal: In any case, it was never anything like as successful as the Beetle itself. 1956 was also the year in which Germany overtook Britain as Europe's largest producer of motor cars and the 'Fifties and 'Sixties also saw satellite plants open in Brazil, Australia and Mexico for the production of Beetles.

In 1961, Nordhoff had another go at widening the company's model range when the Volkswagen (it had long been recognised as the company name) 1500 was introduced. It was based on Beetle mechanics, though with a number of significant differences, but when production finally came to an end in 1973, a 'mere' 2.3 million had been produced: It was no successor to the Beetle! In 1965, Volkswagen tried another approach and purchased Auto Union, which included the defunct Audi name. Volkswagen kick-started the name back into life with the conventionally produced Audi 70 of 1965, giving them another string to their bow and starting yet another motor car dynasty which continues to this day.

Nordhoff's worst fears began to be realised in the mid-'60s

when the German economy began to slow down and when Italy's Fiat took over Europe's No. 1 position as a manufacturer. In 1965, the Beetle's engine size was again increased, this time to 1285 cc and fitted to an additional model, the 1300 Beetle. Then in 1966, a 1500 Beetle with 1493 cc engine and an automatic option was introduced. In 1968, the year in which the legendary Heinz Nordhoff died, yet another attempt to break out of the Beetle shell was made with the introduction of the 411 with a rear mounted 1679 cc flat-four engine. In spite of the introduction of the 1795 cc, fuel injected replacement, the 412 model was Volkswagen's biggest failure and was scrapped in 1974 after only 400,000 were built.

Then, in 1969, an attempt was made to join with Porsche themselves in a bid for both makers to build a low-cost, high-performance car that stood somewhere between Porsche's exotic image and Volkswagen's more workaday appeal. Sadly, there were problems between the two companies and when the car arrived, it appeared as the classical compromise. It was unattractive, it lacked the appeal of either company's main products, but in all just over 100,000 of the VW 4-cylinder cars were produced and a relative handful of the 6-cylinder Porsche engined cars were made.

Over the years, Volkswagen's changes to the Beetle were generally so minor in nature that when front and rear suspension was re-designed, with MacPherson struts appearing at the front and semi-trailing arm rear suspension taking much of the sting out of the rear, the company was moved to designate it as a new model of Beetle called the 1302. Also, two suffixes were added to the numbering of each Beetle: An L after the car's number indicated that it was fitted with factory accessories while an S meant that it was the most powerful Beetle then available. As the decade progressed, model numbering

became incredibly complex as an increasing range of options on the basic theme was constantly being expanded.

In 1974, potential disaster faced Volkswagen as the steam went out of Beetle sales. The replacement that everyone knew was essential seemed to be impossible to find and an international recession induced by the Arab-Israeli war and a huge rise in the price of oil took its toll. The company made it first ever loss – and it was a big one! £142 million was a great deal of money to throw away in 1974, and the company approached the threat of bankruptcy. In the previous year, however, another new model had arrived. The Audi 80-derived Passat was the first in a succession of new-look Volkswagens and then in 1974, the Scirocco appeared, both cars bearing the heresy of front engine and front wheel drive. Neither were conceivably considered as a Beetle replacement and it soon became apparent that the company were intent on replacing one model with a range of cars, following the approach of every other major manufacturer. Their next and most important new model, the Ital-designed Golf (known as the Rabbit in the U.S.) was also front-engine, water-cooled and front-wheel drive and represented as clean a break from the Beetle concept as any that could be imagined.

With the 1976 model year, the Beetle range started to be cut back and by 19 January 1978, when the last German built Beetle saloon left Volkswagenwerk, just four variants were produced. But the Beetle story was far from over! Cabriolet production continued for U.S. spec. cars only until 10 January 1980, but even then production still continued in various parts of the world but principally in Brazil and Mexico. In fact small shipments of South American Beetles, complete with a body styling which had earlier been discontinued in Europe, were continuing to be shipped to

Germany until 1985 at the very least.

Cabriolet – the Fun Bug!

It is not quite accurate to regard the Cabriolet as just a Beetle with a soft-top: In fact all of the cars (but for a small and interesting handful) were built by Karmann, a relatively small firm of coachbuilders who fitted all the best optional-extras currently available on the saloons . They also fitted substantial strengthening box-section which can easily be seen running lengthways between the wheel arches and a little way in from the outer edges of the floorpan.

The firm of Karmann was founded in 1874 as coachbuilders and built their first car bodies at the Osnabruck works in 1902. In 1949, they produced one of the two – only brands of Beetle convertibles recognised by VW. Not only were Karmann in almost right at the start of Beetle production – the first Karmann proposals for a Beetle Cabrio were presented as early as 1946 – they also had the honour of producing the last of the German-built Beetles, constructing Cabriolets to American specification for about a year after Wolfsberg ceased production. From 1970 to 1976, it was very difficult to get hold of Cabriolets in right-hand-drive form.

All of the Karmann-built Cabriolets (they all carry a badge near the fuel filler cap with the Karmann logo) were full four seaters. The soft-top folds down high on the tail in typical German style, but it does leave the rear seats completely unimpeded for the rear passengers.

Not everyone knows about the rather prettier 2+2 seater Cabriolet also based on the Beetle and also factory-recognised, but which ceased production in 1951 after only two years of production. In the following year, the makes, Hebmuller, another established

coachbuilding firm went bankrupt and the Hubmuller Cabriolet was no more. It seems rather sad that only around 700 of these extremely attractive cars were built.

On the other hand, over 315,000 Karmann Cabriolets were built during over thirty years of production but even so, there are not too many available for sale at any one time and the cars have a true cult status among enthusiasts.

Karmann Ghia – the Coachbuilt Beetle

The Osnabruck firm of Karmann became involved with another variant on the Beetle theme when the Italian styling house Ghia designed a new body for the Beetle, the resulting car being named Volkswagen Karmann Ghia. Only small modifications were made to a standard 'export' chassis and to the steering drop arm, to allow for the lower steering wheel position. There was little to choose between the Karmann Ghia's mechanics and those of the standard Beetle, but the sporting looks of the Karmann Ghia also allowed it to cut through the air more efficiently, giving it a top speed of around 89 mph compared with the standard cars' 77 mph.

The body, manufactured by Karmann themselves in a less 'mass-produced' manner than Beetle bodies, was modified in 1960. At the same time, the car was made available in right-hand-drive form and mechanical changes were made more or less in keeping with those for the Beetle.

In 1957, an attractive Cabriolet version of the car was built and in 1962 a Type 3 became available based on the non-Beetle 1500 model, but this was only built in fixed-head form. Production for the European market ceased at the end of 1973 and the U.S. market around six months later.

Transporter Through to Camper

Right back in KdF-Wagen days, a prototype Beetle panel van had been produced by the simple expedient of adding a van rear end to a Beetle car. Unfortunately, the position of the engine made the van virtually useless for the intended purpose so when Volkswagen set to thinking about an all-new Volkswagen commercial vehicle after the war, their thinking had to be dramatically different. They felt that it made sense to stick to the basic suspension and mechanics of the Beetle in order to keep the cost down and, after all, that particular layout was by now all that Volkswagen – and Volkswagen owners – knew! But to squeeze a sensible payload into a rear-engined van meant that some radical rethinking would be necessary.

The answer was found to be in placing the driver and up to two passengers in the 'forward control' position, right at the front of the cab with seats astride the line of the front wheel arches and then, with the engine stuck immovably in the rear position, to provide wide access to the rear via side doors. The Transporter was built a little longer than the saloon and a little wider but with a much larger appearance because of its great height. The result was that a perfectly acceptable amount of load space was available and in the best possible position for the carriage of heavy loads – amidships, between the two axle lines.

(The following section on the history and development of the Transporter was produced for this book by Volkswagen A.G. and translated by V.A.G. (U.K.) Ltd.

"The oldest existing mention of the project for the Volkswagen Transporter in the Volkswagen archives dates back to 11.11.1948. In a memo to the Personnel Department, the

Technical Manager of the Volkswagen works asked for additional staff for the special Type 29. At this time, the project was still in the design and drawing stage, because the first drawings from the Design Office were only handed over to the General Manager, Mr. Nordhoff on November 20th 1948.

The drawings show two nearly identical models, which only differ in the driver's cab and which are labelled A and B. Design B shows a slightly sloping front of the cab, without a projecting roof. A model was made from this drawing. In parallel with this design phase, some parts of the vehicles, particularly those of the axles, were being tested. New shock absorbers, springs and the front wheel tracking angle were being tested.

On February 7th 1949, the General Manager Mr. Nordhoff proposed, from the model, to divide the three seater bench into a single driver's seat and a double seat next to it, so that the double seat could be taken out if required. Two days later this proposal was regarded as impossible by Technical Development, because the seat box lies above the front axle and extends over the whole width of the vehicle, including the front wheel arches as a single bridge.

On April 5th, the trial runs with the first prototype had to be broken off. It was found that the problem could not be solved in this way because the unchanged private car chassis could not withstand the considerably increased stresses, particularly in torsion.

The design change to self-supporting bodywork with a suitable subframe was made immediately. The aims included an improvement in the ratio of total weight: tare weight, which was intended to be raised from 1.85 for the first prototype to 1.91 for the self-supporting bodywork, strengthening the brakes and reducing the fuel consumption by aerodynamic improvement. In wind tunnel tests at Brunswick, it was found that a slight curvature of the front reduced the air resistance by about 40%. This corresponded to a calculated reduction in consumption of 2 litres/100 km. In parallel with this reduction in consumption, the aerodynamic measures also gave an increase in speed.

The stronger springing of the new Type 2 axle with enlarged telescopic shock absorbers also proved useful. When changing over to the self-supporting bodywork, double torsion springs were tested for the rear springs and for the front axle, not least in order to save costs.

The following factors had to be taken into account for the second prototype:

a) A little more space for the pedals because of the curved front.

b) Concentrating the heating on the front left windscreen and the driver.

c) Improved seat profile.

d) Lighter, but stiffer driver's cab doors.

e) Reducing the height of the load floor and better sealing by a sheet metal floor.

f) Removing the corners and angles in the loading space and increasing the luggage space above the engine.

With regard to the foreign competition, a sliding door was provided in the loading space.

The tests on the second prototype were successful. A total of more than 12,000 km of trial runs were driven on the route Volkswagen works — Warmenau — Wittingen — Hankensbüttel — Luttern — Lachendorf — Gifhorn — Volkswagen works, on poor road surfaces, so that the General Manager, Mr. Nordhoff, could decide on a starting date for production on May 19th 1949. This was set for November 1st, or at the latest December 1st 1949, so that the vehicle could be produced in considerable numbers at the beginning of 1950.

The Production Department therefore had a period of about four months up to November 1st to produce machine tools, which was regarded as quite reasonable.

The Experimental Construction Department now received the order to make the first four demonstration models, as well as two further prototypes. One was a normal vehicle, two vehicles with special features still to be decided and a bus for 8 to 9 people, including the driver. The date for these vehicles was October 15th 1949. Before manufacture of the machine tools, the General Manager, Mr. Nordhoff, made the following proposal: "In spite of the well-known and understandable objections to this, it seems to me that it is possible and necessary to reduce the engine space of the Type 29. It is not very bright that the present height is retained only because of the diameter of the spare wheel. I believe that even if the spare wheel is laid flat over the engine, which would give an intermediate layer, which would insulate the inside of the vehicle against heat from the engine, it should be possible to lower the height of the engine space roof." The recognisable second prototype variant of the Volkswagen Transporter resulted from this memo of August 31st. The Technical Development Department found on September 17th that: 'The new shape for the Type 29 resulted from manufacturing reasons together with the omission of the tubular frame and from driving reasons, because the fuel consumption and the acceleration were not satisfactory. In the new design started in March 1949, we relied on the results of the first wind tunnel test, which showed large sub-pressure areas without damping of the broken flow at the sides of the front of the vehicle.

As already mentioned, the resistance coefficient c_D was reduced by the new shape from 0.75 to 0.44. The comparable value for the Volkswagen model is $c_D = 0.39$ (on the original model $c_D = 0.48$ because of projecting parts etc.)

This appeared to have achieved the optimum attainable for a Type 29 van with the best use made of the space. Details can be seen from the enclosed report 49/5 of the Institute of Flow Technology at the Brunswick Polytechnic. As shown in wind tunnel diagram 6, there is good adhering air flow on all parts of the vehicle. The aerodynamically improved shape would presumably require throttling of the engine and the maximum speed for a loaded vehicle went up to 86 km/hour and for an unloaded vehicle up to 92 km/hour. The engine speed was too high at the latter speed. However, an increase of the rear axle ratio of 5:27, for example, could not be considered because of the speed, consumption and for reasons of manufacture.'

The first Volkswagen Transporter was introduced to the public by the Managing Director, Mr. Nordhoff, at a Press Conference on November 12th 1949. The engineers and designers produced the following arguments for using this new design:

VW – Type 29.

A. Main characteristic: Versatility.

From the constructional point of view, the Type 29 was created from the combination of a self-supporting box structure with the main characteristics of the Volkswagen car (air cooled engine at the back, similar components for axles). The shape followed modern trends in design, which prevail abroad for vans of all sizes.

Deliveries and transport of loads is being done increasingly abroad with vehicles which:

a) make the best use of the vehicle area for load space

b) are suitable for versatile use due to the type of box construction

c) make the use of open flat trucks with covers essential

Based on these design trends, the Type 29 is built

for town and country

for long and short distances

for motorways and country lanes

for goods and personnel transport

for trade and industry.

The van type can therefore be used for all lines of business, express transport and transport firms, for example

as a **small bus** for transport for hotels, airlines, schools, private transport companies, occasional transport

as a **special vehicle** for milk floats, caravans, mobile workshops, radio vans etc.

as a **postal van**

as an **ambulance**

as a **mobile station etc.**

B. Individual characteristics.

The versatility of the VW Type 29 is due to the following properties:

Quick and handy in town traffic

due to its small dimensions:

projected road area	6.9 m²
length	4.15 m
width	1.66 m
height	1.9 m
wheel base	2400 mm
track width at front	1356 mm
track width at rear	1360 mm
turning circle	about 10 metres

due to its big output

VW Boxer engine

swept volume	1.13 litres
output	25 HP
max. speed	3300 rpm

due to its low weight:

nett weight – with full tank, tools, spare wheel and 1 driver	975 kg
useful load	750 kg
permissible total weight	1725 kg
permissible axle weights	925 kg each

Economical on long journeys

75 km/hour at only 3100 rpm of the engine

Acceleration from 40 to 80 km/hour in 4th gear:

unloaded 50 seconds

loaded 80 seconds

Fuel consumption:

fully loaded 8 litres/100 km

at 60 km/hour constant speed.

Contents of tank sufficient for about 500 km.

Safe and reliable on poor road surfaces

Stiff in bends due to independent torsion spring wheel suspensions

Ground clearance 285 mm

Good visibility (1.1m² window area in driver's cab)

Headlamps with broad beam effect.

Powerful in hilly areas

Due to rear wheel drive with engine at rear.

(Good adhesion to ground of rear wheels on steep, wet and icy roads).

VW 4 speed gearbox with special ratio for drive wheels.

Transmission ratios:

1st gear	3.6
2nd gear	2.07
3rd gear	1.25
4th gear	0.8
Reverse gear	6.6
Rear axle	4.43
Drive wheels	1.4

Brakes with large areas (braking surface per wheel 170 cm²).

Climbing fully loaded about 22% in 1st gear.

Moderate in maintenance

Due to the accessibility of all parts of the drive. The engine can be removed through the back without jacking up the vehicle, clear separation of driver's cab, loading space and engine space, small tyres (size 5.50 x 16) 5 off, e.g. Conti-Profile SKS tyres.

Small space required for parking and garaging due to small ground area.

Relatively high transport service

Total useful volume	4.5 m³
of which main load space	4.0 m³
length	2.0 m
width	1.5 m
height	1.35 m
additional luggage space	0.6 m³
length	0.7 m
width	1.5 m
height	0.55 m

Driver's cab with three seats.

Easy to load

Loaded from the side, i.e. direct from the pavement by wide doors.

Load opening   1.17 x 1.2 m
Load height, loaded   4.00 m
        unloaded   4.50 m

Easy entry.

Cheap to operate and in taxes

Low price
low operating costs
low weight.

Ready to operate weight (taxable weight) 875 kg

Profitable ratio of useful load

Total weight/own weight: about 2.0:1

Modern construction

Aerodynamic construction (light construction), self-supporting stiff steel box structure (without chassis) with single steel roof.

Aerodynamic shape with low resistance coefficient to 0.44.

Useful load carried between the axles.

Even load distribution over the wheels.

Full use of the brakes (also when empty).

Good appearance

Due to Metro construction, following internal trends in design.

Large side panels for advertising texts.

Reliable in summer and in winter

Automatically controlled air cooling of the engine (no garage required).

Warm air heating for windscreen and leg room.

Generous special equipment provided

Roomy tool shelf under the driver's seat.

Lamps for ignition, winkers, oil pressure, headlamp full beam.

Shelves for documents.

Driver's cab ventilated by movable windows and sliding windows.

Load area ventilated by air pressure device.

Inside lights (also for engine space).

Adjustable driver's seat.

Foot dip switch.

Windscreen wiper.

Pushbutton operation of door locks for driver's cab.

Horn.

Jack for van with 4 inserts.

Handlamp connection.

Supports and spaces for extras of all kinds.

Closely related to the Volkswagen car

Therefore lively, reliable,

economical and powerful **altogether**

a commercial vehicle of universal value for the transport of all goods everywhere."

The Beetle and its brother the Beetle-derived Type 2 Transporter were phenomena the like of which has never been seen before and will, in all probability, never be seen again — that is, assuming the production of Beetles for so-called Third World countries EVER comes to a halt! They retained exactly the same appeal and exactly the same shape right from its concept as developed by the mad genius of Adolf Hitler and the purer genius of Ferdinand Porsche right through to post-war production and as means of moving around 'Folk' and goods the world over at low cost and high reliability they have never been bettered. Amazingly, in spite of its almost unchanged appearance, just one component out of the 5000-plus that went into the Volkswagen car survived right through from first to last, and that was the humble engine bay

rubber. But with such vast numbers made, spares supply can not possibly become a problem in the foreseeable future, except for the earliest cars — which makes the Beetle and it derivative the Transporter truly great vehicles to restore!

H1.   From left to right, 1949, 1943 and 1948 'split-window' Beetles, the '48 and '49 in newly restored condition and the '43 'as found'. (Picture, Brian Screaton).

H2.   The 1943 'split', reputedly found in a barn in Germany, having been hidden by soldiers after the war. Note the unusual number plate and semaphor indicator position. There's not much hope of finding one of these as only a few hundred were built in around 1943 in order to 'prove' the production equipment which was then mothballed until after the war. (Picture, Brian Screaton).

H3. Restored 1948 Beetle. Note the rare 'nipple' hubcaps, small rear lights and grooved bumpers. (Picture, Brian Screaton).

H4. The grooved bumpers are in evidence again at the front of this 'split window' Beetle but the wing/fender mounted indicators are wrong for the car. (Picture, Brian Screaton).

H5. What a difference 10 years makes! 1948 and 1958 Beetles pictured side-by-side. (Picture, Brian Screaton).

H6. This 1952 Beetle, alongside a 1978 Beetle Cabriolet, is said to be in course of restoration. Not all parts are correct for the year but note the single tail-pipe exhaust and 'Pope's Nose' combined number plate light and brake light. (Picture, Brian Screaton).

H7. The small 'oval' rear screen on this nicely restored Beetle denotes a mid-fifties production date. (Picture, Brian Screaton).

H8. Pictured in Norway, this 'oval' includes such accessories as fender skirts and American-style 'towel rail' bumpers. (Picture, Brian Screaton).

H9.   Gathered at Wolfsberg this row of 'splits' lined up in 1985 to celebrate a version of the 50th Anniversary of the Beetle. (Picture, Marco Batazzi, Turin).

H10.   Beetle Cabriolets were built by Karmann, not by Volkswagen themselves. This early 1960's version is little changed visually from the earliest versions.

H11.   On the other hand, the 'nice-in-white' US spec. Cabrio., one of the last Beetles to leave Germany, boasts top-specification in every respect, including fuel injection.

H12. Actually, a handful of Volkswagen-approved convertibles were also built by German coachbuilder Hebmuller until 1951 shortly after which the factory closed.

H13. Rear view of the Hebmuller, pictured here at a 'VW Action' event held at the Royal Showground in Warwickshire, England, said to be the world's largest annual gathering of Beetles. Unlike the Karmann-built car, this was strictly a '2+2' seater.

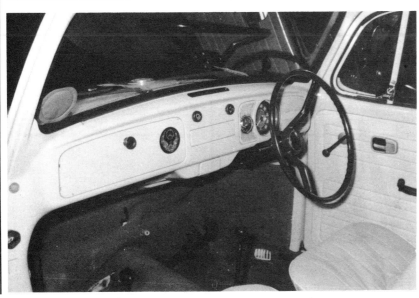

H14. But back to the saloon/sedan models! This shot shows the steering wheel, dash and very rare radio in a 1951 'split window' convertible – except that the rear window wasn't split on drop-head models! (Picture Rich Kimball).

H15. From 1958, the general dash layout seen here was adopted, although this is a later model.

H19. The 'split screen' camper is still regarded as a useful workhorse and is perfect as a dual-purpose vehicle; one that you can use in your spare time as well as taking out on sunny days. (Picture, Jennifer Pedler).

H20. But beware – rear vision IS limited, so reversing can be tricky without the aid of a back-up device as featured elsewhere on these pages. (Picture, Jennifer Pedler).

H16. After the 'oval' rear-screen came an enlarged rear screen but there were still 'sloping' headlamps until U.S. regulations outlawed them.

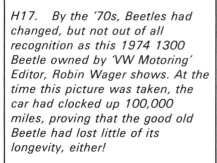

H17. By the '70s, Beetles had changed, but not out of all recognition as this 1974 1300 Beetle owned by 'VW Motoring' Editor, Robin Wager shows. At the time this picture was taken, the car had clocked up 100,000 miles, proving that the good old Beetle had lost little of its longevity, either!

H18. 'Spotting the difference' between the ages and stages of Transporters is a little easier. This is a slightly down-at-heel, but still hard working 'split screen' panel van. (Note that the terms 'split screen' apply to both Beetles and Transporters, but the screens in question are clearly at different ends of the vehicles! (Picture Jennifer Pedler).

H21. Front visibility was much improved on later Transporters and they make much more of an everyday workhorse by today's standards. This is the House of Haselock hack, fitted with 2-litre engine for extra towing power, towing the author's 1973 Cabriolet away from his home for the restoration featured alongside those of other vehicles on these pages. Neat?

H22. When the British sent Major Ivan Hirst to Wolfsberg as Military Governor, he found the factory badly damaged but the southern frontage of this large factory, viewed here from the Administrative Building was still standing.

H23. Other large areas had been laid waste by the American bombers. (Picture W Bradshaw).

H24. REME, the branch of the British Army responsible for repair and maintenance had already taken over parts of the plant following the departure of the US Army and had spent a few weeks maintaining trucks and building Keubelwagens from spares found at the factory. This is 'Cpl Jones; one of the boys' with such a vehicle, photographed in the empty vehicle park. (Picture W Bradshaw).

H25.   Major Hirst, still in uniform but not now 'Army' in the usual way, quickly established his considerable presence. He is seen here in 1946 at a meeting with Herr Carl Schmuecker who was the Secretary and responsible for liaison with 'the German side', as it was then put.

H26.   By the turn of the years 1945-46, there were production line Volkswagens to be seen for the first time in the vehicle park. The few hundred produced in the early days of the war had been to 'prove' the production equipment.

H27.   By March 1946, the Hirst approach was bearing fruit as the 1000th Volkswagen rolled from the line, still with Keubelwagen headlamps. Both men and women worked in the factory and several of the men still wore their armed forces caps. The workforce readily obeyed orders, according to Hirst.

H28. Ivan Hirst, photographed proudly at home in 1986 with the model Beetle presented to him by Wolfsberg when he left in 1949. They had wanted to give him a full-sized Cabriolet, but he declined because of his governmental position. But the beautiful and highly detailed model was said to have cost as much as a full-sized car to build!

H29. The 'Trecker' was a kind of latter-day Keubelwagen, based on Beetle/Transporter components.

H30. Karmann Ghias look terrific but their performance is limited by their use of standard Beetle components. Their exotic bodywork (by Beetle standards) is prone to corrosion and very expensive to repair!

2 Buying

Buying a Beetle
by Robin Wager, the
Editor of VW Motoring
magazine

Buying a Beetle is easy! Buying the right one, however, takes a little patience, a little knowledge and — often — no little time. Even a car such as the Beetle with its justified reputation for reliability and longevity is prone to faults and weaknesses due to the ravages of corrosion, wear and, all too often, downright neglect. On the other hand, the car's ever growing popularity means that unscrupulous sellers are presented with an ideal opportunity to gloss over weaknesses in a problem car and pass it off as a good example of the marque. This chapter aims to provide the prospective purchaser with a sequence of checks on a car under consideration which should be virtually foolproof in ensuring that a car is as good — or only as bad — as it seems. It should also provide the owner who is in the process of deciding whether to rebuild his or her car with the information necessary to make an estimate of the total amount of work — and thus expenditure — required.

There is one point that should perhaps be made before we go any further. Cars are frequently offered in the UK with a 'new' or 'long' MoT certificate. Don't let this fool you into thinking it's automatically a good buy, or even roadworthy at all. An MoT is no substitute for a really sound car!

Take your pick

First of all, the prospective owner has to make the decision as to which model of Beetle to acquire. Some idea of the changes that took place is given in Chapter One, while the Appendices detail the technical and numerical background to the developments. While the Beetle is famous for having been developed by means of only very minor annual changes over almost 40 years, there are certain production landmarks which represent more radical departures from the original Beetle design.

'Split window' models are now so rare, at least in Britain, that anyone contemplating the purchase of one of these falls into a special category at once. Not only must they have a fairly large sum available to spend, but must first *find* their Beetle . . ! Successor to the split window model is 1953 was the saloon with the single oval rear window. These are more readily available, in conditions ranging from 'concourse' to 'restoration project', and at much more sensible prices; though it is the writer's opinion that 'oval window' prices will soon take off, in the virtual absence of anything older to hold them down.

It goes without saying, perhaps, that parts for split-window models are now extremely difficult to obtain, and the same is becoming true of ovals. Without an entry into the somewhat exclusive world of the historic Beetle owners (many of whom are also wheelers and dealers in the related parts), therefore, life can be very difficult.

Once into the era of the large rear window (1957-on) things become easier from the point of view of parts. There is little that cannot be found for most Beetles after that date, thanks to the wide availability of pattern parts and the many swap-meet style events now held every year.

One of the added complications for the potential Beetle buyer is the apparent multiplicity of engines and specification differences. Perhaps the most frequent questions we at 'VW Motoring' are asked by prospective owners is 'What engine is best?' or 'Which model was the most reliable/economical?'

Because of the Beetle's long production history, and the fact that it has been sold in well over 100 different markets, general production modifications have combined with the various local market regulations to spawn many models that differ in various small ways. Further, because of the Beetle's worldwide popularity, many 'oddities' have found their way into Britain through personal importation by immigrants and returning expatriates and soldiers.

The basic Beetle body, however (with the reservations below) remains the same, and it doesn't really matter about the origins of your car provided you acquire it legally and check it out using this book.

Engine and body variations definitely require some clarification. The Beetle has been officially produced with power units ranging from 1.1 to 1.6 litres; in addition, tuning firms

have offered kits to enable the enthusiast to increase these capacities by varying amounts ranging to well over 2.0 litres, while owners have even been known to shoe-horn in a Porsche engine! It is not within our scope to advise on the purchase of such highly modified cars – but check out the engine in your prospective acquisition before you acquire it!

Earliest production cars – split and oval window models – had 1131 cc 25 bhp engines, looking very simple compared with the later versions and fitted originally with a single-tailpipe silencer (now difficult to come by).

The next stage in 1954 was a capacity increase to 1192 cc (the '1200' – long recognised as the definitive Beetle engine size, and the capacity to which it had reverted by the end of its European production), with an extra 5 bhp.

From 1965 a 1285 cc ('1300') engine was offered as well, with the third option, introduced the following year, of a 1493 cc ('1500') unit developing 44 bhp.

Finally in 1970 VW introduced the 1584'cc ('1600') motor with an unheard-of 50 bhp! This engine was available only in a revised body – the most radical restyling of the sheet metal ever seen. The resulting model, known as the 1302S or Super Beetle, had a more bulbous front end, offering greater luggage space. There was another major change under the skin, too – MacPherson strut front suspension, the first time the original Porsche torsion bars spec. had ever been forsaken. This model never had a particularly happy reputation, owing to the early cars' poor engine performance which resulted largely from American-inspired anti-emissions modifications to ignition and carburation.

In 1972 a similar restyled body combined with the 1300 engine was introduced as the VW 1303. Further restyling now endowed it with a markedly curved windscreen and a completely new, vinyl padded dash. The same body was offered with the 1600 engine, designated 1303S. All engines from the 1200 upwards are readily available as replacement short or full units.

To go into the question of the various special edition Beetles which were marketed over the years would require a book in itself. Special editions are, however, generally more sought-after. They were usually identified, quite apart from anything else, by special wheels, although such wheels have developed a market of their own and can now often be found added to otherwise standard models.

Prominent among special editions are the GT Beetle (1200-style body, 1600 engine, swing axles, high gearing); World Champion Beetle (1972 – commemorating the passing by the Beetle of the Ford Model T's former production record of 15,007,033); Jeans Beetle (all-black exterior trim, denim seats, 1200 engine); and Last Edition Beetle, (1977 – numbered series of the final European-produced models).

From 1970 all 1300 and 1600 engines were 'twin-port', i.e. possessed two separate induction manifolds serving separate ports in each cylinder head. This type of engine is readily identified from a glance at the engine compartment; and whilst offering slightly improved breathing it did tend to suffer an increased incidence of cylinder head cracking.

There are other miscellaneous points worth bearing in mind. For example, all Beetles up to 1967 had 6V electrics, which could cause starting and headlighting, in particular, to be feeble. 1200 models retained the 6V system for even longer while the factory used up stocks!

So-called Standard models up to about 1964 (most of them finished in a battleship grey) were equipped with the original-style cable-actuated brakes – efficient enough, but difficult to keep in balance and not really desirable today – so check for these. 1500 and 1600 engines were usually accompanied by front disc brakes, other models having drums all round.

A semi-automatic transmission was offered for a while on 1500 models. Stick Shift Beetles, as they were known, are now very rare and, although the system (which featured a microswitch in the gear lever base for automatic clutch operation) worked well enough, cars thus equipped were very thirsty and had mediocre performance.

Well, if you thought it was going to be easy deciding what Beetle to go for, that might just have given you food for thought! Don't worry, though – if your real aim is just to get a good example, no matter which model it is, we'll certainly be able to help . . .

Where to look

At the time of writing, 20.6 million Beetles have been sold and the model is still being produced in Mexico and Brazil. With this in mind, it shouldn't be too difficult to find one that's right for you!

So where is the best place to start looking? Well, occasionally someone is lucky enough to have a Beetle – one that has been lovingly cared for – passed on by a friend or relative, and that solves a lot of problems. For the rest of us, it's a case of scouring the advertisements of visiting a specialist dealer.

Naturally, I'm going to suggest that the best place to start us with the classifieds ('Compact Ads') in VW Motoring, which you'll find on sale monthly at most main newsagents including W.H. Smith and Menzies in the UK. Apart from my natural editor's bias, the reason for this is that the vast majority of the Beetles advertised there are owned by enthusiasts who are regular readers of the magazine and who therefore know about

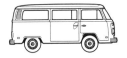

caring for their car. You'll find every level of offering, from the very cheap MoT-test failure (which, with the help of this book, can turn into a rewarding restoration) to the ultimate concours candidate at a correspondingly high price.

Whilst you will undoubtedly find a lot of Beetles in Exchange & Mart, or its American equivalent, we can't really recommend this publication since few of the advertisers are likely to be enthusiasts.

The alternative is to contact one of the firms who specialise in used Beetles — many of whom you will also find in VW Motoring — although they will tend to be offering cars that are already restored to a good standard and will therefore be asking the appropriate price.

Having located what seems like an interesting car, how do you go about ensuring that it represents a sensible buy? We can give you plenty of guidelines here, but I'm going to recommend one invaluable aid: an enthusiast who really knows Beetles.

Finding one may not be so easy, but a good idea is to make contact with your local VW club (see the regular Clubs Register in VWM) — perhaps even become a member prior to buying your car, since you'll almost certainly pick up enough tips about servicing, parts and local traders to more than cover your subscription.

There's been at least one person in every VW club I have ever come across who is a real Beetle buff, and he will probably be only too pleased to 'vet' your proposed purchase for the price of a pint at the next club meeting; he may even know the car and/or its present owner, if you're buying locally. Contacting the local club may make things even easier for you, since one of the members may have just the right car for sale.

Of course, the local newspaper can be an invaluable source of almost any secondhand item, Beetles included, and there's the advantage that they won't be too far away.

Making sure

Let's assume that you have located one or more possible buys. Now comes the really important part — checking them out. This is a procedure that not only can, but should be very time consuming if the 'right' car is to be bought rather than a glossed-over heap of trouble. What follows is an elimination sequence in three separate parts, each one taking longer and being more thorough than the last, this approach having the virtue of saving the purchaser both time and embarrassment. It is always easier to withdraw at an early stage than after an hour spent checking the car over, with the aid of the owner's comments and mugs of coffee!

Thus, Stage A aims to eliminate the obvious 'nails' without having to probe too deeply. Stage B takes matters somewhat further for cars that pass the first stage, while Stage C is the 'dirty hands' stage, the one you don't get into on a snowy February evening unless you are really serious!

Tool Box

Old, warm clothes (if the ground is cold). An old mat or a board if the ground is wet. A bright torch. A pair of ramps. A screwdriver or other probe. Copies of the following pages and a notepad. Pencil. A bottle, trolley or scissors jack. Axle stands.

Safety

Safety should be carefully considered and any necessary steps taken. In particular, do not rely on a handbrake holding a car on a slope or ramps. Never crawl under a car supported by a jack only and remember to chock the wheels on the ground when a car is supported on axle stands or ramps.

Using the checklist

The checklist is designed to show step-by-step instructions for virtually all the checks to be made on a car offered for sale. After each check, the fault indicated is shown in brackets, e.g., the instruction:

"Look along wings/fenders, door bottoms and quarter panels from front and rear of car" is followed by the fault, shown in brackets, as (Ripples indicate filler presence/crash damage. † † †).

The "†" signs require some explanation. They are intended to give a guide to the cost of rectifying the fault if it exists. † indicates that the cost if likely to be less than the cost of a new tyre, † † † stands for the cost of a new set of tyres, or more, while † † means that the cost if likely to between the two. The cost guide relates to the cost of the component/s only, other than in the case of bodywork — allow more if you have the work done for you.

When examining a car you are advised to take this book (or copies of the relevant buying checklists) and a notebook with you. As each item is checked a record can be kept in the notebook. You may wish to record a running cost total for necessary repairs as faults are discovered — this could be a useful bargaining tool at the end of your examination.

It is strongly recommended that the repair and restoration sections of this book and also the relevant Haynes VW Beetle Workshop Manual are examined so that the checker is fully familiar with every component being examined.

Stage A –
First Impressions

1) Is the car "square" to the ground and are front and rear covers, bumpers, door to hinge-pillar gaps even and level? (Closed-up door gaps and rippled panels usually indicate poorly repaired crash damage. † † † +)

2) Look along wings/fenders, door bottoms and quarter panels from the front and rear of the car. (Ripples indicate filler presence. † † †)

3) Check quality of chromework, especially bumpers. (Dents, dings and rust. † †)

4) Turn on all lights, indicators and reversing (back-up) lights and check that they work. (Rear lights earthing/grounding problems plus other specific component problems)

5) "Bounce" each corner of the car. (Worn dampers allow the corners to feel springy and bounce up and down. Each damper – †)

6) Check visually for rust – gain an overall impression at this stage.)From cosmetic, to dire! † to † † † + – see following sections)

7) Check for damage or deterioration of rubber window seals. Genuine replacements are expensive. (Leaks/cosmetic. † to † †)

8) Examine general condition of interior at-a-glance. (Rips, dirt, parts missing. † † or † † †)

9) Cabrio: Check soft-top for: fit around windows, rips and clarity of screen. (Soft-top replacement. † † † +)

10) Quality of paintwork. Does it shine when dry? Are there scratches beneath the shine? Is it chipped? (Neglect or poor-quality, cover-job respray. † † †)

11) Does the seller/his surroundings *look* like those of an enthusiast? (Maintenance. † † †)

Stage B – Clean Hands!

If a car doesn't match up to requirements after Stage A, don't be tempted – reject it! There are always more cars to be seen. Stage B decreases the risk of making a mistake without even getting your hands too dirty!

Check hard for body corrosion in all the places shown below. Use a magnet to ensure that no filler is present – magnets will only "stick" to steel. Work carefully and methodically.

Bear in mind that the Beetle does have one inherent advantage over most post-war cars: a separate chassis/floorpan. So corrosion in, say, the floor that could be terminal in many models is not necessarily so in a Beetle – you can always mount a good body on a better floorpan – which, if it comes with good mechanicals too, can be a very good way of saving a lot of cash!

Bodywork – checklist

1) Front valance, between front wings. This is integral with spare wheel well, which we'll come to later. (Accident damage, cheap repair, corrosion. † †)

2) Front bumper. Severely damaged, badly rusted, or non-existent. † or † †

3) Luggage compartment lid. Accident damage, cheap repair. † †

4) Front wings/fenders. Accident damage, filler, corrosion around headlight rims or at trailing edges. † † each

Note: Excellent fibre-glass moulded, self-coloured wings/fenders are available for Beetles where originality is not important.

5) Front quarter panels (in front of doors). Creasing indicates cheap accident repair. Corrosion at base from water entering boot. † † †

6) Doors. Corrosion at bottom. Filler. Cracking near quarter-light frame. † † each (repair panels). † † † (new)

7) Examine door fit. Hinge wear is common – check by trying to lift an open door. Oversize pins available. After reaming. †. (But shifting old pins is a problem)

8) Door hinge pillar. Corrosion at base may indicate a more widespread problem in sills. † to † † †

9) Door latching pillar (B-post). Corrosion at base, ditto. † to † † †

10) Running boards. Bubbling under plastic covering indicates rusty metal pressing. † pair

11) Side panel (beneath rear side window). Corrosion at base. Filler. (Plate available) † †. Rear wheel arch (wing/fender mounting) panel †

Note: Complete rear quarter panel (inner wing/fender, wheel arch etc up to B-post) available. † † † + +

12) Rear wings/fenders. Stone chipping. Corrosion adjoining body. † to † †

13) Engine cover. Accident damage. Corrosion at base. † to † †

14) Rear bumper. Accident damage, badly rusted or non-existent. † †

15) Rear valance. Accident damage, cheap repair. † †

Interior

1) Examine seats. (Worn, thin or split covers. † †)

2) Check operation of front seat backrests, including angle adjustment (prone to slipping on older cars). Check front/rear adjustment

3) Check dash (scratches in paint, tears in vinyl). Badly fitted additional switches or instruments. Missing or damaged radio speaker grille (around speedo). †

4) Check condition and cleanliness of soft-top headlining. From † if dirty to † † † for renewal. (Hood † † † + +)

5) Examine steering wheel/gear knob. Correct ones fitted? †

6) Test seat belts, if fitted. (If not fitted, plan to do so. † to † †). Inertial reel type should operate freely. All should be free of damage.

7) Check door trim and

interior handles/winders. Wear and scuffing at bottoms, buckling of hardboard backing, broken handles. (NB: some trim colours difficult to match)

8) Wind windows up and down. Binding or excessive looseness indicates attention required to mechanism, possible renewal. (Cabrio rear side window mechanism virtually impossible to obtain). † to † † †

9) Examine rear seat (see 1). Check fold-down facility and backrest latch or retaining hook. (commonly broken)

10) Examine rear luggage compartment (behind seat & parcel shelf if fitted). Dirty, stained, damp? Trim (under window) commonly stained from condensation. † if dirty, † † to renew

11) Lift rear seat cushion. Check for dampness/visible corrosion, especially inner sills and around battery. In severe cases battery can rot through floorpan. † to † † †

12) Lift carpets (if fitted) and rubber floor covering. Many cars have bituminous felt glued to floor, making external floorpan inspection essential). Dampness/corrosion? † or new pan

Mechanical

Don't be in too much of a hurry to start the engine. First of all, take out the dipstick, wipe it, reinsert, and remove again. Is the oil level more or less up to the top mark? (Regular maintenance. Oil consumption). Wipe the dipstick between your thumb and forefinger and smell the oil smear. Does it smell of petrol? (Excessive choke. Leaking fuel pump diaphragm.)

Now ask the owner to start the engine. Is there a cloud of smoke? Don't worry, provided it clears quickly; the horizontal layout of the cylinders can allow oil to remain in the combustion chambers, especially if the car has been parked on a slope. If smoke

persists, especially after warming up, the engine is badly worn.

1) Most later Beetles have an automatic choke which is electrically operated, an integral heating element bringing the choke off (and reducing fast idle speed) after a short time. Check that this happens.

2) Open engine lid (it should say up unaided). Are all the air hoses in place? Is the pressed 'tinware' in position around the base of the compartment? (very important, as running without it can overheat engine). Is the original carburettor (Solex) fitted? A non-standard type is not necessarily bad, the favourites being Nikki, Weber or Reece-Fish (the latter may give problems owing to lack of choke). Twin-carb conversion suggests that the car will have been driven hard, but certainly improves breathing and therefore performance, smoothness (but check insurance rating!)

3) Check engine and compartment for general cleanliness. True Beetle buffs keep engines clean! Check for oil leaks, especially around distributor, fuel pump, generator support pedestal. Slight weeping is common, anything more † to † † †

4) Listen to engine. It should be noisy, but try to separate flat exhaust beat from mechanical noises. Tolerances are greater on air-cooled engines, and a healthy amount of tappet noise and general 'clacking' is OK, but beware very metallic tappings and heavy thumps. † † † † ++. Stop engine. Remove oil filler cap and check for 'mayonnaise' on underside, suggestive of many short journeys (bad for engine — lots of auto choke).

5) Check the pre-heat pipe(s) from the exhaust ports that form a hot-spot at the carburetter. Corrosion (see 6)

6) If the car has a slotted engine lid, is one of the proprietary protective cowls fitted to keep water out and prevent corrosion of manifolds, pre-heat pipes etc? If not, plan to fit one. †

Road Test

If you, the tester are driving ensure adequate insurance cover.

Otherwise simulate the following tests with the owner driving.

1) Operate starter. Is it sluggish (6V system voltage drop, faulty solenoid or worn support bush. †)

2) Is it difficult to engage first gear?

n.b. Expect a long, heavy clutch pedal. (Worn clutch. †. Worn selector mechanism. † † †)

Drive for three or four miles to become familiar with the car and to warm engine.

3) Drive at 30 mph. Does car wander and/or 'tramline' on white lines/road joints? Suspect crossply tyres. All Beetles need radials. † † † for replacements — obviously! Also,

4) — pay attention to the general 'ride' — it should be firm but a little bouncy. 'Crashing' or severe bouncing on road irregularities suggests worn damper(s). † each. Also,

5) Also — brake gently to a halt. A: Does car "pull" to one side? B: Do brakes rub or grind? (A: Worn pads or shoes. †. Seized calipers. † †. B: Worn pads or shoes. †, but more if discs or drums ruined.)

6) Drive at 30 mph in 3rd gear. Apply then release accelerator four or five times, listen for clonk. Worn or broken transmission nose mounting. †

7) In models with double-jointed drive shafts, listen for regular knock on cornering. Worn CVJ. † each.

8) Drive at 40 mph. Lift off accelerator. Listen for differential whine. (Worn differential. † † †, if severe or unbearably noisy.).

9) Does gear lever chatter/vibrate? May just require lubrication or adjustment at base plate, but could mean wear at rear end of shift shaft (inspection plate under rear seat — rear bushings. †.) or selector mechanism († † † for transmission).

10) Accelerate hard in 2nd gear to 30 mph, then lift off. Does gearbox jump out of gear? (Worn internal selector mechanism. †)

11) Drive as in 10 above but lift off in 3rd gear. Does gearbox jump out of gear? (Worn internal selector mechanism. †)

12) Drive at 50 mph in 4th gear. Change into 3rd gear. Does gearbox "crunch"? (Worn synchromesh. † † †. Faulty/worn clutch. † †)

13) Drive at 30 mph in 3rd gear. Change into 2nd gear. Does gearbox "crunch"? (Worn synchromesh. † † †. Faulty/worn clutch. † †)

14) Do front wheels flutter or shake at 40 mph? (Wheels out of balance. †. Worn front suspension. † †)

15) Do front wheels shimmy after hitting bump or pothole? (Worn MacPherson strut where applicable. †. Worn/leaking steering damper. †)

16) When cornering does the steering wheel attempt to return to the "straight-ahead" position when loosed? (If not, this probably indicates tight kingpins (renewal. † †) or balljoints (renewal. † †) or steering box (renewal. † † †)

17) When stationary, operate the brake pedal. Apply light pressure in repeated strokes. (If the pedal slowly works its way to the floor– even over a minute, the master cylinder is faulty. This problem more common to dual circuit systems. † †)

18) Operated the red brake warning light or ensure that it illuminates when the key is turned to the "Start" position (late and N. American models only), then push on the brake pedal as hard as possible. (If the light illuminates the brakes probably leak. Replacement wheel cylinder. †. Sometimes only adjustment is required)

19) Accelerate hard from low speed in top gear, full throttle. (Pinking/spark knock probably indicates maladjusted timing. Can cause piston damage over a long period. † or † † †)

20) If possible descend a long hill on a closed throttle. ("Popping" through the exhaust indicates induction air leak or burnt exhaust valve.)

21) Stop car. Apply brake firmly. Engage 2nd gear. Gently let out clutch – but depress again as soon as car shows any sign of distress. (If car pulls away, worn rear brakes. †. Oil in brake drum. † †. If car remains stationary but engine continues to run – worn clutch. † †+)

22) Facing up a slight incline, allow the car to roll back a little (but don't build up to more than walking pace) and then apply the handbrake smartly. If one side of the rear wheel 'jacks up' the handbrake is out of balance or one cable is broken or faulty in operation. (New cable. †.)

n.b. in severe winter conditions, various parts of the handbrake mechanism can freeze simulating other mechanical problems.

23) Whilst driving at normal speeds with a warm engine, switch on heater (*early cars*: unscrew knob near gear lever; *later cars*: pull right-hand knob in front of handbrake upwards). Check for heat at (a) footwell outlets (b) demist vents at lower corners of screen. (No heat, or heat on one side only. Seized or broken flap cable(s). †.) Check output at rear footwell outlets (later cars: pull up left-hand knob to operate). As for front, above. Does heated air smell of exhaust fumes? Leaking exhaust. † †. Corroded heat exchanger(s). † † each. Oil leaks. † to † † †.

24) With engine thoroughly warm, let it idle. Does oil pressure light flicker? No problem if idle speed set too low, provided it goes out immediately revs increase. Maybe just a weak pressure switch, but could mean main bearing wear. † † †.

25) Check screenwashers (*later cars* – pneumatic operation via pressurised reservoir). Leaks, pressure loss. †. With wet screen, operate wipers (1500/1600: two speeds). Squeaking or grinding, lack of lubrication or worn motor.

†. Odd regular noise can be mechanism contacting radio, where installed in dash slot! Check play at steering wheel. Should be about ¾" at wheel rim in straight-ahead position, up to 4" on full lock. Worn balljoints. † †. Worn steering box. † † †.

Luggage bay inspection

Pull luggage bay lid release (under N/S dash; later cars/Cabrios: inside glovebox). Does it operate correctly? Broken cable. † Lift the front (!) lid and check the general condition of the interior. Does it look like a rubbish tip? A careful owner will have kept it clean. Check condition of fibreboard linings (Replacement of Both † †). Remove cover over rear of dash (not MacPherson cars) and examine wiring. Does it show signs of badly executed additions or overheating? Is there evidence of water ingress (screenwash nozzle or rubber seal). Check for signs of water entering recesses at rear corners of luggage bay (faulty rubber lid seal). Check around seal for bad corrosion in metal flange. Remove spare wheel (may also house screenwash reservoir). Is tyre inflated and with good tread? Replacement † – obviously! Is there a jack (may be under rear seat – later cars) and small toolkit (at least plug/wheelnut wrench, plus jack handle for friction type jack – earlier cars)?

Is base of wheel well intact and free from serious corrosion? (Notorious rust trap). Replacement panel. † †

Examine brake fluid reservoir (*early cars*: under spare wheel; *later cars*: left-hand side of luggage bay). Is level correct? Are rubber pipes from base of reservoir dry? Leakage. †

Remove luggage bay lining if possible, check for dampness/rust in steel panel underneath. Defective seal. †

Check generally for evidence of accident repair (bad welding,

Stage C – Dirty Hands

This is the level at which the car — by now being seriously considered — is given the sort of checks that make as sure as possible that there are no serious hidden faults which could still make the purchaser change his or her mind. It might also throw up a few minor faults to use as bargaining points with the seller!

While Stage A took only a minute or so and Stage B took quite a while longer, Stage C involves a lot more time, inconvenience and effort, but if you want to be sure, it's the most vital stage of all.

Safety: Ensure that wheels are chocked when using jacks or ramps. NEVER go under a car supported only by a jack.

1) Insert jack in one of the jacking points and attempt to raise car. Beware! Jacking point may give way. If it doesn't, and there is no tendency for the running board to be forced upwards when both wheels are off the ground, the car is probably quite solid. If jacking point cannot be utilised, give serious consideration to the amount of corrosion present in body rockers sills etc. Either use this as a bargaining point to obtain an appropriate price reduction, or reject the car at this stage. In any case, you will need a separate jack (trolley type is best) to continue your check.

2) With rear wheel off the ground and first gear engaged (ignition OFF), rotate the wheel back and forth to check the free play in the diff. It should be between 1-2 ins; if more, then the diff is worn and will probably have been noisy on road test. With the gears in neutral, rotate the wheel continuously and listen for a harshness that indicates a worn bearing. Renewal. †

3) Grip the wheel at top and bottom and alternately push and pull, rocking it. Repeat, holding wheel at each side. Axial play indicates worn bearing. †

4) Repeat 2 & 3 for the other rear wheel.

5) Remove car jack (where applicable) then jack both front wheels off the ground together. Rotate steering wheel from lock to lock — it should feel light with no tight spots. Noises or binding suggest over-adjustment to compensate for wear. Replacement box. † † †

6) Move to the front wheels. Use the push-pull routine (see 3 above) to check for bearing wear. Adjustment is free! Replacement †

7) With the front of the car held off the ground on axle stands, have your assistant (where possible) continue to push-pull each front wheel while you examine the steering/suspension swivels with the torch, for slackness. (*Early cars:* king/link pins; *later cars:* balljoints — wear in these is much more dangerous). Replacement. † †

8) At alternate full locks, check the brake backplates or disc calipers for signs of leakage. Inspect pads for thickness via caliper slots, the linings by removing the rubber bung near the rim of the drum. Replacement pads/shoes. †

9) Check the brake discs for excessive wear or deep scoring. Replacement discs. † each

10) Examine the grease nipples on the torsion bar tubes (*earlier cars:* also on king pins) for fairly recent lubrication — a good sign.

11) Check around the frame head for serious sheet metal corrosion (see repair section), also the brake master cylinder and cluster of pipes in same area. Replacement brake pipes. † † plus much labour

12) On MacPherson strut cars, examine the top housings of struts. Corrosion. † each

13) On torsion bar cars, check the tops of the damper towers. Corrosion. † to † † for skilled repair

14) Check around base of fuel tank for leaks, corrosion. Replacement tank. † †

15) Check the condition of the inner wings. Corrosion. † to † †

16) Remove jack, drive rear wheels on to ramps. From beneath the rear end, check underside of the engine.

Check: Oil leaks, likely from sump drain plug/plate. May just require tightening, or new gasket, but securing studs may have pulled or stripped (look for evidence of retaining bolts instead of cap nuts). Usually not serious but † for re-tapping.

Check: Oil leakage from pushrod tubes (common). A small amount is OK but large quantities will only get worse (loose cylinder heads) and cause heater smells. New pushrod tubes/seals. † to † † Telescopic tubes available from Haselocks minimise stripdown!

Check: around crankshaft pulley. Push-pull for endfloat — 4 to 7 thou is OK. If more, suspect rear main bearing — in bad cases, crankcase is U/S. † † † † † . Serious oil leak (engine out) † † † .

Check: around front of engine. Serious oil leak (crank wear) † † † .

Check: around left-hand side of engine. Severe leakage from oil cooler. Tightening or replacement seals. † to † † .

Check: around valvegear covers. Not serious, new cork gaskets very cheap. Any other oil leakage probably indicates careless topping-up!

17) Check generally for corrosion, especially around inner wings, bumper supports (welding, plating. † †) and shock absorber mountings (Replacements. † †).

18) Carry out visual check of exhaust system. Holes or thinness, repairs with exhaust paste. Replacement. † † . Check stubs connecting exhaust to heat exchangers. Severe corrosion. Repair stubs available. † . New heat exchangers † † each.

Author's footnote: You won't find a more thorough, more authoritative buyer's guide to the Beetle than this one anywhere at all. And it all goes to show just how well-versed in all things Beetle the writer, Robin Wager,

the Editor of VW Motoring magazine actually is! *Don't* be tempted by the first shiny coat of paint you see; *Do* use the wonderfully detailed information produced here by Robin and the VW Motoring team.

Split-Screen (Type 2) Transporter
by Jennifer Pedler of the Split Screen Van Club

(Reproduced with the kind permission of VW Motoring).

To some people the Type 2 VW – Van, Transporter, Kombi or whatever you like to call it – is little more than a workhorse, or a vehicle for itinerant Australians. Many owners of pre-'67 'split windscreen' models would hotly dispute this. Immaculate examples of certain models are even regarded as collectors' items. Rarities or not, these vans certainly had more character than their later straight-screen counterparts, despite their more cramped cab and slightly less comfortable driving position.

Type 2 VWs were available from 1954, fitted with the same engine as Beetles of this era – the 1192 cc 30 bhp. Type 1 and 2 models were fitted with the uprated 34 bhp 1200 unit in 1961, and the Type 2 continued to use this engine until 1965 when it was enlarged to 1493 cc for the last two years of the split-screen model production. Most split-screen vans have 6-volt electrics, only those made in 1967 being 12-volt.

The model range has continued virtually unchanged to the present day. There were commercials (pick-up and delivery van) and passenger vehicles (the 8-seater Microbus and the Kombi or estate car). And, of course, there were various caravan conversions available with and without elevating roofs.

One of the most sought-after of the early Type 2s is the model 241 (LHD) or 244 (RHD) *Sondermodell* or *Samba*. Officially this is described as an eight-passenger Microbus, special equipment. It is in fact a luxury bus with a full length canvas sliding sunroof and small roof windows along each side; these give extra visibility and a pleasantly light interior.

Most 'splits' had double opening doors in the side of the rear compartment (left side for RHD vehicles and right side for LHD, apart from the few with doors on each side). Some 1967 models were made with a sliding door of similar design to that of later models. Beware, though, if you are trying to buy a replacement for this, as the later doors are wider and will not fit!

Engine

This is the area liable to give least trouble as, apart from the exhaust, it is the same as that fitted to the Beetle. I have even seen engines complete with Beetle exhausts fitted to these early vans, with the tailpipes either bent down below the level of the bumper or sticking through it via specially cut holes!

Any Beetle engine will fit these vans, so if you feel the 1200 is a little under-powered it is a simple matter to uprate to a 1300, 1500 or even 1600 (Although it must be emphasised that the vehicle may then not be sufficiently safe without appropriate uprating of the brakes). Exhausts for 1300 or 1500 engines will be readily available, as they are the same as those fitted to the later 1600 vans. There should not be any difficulty in obtaining a van exhaust for a 34 bhp engine with fresh-air heater, although those for the non-fresh-air 34 bhp and 30 bhp engines may be in short supply. Any upright air-cooled VW engine to 1600 cc can be fitted although up to 1964 the original was 1200 cc.

Gearbox

The gearboxes fitted to these older vans are much more robust than those fitted from 1968 onwards, but many have at last got to the age when they are starting to give up for one reason or another. The most common problem is jumping out of gear. When this starts to happen, the best course of action is to renew the gearbox.

There were three types of gearbox fitted to the split-screen vans. Up to 1960 a split-case gearbox was used. This was replaced with a tunnel-cased transmission from 1961. The gear ratios in the 1200 and 1500 vans differed slightly; the easiest way to tell them apart (if they are complete with driveshafts) is by the size of the rear hub nuts. The 1200 used a 36 mm nut as opposed to a 46 mm nut on the 1500.

Unlike the later vans, which were fitted with a double-joint axle using CV joints, the rear axle of these vans is of the swinging type, similar to that of most Beetles (apart from the 1302/3 range), but with the added complication of reduction gearboxes at the outer ends of the driveshafts. These house the four rear wheel bearings, which are both awkward and expensive to replace if they fail. Check for condition by listening to them; failed bearings are noisy.

Most 'recon' gearboxes are 'short', i.e. they do not include the driveshafts or reduction boxes. A secondhand replacement, on the other hand, will generally include these and will be simpler to fit. The 1200 and 1500 gearboxes are interchangeable complete, provided the handbrake cables are also changed. It is not advisable to fit a 1200 box into a 1500-engined van, though, as it would probably result in increased petrol consumption.

Gearboxes are generally reliable but if faulty, recon. units are available. Secondhand ones can be difficult to get hold of

although a swing-axle Beetle gearbox can be used if the differential is reversed.

Front Axle

Again these vans employ a similar design to the early Beetles – king and link pins. But those fitted to the van are of a heavier duty construction than on the car. Regular greasing will considerably increase the life of these components, but eventually old age and/or previous neglect will take its toll.

Excessive king pin play, as most early VW enthusiasts will be aware, is a common MoT failure. Dismantling the stub axle is not a D-I-Y job on the Type 2 as the parts are an extremely tight press-fit and specialist tools are needed. The best option is to buy a replacement stub axle. Although this is costly to buy new, be careful if you are considering buying secondhand as play is difficult to detect once the part has been removed.

The steering boxes on these vans gave little trouble, and secondhand replacements should be fairly easy to obtain.

The 1200-engined vans were originally fitted with 15-inch wheel rims shod with 6.40 x 15 crossply tyres. 1966 and '67 vehicles used 14-inch rims (as on the Type 2 from '68 to '71) fitted with 7.00 x 15 crossply or 185 x 15 radial ply tyres.

15-inch commercial tyres can sometimes be hard to get but, as the stud pattern is the same as for the later rims, 14-inch wheels and tyres can be fitted if there is any problem. This may give slightly increased petrol consumption, though, and will make the speedo read somewhat fast.

Body and chassis

Of course, the major drawback of owning, or considering buying, any vehicle so old is the dreaded RUST. This can be considered under two headings – structural rot and body rust. A wide range of repair panels is available so it should be possible to resurrect all but the most rotten of these vans.

Structural rot

Commonly this affects the chassis outriggers and box sections. All these are available as repair panels, and so it is fairly easy for a competent welder to repair this rot provided there is solid metal to weld the new panels to! Other rust-prone areas are the cab floor, the front wheel arches, and the sills.

Body rust

Rusty doors will not mean an MoT failure, but do spoil the look of the van. Secondhand replacements will be the order of the day here although, as I have already mentioned, you could be in trouble if you own a '67 sliding-door model. Common problem areas are the rear wheel arches and the corners of the van under the rear lights; there are repair panels for both of these.

Models to choose from

Most vans offered for sale now are camper conversions (with or without elevating roof) – Devon and Canterbury-Pitt being the most common in the UK. There are also DIY conversions of varying standards. The Samba de-luxe microbus (with full length sliding roof and roof windows), panel van and pick-up models are rarer, and almost always more expensive. You can still pick up a restorable split quite cheaply but vehicles in excellent condition are now fetching about half the price of the cheapest new small car!

Conclusion

A priority consideration when buying a 'split van' should be the condition of the bodywork. Items such as doors, especially sliding doors for '67 models, may be difficult to get. Repair panels are made for most rot-prone areas of the van, but extensive welding can be very expensive. Other expensive trouble spots can be the front stub axles (king pins) and the gearboxes. The rarer models are appreciating assets, but even an old 'split' delivery van can provide you with a workhorse of character!

Author's footnote: House of Haselock take a special interest in restoring these vehicles and in having replacement 'impossible to find' panels made.

Buying a Cabriolet by Ronan Sill of the V.W. Cabriolet Owners Club G.B.

Be under no illusion, buying a Cabriolet means spending a fair amount of money. However, experience has proved time after time that it is money well spent. Either you recoup it when you sell the car or better still depending on mileage and model you make some money. So from that angle one can argue that a Beetle Cabriolet is good value for money. How many mid-range modern cars will be worth as much or more in a few years time? The added advantage is that a Cabriolet is a very practical car. In the winter it is as waterproof, draught proof and cosy as its saloon counterpart and when the sun shines, you can take full advantage of what nature has got to offer. Finally with its roof down it is a real charmer! And while beauty is in the eye of the beholder, one thing is certain; it attracts a lot of envious looks.

The first advice before purchasing a Cabriolet is to look at its chassis number. Lift up the rear seat and on the tunnel you will notice a row of numbers. Now since 1965, Cabriolets have been very easy to identify, the first two digits are/should be 15. This denotes a Cabriolet chassis. I say should, because I do know of

many a Cabriolet with saloon chassis and when you are spending several thousands you are entitled to the genuine article I feel! There is no difference between a Cabriolet and a saloon chassis but it's best to keep away from rogues. There are a few around and I shall come back to that point later! The thing uppermost in our mind being the chassis number, let us bear in mind that between 1965 and 1970 the chassis number begins with 15 then the 3rd digit tells you the model year of manufacture. Thus 155 followed by six other digits will indicate a 1965 Cabriolet. After 1970, it is the same system but you add an extra digit. Therefore a 1971 Cabriolet will read 151 + 7 digits. You cannot have a 1965 chassis on a 1975 shell because they are not compatible but you can have a 1973 saloon chassis married to a 1976 or later shell! I know of such cases.

If the car you are inspecting is a pre-1965 then you will have to refer to the Production Modification section of this book.

Having ascertained that you're dealing with a Cabriolet mounted on a proper chassis, you might as well inspect the space either side of the tunnel. On the far side you'll see the battery, but look behind and around it for rust. Water ingress begins in that area where the chassis and bodywork join. Between the two is sandwiched a foam seal which does age quickly and lets in water in winter. You may never notice it but it might still seep in. (Here's a tip for when you've purchased: To avoid this when everything is nice and dry, coat the seal with plenty of diluted rust-proofer inside and outside. You'll have to roll under the car for the latter part of this useful exercise. Normally this suffices. It it does not, then apply a coat of black underseal covered when it is dry by a coat of rust-proofer. It is not unusual to see that the rust bug had a feast under the rear seat and holes are therefore quite common if the car

has been neglected.

The second point I would look at is the gap between the door and rear panel. On a bad example you can put your finger in the gap. I have never seen such a phenomenon on a 1303 Cabriolet, but it's best to check if it is not too obvious anyway. If the space at the top of the door is wider than at the bottom, then it can be rectified, possibly by lifting the bodywork off the chassis and changing some rear rubber mountings. This sagging usually begins when the sturdy girders running under the running-boards have been attacked by rust. This brings us to the third item of importance: The state of the girders. On Cabriolets up to 1970, the rear end section is of a squarish shape whereas on 1302s and 1303s it is rounded. 90% of all pre-1971 Cabriolets seem to have had work done to that part of the car. This is a vital point to check as it substitutes in great part the strength lost by the lack of a steel roof. New girders can be had at any VW dealer at a high price, but it's worth it! Naturally such a box section can be fabricated but it usually shows and to my eyes it is a real eye-sore to see non-original girders, especially on a car which has undergone major restoration in other departments. To repair girders properly you need to lift the bodywork off the chassis. Otherwise you will be welding bodywork and chassis together which can spell problems in future years if you wish to restore the car properly. (Check when examining a car that it hasn't already been done). There are other strengthening panels but they are to be found inside the car, so they do not really get damaged by the weather quite as badly as the outer panels.

If the car has passed on all these three points then you can start worrying about the top of the car. How good is the whole soft-top? A headlining which is torn means that you really need to take the other layers off too for a

proper job. The padding is wrapped in a black material which, with age, often disintegrates on the sides. Pre-1974 Cabriolets have horse hair for padding. In mid 1974 this was replaced by a foam padding. The external layer is very durable, but eventually it will have to be changed: A costly item! From a dealer it costs £400 in 1985. From the Cabriolet Club G.B. it costs £150. Interestingly V.A.G. no longer supply the original material whereas at the moment the Cabrio Club still supply the original hood skin. (Membership therefore seems to be a must!) Soft-tops can also be had from other sources in particular from the U.S. though not all are perfectly original in appearance. Mohair soft-tops should be fitted to Cabriolets up to 1964. From 1965 onwards a thick, very durable P.V.C. of a similar grain right through to 1979 was used, even though the hood construction and glass area changed several times during the last 15 years of its life.

(Author's note: Read carefully the section on soft-top repair in this book.)

Earlier on, I said the Cabriolet is a draught-free vehicle. In fact I shall advance that by saying it has got the best soft-top in the world. It does not even get the pregnant look at 70 mph on the motorway. On the other hand the Golf Cabrio and the Rolls Royce Corniche do! Also as from 1974 it was possible to get an electrically heated rear window, something the Rolls Royce cannot yet boast about.

Since 1972 hoods are easier to handle and less cumbersome when folded down. Talking of hoods down, beware if you buy a hood-bag for a 1303 Cabrio. There exists three different hood bags and if you swop them round you will find they do not fit well! Upholstery trims apart from black are mostly unobtainable, something worth bearing in mind if originality is important.

If you are presented with a R.H.D. Cabriolet, the question

should be, is it a genuine one? Between 1971 and 1979 about 200 have allegedly been officially sold in the U.K. Yet you will find that more than 200 can be found because quite a few cars have been converted. It is therefore possible to do so but it is a costly job and in the end if you must have a R.H.D. car, you may as well pay the difference now and get the genuine model. For 1303s two conversions can be found. An expedient way which will leave you with wipers wiping the wrong way and the bootlid catch under the dashboard when it should be found in the lockable glove box. Even this method will set you back several hundred pounds. The correct way will naturally cost nearly twice as much. It is fine if you wish to keep the car indefinitely otherwise you are likely to loose out on the money invested in the conversion.

Most Cabriolets have been imported from Italy and are mostly 1303s. Here is a word of caution. Between 1973 and 1975 Italian 1303s were mostly fitted with a 1300 engine. The occasional genuine 1600 model can be found, but you'll have to search hard. From 1975 on they are mostly fitted with a 1200 cc engine because Wolfsburg had stopped the 1300 engine and due to the Italian road tax system, the smaller engine was preferred. It is fine if you use the car as a trendy shopping vehicle which is what rich Italians seem to have chosen to do with the Cabriolets. As a road car the 1300 engined car is underpowered, so needless to say the 1200 feels somewhat asthmatic. Some owners have discovered that changing the engine is not sufficient as the gearbox is also different. The advice it would seem is to save money and be patient rather than have a Cabriolet at all costs. Many, after a time, find that a 1200 is not really suitable for such a heavy car as the 1303. Beetle engines are very reliable and long lasting but with the 1600 engine it is useful to fit an oil temperature

gauge as it tends to run very hot in the summer. Cabriolets have less ventilation to their engines to the extent it is not possible to use the 83 mph top speed of a 1600 engined 1303 as cruising speed on the motorway. After a while the oil gauge would read over 120 degrees centigrade. This is not very healthy for the engine. A 1600 engine will last just as well as the unburstable 1200 but it does need some consideration.

One final word on running a Beetle Cabriolet is the often exhorbitant price of body and trim parts which are particular to the Cabriolet. Only 300,000 Cabriolets were built between July 1949 and January 1980. This is a limited number compared to the several millions of saloons/sedans built. It must also be borne in mind that Cabriolets were coachbuilt by Karmann with quality in mind.

What is the best 1303 Cabrio to go for? Definitely a post 1975 1600 engine Cabriolet. At that time they lost the LS suffix on the engine lid but they gained excellent front seats with adjustable headrests (optional) and the rack and pinion already fitted to 1975 models. Italian Cabrios do not get the 1303 badge, instead they read "Volkswagen" while U.S. models sport a "fuel injection" badge. It is interesting to note that whilst the 1303 saloon/sedan was deleted in 1975, the Cabriolet counterpart was improved in the following year and then remained unaltered until July 1979 for Europe and January for the U.S. market.

Running and Buying an early ('Split-Window') Beetle
by Richard Cotton

Driving a split-window

Despite the apparent shortcomings, a 'split-window' is

very easy to drive, provided one doesn't choose a city centre in which to practice. It takes some time to learn silent gear changes on the "crash" gearbox, but the box itself is very rugged and usually outlives the 25 hp engine. Cable brakes need to be treated with care as they operate with delayed action as the cables take up the slack, but the hydraulic brakes on the deluxe models are perfectly adequate.

The Beetle has always been a heavy car and the early engine is desperately under powered, with third gear being required for the slightest hill. However, the low revving aspect of it means that it does last a very long time — a fair few original engines and gearboxes survive in rusted — beyond restoration Beetles. Like most cars of the forties and fifties, the VW used semaphore-type trafficators, but operation of these is awkward in that the switch is in the middle of the dashboard under the windscreen. The decision to turn left in dense traffic requires about ¼ mile of hand and foot movements and a silent prayer that the driver behind will see the dim single brakelight and almost invisible semaphore!

Bodywork

The bodywork on the 'split-window' Beetle is very simple, with the bodyshell being bolted straight onto the single backboned floorpan (there are no cross-members). The floorpan forks at the rear to support the engine, gearbox and axle assembly. Each wing/fender is held to the body by ten bolts, making do-it-yourself repairs much easier than on many cars. Although very often one or more of these bolts will a) shear off or b) take out a large piece of rusty metal with it, only five or six bolts are necessary to keep a Beetle wing firmly in place, so check the mountings carefully.

Principle rust areas on the body are the spare wheel well, front and rear bumper hangers, bottom rear quarter panels (and

wing/fender mounting bolt holes) and bottom front door pillars. Body rockers/sills, which are hollow to carry heat from the heat exchangers, also rust, mainly where the running boards are bolted to the car. As they are an important part of the car's rigidity, to do a proper repair requires removal of body from floorpan — consequently, there are a lot of bodged repair jobs around! The bolt-on panels rust too, bottom of the passenger door being first, the extreme bottom front of all wings/fenders and the three "corners" of the front cover. All bolt-on panels are replaceable with later items which are readily available from Volkswagen themselves, but finding, in good condition, early original doors (no quarterlights (vents) pre Oct 52), front wings/fenders (no cut-out for indicators, no apertures for horn grilles), rear wings/fenders (recess for rear light fittings, pre Oct 52) and front cover (without raised area for VW emblem) is becoming very difficult. In general though, the Beetle doesn't have a particularly serious rust problem, and some remarkably rust-free examples survive. As a sweeping generalisation, it's true to say that if you find a car with sound, useable side members (heater tubes), then you've found a sound 'split-window' Beetle!

Steering & Suspension

Steering on the split-window was by worm and sector steering box via track rods to king and link pin suspension. Very primitive, but also very simple to work on. The boxes last almost indefinitely if regularly adjusted. It is generally easier to replace king and link pins as a complete stub axle assembly rather than go to the trouble of having new king pins and bushes renewed — this way the job takes only an hour. Very early models (up to 1949) had lever arm shock absorbers (tiny 8 inch hydraulic ones were an optional extra) — both are virtually unobtainable now, an expensive rebuild of the existing units being the only way round. There is a tendency for the top mounting bolt of the front shock absorber to shear off, leaving the nightmare of drilling and retapping two inches of toughened steel bolt — better to use heat than brute force in this area.

Brakes

Hydraulic brakes on the split-window are easy to maintain, although they used a master cylinder with reservoir directly above whereas later cars had a remote reservoir. The size of the wheel cylinders had also changed several times over the years, the 16 mm rear ones used between 1949 and 1952 being particularly hard to find now. Front cables for the cable-operated brakes are now no longer available, and setting up cable brakes so that they'll pass an MoT takes a lot of patience. Whether cable or hydraulic, the rear drums are held on with a 36 mm nut tightened to 217 1bs/ft, and it is essential to use a ¾ inch square socket wrench and at least a three foot extension — a great many ½ inch socket wrenches have been broken in the name of economy!

Engine

The 25 hp engine is the easiest of all Beetle engines to work on, as it is the smallest, leaving plenty of room to reach the spark plugs, It is also very light and therefore easily removed, taking no more than ¾ hour even for the novice working alone with just a small trolley jack. This is just as well, as any overhaul greater than fitting a new rocker cover gasket or checking the tappets requires removal of the engine. Air cooling means very efficient, but not easily regulated, heating system (operated via heat exchangers). It also means that temperature is critical, and a broken fan must be repaired immediately — it takes less than ten miles without the fan turning to melt the HT leads and do severe damage to the engine!

Interior

For a small car, the interior of the later, deluxe split-window is surprisingly luxurious. Seats were cloth, in several different herringbone patterns, and the headlining was beige or grey cotton. The standard models, particularly early ones, had more primitive seating which gave the car a very spartan appearance. Neither did standard models have any insulation behind the rear seat, so noise at speed (65 mph flat out) is considerable. All models had an interior courtesy light and most had ashtrays, both of which are the first things to disappear from the car over the years.

Buying a split-window

The greatest problem for the potential split-window owner is simply the lack of split-windows available. Only about sixty are definitely known to exist in the U.K. for instance, with an unknown number still lurking unknown in barns and garages. Most of these are in fairly rusted condition; one must expect to pay a great deal of money just to get the necessary welding done (unless doing it yourself). They vary in originality too. Bumpers and rear lights are the most commonly sought-after items as both were only used up to October 1952 and have long been unavailable from VW. A number of people have started re-making early parts, but good repros can be very expensive. Nevertheless, good examples can still be found. Just recently a 99% original 1951 Beetle with sunroof was found in Devon (now being restored to concours condition). Prices vary enormously too. Unfortunately, the days of finding an early car for a few pounds are long gone; everyone expects them to be worth a lot of money just because they're old. Things to look for, apart from the obvious rust areas

mentioned above, are the front end inside the spare wheel well — very often this has suffered accident damage and may be badly bent. An external sign of this is front bumper hangers at an odd angle. Look also at the rear end for accident damage. The rear skirt, above the tailpipe, if often replaced with a later panel. The best way to tell is to look at the tailpipe(s) themselves and where they emerge from under the car. All split-windows used only one, non-chromed tail-pipe, but if a later engine or exhaust has been fitted, cut-outs will have been made in the skirt. If these cut-outs are crudely done (as if done with a knife & fork!) then the panel is probably original. Later panels have smoothly rounded cut-outs and are strengthened.

If you are after a restored split-window, you may have a long wait, as there are not enough around for them to become available very often. Restoration is a very expensive business, even on a Beetle, and restorers rarely recoup the money they have spent when they sell their cars. On the Continent, particularly in Holland and Germany where standards are higher, a good restoration job will be more expensive than in Britan and in the USA the cost will be even higher. All this can sound disheartening, but there is still plenty of scope for the amateur with limited funds — it just takes a lot of patience!

B1. This transporter looked really ragged and would require a lot of work, but as one of the rare 'Samba' models (note all the extra glass), it could be worth considering as a proposition if you come across one.

B2. When it arrived at House of Haselock, the author's Cabrio. still looked pretty smart, but you would be well advised to look at what needed to be done, depicted in many of the pictures in this book, to see how external appearances can be deceptive. Then look at picture FAL2 under 'Modifications' to see the sort of transformation that can be wrought!

B3. Vehicles can often be bought in an unfinished state at knock down prices, but you can end up with the worst of all worlds. You won't know where all the bits are or where they went, you won't be able to check whether the work carried out has caused distortion and finishing off a job is far more time and money consuming than the more dramatic job of stripping down, anyway. This one, under restoration at Haselocks, was not for sale, but note how the front wheel arch had (typically) rotted away. Replacements are available from Haselocks who have them specially fabricated.

B4. This 1302S interior would need careful checking over, too. Padded dash covers are still available from Volkswagen at the time of writing, but for how long? STP make a plastic protector called 'Son-of-a-Gun' which prevents the sun from drying out and cracking the plastic, so they say.

B5. Many seat covers are available from Volkswagen and many more from specialist suppliers in the USA, but check that the pattern you want is still around if the car you want has ripped seats and you prize originality. One good thing is the availability of second-hand parts for later cars.

B6. A Holley carb. may or may not be to your taste. Check out engine originality, too, if that matters to you.

B7. Some faults just can't be spotted without some dismantling, such as the corrosion in these rear light pods, hidden beneath the lenses.

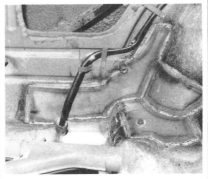

B8. On a larger and much more dramatic scale, corrosion in the rear inner wing/fender and floor beneath the rear seats should be checked carefully. Corrosion can need this much patching, or even more.

B9. One thing you don't need to worry too much about is the state of the wings/fenders because replacements are readily available for almost all cars and they're remarkably inexpensive. So don't worry as much about superficial damage as about structural rigidity.

B10. The importance of the condition, and even more important, the completeness of interior trim in early cars can't be over emphasised, although 'Bugs for You' in the USA can help here.

B11. Earlier Cabriolet's soft-tops pin down to a wooden bow at the rear. Like all timber, it can rot out so check it as thoroughly as you can by pushing through the cloth, inside and outside the car to see if you can detect sponginess.

B12. This jacking point has collapsed under the pressure of the workshop lift. It indicates rotted body rockers/sills.

42

3 Bodywork

Types of Repair

Beetle bodywork repairs can't all be categorised in the same way. Some are as simple as body repairs could ever be, some are more difficult while others are really tough going! Wing/fender replacement couldn't be easier and bumpers, doors and engine bay/luggage bay covers are easy to remove and replace — always assuming that the demon rust hasn't decided to grab hold and not to let go of the fixing bolts — but from then on, things are not so easy without specific step-by-step instructions on how to proceed. But then, that's where this book comes in! Transporter bodywork can be just as tricky if not trickier to repair because there are no bolt on major panels at all, apart from doors.

However, Beetle bodywork is by no means all doom and gloom; there are certain advantages in its construction, too. One is that there is a full range of repair panels available and that House of Haselock, Nuneaton (see Appendix for address), for instance, where the photo-research for this book was carried out, can supply full Volkswagen-produced panels, mass-produced repair panels (more of these anon) or a range of purpose-designed panels for both the Beetle and Transporter

restorer. Another is that the Beetle is a chassis-based car and the advantages of that for the DIY restorer are immense! Fully professional body shops are familiar with the problems of distortion when restoring chassis-less cars: they can twist out of alignment and cause very major problems where there are no facilities for locking the structure in shape on a jig or for pulling it back into alignment with hydraulic rams. The Beetle is less prone to distortion when body panels are removed, although having said that, the body can still sag to a degree; the chassis/floorpan remaining rigid and the body sagging a little around it, unless you remember to leave doors in place as long as possible so that the door aperture and door gaps can be regularly checked when major panels are being replaced and unless you only ever remove one panel at a time. If you go hacking a lot of bodywork away at any one time, you'll be sure to lose the shape with disastrous results. Cut-out and let-in a section at a time as shown here! Naturally enough, the Beetle Cabriolet is most prone to the 'sag' problem because it doesn't possess the closed car's strong roof structure to help keep it in shape.

It was mentioned earlier that a number of different types of

repair panel are available for the Beetle or Transporter restorer. As with any other car you care to mention, the original manufacturer's own replacement panels are a better fit than any one else's, as well they should be. The reverse side of this coin is that Volkswagen's panels are generally those that would have been used on the now-defunct production line. In other words, they are not necessarily designed for the repairer or restorer and they can be difficult and time-consuming to fit. On the other hand, once they're on, Volkswagen's own panels, where they are still available must be able to do the job better than any others. Several Volkswagen panels were fitted to the author's Cabriolet featured in this book and they do a terrific job — provided that you are willing to pay the high cost of these superb panels and provided that you intend doing the job as thoroughly as it can possibly be done.

Some repair panels don't fit as well as Volkswagen's, but the better ones have other huge advantages that are worth bearing in mind. If the Bug or Beetle's rear inner wheel arches are corroded in the area of the chassis mountings only, you can purchase a repair panel just for that area. The Volkswagen alternative would be to use a full quarter panel — the

one that stretches from the door shut pillar right round to the rear of the car including the rear window surround. It's a very large-scale job to fit and it would cost over ten times more than the non-Volkswagen repair panel. Clearly under these circumstances, it would be silly to fit the full Volkswagen panel when House of Haselock, for instance, could supply a small, inexpensive panel made specially for the job at a small fraction of the cost.

The third type of panel mentioned earlier in this introduction is the specialist restorer's panel designed and commissioned specially for the Transporter or Beetle restorer. Mass-produced panels are made with the repair trade in mind and the range has to be restricted to the fast moving panels. Consequently, parts of these vehicles such as the rear floor and beneath-the-seat of the Bug/Beetle and the front wheel arches of the Transporter are not obtainable and have to be fabricated unless purchased as full-scale VW panels.

You can restore a Bug/Beetle without taking the body off the chassis, but if you want to do an as-good-as-new job, off the body will have to come. Do remember that the cardinal rule is to restore the body first, THEN take the body off the chassis. If you take the body off first, the dreaded distortion mentioned earlier will set in and there will be a good chance that you will repair the body, but lock it into the wrong shape so that it won't seat back onto the chassis/floorpan at all! Leave the body on the chassis, follow the procedures shown in this book and there shouldn't be a problem at all.

Hints, tips and equipment

More and more DIY restorers and enthusiasts are discovering that doing their own welding not only saves them a great deal of money, it also gives them a great deal of satisfaction. Of course, no one can expect to pick up a piece of welding equipment for the first time and make a perfect weld, but there are welding sets that make life so much easier for the DIY-er. Those recommended here are not necessarily the cheapest on the market, but they are considered by the author to be the best having been used extensively by him, while many of them were built for light professional use rather than down to an 'occasional use' standard, which means that, like all good tools, they should last some time.

And of course, the home restorer has to invest in a certain amount of other equipment too, although most people wishing to carry out a full-scale project will already have acquired much of it. Those who have to buy gear from scratch can console themselves with the knowledge that the equipment they buy should cost far less than the labour costs of a rebuild plus the fact that they will still own the equipment for future use. Hand tools receive the largest amount of use and it is always well worth investing in the best that are around, because poor tools make a good quality job well-nigh impossible. Sykes-Pickavant produce a huge range of bodyshop panelwork tools and are developing an increased range at lower cost suitable for the DIY repairer and restorer. An electric drill is invaluable, of course, but so is a mini-grinder which is useful at almost every stage for cutting out rusty metal, sanding paint and surface rust away from weld surfaces, dressing welds and dressing the edges of repair panels. A major manufacturer in both the UK and USA of good quality electrical tools is Black & Decker.

With these basics plus the more obvious hammer, bolster chisel, screwdrivers and spanners, as well as a means of cutting out sheet steel (a good pair of universal tin snips will do for a start) the first-timer could get under way. He or she would have to fit panels together with self-tapping screws and/or clamps until a 'mobile welder' could be dragged out of Yellow Pages or the bodyshell trailered to professional premises. Several such visits would be necessary as some panels have to be closed off before others can be welded into place, but the procedure is not impossible given the co-operation of a friendly welder or bodyshop. If restoration is to be taken seriously it would be best to learn to weld at some time or other. It is possible to hire arc welding equipment from most tool-hire firms, but this type of welding is too fierce for outer body panels in even the most experienced hands. For work on thicker chassis members and for tack-welding some components, arc welding can be acceptable. Arc-brazing, which is more versatile, but less strong can also be carried out with an arc welder with the addition of a special accessory but should never be used in conjunction with modern high-strength steels or for structural components: it isn't acceptable for the British annual 'MoT' test, for instance.

In the UK most Technical Colleges and Evening Institutes run evening classes where, amongst other things, beginners can learn the rudiments of gas or arc welding. 'Gas' or oxy-acetylene welding is far more versatile than arc welding as far as car bodywork is concerned, but gas cylinders (widely called 'bottles') are more expensive to obtain and less safe to store. A company called Murex, owned by the welding rod firm ESAB now market a range of welding products including 'Portapack' (nothing to do with the author!) welding kits. Shown being used in this book, they are small-scale oxy-acetylene welding kits which the user buys outright and then rents the mini cylinders for a renewable seven year period, the cylinders being exchanged at a British Oxygen Company centre in

the normal way when the gas is used up. This means that the cylinders undergo stringent safety checks every time they are exchanged, making this source the safest and most reliable. There are a number of manufacturers, producing cheaper alternatives which may be perfectly adequate, particularly if you only intend using 'gas' for a little cutting, heating stubborn nuts plus a little brazing or welding. These kits can include a first class welding torch run from a replenishable oxygen cylinder and a discardable container of Mapp gas which burns almost as hot as acetylene, but without the storage risks. Other sets sometimes have cheaper welding torches which can be a real pain to use but 'you pays your money and takes your choice . . .'.

The author's favourite way of welding body panels is using MIG. MIG stands for Metal Inert Gas and is technically a form of arc welding, but it's far easier to use without 'burning through' and creates far less distortion than 'gas'. MIG welding sets were once rather expensive which made it difficult for the DIY-person to justify the high cost, but now firms such as SIP (Industrial Products) Ltd produce 'mini-migs' which don't fall all that far short of the larger seat in performance terms and are far cheaper to buy, costing about the same as half-a-dozen good quality Beetle tyres. You'll see MIG sets being used at House of Haselock throughout this book and really no self-respecting bodyshop would use anything else! If you were trying to equip yourself with the sort of welding equipment that would enable you to have a chance of doing a first class job, the author's advice would be to go for a MIG set and a cheaper oxy-acetylene or oxy-Mapp set as a fill-in and for all those unforeseeable cutting, bending, freeing and brazing jobs for which the MIG is, frankly, useless. Alternatively, if your pocket runs to it and you feel you can afford the best around, supplement the MIG with a

Portapack. On the other hand, some folk prefer to go the other way and to buy the good-quality oxy-acetylene set first and to buy a MIG later – it's all a matter of personal preference.

All of the jobs shown throughout this book, apart from the major respray section, which was carried out on behalf of ICI Paints by a Leicester-based company, Graham Maurice Cars Ltd, were carried out at House of Haselock, Nuneaton, a firm with a highly recommended reputation for considerate, friendly service. Naturally, skilled mechanics are shown at work, but the photographs and captions have been presented in such a way that the home restorer can make best use of the House of Haselock skills on display. Please read carefully both the 'Tool Box' and (especially) the 'Safety' sections before commencing work. But remember that there will always be new and individual ways of

having accidents and that safety is entirely YOUR responsibility!

BOD1. MIG welding is most certainly the best way of welding together car body panels since it is quick, much easier to learn than any other welding method and causes far less distortion than any other method. SIP market a full range of welders on both sides of the Atlantic, right down to the 'Migmate' shown here on the left, up to the 'Autoplus 150' shown right and on up to very heavy duty, heavy industrial machines. The inexpensive Migmate is ideal for DIY work while the Autoplus is an inexpensive 'professional' machine that would last the DIY-er a lifetime and is capable of heavier-duty work. Check when buying an inexpensive MIG that the torch isn't permanently 'live'. There isn't room to go into it here but a non-live torch (such as those on SIP machines) is almost essential.

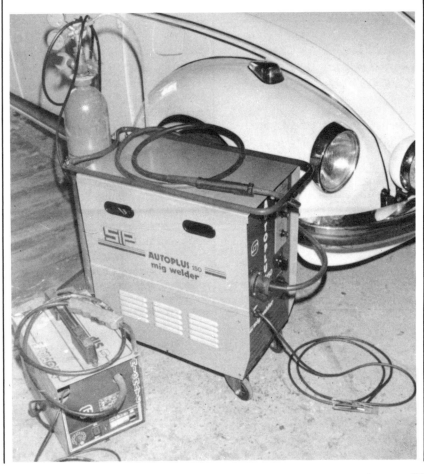

BOD2. 'Gas' welding is much more difficult to use in inexperienced hands, but sometimes, there's no alternative and in fact it's much more versatile than MIG. There are cheap sets around — OK for brazing or freeing stubborn nuts — but the 'Portapack', available in the UK from BOC (who supply the gas) and Murex (who supply the hardware) is a fully professional quality kit in a DIY or portable package.

BOD3. This is one of BOC's many Cylinder Centres where Portapack cylinders can be changed (find your local centre in the telephone directory). Portapacks can be purchased there or at many motor factors.

BOD5. This Sykes-Pickavant tool is ideal for letting patches into Beetle bodywork. It allows you to join two flat pieces of metal with all the smoothness of a butt joint but with the strengh and ease of welding of a lap joint. The two rollers pull the steel between themselves and form a 'set' or shoulder in the edge of the steel.

BOD6. Although a little more expensive, the Sykes-Pickavant sheet metal folder enables you to create perfectly formed folds and box-sections in sheet steel.

BOD4. This cutting tool, made by Sykes-Pickavant, consists of a pair of cutting wheels which pull the steel between themselves as they cut. It works really well but takes up far less room than a guillotine.

BOD7. Metrinch sockets, available in both the UK and USA have the unique virtue of fitting both AF and Metric nuts and bolts perfectly well. Ideal for those with cars of both domestic and imported variety in the stable.

BOD8. Electric power tools are an invaluable aid in the workshop shown here on the Black & Decker workmate, which makes a useful portable workbench, are (from right-to-left) the Professional's rechargeable electric drill, palm-grip sander, mini-grinder (a tool you can't do without for bodywork repairs) and random-orbit sander which is worth its weight in gold when preparing for a respray. All are by Black & Decker.

BOD9. Another tool which finds lots of domestic uses as well as those in the workshop is the KEW 'Hobby' power washer which operates from the mains water supply and the electricity supply to give variable levels of power of water jet to which can be added detergent or grit for grit blasting. Superb for cleaning down both before and after restoration!

BOD10. We came across this tool only after most of the restoration was completed but it is shown under 'Rustproofing'. It's amazing! Made by AutoVip, the cage is bolted to the hubs after lifting the car on the beam provided, and after removing the battery and blocking the sealing brake fluid reservoir with a piece of plastic sheet under the cap, one person can tip the car right onto its side giving incredible access for restoration or repairs.

See 'Specialists' section for addresses of all the euipment shown here and that shown throughout this book, where it has been found useful.

Tool box

At the start of every section a 'Tool Box' section appears listing most of the tools and equipment needed to enable you to carry out the work. No list of 'essential' tools is presented here, but refer to the foregoing advice on the sorts of tools you might expect to have to use.

Safety

At the start of most sections is a 'Safety' note. Naturally, safety is the responsibility of each individual restorer or repairer and no responsibility for the effectiveness or otherwise of advice given here nor for any omissions can be accepted by the author: After all, the jobs you will be carrying out will be YOUR responsibility so do take care to familiarise yourself with safety information available from the suppliers or manufacturers of the materials or equipment which you use. 'Safety' notes are intended to supplement this information with useful tips as is the additional information on workshop safety and workshop practice in the appendix — you are strongly advised to read the appendix before commencing any of the tasks detailed in this book.

Stripdown and examination

Before attempting to carry out any major body repairs, all or part of the bodyshell will need to be stripped of its lights, trim and ancillaries. Removal is a common sense procedure in many instances, but where there are complications, the accompanying photo-sequence aims to point them out. Other dismantling procedures may be found where they fall naturally into one of the repair sections of this book such as that on bumper removal. Be sure to have sufficient storage

space available — cars 'grow' amazingly when they're taken apart! — and store large components logically in cardboard boxes with smaller items being placed in labelled plastic bags. Often, stray nuts and washers are best stored by fitting them temporarily back onto the component from which they came. At the time of taking parts off it may seem as though you couldn't possibly forget where all the various bits and pieces belong, but it won't be quite like that in a few days or weeks time! Discipline yourself to thoroughly label components as they are removed and tag wires and pieces of masking tape which can then be written upon to give positive identification.

Before starting work, store any stripped out glass under cover and mask off any glass that remains in place including the interior mirror and dash gauges. Sparks from a mini-grinder will embed themselves into any glass they hit and be impossible to remove, requiring replacement of the damaged glass.

As you remove parts, make a list of any that may need replacement. Some may be easy to obtain from your main agent, but others may have to be searched for. Owners of older Bug/Beetles can find hard-to-get detail parts such as mirrors, lamps and lights, chrome, trim and steering wheel from a company called 'Bugs For You' run by Rich Kimball in California. Details of what Rich can supply are shown elsewhere in this book in the section with which he assisted on 'Fitting the Right Parts' and his address is shown in the Appendix.

Techniques

The bodywork section of this book shows how to repair all of the major sections of the car but there will inevitably be small areas of additional damage which will have to be repaired as they are found using simple patch repairs. In general the techniques shown

here for fitting let-in panels can be applied to the repair of DIY-patch panels. For more specific step-by-step information on bodyshop techniques including all types of welding and panel beating through the use of body solder, filler and touch-up paint repairs right through to the full blown respray (so to speak!), see Haynes 'The Car Bodywork Repair Manual' by the same author, containing almost 300 pages and 1,000 illustrations.

Before starting on the bodywork, you'll want to remove all vulnerable items, both inside and outside the car, as well as those that would get in the way of body repairs. It's obvious how most of them come off but here's a look at some typical stripdown procedures.

Safety
Never drain a fuel tank indoors or where the highly flammable petrol vapours can gather, such as over a pit. Store petrol drained from the tank in safe, closed, approved containers. If the empty tank is to be stored, have it steam cleaned to remove petrol vapours. Place a damp rag into any openings and keep tank out of doors for very short-term storage. Keep all sparks and flames away from the fuel system whilst working on it.

Battery and wiring

S&E1.   To avoid the risk of a short and because batteries create highly combustible hydrogen gas, the battery should be removed first. Keep the clamps in a safe place.

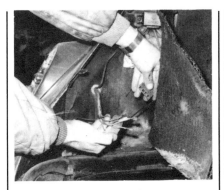

S&E2.   On later Bug/Beetles, some wiring connections are of the plug-type. Your first entry in your stripdown log may be to show the correct positions of wires for re-assembly.

S&E3.   Where lamp units are to be removed, ease out the grommet protecting the cable and pass the wiring through the panel. New grommets needed? Make a note!

S&E4.   Also, where wiring has frayed, now is the time to note the fact so that you can be sure to have replacement wiring of the right type available for reassembly.

For details of how to remove light units from wings and front and rear lids, refer to the later section which shows how to replace those components.

Exterior Trim

NEVER assume that you will be able to find replacements for exterior trim; and the older the car or Transporter, the more you have to take note of that warning. In other words, no matter how time consuming it is to work out how to take off exterior trim or how difficult it is to free seized nuts, take the time to do the job without damaging trim whenever you possibly can.

S&E5.   The '1302LS' badge on this Bug/Beetle is held on with pins cast into the rear of the badge. The pins pass through the panel and on the other side, clips are pushed over the pins to hold the badge in place. Some older models have gaskets and base plates as parts of their badge assembly. Others have retaining tongues which must be bent straight to remove the badge.

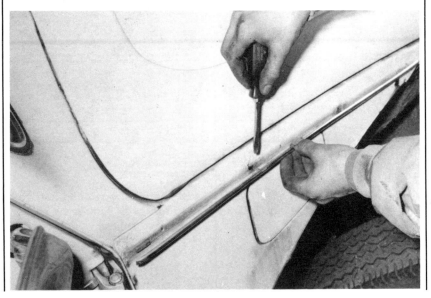

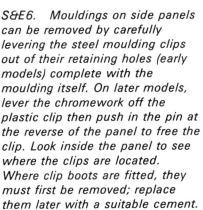

S&E6.   Mouldings on side panels can be removed by carefully levering the steel moulding clips out of their retaining holes (early models) complete with the moulding itself. On later models, lever the chromework off the plastic clip then push in the pin at the reverse of the panel to free the clip. Look inside the panel to see where the clips are located. Where clip boots are fitted, they must first be removed; replace them later with a suitable cement.

S&E7. Side mouldings on the Cabriolet are no different to remove, but those at the door top are integral with the glass rubber and must be removed by undoing the (probably thoroughly rusted) retaining screws.

Later heater fan unit removal

S&E8. Although it should have been, no connector was fitted between the tubes on this car. It would normally be pulled free from the blower unit tube.

S&E9. Three screws hold the unit to the scuttle top.

S&E10. This drainage pipe slots downwards into a drainage tube in the body.

S&E11. The blower unit can be pulled forwards and the wiring connectors removed and tagged for correct replacement.

Interior

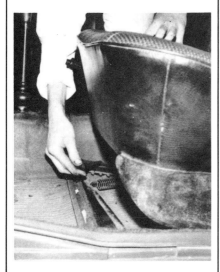

S&E12. Early cars' (De Luxe) seats (and all those prior to the '3-point fixing' seats) are removed by sliding the seat forwards until it can be lifted from its runners; Standard models' seats are taken out after removing the two wing nuts and taking off the seat clamps. Later Bug/Beetles' seats are of the three point fixing type. Push the seat back to the last but one position, take the covers off the runners then insert a screwdriver into the bracket from the front and push the locking plate down. Now pull the longitudinal position adjusting lever on the frame tunnel and slide the seat out to the rear.

S&E13. Seat belts are held in place by bolts concealed beneath plastic caps. Keep all washers in the correct order for reassembly and store the belts themselves in a plastic bag so that they're kept clean.

S&E14. To remove the rear seat base, lift it up at the front and pull forwards.

S&E15. The backrest is held in place by two hexagonal head screws on each side. After their removal, the backrest can be lifted away.

S&E16. Window winder handles and door opening handles are held in place with cross-head screws on later models. Early cars have concealed fixings: Push back the trim and you will see a pin through the shank of the handle. Push out the pin and pull off the handle.

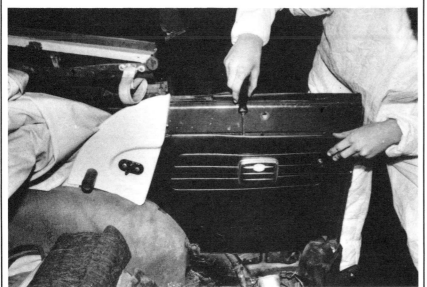

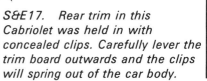

S&E17. Rear trim in this Cabriolet was held in with concealed clips. Carefully lever the trim board outwards and the clips will spring out of the car body.

S&E18. Further trim panels cover the Cabriolet soft top hinge mechanism. For details of removal, see the section on 'Soft-tops'.

S&E19. Carpets are glued to inner sill structures, but rubber mats can be lifted out. Don't forget to remove the beading from the seat runner.

S&E20. Sound deadening is often stuck down to the rear floor area. It will have to be scraped off so that the whole area can be carefully examined. This area is very prone to corrosion, but it is often poorly repaired and the only way to check for fibreglass or pop-riveted repairs is to clean this area thoroughly. Any other floor areas covered with stuck-down sound deadening will have to be scraped clean before any welding is carried out in the vicinity to reduce the fire risk.

Fuel Tank Removal

Safety

If the fuel tank is to be stored for any length of time, have it steam cleaned to remove all traces of fuel vapour; it is the vapour that ignites and explodes, so simply draining the fuel out is not enough. Also, in time, sediment tends to collect at the base of the tank and, especially after disturbing the tank, this can easily find its way in to the carburettor and block the jets. Having the tank steam cleaned is an excellent way of getting rid of this sediment and if the outside is also steam cleaned the base can be examined for corrosion; or the tank could be vigorously flushed out with a hose — but be sure to dry it thoroughly before storage (to prevent rust) and before fitting. For very short-term storage, always store the tank out of doors and seal all openings. When draining the tank, always do so out of doors and well away from possible sparks or any other potential sources of ignition.

Bug/Beetle Car

FT1. Early cars differ from later ones in a number of minor ways, one of them being that there are more pipework connections to later tanks. They must all be removed, of course, and here the filler and breather pipes are being removed from the author's 1302 Cabriolet.

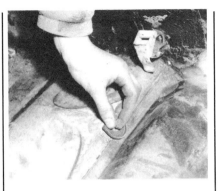

FT2. The retaining bolts hold down plates which in turn bear on the fuel tank flanges.

FT4. The tank can be lifted away but note the additional procedures in the following section:

It will often be necessary to remove lining material from over the tank and from behind the dash.

Early models without a gauge

Close the fuel tank and disconnect the fuel hose from the fuel pipe. Take off the right-hand front wheel and, with the car supported on an axle stand and the wheels chocked, remove the fuel tap operating rod — take out the split pin first. Four mounting screws hold the tank in place.

FT3. Lift the tank and clamp the fuel line at the base to prevent spillage.

Front & Rear Bumper Removal

The following section is compiled from the repair of a number of different Beetles as they passed through the House of Haselock workshop. Don't get hung up on different colours or body styles; the principle is the same for all!

FRB1. Bumper removal follows a similar pattern on all models and is also similar front and rear. Here a front bumper is being removed at Haselocks from the author's 1302 Cabrio.

FRB2. A front bumper on a late-model Bug/Beetle is being removed from beneath the wing/fender. Note that the horn mounting bracket is located by the same mounting bolts.

Clearly some repair work will be necessary in this vicinity — see appropriate section. On earlier model Bug/Beetles, these mounting bolts are found inside the spare wheel well.

FRB3.   It is possible to remove the bumpers while leaving the body mounts on the car. This is a later type mount, but earlier ones are similar and the principle – involving the removal of mounting bolts from the bracket – is the same except that there are sometimes separate reinforcement plates which must be retained.

FRB4.   Rear bumpers are removed in exactly the same way. Note that here the body grommets are coming out with the brackets. They must be replaced before the bumper brackets are inserted.

FRB5.   Bumper mountings for later U.S. models incorporate a telescopic impact-absorption device and the mounting system is slightly different. (Drawing courtesy Volkswagen).

Front & Rear Wing/Fender Replacement

Changing the wing/fenders on these cars is one of the most straightforward body jobs around. Naturally, all of Volkswagen's wing/fenders fit virtually perfectly

and some of the 'independent' suppliers' wings are pretty good, too. Haselock's used excellent quality panels supplied by the independent supplier Uro Autoparts for this sequence. Do remember that if the outer panel is corroded so badly that it requires replacement, chances are that inner panels will be corroded too. And repair of those panels will

require some welding to be carried out.

Before either front or rear wing/fenders can be removed, the bumpers must be taken off as described in the previous section.

FRW1.   The headlamp unit must be removed and the wiring disconnected from the headlamp bulb.

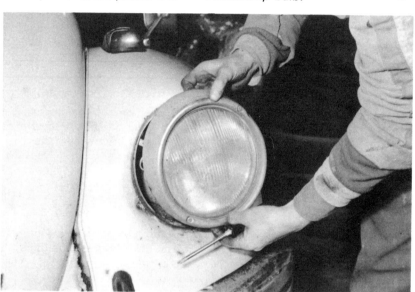

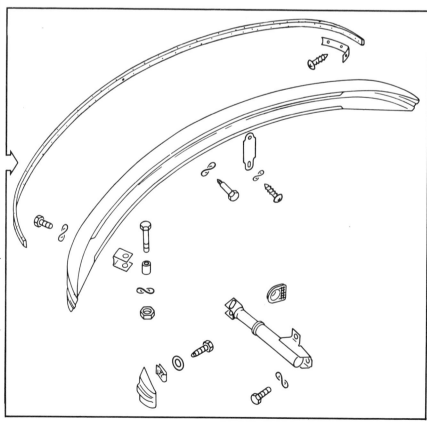

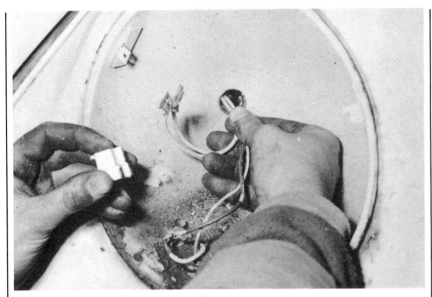

FRW2. When there is a terminal fitted to the wiring, this must be unclipped so that the wiring can be withdrawn through the rear of the headlamp bowl. Early models also have a headlamp support bracket which must be unscrewed from under the wing/fender.

FRW3. Wiring to the rear lamps is a little more complicated. Here, Stuart at Haselock's is jotting down the correct wiring positions for simple reassembly.

FRW4. The simplest part of the job is theoretically to undo the mounting bolts as shown here. (It is actually somewhat easier with the road wheel removed.) In practice, these bolts are terribly prone to seizure and breaking off. It would be wise to apply releasing fluid to each captive nut each day for a couple of days before the job is tackled to attempt to break down the rust bond.

FRW5. Where the wing/fender bolts to the front or rear panel there is no captive nut, but a nut and bolt which must be removed with a pair of spanners.

FRW6. At the inner end of the panel, where it bolts to the running board or sill panel, there lies another nut and bolt. There should be a rubber washer between the two and this may have to be replaced. (Here the outer part of the panel has been cut away.)

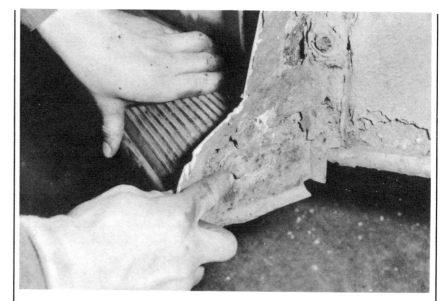

FRW7. Here the front wing bolts are being slackened at Haselock's using a power ratchet but the principles are exactly the same using hand tools.

FRW9. Now, having said all that, it is only worthwhile unbolting a wing/fender if you intend keeping and re-using it. If the panel is scrap, there is a much quicker way of taking it off — by cutting it off!

FRW10. This rear wing/fender has been cut from the author's Cabriolet and is just lifted away.

FRW8. Once all the items mentioned have been disconnected, the wing is simply lifted away.

Safety

Cut steel edges can be a real safety hazard. Always wear thick, industrial quality gloves when handling metal in this state and dispose of the scrap metal safely. Follow normal good workshop practice when using hammer and chisel and remember that a really sharp cold chisel is actually safer to use than a blunt one.

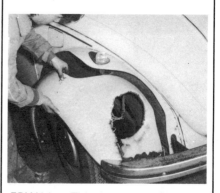

FRW11. This front wing/fender on a 1302 saloon/sedan is being treated in the same way, but note that the side light and bumper have both been left in place . . .

FRW12. ... because it is actually much easier to remove them without the bulk of the panel in place.

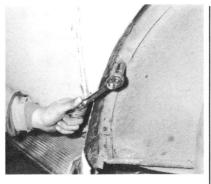

FRW13. It is also easier to remove the fixing bolts in this way – especially important if, the bolt heads have corroded away so that you have to force on a smaller size of socket, or if the bolt has to be drilled or ground away.

FRW14. The remnants of the rear wing are lifted away (it would have been best if thick gloves had been worn!) to expose ...

FRW15. ... some pretty fearsome looking holes where damp had been trapped behind the wing mounting flange. If the rest of the quarter panel was sound, it would be sufficient to patch-repair these holes, but see the appropriate section for more information on rear quarter panel repair.

FRW16. An even more common repair involves drilling out a sheared-off wing mounting bolt. Start by centre-punching as close to the centre of the bolt as you can then drilling through with a small diameter drill to provide a pilot hole. (If your centre-punching is just a little off centre, you can angle the drill for the first few seconds of drilling to take the position of the hole back towards the centre of the bolt before restoring the drill to its position in-line with the bolt.) Then drill out the bolt in such a way that the core of the bolt is removed while the threads are left undamaged. You may wish to go up in small size increments until reaching the required size.

FRW17. The shell of the old bolt will then tap out with the centre punch or a small drift and the captive threads can then be cleaned up with a tap. If the bolt was in any way tight, it's as well to tap the threads out to clean them up in any case.

FRW18. Sometimes the bolt seizes in the captive nut, but instead of shearing, the whole captive nut twists out of the body like the one here just in front of the door hinge.

FRW20. ... then welded onto the quarter panel.

FRW21. This is a new wing/fender from Uro being offered up and checked for fit and alignment.

FRW19. New captive nuts are straightforward to get hold of (See Haselock's address in the Appendix) and here a new one is being offered up. After ensuring that the nut is properly located, it can first be bolted in place ...

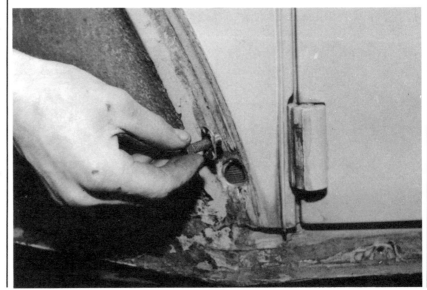

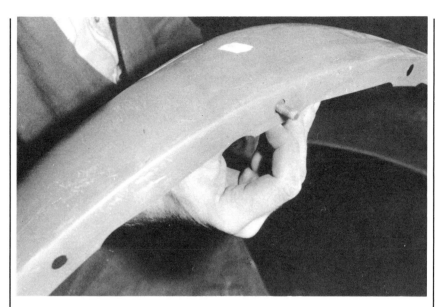

FRW22.   Then a bolt is popped through one of the top mounting holes . . .

◄

FRW23.   . . . and the bolt inserted, the wing/fender being suspended in place. The bolt should be loosely inserted only at this stage. It is best to use 'bright-zinc-plated' bolts to avoid any future rusting problems and the thread should be greased before assembly.

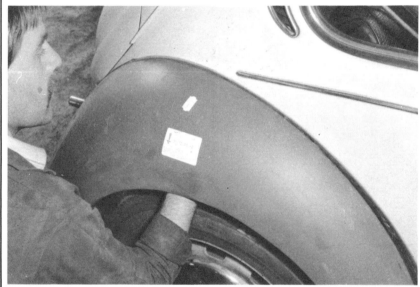

FRW24.   Procedure for front wings is the same as for the rears. After the first bolt has been inserted, the others can be screwed loosely into place and the wing/fender pulled and pushed into alignment.

FRW25.   Sometimes, a little filing of the mounting holes is needed to get the panel into exactly the position you want it, but remember that well fitting panels are one of the hallmarks of a well-prepared motor car, so take as much time as necessary to get it right.

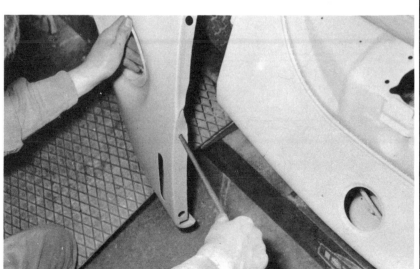

FRW26. The author's car's wing/fenders were removed again at this stage and, once the fit was assured, were painted with a two pack epoxy paint which Haselock's like to use for special jobs because of its extremely tough, resilient properties. Body colour paint was to be sprayed on later.

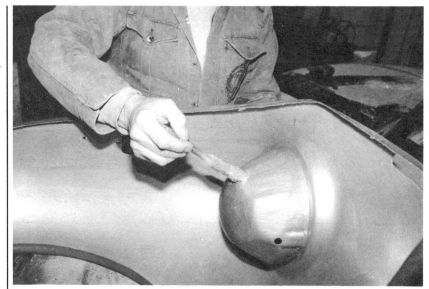

FRW27. When the wing/fender has been fitted up loosely and you are satisfied that the fit is correct, the beading can be re-fitted, pressing it into the space between wing/fender and quarter panel. If the old beading has deteriorated at all, new can be bought quite cheaply and should be trimmed to length after the panel has been fitted up.

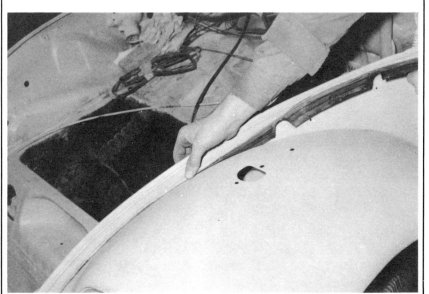

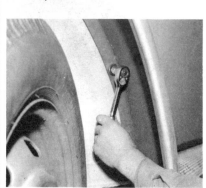

FRW28. New wing/fenders, sound inner panels and, as always at Haselock's, new bolts and washers to hold things in place.

FRW29. It then remains to re-fit all the fixtures and fittings, not forgetting to replace rubbers where necessary and taking the time to fit the rubber protective covering to the wiring — Volkswagen took the trouble to fit such good quality parts when the cars were built; it's up to you to maintain their high standards now!

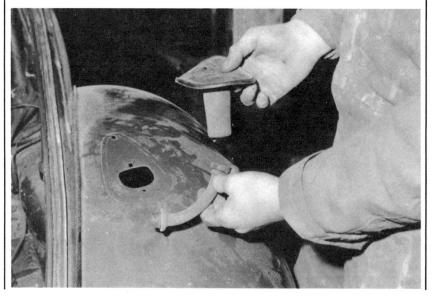

Running Board Replacement

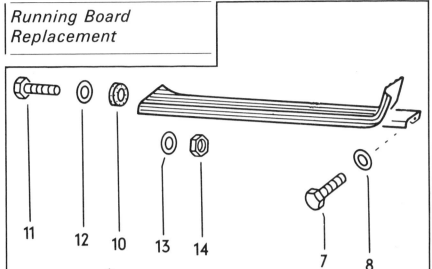

11   12   10   13   14   7   8

LEB3.   If the cover is a good fit, carefully mark the positions of the hinges before taking out the fixing bolts and lifting the cover carefully away from the car.

RBR1.   Running boards are screwed to the body with a line of bolts (parts no. 7 & 8).

RBR2.   And at each end a nut and bolt (RBP1. part nos. 10 to 14) including a rubber buffer which should be renewed with the running board, hold the panel to both the front and rear wing/fender panel.

Front (Luggage) Cover and Latch

The front and rear covers are lifted via a pair of hinges to which each cover is bolted. A little dismantling is necessary before either can be removed. Refit the components in the reverse order of dismantling.

LEB1.   If the luggage bay cover is to be stripped down, it is a good idea to remove the lifting handle and latch assembly before removing the cover itself. Two bolts pass through both the latch and the cover and screw into the lifting handle; remove them from the inner face of the cover.

LEB2.   Lift the cover and take off the C-clip that holds the spring in place. Remove the spring end from the mounting pin and replace the clip to keep it safe. If a telescopic prop is fitted, remove the bolt from the top end of the prop and detach it. ▶

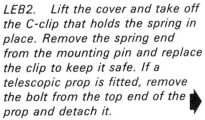

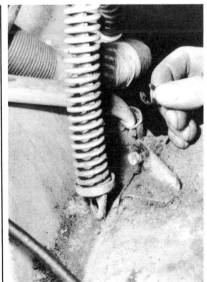

LEB4. When replacing, refit the hinges to the positions previously marked or, if realignment should be needed, tighten the hinge bolts until they just grip, but so that the cover can be moved by applying pressure one way or the other. Adjust the fit of the cover until it is perfectly centralised.

LEB5. If adjustment of the latch is needed, the locknut can be freed and the striker screwed in or out until the correct position has been obtained. If the sealing rubbers have deteriorated, replace them before adjusting the striker. Retighten the locknut.

The front (luggage) coverlock is installed in the front cover and on early models is bolted in place while in others it is held in by pop-rivets. For removal/ replacement of the latter type, see section on Front Panel Replacement. The cable can be removed from the lock after loosening the clamping screw and it can then be pulled out from the conduit tube. If the lock bolts on to the front panel, it can be lightly fitted and adjusted a little for fit.

Rear (Engine) Cover and Latch

LEB6. The rear, engine cover latch is held in a similar way, by screws fitted from the inside of the cover. On early Bug/Beetles, the rear latch is held by a single nut from the inside. When replacing this type, the nut should not be overtightened or the handle will become stiff or impossible to turn.

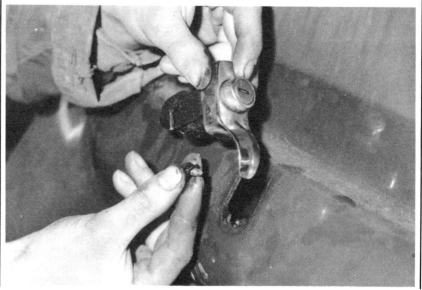

LEB7. If the rear licence plate light has to be removed, this will involve opening up the wiring clips and removing the wiring, too. All types have integral threaded studs which pass through the cover and are held by nuts and washers on the inner side.

Again, the hinge position should be carefully marked before removal or a similar procedure can be followed to ensure their realignment. The cover is held open by a strong spring. Remove the spring by squeezing the two 'L' shaped ends out of their holes. Alternatively, and more safely because there is then no risk of the spring flying off, leave it where it is, undo the cover bolts and use the cover to hold and eventually ease the spring tension. The hinge brackets can be unbolted if the engine fan cover is being removed.

When replacing the engine cover and spring, use the reverse

of the 'safe' procedure shown above. A weak spring can be given added tension by replacing it in the lower of the two slots available. It is much easier to first fit the hinge brackets to the body rather than to the cover. Striker plate adjustment can be carried out by slackening the fixing screws and sliding the plate on the cover. Do ensure that the cover is properly centralised first. Both front and rear striker plates should be greased when refitted and as a regular servicing job.

Front & Rear Panel and Spare Wheel Well Renewal

The Bug/Beetle not only has a push-me-pull-you appearance, but the fit of the panels front and rear is also remarkably similar. Both front and rear panels form a closing plate between the wing/fender panels, but the front panel is the more complex to fit because it is enclosed along its lower edge and, on earlier models, forms part of the vertical spare wheel well. The panels shown here are supplied by Uro Autospares and it would seem that panels for the earlier model cars are not available from Volkswagen. More than one car is shown being

repaired here at Haselock's in this sequence. *Don't* chop away more than you absolutely need to at any one time otherwise you will loose vital fitting-up reference points!

Safety

Replacement of this panel will require welding in the area of the fuel tank. To avoid risk of fire or explosion, remove the tank (see earlier section) and store safely. Wear thick industrial gloves when handling sharp or jagged metal.

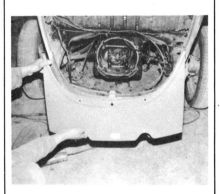

FRP1. Rear panels are substantially the same for early and late model cars although there are detail differences. Like the front panels, they attach to the quarter panels and the wing/fenders bolt through parts of them.

FRP2. Start by pulling out the rubber sealing strip from the channel in the panel. The Volkswagen manual recommends easing it open in order to remove the strip, but it may be possible to carefully pull the strip out otherwise it may be difficult to close the channel back up again satisfactorily; but that approach may be the only one available. The steel grip channel is a natural water trap and some owners of non-show cars leave the grip channel off after restoration and glue the rubber to the channel.

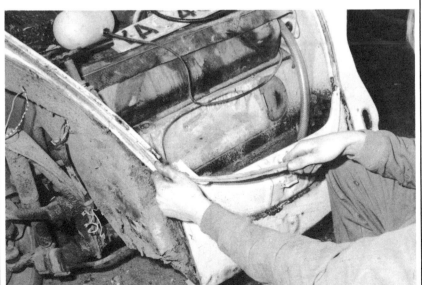

FRP3.   The pop-rivets holding a later-type lock mechanism in place are drilled out . . .

FRP4.   . . . and the lock mechanism complete with cable – it may not be necessary to dismantle it here – is placed carefully out of the way.

FRP5.   The front end of this car was particularly rotten so the old front panel came off without too much trouble! Normally a hack saw would be used to cut through the heavier top section while the sides of the panel are cut with a cold chisel. If the front panel is corroded, the spare wheel well on this type of body is also certain to be rotten, but if the front panel is to be removed because of light accident damage, cut carefully along the flange where the two panels join, grinding back to sound metal at the flange.

FRP6.   If you want to save the manufacturer's number on the plate hidden in this area, now is the time to remove it!

FRP7.   Uro Autospares also supply a repair panel for this section but, as is quite possible, corrosion is even more extensive, you may have to make up patch panels of your own or attempt to find sound second-hand panels.

FRP8.   Stuart, one of Haselock's body men, spent some time cleaning up the surrounding panels after cutting away the corroded spare wheel well. The new panel was perfectly aligned, clamped into place and then MIG welded in.

FRP9.   Provided that the quarter panels were in good shape, it would then be OK to offer up and fit up the new front panel.

FRP10.   Then the new panel could be bolted into place through the wing/fender mounting holes to align it perfectly before being MIG welded into position.

FRP11.   But sadly, life 'aint usually that simple! The reality – corroded leading edges to the quarter panel – is more likely to look like this.

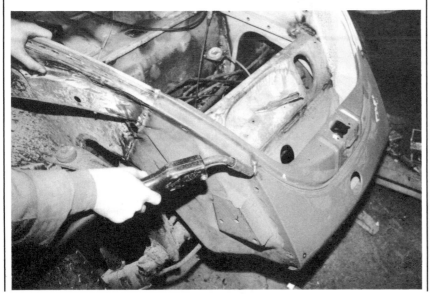

FRP12.   Then, if you were REALLY keen, you might decide to fit a complete new quarter panel, but that's a dramatically large job! The option is to fit a repair panel made specially for the job and sold by people like Haselock's. (See appropriate section for details.)

FRP13. Where he has to fit a new front panel repair and a new front panel, Stuart fits a new wing/fender in place to assure himself of exactly the correct location for the front panel.

FRP14. Then and only then does he MIG weld the panel into place.

FRP15. Next, the front lock can be restored to its former position.

FRP16. If the lock is to be pop-riveted into place, its position must be carefully established first because, unlike the earlier bolt-on type, adjustment is clearly impossible without drilling out the rivets and repositioning.

FRP17. Positioning the new rear panel is in many ways simpler than the front panel because there are no welded joints along its lower edge. However, the same points apply concerning corrosion of surrounding panels — see section on rear quarter panel repair for details — and the temporary fitting up of the rear wing to ensure perfect alignment before welding into place.

Rear Quarter Panel Repair and Replacement

This is undoubtedly one of the most complex and difficult parts of the Bug/Beetle to repair fully, the rear quarter panel forming a very large part of the outer body of the vehicle. Its strength is extremely important and so is its correct and accurate fitting. It is a very time consuming repair to carry out fully and the temptation is to cut

corners and use sub-standard repair techniques.

Mind you, there is no need to assume that every rear quarter panel will require complete replacement just because it is partly corroded. Putting in a full Volkswagen panel is the purists way of going about repairing it and gives a replacement that is literally as good as new. On the other hand, Haselock's have been fitting Uro panels in this area for many years and there are relatively few cases where you absolutely HAVE to fit the full Volkswagen panel — which is not to say that some enthusiasts haven't been prepared to pay the extra expense and specify the full panels anyway.

It is worth noting that Volkswagen supply inner repair panels to compliment the outer panels and that while all of them are far more expensive than the repair panels sold by the specialists, the fit is superb — provided that you have the time and the somewhat higher level of skills necessary to fit them.

This section describes both approaches to repairing this part of the car, starting off with showing how Haselock's tackle the patch panel approach then showing how they fit a pair of Volkswagen's rather expensive full rear quarter panels. By crafty means, we saved quite a lot of money over the normal extremely high price of the proper Cabriolet panel — each one costing around the price of three full sets of tyres!

Note. NEVER chop away more than you absolutely need to or you can easily lose the shape of the body. Only repair one panel at a time!

Rear Quarter Panel Patch Repairs

RQ1. One of the reasons for the importance of this part of the car is the fact that if incorporates a major mounting to the rear chassis. After removing the road wheel and supporting the car on axle stands, start by removing the chassis mount bolt.

RQ2. Very early cars do not have rear anti-roll bars fitted to them. For those vehicles that do remove the anti-roll bar mounting plate nuts . . .

RQ3. . . . and take off the outer plate, rubber bush and inner plate to release the anti-roll bar from the inner panel.

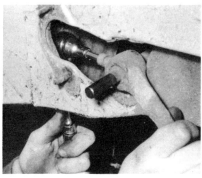

RQ4. Later models have an arm mounted on the anti-roll bar and this must be removed after unscrewing the Allen (internal hexagonal head) screw.

RQ5. Remove the damper top mounting.

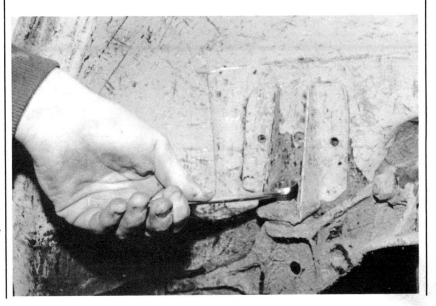

Chassis Mounting Repair

RQ6.   Corrosion frequently takes place in the seam joining the chassis mount reinforcement plate to the inner panel. Scrape all along the seam to determine whether this panel is weak or not, even if it looks superficially sound.

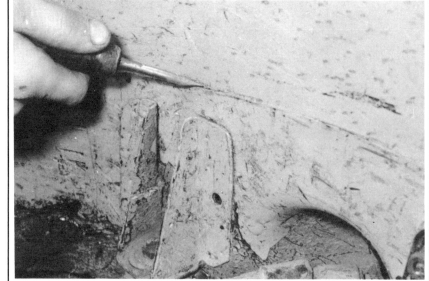

RQ7.   The Uro repair section for this area is designed to replace the reinforcement section, but to replace also a surrounding area of the inner panel which may have corroded. Where weakness lies only in the reinforcement, it may only be necessary to remove that section. Haselock's start this repair by chiseling off through the spot welds . . .

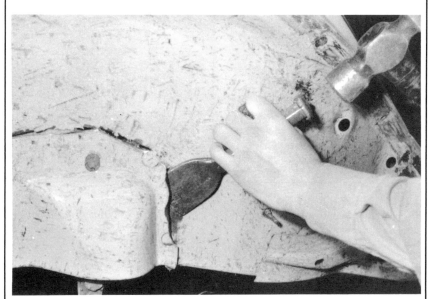

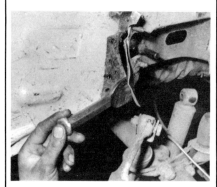

RQ8.   . . . Working all around the panel until it is removed whole.

RQ9.   Don't forget that the panel will also be secured to the rear seat panel area and will also need to be cut free there. (Needless to say, it is essential to strip all of the upholstery out of this area to avoid damage or fire.)

RQ10.   This is the size of the scrap panel that will have been taken away.

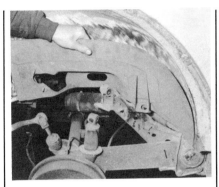

RQ11. On the other side of the car, the replacement panel is offered up and . . .

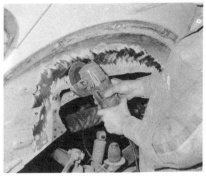

RQ12. . . . the area in which it is to be welded is thoroughly cleaned back to bright metal with a coarse grit sanding disc.

RQ13. Then the panel can be bolted down to the chassis mounting, tack welded and pushed into shape (it's unlikely that the curvature will be absolutely right first time). It is then seam welded all the way round both inside and out to make a really strong job. As usual, MIG welding produces the best results.

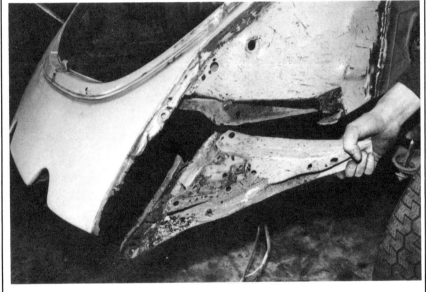

RQ14. In the section on rear panel repair, it is mentioned that this area of the rear quarter panel, the bumper mounting, is also prone to rotting out. After carefully comparing the shape of the replacement Uro panel and scribing around it, the Haselock's body man has cut out the corroded section.

RQ15. The bumper mounting repair panel is a full section and there are identifying holes to ensure correct alignment. However, if all of the panel is not required, it can always be cut down to suit. It's far better to have too much metal in your repair panels than not enough!

69

RQ16. The other rear quarter panel repair section available covers the remaining area most prone to corrosion. The corroded metal should all be cut out first. Be warned that it is extremely difficult to run a seam weld along the top edge of this repair panel without causing heat distortion. It would be best to weld in short runs, spread along the joint until they all join into one seam, but allowing plenty of time between each run for the panel to cool off.

Full Rear Quarter Replacement

Note! NEVER replace more than one panel at a time or you can easily lose the shape of the body!

RQ17. One of the first jobs I did to my Carbiolet when it got to House of Haselock's was to attack the rear quarter panels with a coarse sanding disc on the mini-grinder. Quite amazing amounts of filler came off! The quarter panel had been replaced once before AND a patch repair had been fitted to the front lower part of the panel. It was fairly sound, but the work had been crudely done.

RQ18. This is the full saloon/sedan quarter panel available from Volkswagen dealers and as can be seen, it includes the full rear side window section. If this part of the panel is perfect, it could be cut and joined as in the following sequence. If there is any deterioration there it will be necessary to cut the old panel away from the roof section. (Drawing courtesy of Volkswagen, from their parts manual.)

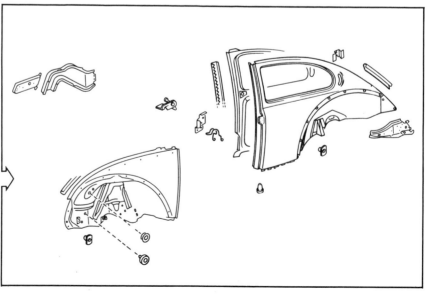

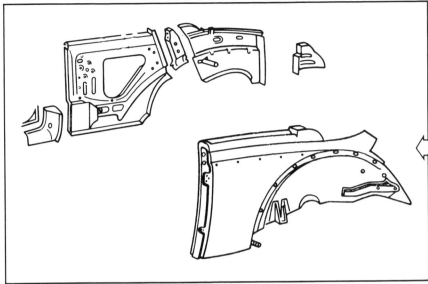

RQ19. This is the 'Karmann' Cabriolet panel also available through Volkswagen dealers although invariably 'to order'. It includes the slightly complex waist rail section, but it is a very expensive panel and it may not be necessary to use it even for the Cabriolet, because a cut-down 'Beetle' 1200 panel can be used as shown in the following sequence, provided that the waist rail section is perfectly sound. (Drawing courtesy Volkswagen, reproduced from their parts manual.) The complete set of inner panels, also expensive but fairly complex, are available from the same source and it may be that the complete inner and outer assembly is available (both together) but it would undoubtedly require a bodyshop with the correct jig to use it.

RQ20. The panel was cut just below the rear side window after comparing its shape with that of the original panel.

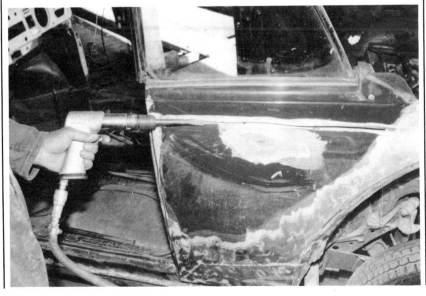

RQ21. Then, after stripping out the interior, trim, wings and soft-top, the quarter panel on the car was marked out with reference to the edge of the repair panel and after leaving a generous overlap — it can be trimmed back later — the air chisel was used to cut along the panel. Especially for home users, some sort of non-distorting cutter such as a 'Monodex' or 'Niblex' would be preferable or even a hacksaw blade in a pad saw. You must remember to detach and remove the main wiring harness from this area and to take the sound deadening material from behind the reinforcement plate in the engine bay. It's recommended by Volkswagen that the side panel is cut out first before tackling the whole quarter panel. This gives you a 'window' so that you can see to avoid damaging the seat support between inner and outer panels.

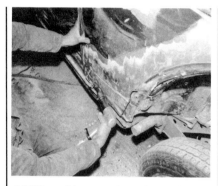

RQ22. After cutting along the front edge and the bottom of the panel . . .

RQ24. If you are working on a Cabriolet, this gives an unrepeatable opportunity to work on and overhaul the rear side window sliding mechanism. The glass should be removed to avoid damage.

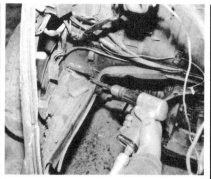

RQ26. The Volkswagen panel includes this rear reinforcement box-section which must also be neatly cut out after stripping wires and fittings from the area.

RQ23. the side of the panel was removed leaving the wheelarch in place, the section-at-a-time approach allowing you to be more meticulous about where to cut.

RQ25. Whether or not the rear panel is to be saved, leave it in at this stage as a reference point for fitting up. Haselock panel-beater Ghenti is cutting the quarter panel away from the flange with a sharp chisel.

RQ27. With the old quarter panel out of the way, there's then a great deal of tidying up to carry out. Flanges must be cleaned to shiny metal to make them weldable, corrosion in the inner wheel arches may have to be trimmed out and then flanges have to be trued up with the hammer and dolly.

RQ28. The cut-down left-hand panel was offered up to the car so that the job of checking for correct alignment and fit could commence.

RQ29. It is essential that no rippling has been introduced into these panels whilst cutting, this risk being the biggest disadvantage of not using the full Cabriolet or saloon/sedan panel, both of which include the full reinforced shape of the top of the panel. About 1 in. to 1½ in. overlap should be fine, so cut back to that, then clean the panel beneath back to bright, shiny metal.

RQ30. Here the right-hand panel is being bolted to the frame — that's one alignment that you can't argue with, so start from there.

RQ31. Back to the left-hand panel, clamps are used to fit it to the engine bay rain channel.

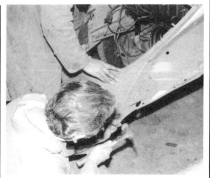

RQ32. This rear valence was retained, so the quarter panel was carefully panel beaten until the joining flanges fitted perfectly.

RQ33. At this stage, the odd tack weld may have been used here and there, but there should as yet be no extensive welding at all. In spite of the car's chassis, you will undoubtedly have experienced some sagging in the body, particularly with the open topped car, so check the panel level here . . .

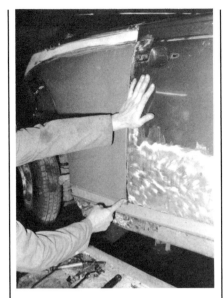

RQ34. . . . but most importantly of all, refit the door and check that with the door properly aligned to the sill and the front of the door aperture, the rear door gap is perfectly even all the way along and that the bottom corner of the door tallies with the leading lower corner of the quarter panel. Check also that the curvature of the leading edge of the quarter panel matches that of the door before the quarter panel is welded to the door pillar. Volkswagen's own figure for the correct door aperture is 945 mm (37.2 in.) measured immediately above the sill.

RQ35. Haselock's panel beater Ron helps Ghenti by holding the top of the panel whilst Ghenti tack welds it. The avoidance of distortion is all important here and it's best to clamp then weld from the centre, working out. A spot welder, where it arms can be fitted in, creates little or no heat distortion.

RQ36. Then Ghenti welded the lower edge of the quarter panel to the sill . . .

RQ37. . . . and the leading edge to the door shut pillar. MIG welding is best here because of the reduced risk of distortion, but the raised nature of MIG welds means that some grinding off will be necessary.

RQ38. It would be ideal to 'lead load' this joint to seal it so that no future corrosion could possibly get in but then the most sensible way for the DIY-er to obtain a smooth finish is to flash over the joint with a thin coat of plastic filler.

*If an earlier Cabriolet is being worked upon, it will naturally be necessary to remove the rear body bow, the wooden strip around the rear of the tub. Before replacing it, glue a strip of material to the bottom half of the inside of the bow before screwing it in place to prevent it causing rubbing noises when the car is travelling along.
*If full Volkswagen quarter panels are being fitted, you can remove the old one from the rear of the car by melting the lead out of the leaded joint at the rear of the tub (see where this will be by reference to the rear edge of the replacement panel) then cutting along the old joint.

Rear Inner Wheel Arch

RQ39. This shot of the wheel arch just ahead of the engine bay shows how the author's Bug/Beetle looked tatty but reasonably sound, until . . .

RQ41. Equally prone to corrosion are the bracing sections beneath the rear seat base. Repairs have to be fabricated from sheet metal.

RQ43. . . . before folding flanges to fit on the bench. Accurate marking out, cutting and frequent offering-up to the car are the key to making this sort of repair fit well.

RQ40. . . . after the fibreglass and pop-riveted plates had been stripped away, there was little but thin rusty metal, some of which has been cut away here.

RQ42. And actually, at the time of writing, the same is true of all the other inner wing areas, unless you buy the full thing from Volkswagen. Here Haselock's panel beater Ron is cutting out a DIY repair patch . . .

RQ44. Ron locates one of his repair patches in place to check for fit against the edges of the existing metal although he wasn't able to fit the patches properly without the new rear quarter panel — they hadn't arrived from the Volkswagen dealer at this stage.

RQ45. When the quarter panel was in place, the patches were fitted up to it. Make them fit without any pulling so that they lie perfectly in place before being welded if you wish to avoid distortion. It is understood that House of Haselock's have made repair panels for these areas available for sale: They'll be extremely useful!

RQ46. There's no real knowing where the corrosion on an older car will stop. You will invariably have to make up at least some of the repair patches needed for your car if it is badly corroded. Make up a complete card template first and NEVER leave corroded metal behind the repair or it will quickly break through again.

FQ2. After the paint has been sanded off the weld edges, the new panel can be fitted into place — always check it at this stage against the luggage bay cover line and the front panel —

FQ4. . . . and you can see that the front panel/spare wheel well has been welded to the new metal all along its inner flanges, too. Seal all welded joints with seam sealer as extra protection against corrosion.

FQ3. Then, when everything is perfectly lined up, the panel can be welded in place with a long seam weld; one which will keep out damp and thus corrosion . . .

FQ5. Corrosion is quite common in this area and you can see where a plate has been welded on here in the past.

Front Quarter Panel Repair and Replacement

Bumper Mounting Area

FQ1. Here there's a similar situation to that at the rear end of the car. There's a choice between fitting the complete, excellent quality and very expensive full quarter panel; or the sorts of excellent repair panels that Haselock's use and sell, many of them marketed by Uro Autospares and others produced uniquely by House of Haselock themsleves. This is the Uro front bumper repair panel being offered up by body man Stuart after the old one has been cut away.

FQ6. And the suspension towers and tower tops on models with MacPherson strut front suspension can corrode, too.

FQ7. Where severe corrosion is found, it may be best to cut your losses and fit a full Volkswagen front quarter panel.

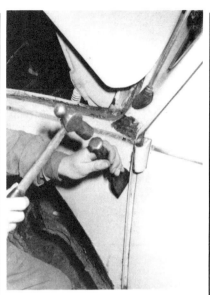

FQ8. After comparing the new panel with the attachment points of the old, you can start cutting the old one away. Here the first cut to remove the old panel is made ahead of the door hinge pillar seam.

FQ9. It's essential to study the new panel closely to find out which struts and box sections are part of the new unit and which have to be left in place. Stuart is using a special tool to drill out the spot welds before tapping in a thin bladed, sharp bolster chisel to finally make the break although in the event, this box section had to be taken out anyway. A twist drill handled carefully will do the job just as well as long as you i) centre punch and drill as close to the centre of the spot weld as possible and ii) when you can, your drill through the spot weld in the panel you are taking off, but not the one that remains. Of course, this is not always possible, in which case the hole should be used to make a strong plug weld with the MIG or gas welder.

FQ10. Before the wheel arch part of the panel can be removed from the left hand side of the car, the speedo. cable which is driven off the front left-hand wheel bearing dust cover, must be removed.

FQ11.   Then, after more drilling out of spot welds, the wheel arch can be cut free . . .

FQ12.   . . .leaving all the weld flanges on the inner panels in place.

FQ13.   When all of the old panel has been removed, the weld flanges can be sanded back to bright metal and trued up very carefully with the hammer and dolly after patch-repairing any other areas of corrosion that may be found, such as at the end of the heater channel. Note that if the spare wheel well (early models) has to be replaced, it is best done with the old front quarter panel still in place so that it can be perfectly aligned before cutting the quarter panel away.

N.B. New demister ducts can only be fitted at this stage. See FQ28.-on for detais.

FQ14.   Stuart offers the new panel up to the car . . .

FQ15.   . . . and checks the fit against the luggage bay cover, the spare wheel well, the door hinge pillar and the body flanges left in place. You must also be **certain** that the door hinge pillar has not moved out of position at this stage, especially on the Cabrio.

FQ16. After clamping the panel securely in place and, where necessary, re-dressing the flanges with the hammer and dolly to ensure a good fit, he tack welds the panel to the hinge pillar seam. The best way of joining these two together is actually with a spot welder.

FQ17. Seam welds are the order of the day where the new panel meets internal members.

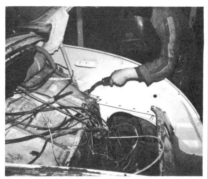

FQ18. Where you're joining new metal to existing like this, it is essential that the old metal is bright and clean otherwise the weld will be untidy and weak, being full of impurities.

FQ19. Another joint is to be found where the footwell heater channel (sills) meet the new panel.

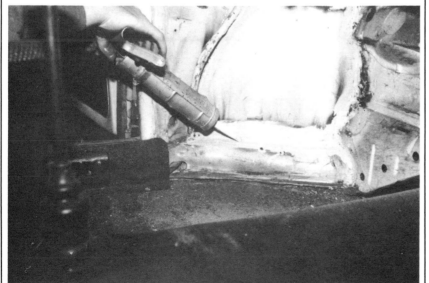

FQ20. Always seal all welded joints with seam sealer, brushing into the joint after it is piped on, with a brush dipped in the correct solvent for the seam sealer-check with your supplier.

Using Sound Second-Hand Front Quarter Panels

Although some don't like the sound of it, the use of second-hand panels, as long as they really are sound, is a perfectly respectable process. After all, cars are nothing more than pieces of metal welded and bolted together and if you happen to weld on a part that's been in use previously,

but which is as good as a new one, what's the difference?

When it comes to the really expensive and complex items like the quarter panels, you've found the ideal use for this type of repair, provided of course that corrosion in the old panel is limited to the area being replaced. First, clean back the old panel to bright metal all over so that you can be certain how much of it is in need of replacement. Then, cut off the new-old panel to give yourself a very generous overlap, cutting the repair patch down to scale when you can mark it up with reference to the car.

FQ23.   Similarly, at the back . . .

FQ26. Back on the other side of the car, the scrap part-panel is shown being removed.

FQ21.   You may not be joining the new panel to the old along a 'natural' line, so be sure to include this sort of no-argument reference point for correct alignment.

FQ24.   And then chisel the rest of the panel away (this is a professional air chisel, but a hand held bolster chisel would be as good although slower).

FQ27.   Ghenti points to a bracing piece that you have to be careful not to cut through when taking off the old panel.

FQ22.   After marking out the panel to be cut away, cut through the top of the quarter panel, including the rain seal moulding with a hacksaw, cutting well inside the area required.

FQ25.   Here you have to work carefully to the marked-out line, allowing about 1 in. or so to lap the joint.

FQ28.   New demister pipe can only be fitted now, while there's access to the heater channel (sill) top. Fit a new hose clip and branching piece whilst access is available.

FQ29. The replacement panel is offered up several times and the patch panel and existing panel are both trimmed until there is a good fit with the right degree of lap.

FQ30. The panel is clamped and fitted both front and rear . . .

FQ31. . . . and those alignment holes mentioned earlier are used to bolt both panels together.

FQ32. Then it's back to fitting the luggage bay cover as a final but essential check for accurate fit.

FQ33. The only major difference between new panel and old was the operation of the fuel filler flap, the old one having an internally released latch. The filler neck, complete with holes and pressings for the latch was taken from the old panel . . .

FQ34. . . . and spot welded to the 'new' one. This sort of moving around of minor details is something that you have to be prepared for when you're restoring older cars with a view to keeping them looking original!

FQ35. To finish off the hinge pillar flange, Haselock's make a capping piece pushed over the flange. It is being spot welded at the top . . . ▶

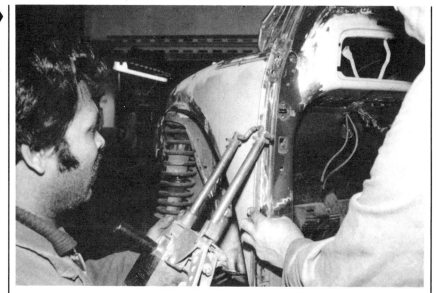

FQ36. . . . then eased into place down the seam, following its slight curvature, before being welded again with the SIP Spotmatic. This follows the approach of the original panel which was folded over at the seam during manufacture. ▶

Sill/Body Rocker Patch Repair

Sometimes just the outer section the sill/body rocker panel rots out, in which case . . .

SPR1. You can cut out the rotten and vertical faces of the panel . . .

SPR2. . . . and, just as the House of Haselock panel beater is doing here with the Spotmatic, spot weld the new panel across its ▶ bottom flange and MIG it across the top of the step.

Luggage & Engine Bay Cover Removal & Replacement

The front and rear covers are lifted via a pair of hinges to which each cover is bolted. A little dismantling is necessary before either can be removed. Refit the components in the reverse order of dismantling.

DHP2. The lower hinge pillar is rather prone to rotting out. A repair section complete with threaded plate for the hinge is available. Offer it up to the pillar and use it as a template for cutting out the corroded steel.

DHP3. Accurately cut out the unwanted steel . . .

Door Hinge Pillar Repair

DHP1. Even though the lower hinge pillar may be in excellent condition, always run a tap through the thread in order to prevent jamming and seizure when the hinge is replaced. If you don't have the correct size of tap available, make a saw cut down the length of a bolt and run that in and out of the thread with releasing fluid as lubricant.

DHP4. . . . and tack weld the new panel into place. Use strong tack welds, but don't seam weld the panel in place until after the door has been fitted and checked for fit. Then, if the pillar repair has to be moved, the tack welds can be broken or ground off and the adjustment made. Needless to say, this repair should be made when the other outer panels are in good shape so that there is a reliable reference point against which to fit the door accurately.

Removing The Body From The Frame

The combination of a welded body 'tub' and a separate, strong frame gives the Volkswagen an immensely strong structure. At the same time, the absence of nooks and crannies means that the body is less rust-prone than those of most cars, although many of the cars are by now rather old and in the end, rust will always have its way. It is also said that the Karmann-built cars, which includes the Cabriolets, were more rust-prone than the saloon/sedan models.

A complete restoration really requires that the body is taken from the frame and, needless to say, this is quite a major task! But first, a word of warning! Don't ever take off the body in order to repair it because, although it may make it easier to 'get at', there will be a very real risk, or even a likelihood that the body will become distorted and so not fit properly back onto the frame. Always carry out all the body repairs before lifting it off so that its inherent shape is not altered and so that the 'tub' is strong enough not to distort when lifted up. This advice is particularly important when

dealing with the Cabriolet, of course. Note that there is no difference between the saloon/sedan models and the Cabriolet when it comes to body-to-frame mountings.

In the photographs illustrating this section, you will see how House of Haselock lift off and replace the body using a power hoist. Naturally, home mechanics won't have access to this type of equipment and so the body will have to be lifted by hand. This is a job best treated as a social occasion and it could be that it will require the offer of liquid refreshment following the big event to get sufficient lifting power together! Four of us carried the Cabriolet body around after it had been removed at Haselock's and after it had been completely stripped out to the barest of bare shells, but two more pairs of hands would have made the job more comfortable, especially since when lowering and lifting it is all too easy to cause an injury. Where a saloon/sedan body has to be lifted high enough to get it off a chassis. I would recommend getting eight lifters together.

The body is held to the chassis by countless bolts, most of which pass upwards from beneath the car. Take out the bolts which are removed from beneath first of all, after raising the car up on axle

stands or by driving it up ramps, not forgetting to chock the wheels on the ground. DON'T work underneath a car supported by a jack.

Provided that you lift and lower the car via the chassis, there will be no problem with having the underneath body bolts undone. then, with the car on the ground, the bolts reached from above can be removed, any other dismantling that is necessary can be carried out and the body lifted straight off. Have some trestles ready to lower the body onto, in order to save having to lift or lower to ground level and to make work underneath easier to carry out.

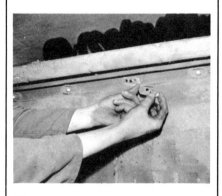

BR1. Beneath the sills, all along the edges of the car there are M8 bolts (i.e. 8 mm) and special washers tying the body down.

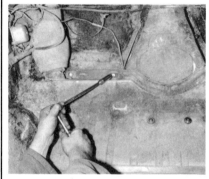

BR2. Other M8 bolts are found beneath the rear seat area . . .

BR3. . . . while, M10 bolts hold the centre tunnel to this body bracket alongside the foot pedals.

For the full removal sequence, see the paragraphs following these picture captions.

BR4. The frame and floorpan form a self contained unit capable of being moved easily around. Later models, those with MacPherson strut front suspension have to be picked up at the front with a trolley jack and 'wheelbarrowed' around because the front suspension is located on the bodywork and without the body in place the front wheels are free to flop drunkenly about. The bolts in the centre-side and rear-cross joints are, as stated in the previous captions, M8 whilst all the others are M10. The numbers superimposed here indicate the tightening order of the M10 bolts on early models. See the re-fitting sequence at the end of these picture captions for full details.

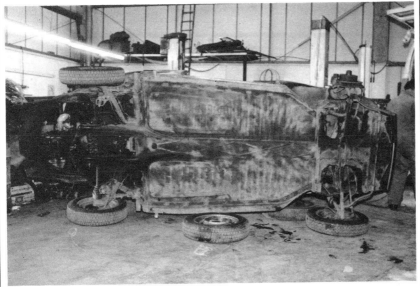

BR5. One of the great advantages of having the body off the frame is that so many things become so much more accessible. You can tip the frame onto one side like this in order to clean it and paint it while mechanical components like brakes and steering become twenty times easier to work on.

BR6. One job that you are strongly recommended to carry out is to clean out all the body mounting threads while the body is off. If you haven't got access to a tap, take a bolt, make a saw cut down its length and run it in and out of the thread a couple of times using releasing fluid as a lubricant.

BR7. The body can also be tipped and cleaned up at this stage. First I hosed the underside down with the KEW 'Hobby' pressure washer, which is the only type of washer affordable by the DIY-er, and this removed all the dirt and, when connected up to a detergent supply via the pipe fitted to the unit, most of the grease came off, too. The heavier stuff had to be worked off with a brush and degreasant while the really heavily encrusted stuff had to be scraped away.

BR8. There were one or two lightly rusted areas on the frame head and these were also cleaned back to bright metal using the KEW by adding on the sand blasting attachment. This was excellent for stripping off paint but very heavy rust was beyond it. It may be worth having a heavily rusted frame professionally sand blasted, but you would have to strip off all of the mechanical components first. All of the metal was treated with rust-proofing treatment and then all the body-to-frame joining areas were painted with ICI Autocolor metal primer.

BR9. At Haselock's they were able to lift the bodyshell on the hoist but you'll have to devise some other means as discussed earlier. Some areas of the underbody, where they meet or are concealed by the frame, must be painted whilst the two are separated. Here the sprayer is using an air-fed mask because he's using ICI Autocolor's 2K paint which gives the hardest and most resilient finish of all, but there are ICI cellulose base paints which are safe for the home sprayer to use with a standard face mask.

BR10. Just for once, the author gets himself into the picture — it's hard being both the photographer and the subject! I'm injecting body sealer into all seams to prevent any possibility of water or damp ingress and so improving the life-expectancy of the panels. After injecting the sealer I wiped it over with a small brush dipped in the right solvent for the sealer — different ones require different solvents so ask your supplier about it — to give a better finish. The sealer was applied after the undercoat had been applied, but before the body colour was sprayed on.

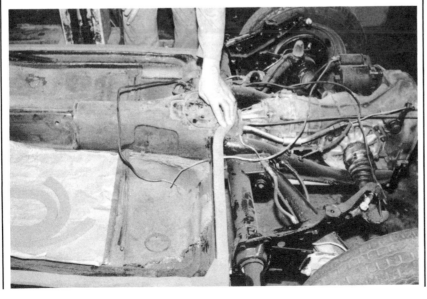

BR11. It's important to use a new body gasket on the frame before lowering the body back into place.

87

BR12. Here's my Cabriolet body on the hoist before being lowered back onto the frame. Note how the underbody and wing joint areas have all been painted in body colour and the frame painted in semi-gloss black, again using ICI Autocolor 2K for longevity. Because of the MacPherson strut front suspension, the front end of the car has had to be supported on axle stands.

BR13. The body must be lowered slowly and carefully into position, taking note of all the points raised in the notes at the end of these captions including the use of guide studs.

BR15. . . . and the studs passed through the inner wing/fender. Nuts can be fitted and tightened later.

BR17. . . . but don't tighten it down hard yet. See the section at the end of these captions for tightening details.

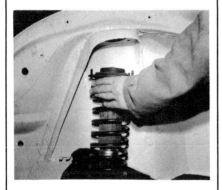

BR14. Even more pairs of hands are needed when lowering on a 'MacPherson strut' body because the strut has to be aligned with the tower on the body . . .

BR16. You may find that the bracket down in the footwell doesn't align with the bolt holes straight away in which case insert a bar into one of the holes, lever the bracket into position and insert a bolt into the other hole . . .

BR18. Just as reminders, mounting bolts also go on the rear wing/fender mounting . . .

BR19. . . . at the ends of the front cross member there are two M10 bolts . . .

BR20. . . . two more bolts in the spare wheel well (later models – those on earlier models are further forwards than this, on top of the front axle; see BR4.) . . .

BR21. And there are those that go down into the frame end plate beneath the rear seat area.

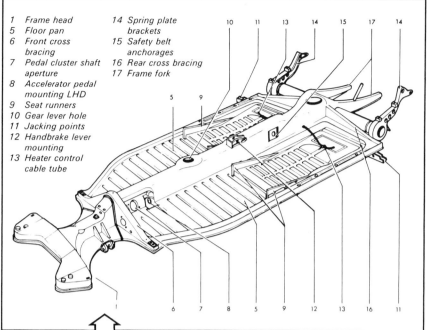

1 Frame head
5 Floor pan
6 Front cross bracing
7 Pedal cluster shaft aperture
8 Accelerator pedal mounting LHD
9 Seat runners
10 Gear lever hole
11 Jacking points
12 Handbrake lever mounting
13 Heater control cable tube
14 Spring plate brackets
15 Safety belt anchorages
16 Rear cross bracing
17 Frame fork

BR22. The sturdy underframe is not in itself totally rigid, but relies upon combination with the so-very-strong body for its rigidity. Here you can see what's included – and it's virtually the same for every Bug/Beetle that has been built except that this is the 1600/1302/1303 front end. See BR4. for other type.

Body Removal – Summary

1) Remove the front and rear seats and the battery.

2) Disconnect the speedo, drive shaft from the left-hand front wheel hub.

3) Remove the fuel tank. (See relevant section).

4) Disconnect the choke control cable from the instrument panel and remove it from the body.

5) Take off the steering column together with the steering wheel.

6) Disconnect the cable from the stoplight switch.

7) Remove the heating pipes.

8) Detach the cables from the starter motor, the generator and the ignition coil. Label them to ease reconnection.

9) Remove the 18 M8 body bolts from beneath the car.

10) Remove the remaining body mounting bolts in the reverse of the order shown in picture BR4.

Body Replacement – Summary

Generally, you should follow the reverse of the procedure outlined for 'body removal', but there are also some extra points to watch out for:

1) Fit a new weatherstrip gasket onto the frame (it's available from Volkswagen), if necessary glueing it down to prevent it from moving. Fill any depressions or gaps at corners with sealing compound.

2) Place rubber packings on the front axle and rear cross tubes.

3) To help the body into its correct position, it helps to screw studs into the holes in the rear cross tube; remove them when the body is on the frame.

4) First lightly tighten all the M10 bolts in the order shown in BR4, tightening the bolts on one side and then the other, and then add the M8 bolts.

5) Note the position of the earth (ground) cable. The bolts which pass through the front cross member are screwed into a plate with two tapped holes in it, the

plate being free to move within a 'captive' guide.

6) If the front M8 bolts don't fully cover the slotted holes, seal the resulting body-to-frame gap with rubber shims or with mastic.

7) If the front axle leaves a gap at the mountings, compensate with two rubber packings. The gap should not exceed 0.12 in.

8) NOTE that the bolts should only be tightened to the following figures: M10 bolts, 22 lb. ft.; M8 bolts, 14 lb ft. It is strongly recommended that a torque wrench is used and that the bolts are not over-tightened.

9) Re-install the components removed when dismantling.

Glass Removal & Replacement

Front and Rear Screens and Fixed Side Windows

The basic procedure is the same for all three types of windscreen, but different models of car may be fitted with different types of trim or moulding around the screen. This must be removed before the glass is taken out.

Make sure you know which type of glass is fitted before attempting to remove it. 'Toughened' glass will stand a

certain amount of thumping before breaking, but other types crack or shatter much more easily.

Safety

The dangers of broken glass should be self evident! The Haselock mechanics photographed in this sequence were happy to work without gloves or goggles; you should wear both. Also, be sure to apply masking tape to the windscreen demister vents to prevent any broken glass from dropping in. It could blow out later and get into the eyes with pretty dire consequences!

W1. After removing any trim or mouldings (and after taking off the windscreen wiper arms if the front screen is to be removed), you should use a chisel shaped piece of wood with a rounded end to ease the rubber free all the way around both inside and out taking care not to split the rubber if it is good enough to be re-used. You may, if you wish, use a garden sprayer/atomiser to spray a mist of detergent in water into the inside of the joint to help the rubber to slide. With two assistants on the outside to prevent the screen from plopping onto the floor, push the screen carefully but firmly from the inside (use your foot if you like!), starting with one top corner and then the other.

W2. The safest way of working is to cover the glass with broad masking tape which is what Haselock's did when removing the screen from this fully restored Bug/Beetle. Then even if the glass should crack or shatter — and you can never guarantee that it won't — the danger to say nothing of the mess and inconvenience will be much less. Note that a cloth has been used to cover and protect the bodywork.

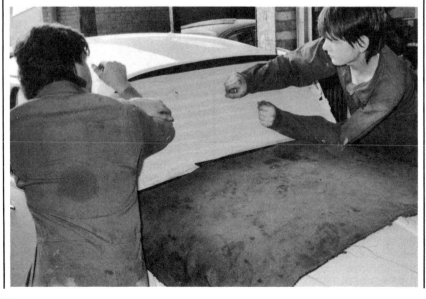

W3.   When the glass and rubber start to come free, they can be pulled clear from the outside. With the screen out of the way, clean off any stuck-on remnants of rubber or adhesive, scrape off any rust back to shiny, bright metal before painting — and don't be amazed if you even have to carry out a small patch repair, cutting out corroded metal and replacing it. And be sure to seal the screen properly next time to prevent this happening! Make sure there are no sharp edges on the screen aperture — see W5.-on.

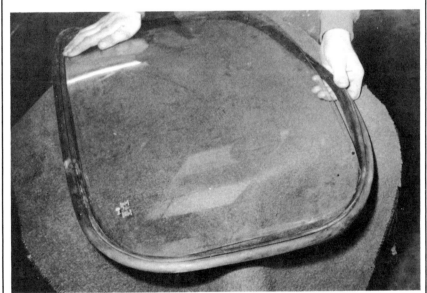

W4.   Clean the edges of the glass, to be fitted, pretty thoroughly too. Old rubber which has gone hard and started to crack is no use so be prepared to replace it. Fitting is much easier with new rubber, too!

W5.   Identify for yourself the flap in the rubber that folds over the metal screen aperture. Take some thin cord — nylon is ideal — and push it under the flap all the way round. (A 'quick-tip' is to use a short piece of brake piping through which you thread the end of the cord. Push the end of the tube under the flap and draw it along, laying the cord into place).

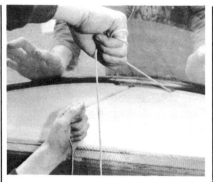

W6. Aim to make the two ends of cord join then slightly overlap at the base of the screen. Have the screen propped into place from the outside, locating the base of the screen as well as possible. Whilst the screen is pushed inwards fairly hard at the bottom, pull one end of the cord . . .

W7. . . . so that your hands cross and the rubber lip is pulled over the edge of the metal window aperature.

W8. Your assistant (or better still, two of them) can make all the difference between success and failure here. The glass must be pushed downwards so that the lip is held well onto the window aperature while first one end of the cord is pulled for a few inches and then the other. Two snags are likely to occur unless you're forewarned. One is that you may tug too energetically on the cord and pull a cut into the rubber, and the other is that the cord may catch on a snag on the metal aperature and break, although this is less likely with nylon.

W9. The tricky point will come when you go round the corners and into the finishing straight at the top. It will help enormously if your assistant gives the screen regular (judicious!) smacks with the heel of the hand (wear thick industrial gloves!) to push the rubber well into position, otherwise the cord may easily pull out of the rubber lip without it having been pulled over the steelwork. Pull the cord up (for the lowering; and down for the top run) to further discourage the lip from failing to pull over the steelwork.

Finally, refit any chromework or trim to the screen surround.

New rubbers should not be prone to leakage but VW used to recommend some use of windscreen sealant on the screen surround. If you wish, you may inject screen sealant into the rubber where the screen glass is seated before pushing it onto the glass and into the rubber where it flaps over the screen aperture before inserting the cord. Needless to say, this will create a lot of mess on hands and glass! After you have finished, scrape the excess off the glass with a plastic scraper and wipe the glass clean with paraffin/kerosene followed by a strong mix of detergent and water.

Cabriolet Rear Vent/Quarter Light – Refitting

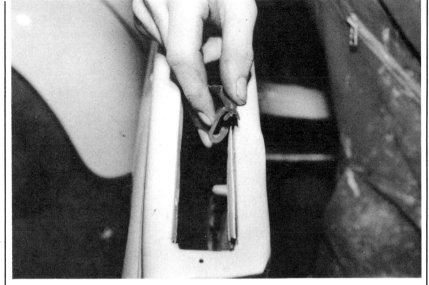

RVR1. Start by fitting a new sealing rubber to the inner edge of the vent aperture, clipping it over the lip provided as shown . . .

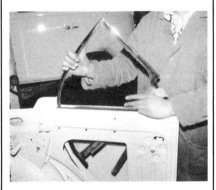

RVR2. . . . then slide the vent (ready cleaned and polished!) into place.

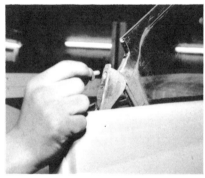

RVR4. The pivot bracket is mounted on the lower front corner of the vent and the mounting screws go in here . . .

RVR6. You can tighten them up now, but remember that you may need to slacken them for up-and-down adjustments later.

RVR3. Locate the runner on the operating arm into the channel.

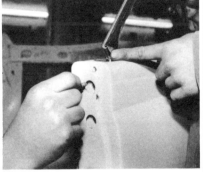

RVR5. . . . but only after the vent has been pushed into place, when the screws can pass through the two holes in the door pillar.

RVR7. A new rubber is slipped into the leading edge, sliding up from below as shown – House of Haselock fitters use a smear of hand cleanser to help things along.

RVR8. Then, with the glass wound right down, you can fit the outer rubber seal, using new self-tapping screws.

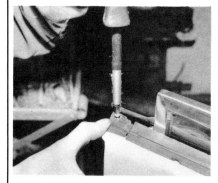

RVR9. Finally, the end finisher can be screwed into place.

Cabriolet: Rear Side Window & Regulator

W10. This exploded diagram, reproduced courtesy Volkswagen from their 1302/1303 parts book, shows the components of the Cabriolet rear side windows and mechanism.

Removal

1) Raise the soft-top.
2) Take out the rear seat and back and the side trim.
3) Above the striker plate on the door shut pillar there are two window anchor bracket screws behind a rubber plug: remove plugs and screws.
4) Remove the four screws attaching the regulator then press the regulator towards the outer panel. Detach the roller arm from the glass retaining channel and pull the regulator out through the opening now exposed by the removal of trim.
5) The window glass can now be lifted out.
6) The weather strip and rubber on each end are removed by taking out the three retaining screws. They are highly likely to be well rusted in. Soak them for hours beforehand in releasing fluid and/or apply heat from a large soldering iron. If the body is yet to be restored, apply stronger heat.
7) The window guide is held in place by two screws in the window compartment and one in the inner panel.
8) When replacing, renew any broken or cracked rubbers and grease and check the operating mechanism and the condition of the channel runners.

Cabriolet Rear Side Window Dismantling

1) Take off the weather strip from the vertical edge of the window.
2) Unscrew the anchor brackets, take off the window lift channel and pull out the glass.
3) Remove the glass weather strips.
    If the side window leaves a gap at the door window even when fully raised, remove the stop at the roller arm and file it until the window gains sufficient travel.

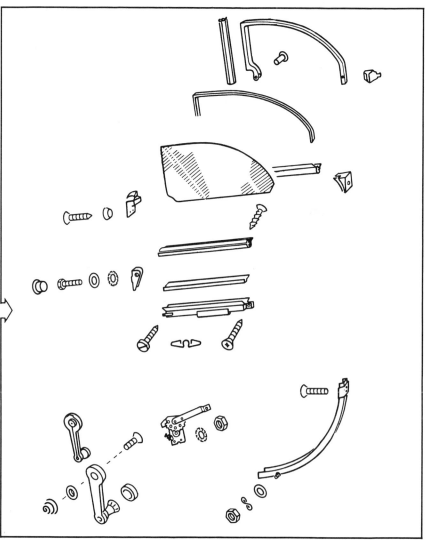

If there's too much travel, screw on a 6 mm nut to the rear upper regulator attaching screw. Final adjustment may have to be made as already described with the file.

Door Glass

See section on 'Doors' for details.

Side-member (Heater Channel) Replacement

This area of the car is sometimes known as the 'sills' or 'body rockers'. But forget all you have ever known about the replacement of body rockers or sills on other cars: These parts involve some pretty major surgery!

SMR3.   And here's a look-in to a similar job being carried out on a closed Beetle showing the plain shape of the side-member top.

SMR4.   Ron cut the side member away from the door hinge pillar . . .

SMR1.   The main side-member (part no. 1) is a complex panel because it includes not only the mighty structural box-section, but within it there is another tube, the heater air pipe, which adds even more strength to what then becomes a massively strong structure. Unfortunately, like any other mild steel part, it can and does rot away in time. Between the side-member and the frame is sandwiched a closing section (part no. 6) through which the main mounting bolts pass. (This drawing is reproduced with thanks to Volkswagen.)

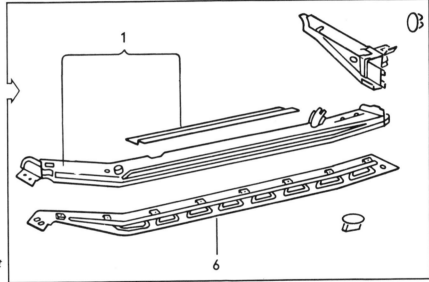

SMR2.   This work was carried out at Haselock's by panel beaters Ron and Ghenti. Although the vehicle shown here is a 1302 Cabriolet, which has the extra strengthening 'girder' box-section running beneath the side-member and a few extra strengthening gussets, the work on a saloon/sedan is very similar and if anything easier to carry out. Here Ron cut the side-member outer away from the strengthening gusset.

SMR5. . . . and took a piece of the lower inner part of the front quarter panel in order to gain access to the side-member where it extends into this area.

SMR7. . . . and another just ahead of the rear one. These cuts could be made at the hinge pillars on saloon/sedan models.

SMR9. . . . and since this has also been sawn through, out it came!

SMR6. Then, with wiring and any other damageable stuff out of the way, a cut was made just behind the front strengthening gusset . . .

SMR8. The outer section was then cut away from the floor, exposing the reinforcement-cum-heater channel . . .

SMR10. Next Ghenti tackled another complication found on the Cabriolet. The rear pillar reinforcing gusset covers the area in which the side-member has to be introduced and welded. Here he made a horizontal saw cut to neatly chop the panel out.

SMR11. He cut out the gusset, chiselling it from the seat support frame. The bottom of it had corroded along with the rest of the side-member, so a localised repair had to be let in later.

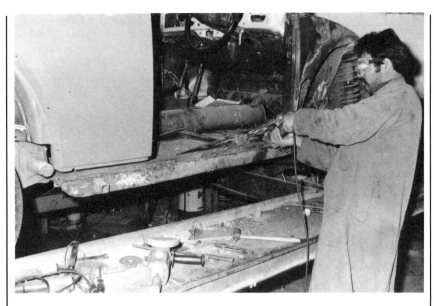

SMR12. Ghenti spent some time with the mini-grinder cleaning up all of the flanges back to bright, shiny metal (but without sanding right through!) and removing any rags and tags of 'dead' steel that were still hanging around.

SMR13. Here, the new Uro Autoparts-supplied side-member is shown being offered up to the side of the car. You can see that it extends right back to the rear wheel arch and right up to the front one. Now, a snag! At the front is the stub which takes the hot air up to the screen surround (the one at the rear is just above Jenti's left hand, but that's no problem). You'll see from the section on 'Front Quarter Panel' replacement how the screen surround hot air pipe is connected to this stub. And you'll also see that you will have to cut a hole in the front quarter panel in order to get the side-member into position at the front, making the cut large enough to fit up the pipework properly.

SMR14. The side-member is pushed between the floor and quarter panel at the back and then slotted in at the front.
    *Now is the time to insert the closing section (SMR1. part no 6), if you're replacing it.

SMR15.   The side-member is clamped into place . . .

SMR16.   . . . and the frame-to-body bolts, which screw into the side-member are re-inserted.

SMR17.   But before anything is welded into place, you must check that nothing has sagged or dropped while the side-member has been cut out. This can easily happen in spite of the strength of the roof or the strength of the Cabriolet's reinforcement 'girder', so you should now re-fit the door and check that the detail pressings line up and that the door gap is even all the way around. You may need to place a jack with a piece of timber above the head to lift the body and take out the sag, or even to use a hydraulic ram to push the body into shape. This latter course of action is not likely to be required (unless you have taken off too many body panels at once and lost sight of what the shape ought to be) but, unless you regain the correct dimensions easily, it would be sensible to have the car trued up by a specialist with the experience to put matters to rights: DIY body repairs are absolutely fine, but one thing you mustn't risk is a distorted body. It

could be dangerous on the road and, once welded up, would be horrendously expensive to have put right!

SMR18.   Check also that the distance between the faces of the door opening (dimension 'a') measures 945 mm (37.2 in.). (Drawing courtesy Volkswagen)

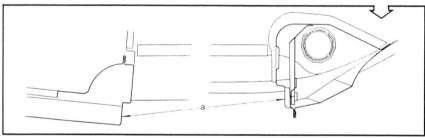

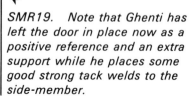

SMR19.   Note that Ghenti has left the door in place now as a positive reference and an extra support while he places some good strong tack welds to the side-member.

SMR20. On the inside of the car, strong seam welding has to be placed around both door pillars and, on the Cabriolet, the extra strengthening gussets. The one that was cut out has to be repaired and re-fitted.

SMR21. Here from beneath the wheel arch looking forwards you can see how the rear end of the side-member fits neatly into the wheel arch. The base of the rear seat support area has to be welded up and the small cross-member (SMR1. part no. 9) may have to be repaired, as with this car, or replaced entirely. It includes the closing-off plate for the end of the side-member.

SMR22. Volkswagen, of course, make panels with the correct individual features for contemporary saloon/sedans and Cabriolets. Here, a non-Volkswagen part, supplied by Uro Autoparts was used, but it meant that their saloon/sedan panel had to be adapted for the Cabriolet. This involved chiselling off the carpet clamping strip from the panel top and letting on a new one. You can expect to have to make minor modifications of this sort when using later panels, if they're the only ones available, for early cars. But at least there are parts available! How many other cars of this age and even newer could make such a boast?

Beetle Door Removal

1) The hinges are welded to the door, so you have to unscrew the two countersunk crosshead screws holding each hinge to the door pillar. First, the plug over each screw head has to be removed, then each screw has to be removed with an impact screwdriver set to 'unscrew'. Whatever you do, don't risk rounding off the heads.
2) When refitting, take off the latch striker plate, have an assistant help to manoeuvre the door level into the door opening and only fully tighten the screws when the door fits properly.

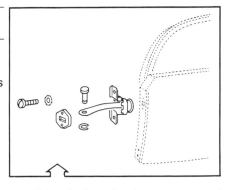

BDR1. Before the door can be taken off the stay has to be removed by taking out the screws holding it to the door pillar or to the door itself as shown in this drawing reproduced with the kind permission of Volkswagen.

Beetle Door Stripdown

The door being stripped down at Haselock's is from a 1302, but differences over earlier and later cars — surprisingly few in number — are mentioned in the text.

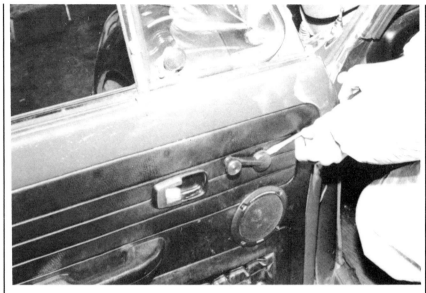

BDS1.   Lever off the shaft end of the plastic cover placed over the window winder handle. (Not early cars.)

BDS2.   Take out the screw holding the handle to the shaft.

BDS4.   Take out the recessed trim plate from the inner door handle lever . . .

BDS5.   . . . and remove the screw.

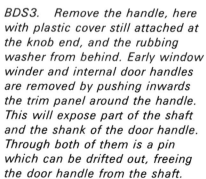

BDS3.   Remove the handle, here with plastic cover still attached at the knob end, and the rubbing washer from behind. Early window winder and internal door handles are removed by pushing inwards the trim panel around the handle. This will expose part of the shaft and the shank of the door handle. Through both of them is a pin which can be drifted out, freeing the door handle from the shaft.

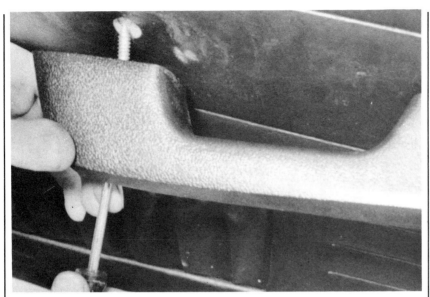

BDS6. Take out the screws holding the door pull . . .

BDS7. . . . and prise the trim panel clips out of the holes in the door frame. The clips are liable to pull out of the trim panel itself on older cars or where the panel has become damp and there is also a chance that the panel could split if bent too sharply.

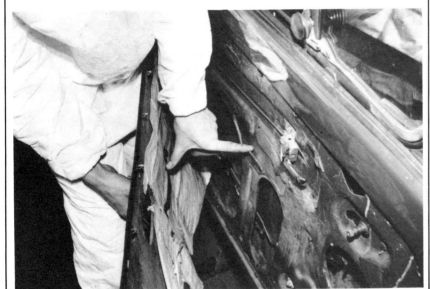

BDS8. In this case the door pull is screwed to the trim panel and has been left on the door and the bar by the mechanic's thumb hooks over the plate by his index finger. So the trim panel has to be lifted to remove. Don't forget, on all cars, to retrieve the spring that sits behind the winder and door opener handle (the latter only on early cars).

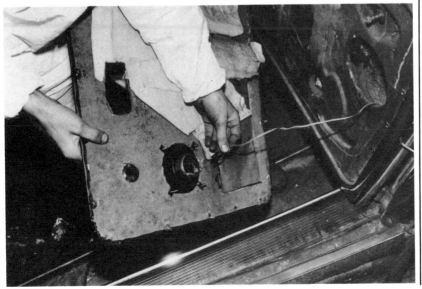

BDS9. If radio speakers are fitted to the door trims, disconnect them, taking note of which way round the wires went! Protect the speaker cone against damage — it may be best to take it off.

BDS10. There should be a plastic sheet stuck either to the door itself or to the door trim. Peel it off carefully and, if it's good enough, re-use it or if not, replace it to prevent water from running down and rotting the door trim panel.

Door Gear

BDS11. This drawing, shown here with the kind permission of Volkswagen, shows the outside door handle (bracketed 1 plus 2, 3 and 4) and also the door alignment dovetail.

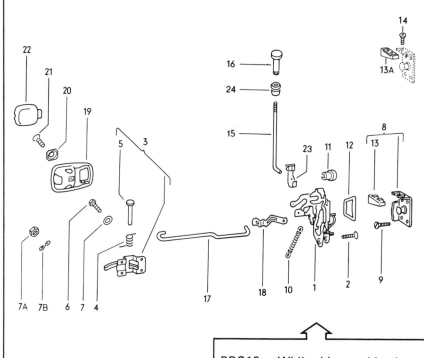

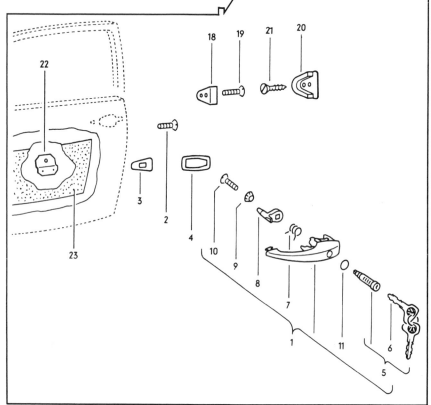

BDS12. While this one (thanks again, Volkswagen!) shows the latch mechanism, the lock mechanism and the interior door handle. The door pillar mounted components (part no. 8 & 9) are also there.

1) Take out the four screws (BDS12. part no. 6) holding the interior door handle (3) to the door frame.

2) The remote control rod (17) with its packing can be taken off and the inside lock control unclipped (23).

3) Undo the screws holding the lock/latch to the door edge (BDS12, part no. 2) and the one holding the handle (BDS11, part no. 2). You will have to ease the door sealing strip away to get at them. The lock/latch mechanism (BDS12, part no. 1) is quite complicated so, if it goes wrong, you may have to invest in a new one.

4) Early lock mechanisms are removed in a similar way except that there is no push-button interior locking mechanism to undo and the inside handle mechanism is linked to the lock/latch with a bar which need not be removed; and two parts are taken out still linked together.

BDS13. *The outside door handle can now be lifted away.*

Saloon/Sedan Door Glass & Gear

BDS14. *These drawings, reproduced with the kind permission of Volkswagen show the door window frame of the saloon/sedan (above) and the Cabriolet (below).*

BDS15. *The top set of drawings show the window regulator used on most Beetles while the bottom set of drawings show the regulator used on Cabriolets.*

1) Lower the window and undo the bolts holding the window frame to the winding mechanism — they pass through the plate shown on the right-hand side of part no. 1, BDS15.

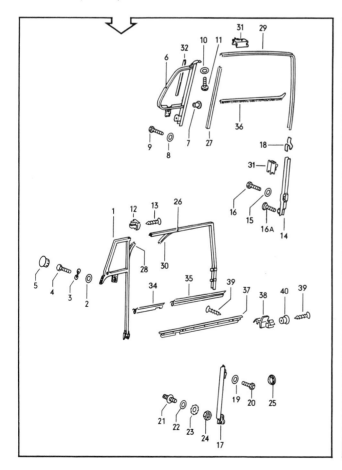

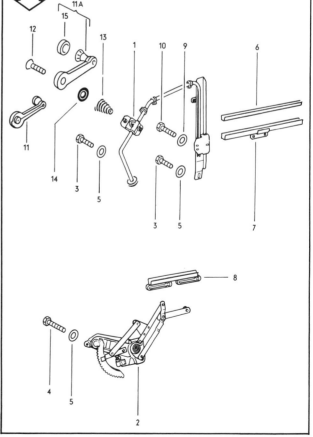

2) Undo the screws holding the winder to the door, ease the winder forwards and draw the glass out downwards.

3) Take out the bolts holding the winder to the door – see BDS15, part no. 1 again, the plate on the upper, left-hand section.

4) Mr Haynes' manual says, 'The refitting is quite a struggle. We are sure the winder goes in, in seconds, at Wolfsburg; but it doesn't when you are on your knees apparently praying to the door.' Don't YOU crack up! Fit the winder in through the slot with the winder hub end first. Wriggle the winder mechanism until you can pick up all the securing bolts' thread holes, but don't put the bolts in yet. With a second pair of hands in the vicinity, insert the glass as the reverse of how you took it out. Plus: either make certain that the top of the tube tucks behind the quarter light (vent) bottom swivel pin, instead of in front of it where it tries hard to go; OR take out the quarter light (vent) first.

5) Holding the glass in position, fit the bolts loosely, try the mechanism to line things up, tighten the bolts, but be prepared to loosen and reposition the window's position on the winder.

6) Take great care not to kink the pipe or you'll get an awful tight spot. Oil but don't grease the mechanism.

Cabriolet Door Glass & Gear

1) Part no. 2, BDS15 shows the window regulator (winder gear) for the Cabriolet. To remove, proceed as follows (assuming the door trim has already been taken off as already described):

2) On the passenger side, take off the arm rest support bracket after taking off the upper support screw.

3) Remove the lower screw from the bottom of the front window run channel (BDS15, part no. 1).

4) From now on, have someone support the glass to prevent it falling. Take out the six bolts holding the regulator (2) in place.

5) Press the regulator inwards and push the window lifting linkage towards the lock until the two rollers in the lifting channel are free.

6) From the rear edge of the door, loosen the upper and lower retaining screws of the rear window run channel (BDS15, part no. 26).

7) The window complete with the rear run channel can be lifted out of the door.

8) The rear channel screws go into captive nuts which can be moved around to adjust the position of the window.

9) The front channel is cemented into position and can be replaced when the vent frame is removed – see next section.

10) It would seem that early Cabriolet window sealer strips (BDS15, part no. 37) are just clipped into place while later ones are held with screws as well. These are prone to seizing solid so apply plenty of releasing fluid well beforehand.

Vent (Quarter-light) Removal

BDS16. If just the glass and frame are to be removed, the top rivet (13) must be drilled out after which the glass and frame can be lifted out. The Cabriolet glass and frame, however, can be taken out after unscrewing the top pivot (11).

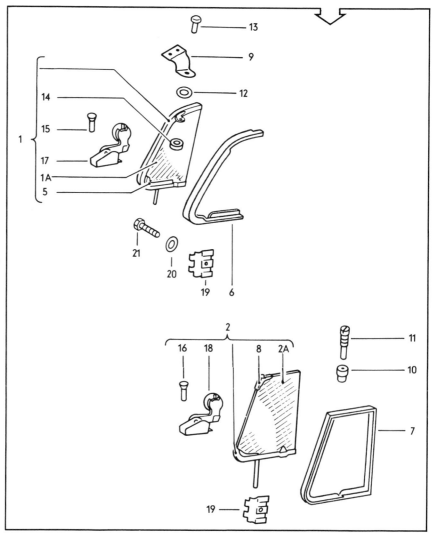

104

If the bottom needs attention, you'll have to take out the whole frame, with reference to BDS14. It is possible to adjust the clamp if the pivot has simply become loose, allowing the vent to slam shut when the car is on the move.

Fitting a Beetle Door Skin

This is essentially similar to the process described under 'Fitting a Transporter Door Skin'. See that section for more details.

Safety

Always wear goggles when using a mini-grinder. The cut off edges and flanges from an old door skin are among the sharpest and most dangerous. Wear thick industrial gloves and dispose of the old panel safely.

BDS1.   After removing the door, the edge of the door skin is ground through then cut with a sharp chisel. Wear thick gloves!

BDS2.   This Cabriolet door skin was cut away just below the waist rail. You have to decide for yourself whether to replace the whole skin, including the waist rail on the Cabrio or including the window surround on the sedan/saloon models.

BDS3.   The door base had rotted out, but full repair panels are available. Here, a bracket in the front lower corner is being cut around to retain it as the old base is removed.

BDS4.   The new panel was clamped carefully in place then welded with a series of MIG tacks to cut down the very real corrosion risk.

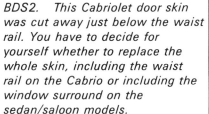

BDS5. The Volkswagen door skin, made for the saloon/sedan models (Cabrio. door skins are far more expensive) was cut down and then fitted as shown under 'Fitting a Transporter Door Skin'. Note that the skin should be lightly fitted, the door re-hung and the fit and shape checked meticulously before further welding with the door on the car, if possible.

Camper/Transporter Bodywork

The history of the Transporter includes so many types that they are just too numerous to list fully here, but they include Van, Kombi, Station Wagon, Pick-up, Bus, Camper, Caravette, Campmobile and Continental. Real buffs refer to the 'Type 2' (Type 1 being the saloon/sedan, of course) but it's easier to just call them by Volkswagen's own name of 'Transporter'.

Before 1979, the Transporter was made in two basic body types: From 1949 to 1967 as a 'split screen' model and from '67 and '79 in a much modified, but still recognisable form with one-piece screen. As indicated, these two body types had almost innumerable variations on the same theme applied to them but, with the exception of parts of the rear end of the Pick-up models, the bodywork repair procedures shown here apply to nearly all of

them. One reason is that the basic structural principles were so similar all through, including the fact that there are even fewer bolt-on parts than for the Beetle. Therefore, whenever body parts are replaced, it involves similar sets of operations. The most common body repairs carried out in the House of Haselock body shop are shown in the following section, most featuring 'split-screen' Type 2 Transporters, others involving later vehicles.

Transporter Body Panels

Body panels for the 'split-screen'

Transporter are available as reproduction repair panels made to a high standard from Haselock's and many of them are shown through this book. Also, many of Volkswagen's own panels are shown throughout the book and the full range of post-'split-screen' Transporter panels are still available from your Volkswagen dealership.

TBP1. For instance, these are the later Transporter front-end panels, this drawing being reproduced with kind permission of Volkswagen from their 'Type 2 '68-79' parts list which you will be able to see in microfiche form at your Volkswagen dealership.

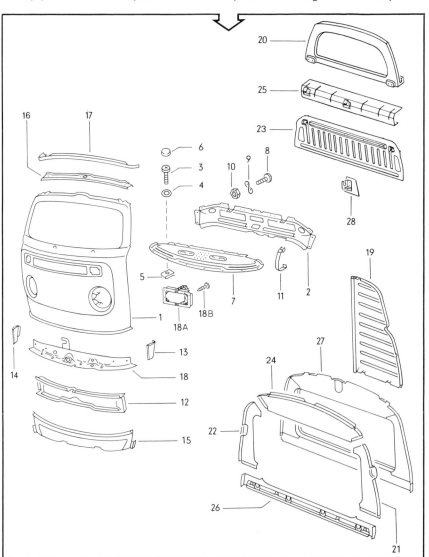

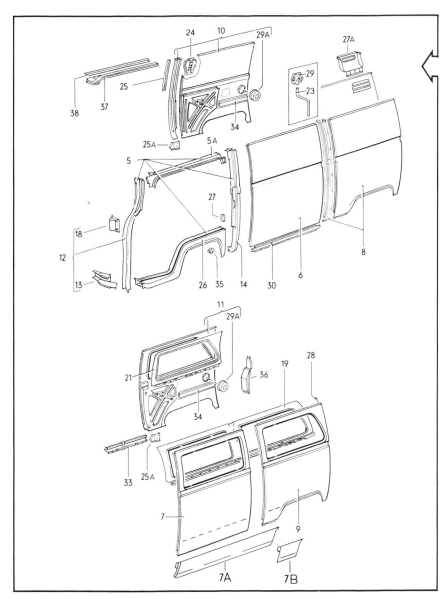

TBP2. These are the side panels and door surround panels available from Volkswagen (and taken with thanks from the Volkswagen Transporter parts book), but note that they are not interchangeable with 'split-screen' Transporter panels.

Fitting a Transporter Door Skin

Safety

Always wear goggles when using a mini-grinder. The cut off edges and flanges from an old door skin are among the sharpest and most dangerous. Wear thick industrial gloves and dispose of the old panel safely.

Later models — full door skin

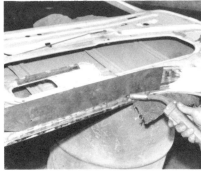

DSR1. Haselocks repaired corrosion in the base of this Transporter door before removing the skin to lessen the risk of distortion to the door shell.

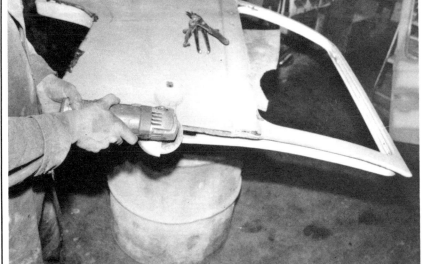

DSR2. The old skin was removed by grinding the edge of the flange all the way round ...

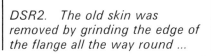

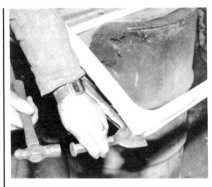

DSR3. ...then cutting through the thin edge of steel with a sharp bolster chisel. You really **MUST** wear thick industrial gloves here because the edges of the steel will be razor sharp.

DSR4. Inside the window opening, it was necessary to use a cutting blade on the mini-grinder to separate the skin from the frame.

DSR5. Haselocks remove the lower part of the skin separately from the upper part.

DSR6. Spot welds holding the flange around the edge of the door in place are ground through and the door edge left level and smooth; clean off paint or contaminates.

DSR7. The new door skin is lowered into place . . .

DSR8. . . .and the flanges re-spot welded all the way around after clamping down. In fact, the door was spot welded in a few places, then fitted back to the vehicle to check for perfect fit — it's far easier to twist and pull it back to shape now rather than after it's been welded up — before final welding. You could tack weld with a 'gas' or MIG welder if you don't have a spot welder.

'Split-Screen Transporter door skin repair

DSR9. Where there's corrosion in a 'Split's' door skin, the only option is to fit a door skin repair patch made by Haselocks since full door skins are no longer available.

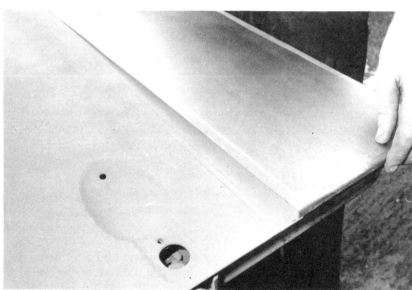

DSR10. The repair patch comes complete with 'shoulder' to lap under the edge of the existing skin. After removing the door, mark out a line against the top edge of the repair panel, then draw another line just below it to allow for the overlap.

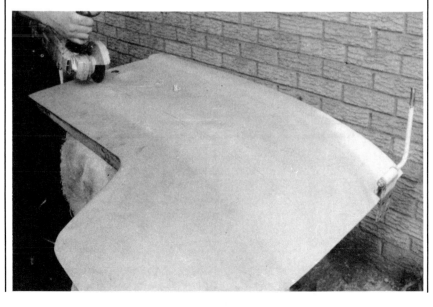

DSR11. Cut with some form of non-distorting cutter. Here a cutting disc on the mini-grinder was used with great care. When welding, use only tack welds with a MIG otherwise the panel will distort and buckle horribly.

Transporter Front Panel

Damage Repair

TFP1. Even a relatively small amount of accident damage can cause problems to the front end of the Transporter because of the size of the panel and because the strengthening panels behind make it impossible to get ordinary panel beating equipment onto the inside. It may have been possible to pull the dent out, but the panel is so large that it may have buckled, stretched and made matters even worse.

TFP2. The Haselock solution was to cut around the damaged part of the panel . . .

TFP3. . . . and to remove it completely.

TFP4. Then supporting strips were welded along the edges of the opening . . . (if they had been spot welded, the process would have been quicker and there would be less risk of the home welder distorting the panel but it would be difficult to insert spot-welding arms).

TFP5. And after being trued up with hammer and dolly . . .

TFP6. . . . and the bent section of the panel beaten back to its former shape . . .

TFP8. . . . and after the MIG welds had been ground off flush, it only remained to lead load the seams or to wipe on a skim of filler and refinish the job.

Front Panel Replacement

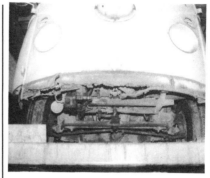

TFP10. As always in these cases, things looked even worse as parts began to be stripped off. Removal of the front bumper revealed just how nasty the front apron had become.

TFP7. . . . it was welded back into the front panel . . .

TFP9. When this 'split-screen' Camper came into Haselock's, the front end was a total mess, having been crudely repaired in the past.

TFP11. First, it is good practice to cut a 'window' into the panel to be removed. Here, the window was a full length one, stretching from screen to apron and from side to side. This approach shows clearly how many small ancillaries may still have to come off and, most importantly, it enables you to cut off the panel joints without having to wrestle with a major piece of motor vehicle.

TPF12. On this Camper, the screen pillars had started to corrode, too. If they were sound, but the rest of the front panel was rotten, it might be possible to cut the new panel just above the lip which joins on to the screen base and avoid having to work on the screen pillars at all. On the other hand, if you're going this far down the restoration route, perhaps you should be prepared to do the job in its entirety.

TFP13. Old spot welds have to be drilled out to remove the old panel and are then separated with a thin bladed bolster chisel. The new panel is best spot welded into place, but could be plug welded with MIG or gas. See later section under Transporter Bodywork or read the sections on quarter panel replacement under Beetle Bodywork.

TFP14. The same applies to the base of the window flange, viewed here from the inside.

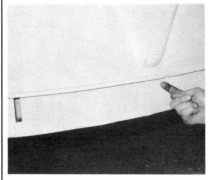

TFP15. The base of the front panel lips under the new front apron.

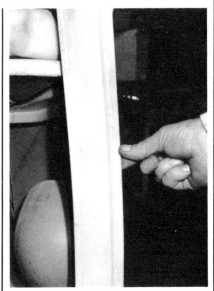

TFP16. This is the front door pillar viewed from the rear of the Transporter. The new front panel laps around this edge rather like the edge of a door skin and in fact, it's fitted in exactly the same sort of way. See section on Doors for further information.

TFP17. The renewed front end gives the appearance of this part-restored Camper a flying start, especially when compared with the mess photographed earlier!

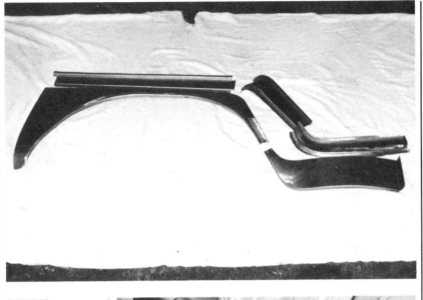

Front Wheel Arch Replacement

FWA1. This part of the Transporter is particularly prone to corrosion because of the way it sits just over the front wheel and beneath the front doors, trapping in mud and damp. It's quite a complex component and extremely difficult to fabricate on a one-off basis, while the parts suppliers haven't got round to making replacement panels. Or rather they hadn't because Barry Haselock, the Big Daddy of House of Haselock, has designed jigs for the production of replacement panels for this area of the split-screen Transporter. Here's how to fit these Haselock panels.

FWA2. As you can see, the front floor is prone to corrosion too, but at least the front panel, repaired in the previous section presents a clean surface to work up to.

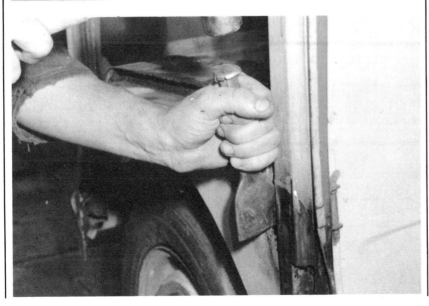

FWA3. Cutting away the old panel follows exactly the same procedure as for other panels shown through this book. Drill out spot welds where you can or chisel alongside a seam and use the mini-grinder to grind back to a clean flange on the surrounding panel. Quite often, of course, this flange has corroded too, in which case it will have to be re-made with a piece of folded steel sheet.

FWA4. At the rear of the wheel arch is a large closing plate. This one had also corroded out badly and so, with the old wheelarch cut clear, the corroded metal was cut back to sound steel . . .

FWA5. . . . and a repair panel made out of flat steel to replace it. This was tucked behind the flange on the side panel before being welded in and cut to fit around the cross-member at the base. Originally there was a pressed fluting half way up, but reproduction of that sort of shape is too difficult for most DIY repairers to carry out.

FWA6. The seat base lacked a flange and so one was made up from folded sheet, clamped and then spot-welded in place.

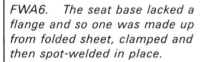

FWA7. Here on the left-hand side, the Haselock repair panel, shown in its made-up form as it is sold, is shown being compared with the corroded part. This new panel is simply spot or seam welded in place at the top and at both ends.

Front Floor Repair

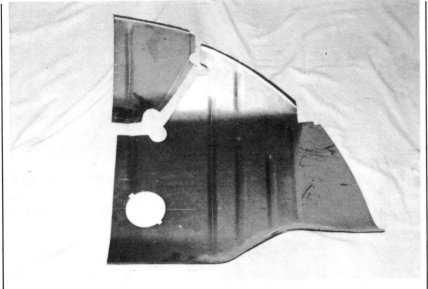

FFR1. House of Haselock have also developed a repair section for the front floor of the Transporter. These come in two pieces and include correct holes and fluting pressed into them. They cover the most common area of corrosion but, depending upon how badly this area has rusted, you may need to make up some extra repair patches to complement this one. Place the repair patch over the floor, scribe around it and cut out the floor, allowing for the flange on the repair section.

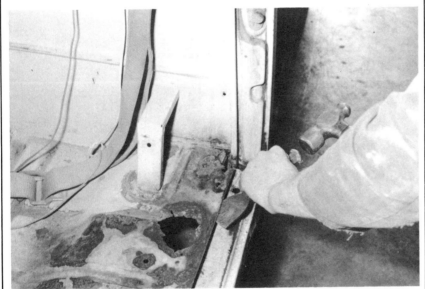

FFR2. Chisel the floor away from the wheel arch. If that has also corroded, it is best replaced with the old floor still in place, to ensure accurate lining-up. Then the new floor can be fitted to the correctly aligned new wheel arch.

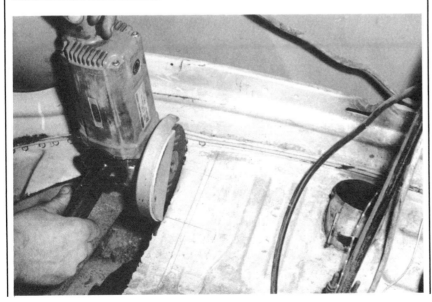

FFR3. It can be tricky to cut through steel in an area like this without distorting it. But a successful way of doing so is to use a cutting disc (made specially for the job, but not too expensive) in a mini-grinder. You can cut accurately and without twisting up the steel that stays behind, although you can't get into awkward spots. Take careful note of manufacturers' safety notes when using a mini-grinder because a wheel that shatters in use can cause severe injury. Always wear suitable shatter-proof goggles and preferably a full face mask.

FFR4. Here there's another of those situations where panels have been spot-welded into place. This tool is made specially for cutting out spot-welds and consists of a central pin which holds the tool into a centre punch mark that you will have previously made, and a cutter which cuts a ring around the spot weld.

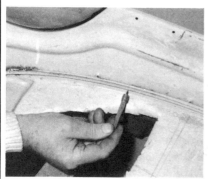

FFR5. You may have to look quite hard for the spot welds, although cleaning the metal with abrasive paper will show them up. Place a centre punch mark in the centre of each spot weld.

FFR6. As usual, the bulk of the old panel has been cut away leaving the joint area to be removed separately. You can see that where the tool was used first of all, to the right, the operator made the mistake of drilling right through, which is easily done. You should take extreme care to only drill through the panel to be removed; having an assistant push a screwdriver into the joint so that there is a clear movement and sound when the two panels separate is a big help. On the other hand, if you don't have a spot welder to replace the panels and intend plug welding or brazing, a larger hole may give a stronger joint.

FFR7. The spot welder cutter leaves the remains of the old spot weld attached to the panel that is left behind. These have to be ground off.

FFR8. Then the edges of the cut panel have to be ground and trimmed back to exactly the right position so that the repair panel flange tucks underneath and leaves a flush fitting panel when it is welded into place.

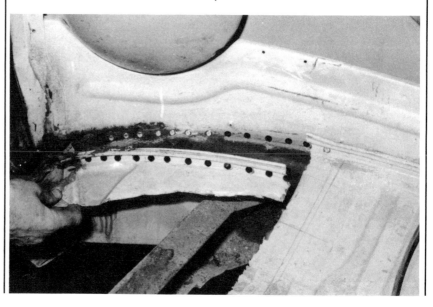

Rear Lower Quarter Panels

RLQ1. Just as the Transporter's front wheel arches are prone to corrosion from damp and rubbish thrown up by the front wheels, so the rear quarters are also vulnerable.

RLQ2. This repair section is available from Uro Autospares for repairing the area. As with the use of other repair sections shown in this book, you mark the edges of the section, using it as a template, cut inwards of the mark to allow a little overlap . . .

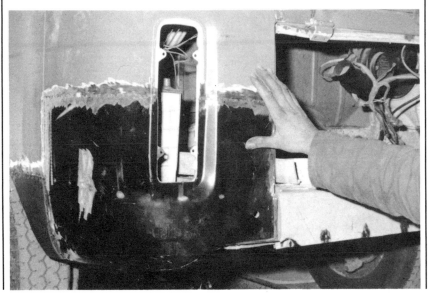

RLQ3. . . . and weld the new panel in place. But note that, as pointed out in other sections, there's almost always more to it than that! Haselock's have had to add a one-off repair just ahead of this repair section, leading up to the wheel arch, and it's also very common for the closing plate inside the repair panel, sitting just below the level of the rear light units, to rot out as well. Make a card template the shape of the repair panel before fitting it, make the steel repair panel to suit and then weld it in place after the quarter panel repair is in place.

RLQ4. The joint can be finished off with filler, but be careful not to lose the seam between the full rear quarter panel and the side panel which should run from top to bottom.

Transporter Sill/Body Rocker and Rear Floor

TSF1. The Transporter's sill or body rocker sections are straightforward in construction and easily available. After the old one has been cut off and the flanges cleaned back to shiny metal, the new sill is clamped accurately and welded into place. But, yet again, be prepared to repair other areas beyond the sill, exposed when the old one is cut away.

TSF2. Transporter bodies contain such a wide variety of internal fixtures and fittings that it wouldn't be possible here to detail their removal. Needless to say, such stuff will have to come out before the floor can be repaired! You'd be strongly advised to make careful sketches of where everything goes and to pencil a number on each separate part of the interior as it comes out, even the bits you know will require replacement: Campers can be particularly complex and you'll never remember where everything went!

118

TSF3. Upper floor repair sections are available from the VW specialists such as Uro. Here the House of Haselock team are offering up the corrugated section and checking it for fit after cutting it to slot around the vehicle's internal supporting struts.

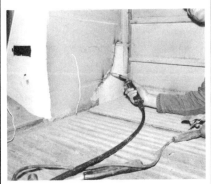

TSF4. The part bulkheads behind the front seat had corroded on both sides and both had to be repaired with one-off repair patches.

TSF6. Once again, there's the business of cutting away the old panel and this time the chassis frame itself could be inspected, cleaned and painted. The new panel is lifted into place . . .

TSF7. . . . and welded in to complete a thoroughly sound job beneath the vehicle.

TSF5. The frame is boxed in above, with the van floor and along the edges beneath. Naturally the lower 'floor' is prone to rotting away but there were no repair panels available. Once again, House of Haselock came to the rescue, designing and producing replacement panels which are now on general sale.

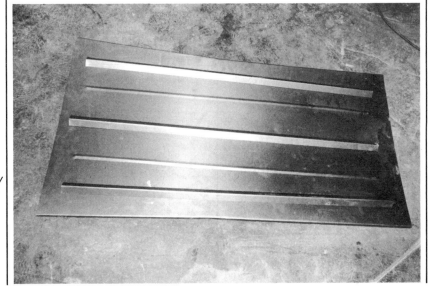

Transporter Doors

Cab and Hinged Side Doors

TDR1.   There are strong similarities here with the Beetle doors. First remove the check strap pin. (Or take out the check strap retaining screws – side doors.)

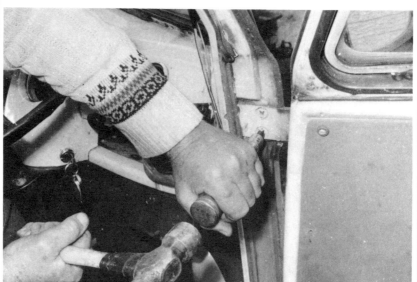

TDR2.   Then get someone to take the considerable weight of the door as it is freed and use an impact screwdriver to remove the screws into the door pillars.

Sliding Doors

TDR3.   Remove the outside runner cover. The retaining strip (19) is held in place by a crosshead screw. The cover itself is held by the two screws 2 and 14 and the retaining bolt (11) which is accessible from inside the passenger compartment. Drawing reproduced courtesy Volkswagen.

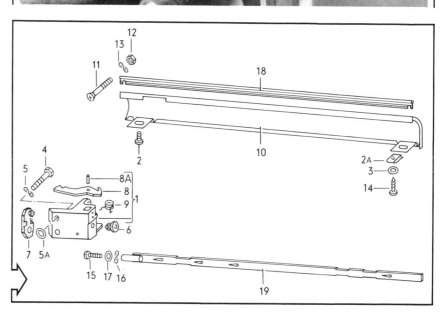

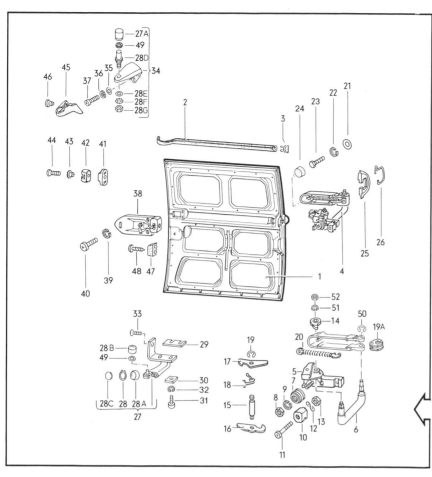

1) Down the length of the door is a cover. In the end of it is a tensioning screw which is unscrewed about 15 turns then tapped smartly to the rear. The cover can now be lifted up and out.

2) Move the door back until the guide piece and roller on the hinge link can be disengaged from the channel. Next, push the door to the rear until the upper roller clears the top channel. Now swing the door out a little so that the lower rollers can be moved out of the gap in the bottom channel.

3) Note that the door is very heavy and that you must have at least one extra pair of hands to help handle it whilst it is being removed.

TDR4.   The complex layout of the Transporter sliding door, hinge and roller guide is laid out here in this drawing reproduced here with thanks to Volkswagen.

TDR5.   And this drawing, also reproduced with the kind permission of Volkswagen shows the lock and latch mechanism of the sliding door.

Preparation & Paint

The importance of getting the paintwork right on a restored Beetle or Transporter can't be over-stressed! You may have spent weeks of your life making your vehicle as sound as the day Volkswagen conceived it, but unless the paintwork is right, the whole effect will be spoiled. Re-painting a car is actually a major subject in itself, but provided you keep things simple, there will be enough information here to enable you to have a go at doing it yourself. If you feel you need to know more, I've written another

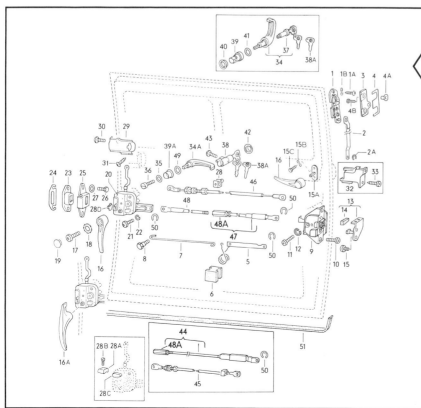

book with Haynes called The Car Bodywork Repair Manual which is around the size of this book, but which does nothing but give information on how to fix car bodywork, so there's a very large amount of information in there on all aspects of paint spraying for the home sprayer.

But back to the specifics of the Beetle and Transporter: Your first decision must be to pick the type of paint you wish to use. The very best paint is not at all suitable for the home sprayer unless you possess well above average levels of equipment. It's known generally as 'two-pack' paint because the paint is mixed with a hardener before spraying and it then sets like an adhesive. The finish from the gun is superb, the paint film is much harder than anything else on offer and it doesn't need polishing for many years, a wash and leather down restoring its shine. The snag is that the air-borne particles of paint are toxic, containing iso-cyanate; the family connection with the word 'cyanide' not being coincidental! Professionals use an air fed mask when spraying with this type of paint, but the home sprayer would also have to be certain that the spray mist would not cause anyone else potential harm. This would clearly be impossible where you would be working in a high population-density area, where the garage is attached to the house or where children or other inquisitive souls could be in the vicinity.

My Cabrio. and the House of Haselock Baja Bug are shown being sprayed in this section by Graham Maurice Cars and Autoprep respectively using ICI 2K paint in a professional booth, and that may be another option open to you; to go as far as you can in preparing the car then take it to a specialist (who will invariably criticise your preparation and want to do more – if he doesn't, ask yourself why!) and have the paint put on. This is actually quite a cost-effective thing to do because the most time-consuming part of

the job is the preparation. ICI Autocolour paints are supplied to Volkswagen as 'original equipment', by the way, so its use for refinishing is perfectly appropriate here!

The only other type of paint that I could possibly recommend is Cellulose Enamel paint. Cellulose isn't and hasn't been used by any of the manufacturers for many years, but it is more suitable for DIY use. If a face mask of the correct type is used and the spray area kept ventilated, the fumes are not especially dangerous (but take a look at the 'Safety' notes) and the finish will be quite durable. It also has two advantages for the home restorer. Any home paint job is almost certain to have bits of dust or kamikaze flies land in it and these can be most easily polished out from cellulose, and so can any runs that the unskilled sprayer might have induced. Also, if cellulose is 'cut & polished' (rubbed down with extremely fine abrasive paper then with polishing compound) it is possible to obtain the sort of 'mirror' finish that no other paint will give. Trouble is, it doesn't last, and you have to polish the shine back again, in the end polishing right through the paint over a period of years, necessitating a full respray all over again.

Safety

Cellulose paint:
The spray is volatile – keep away from all flames or sparks – and so are the fumes from paint and thinners while thinner dampened rags are also a fire hazard. The spray can cause you to lose consciousness if inhaled in a confined area. Always use a suitable face mask (see your supplier) and ventilate the work area. Protect hands with a barrier cream or wear

protective gloves when handling paint. Keep well away from eyes.

'2-pack' paint:
Spray from this type of paint is toxic to the degree that it can be lethal! (The hardened paint on the car is not dangerous, of course!) Only use with an air-fed mask from a clean compressed air source (i.e. not from within the spray area) and never use this type of paint where the spray could affect others. It can also cause eye irritation and eye protection should be worn. Protective gloves should be worn when mixing and handling paint. Those who suffer from asthma or other respiratory illness should have nothing to do with this type of paint spraying! There is also a fire risk with peroxide catalysts.

General:
Don't eat, drink or smoke near the work area, clean hands after the work is complete, but never use thinners to wash paint from hands. Always wear an efficient particle mask when sanding down. OBTAIN AND THOROUGHLY READ THE MANUFACTURER'S DATA AND SAFETY SHEETS BEFORE USE.

The following picture sequence shows how the preparation and painting of a Cabriolet and a Baja Bug plus several shots of Beetles and a Transporter being prepared for refinishing. The principles of spraying the Baja Bug are the same as for an ordinary saloon/sedan.

P&P1. Whilst still at House of Haselock, my Cabrio. was examined all over to look for defects that would have to be put right, including dents and dings. These were marked so that the job could be assessed in terms of time and materials required.

P&P2. Suspicious areas were ground back as described under 'Stripdown', revealing large areas of filler. To say that this set back the respray is something of an understatement if you take a look at what else was done to it, shown in this book . . .

P&P3. All of the old paint was removed – it's the only way to carry out a really high-class respray. Here stripper is being brushed onto the front lid, the guy doing the work wearing tight-fitting rubber gloves. Eye protection is a 'must', too.

P&P4. Once the paint has wrinkled, it can be scraped away easily with a metal scraper. Keep wearing the gloves because the stripper is still corrosive. When you're dealing with old paint, you may have to leave the stripper, thickly coated, quite a long time to wrinkle the paint and then strip several layers away, one at a time.

P&P5. The remains will have to be sanded away using a random orbit sander. This is an air tool but Black & Decker produce an excellent electrically operated machine suitable for the home workshop.

P&P6. Ridges and fluting have to be cleaned up separately. You'd normally, if you weren't demonstrating for the camera, strip the whole panel before sanding!

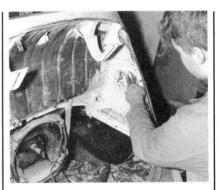

P&P7. One of the hardest parts to strip is inside the engine bay – but there's nothing for it but to persevere.

P&P8. And again, the luggage bay area can be a fiddle to clean up although again, the random orbit sander can save a lot of finger-ache and time!

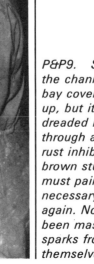

P&P9. Surface rust in places like the channel around the luggage bay cover can be difficult to clean up, but it's essential work if the dreaded rust isn't going to break through again. You could also try a rust inhibitor to try to hold the brown stuff back a little, but you must paint it, with a brush if necessary, before it gets damp again. Note that the screen has been masked to prevent sanding sparks from embedding themselves into the glass.

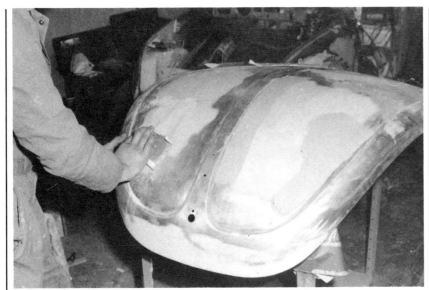

P&P10. The next stage is to apply a thin skim of body filler to any minor imperfections in the body. It's important that all blemishes are taken out now; the trouble is that they won't be apparent now because a matt surface hides blemishes, but they'll show up like several sore thumbs once the gloss coat goes on.

P&P11. Here's a typical area for filling and flatting carefully; it's the place where a new rear quarter panel repair was welded to the existing panel at the top.

P&P12. And here, the surface of a new wing is sanded, taking care not to go through the protective paint, but just far enough to 'etch' the surface to give the primer a key. You really should wipe the panels with spirit wipe before sanding down because otherwise the sander can push contaminants into the surface.

P.&P.13. Tiny blemishes have been smeared with a really thin coat of stopper (smoother than normal filler) before being carefully hand flatted.

P&P14. You may want to sand panels down before fitting them. That way, they're much easier to get at. Theoretically, you should sand with your hand held across the angle of sanding, as shown here, so that your fingers don't create grooves in the surface.

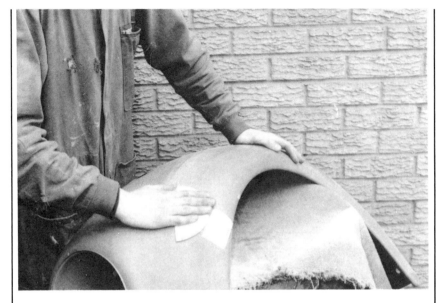

P&P15. Flatting with the panels off means that you can get right into the joint area, but you can't check for accurate fit, unless you fit up, remove the panels, fill, flat and prime the panels, re-fit and re-flat.

P&P16. Doors are large, heavy things to flat off the car and you'll need to support each one on a trestle or table of some sort whilst working on it.

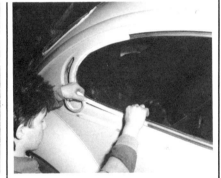

P&P17. Once you are happy that every surface is blemish-free (and you must be prepared to spend hours and hours getting there) you can mask-off ready for priming. If you're not taking the glass out — you'd need to for a tip-top respray — you may have to paint tyre black onto the rubbers if the tape refuses to 'stick' down in place. Tape carefully around the edge, then fix tape half way over the edge of your masking paper and stick the edge of tape and paper to the first lot of tape.

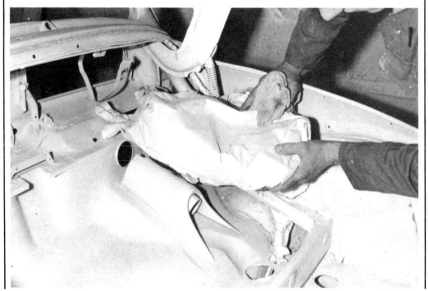

P&P18. You won't have to remove the wiring loom completely from the car. Disconnect it back to where it appears through a grommet, bundle it together and 'bag' it for protection.

P&P19. To avoid getting paint onto suspension components, you'll have to take great care to mask off, remembering that spray can, and does, blow some little way beneath the car.

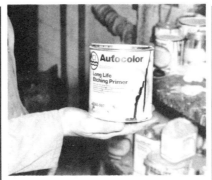

P&P20. At the end of this picture sequence, you'll see a breakdown of paints and primers used. One of the most important was the ICI Autocolour Etching Primer which eats its way microscopically into the surface of any bare metal . . .

P&P21. . . . giving excellent 'stiction' and helping to prevent the spread of rust should the paint film become broken through chipping or scratching. Good stuff! It's shown being used here to spot prime areas that have broken through to bare metal after flatting.

P&P22. Then, after a couple of coats of primer have been sprayed over the top and allowed to dry, the random orbit sander could be used with a fine grade of abrasive to smooth the surface. (You should always wear an efficient particle mask because inhaled dust can be dangerous.)

P&P23. You'll invariably have to finish off by hand, or you could flat the whole lot by hand using a rubber block to support the wet-and-dry paper, dipping it into slightly soapy every now and again so the dust comes off as a slurry.

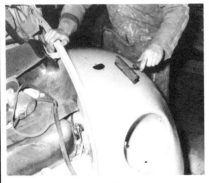

P&P24.   A good House of Haselock tip is to use a rubber squeegee to wipe off excess slurry every now and again. Be sure to wash down after flatting.

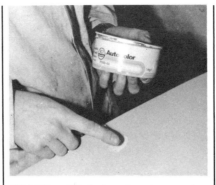

P&P25.   ICI Autocolor stopper is used at this stage to fill in final blemishes; wipe it over a wider area with a spreader or use your finger to dab a little into a pin hole or other small blemish.

P&P26.   Don't forget to prepare any accessories that are to be painted in body colour. Here the lenses have been taken out of the Cibie 'Oscar' dipping spot lamps and the shells, supplied in a neutral grey, are being flatted for spraying.

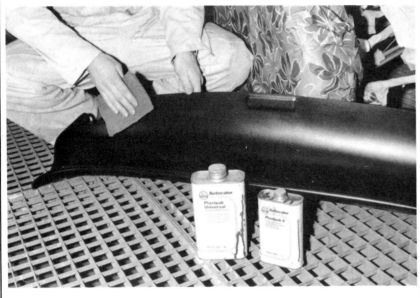

P&P27.   And here the Kamei spoiler, made in impact resistant plastic, is being rubbed down with an abrasive pad prior to the use of Plastpack. See P&P 53 at the end of this section.

P&P28.   It's very important that every square inch of the surface is wiped down with spirit wipe, such as the ICI Autocolor Spirit Wipe used here. This ensures that there are no contaminants on the surface of the paint that can cause a paint-finish (and morale!) – destroying reaction.

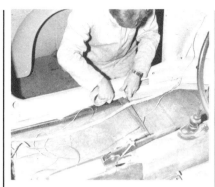

P&P29.   Now, it's important when masking off, to prevent dust flying around as it is to avoid overspray. The floor is shown being masked around the edge as in P&P17 . . .

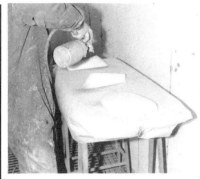

P&P32.   The car was sprayed in perfect conditions in Graham Maurice Cars' heated spray booth. All of the 'bits and pieces' were laid out around the walls on clean paper and sprayed in turn.

P&P35.   Mick, the sprayer, started with the dash and the area beneath working from one side of the car across to the other . . .

P&P30.   . . . then paper is used to 'fill in'.

P&P33.   Some needed to be turned, but it's best if you can suspend them. If you wish to hold parts being sprayed, wear gloves.

P&P36.   Then he sprayed one half of the screen surround. If the car had had a roof, he'd have started the outside of the vehicle with that. See the sequence covering the Baja Bug for details.

P&P31.   The amount of paint to be used is carefully measured into a mixing tin and the correct amount of thinner and activator (hardener) added to it. Note the protective clothing.

P&P34.   The doors were painted, suspended, off the car so that there was access to every part of them. The gun was used in horizontal 'passes', starting with the top and working downwards.

P&P37.   Then he moved forwards, spraying the front quarter panel in horizontal bands, working down from the top.

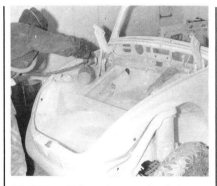

P&P38. When he reached the front, he stopped and transferred his attention to the inside of the luggage bay.

P&P40. . . . onto the other front quarter panel . . .

P&P42. . . . the rear quarter panel . . .

P&P39. Then, it was on with the front panel . . .

P&P41. . . . the sill/body rocker area . . .

P&P43. . . . and the engine bay (note the masked-off gearbox). Then it was down the rear side of the car and back to the door apperture. After the paint solvents had 'flashed off', the next coat was put on and then the next until Mick was satisfied that a good coat had been applied. And there's another advantage of 2K paint over cellulose: it gives a thicker build of paint and, because the paint hardens rather than simply drying, it is far less prone to shrinkage, thus preventing old blemishes and scratches to show through.

P&P44. Back at House of Haselock, the car with doors back in place was taken from the trailer ready for the next stage of its total restoration.

Painting a Sedan/Saloon Model

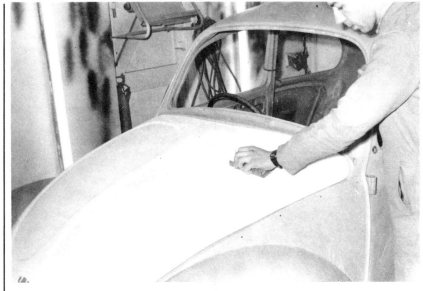

P&P45.   The Baja Bug shown being built up in another part of this book was painted at Autoprep of Martley, near Worcester. Here the fibreglass bonnet is being flatted in the normal way prior to painting with primer.

P&P46.   And, of course, the rest of the car was also flatted in the same way. Paul of Autoprep is seen flatting with a rubber block around which his flatting paper is wrapped.

P&P48.   Now here is the bit that wasn't shown in the previous section. When painting the roof of a sedan/saloon you start working in front-to-rear strips from the centre of the roof coming back towards yourself, a strip at a time.

P&P50.   Next, it is back to one of the corners of the car. Paul started spraying at the rear left-hand corner where the spray procedure is identical to that shown in the previous section.

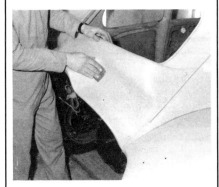

P&P47.   For the curvacious bits you can throw the block away; your fingers are much more versatile and blend to the concave curves of the panel.

P&P49.   Then you hightail round to the other side and repeat the procedure from centre of roof to gutter line.

P&P51.   The Baja fibreglass front end is sprayed in exactly the same way as that of a steel-bodied car.

Both Graham Maurice Cars of Leicester and Autoprep of Martley, near Worcester, made a superb job of spraying these two cars and both got on extremely well with the ICI materials. Now, here's a resume of how to go about spraying your car, using either 2K (2 pack) paint or cellulose, bearing in mind that, for safety reasons, 2K isn't suitable for the home sprayer unless he/she is lucky enough to possess some very specialised equipment.

2K (2 pack) paint

Step 1: Long-life Etch Primer
    5 minutes drying time
Hi Dur Rapide
    1 hour drying time
Wet-or-dry flat
2K finish
    Bake, or cure overnight
Polish where necessary

Cellulose Paint

Long Life Etch Prime
    5 minutes drying time
RPF (see data information that follows)
    30 minutes to 1 hour drying time
Wet flat for best results
Belco
    4 hours or overnight drying time
Wet flat with P 1200
Then double coat Belco and allow 4 hours drying time

Polish

A large number of different materials were used in the spraying of the author's Cabriolet and the Baja Bug shown here. Here's a run-down of what they were and what they have to offer. Each one includes "Data Sheet" number. This is the number of the Data Sheet supplied by ICI and obtainable from their suppliers by anyone who uses their materials.
1) Zinc Rich Weldable Primer Data Sheet B13. Used in joints before welding/jointing.
2) Polyester Stopper Data Sheet B1. Used to fill dents and imperfections over bare metal.
3) 2K Etch Primer Data Sheet B15. Used on chassis to etch all bare metal areas and to prime chassis.

Can be left overnight before flatting and applying colour or can be used as non-sand primer given 20 to 20 minutes to dry and colour applied directly over it.

Only for use with 2K not Belco. N.B. Allow 10 minutes to stand before use.
4) Stone Chip Primer Data Sheet B11.

Chip resistant coat for use on chassis and areas liable to stone damage.
5) Cleaning solvent 61. Data Sheet C2. For cleaning off any contamination from bare metal areas before any priming/painting is carried out.
6) Spirit Wipe Data Sheet C2. For degreasing panels before spraying.
7) Long Life Etch Data Sheet B4. Allow 10 minutes to stand when mixed together before using. Apply to bare metal areas. N.B. DO NOT LEAVE UNPRIMED OVERNIGHT I.E. APPLY PRIMER IMMEDIATELY AFTER ETCH IS DRY. *If you need to leave panels in etch and you are equipped to use 2K (see "Safety" notes at the start of this section) you can use 2K Etch primer instead of Long Life Etch. But note that if cellulose is to be used afterwards RPF must be sprayed between the 2K Etch and Belco coats.*
8) Hi Dur Rapide Data Sheet B19. Excellent filling properties, excellent flatting properties. Ready to flat in 1 hour. You can use Hi Dur Rapide to fill scratches. Apply as many coats as you wish and then flat smooth. If you have a small area of severe imperfections you can brush Hi Dur Rapide unthinned straight out of the can and then flat carefully afterwards. *N.B. This is a 2 pack material and an air fed mask must be worn.* (See "Safety" notes at the start of this section).
9) RPF Data Sheet B6. Fast air dry primer for use in open shop conditions. In other words, you don't need a spray booth and RPF is dry in 20 minutes. This was used for repriming small breakthroughs on the previously primed panels of the Cabriolet's body shell. It is the best primer for use under Belco.
10) 2K Data Sheet A1. Although for the safety reasons already discussed it is MOST IMPORTANT that the DIY-er doesn't use 2K at home, it does give the most durable finish and the one most similar to the original enamel from the production line. If the professional refinisher is using a low bake process he will mix the paint in the following proportions:

2K, 4 parts; Hardener 770, 2 parts; Thinner 1275, 1 part.

Apply 3 coats then put on bake for 30 minutes at 60 degrees Centigrade. For an air dry process he will use:

2K, 4 parts; Hardener 760, 2 parts; Thinner 1196, 1/2 part. He will apply three coats and allow to dry overnight.
11) Belco Data Sheet A3 and Supplement. This is an air drying paint. Application:

Belco, 1 part; Thinner, 1 part.

For cold conditions use Thinner 246. For best gloss, use Super Thinner 151.

For best results spray three coats, allow to dry then wet flat with P1200. Next, apply one double coat of Belco, allow to dry then polish.
12) Polishes and Compounds Data Sheet C3. You can buy coarse and fine grades of compounds in just the same way that you can for flatting paper. The grades go as follows: 2A (very coarse); 2B (coarse); Compound 41 (medium); Super Cut (fine); No 7 (very fine). It is only normally necessary to use two of these compounds to bring up the perfect finish to your paintwork. Here's how it's done.

2K Paint

First wet flat with P1200 Superfine then use Super Cut followed by No 7.

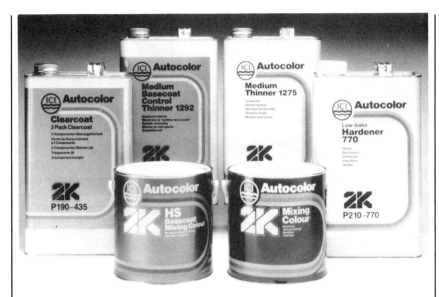

Belco

First wet flat with P1200 Superfine then compound with 2b followed by Super Cut or No 7.

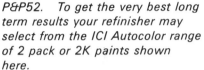

P&P52. To get the very best long term results your refinisher may select from the ICI Autocolor range of 2 pack or 2K paints shown here.

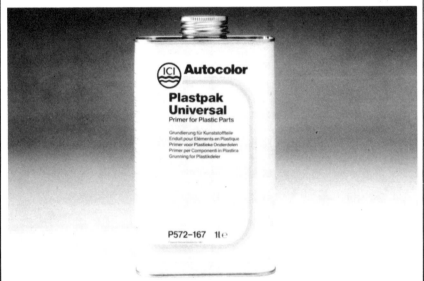

P&P53. If flexible plastic components are to be painted then Plastpak Universal Primer has to be sprayed on first. If you try to get away without using Plastpak things like your Kamei spoiler or engine vent cover will simply not allow the paint to stick properly allowing it to peel and look ragged in no time.

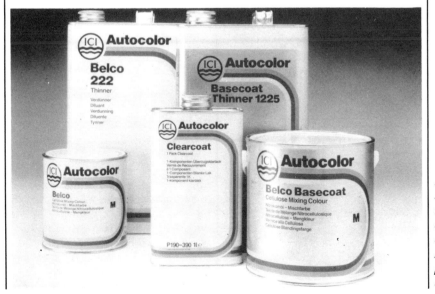

P&P54. Most DIY refinishers will select from the Belco range. The finish isn't as durable as 2K, but it does have the advantage that it's capable of being brought up to a higher gloss than any other type of paint although it takes plenty of elbow work.

Rustproofing

For anyone to spend time and money on repairing or rustrpoofing a car then fail to protect it against future rusting is surely unthinkable! You can protect outer surfaces with paint (which I prefer) or underseal, but hidden and enclosed sections have to be covered with an injected and sprayed fluid of which there are several on the market. I chose Comma 'Wax Seal' because it flows well and because it is said to contain corrosion inhibitors which stop existing rust in its

tracks as well as sealing out new. Do remember that partial coverage of any corrosion inhibitor is actually worse than none at all — it concentrates the corrosion in other areas, so it's best to invest in the best of injection equipment and not rely on the low-cost hand pump equipment which most manufacturers sell to the DIY market. I use a SATA injection kit which runs at high pressure from a compressor (you could hire if you don't own one) and costs about the same as three or four tyres to buy, which is about the same as the cost of having the work done. But you can be sure of doing the

work thoroughly, you still own the equipment and some folk have recovered the cost by doing friends cars for them . . .

R1.   I tipped the car onto its side using the AutoVip roll-over cage which is a remarkable piece of gear — see 'Hints, Tips & Equipment', and spent many hours scraping all underseal and surface rust from beneath the floorpan. Then I painted Comma 'Rust Stop', a metal primer with rust inhibitors, onto the surface, following up with two good coats of 'Hammerite' hammer finish black paint. This is non-original but easy to wash off and very hard wearing.

R2.   The SATA gun comes with a flexible lance which was used inside the long box-sections along the sides of the Cabrio.

R3.   Then the rigid wand with hook end was used to cover all the areas inside nooks and crannies at the front and rear. A few box-sections are totally enclosed and can only be got-at by drilling holes in strategic places.

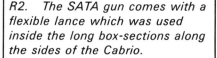

R4. The frame head and the area behind it was covered with great care with the Wax Seal fluid. It must be emphasised that there are many nooks and crannies that have to be sought out carefully but that there isn't room to cover them all in detail here.

R5. Young Richard, a neighbour helped with these shots: The running boards were removed, holes drilled and the body rocker/sills injected with the flexible SATA lance.

R7. Door hinge pillars were drilled and injected both upwards and downward.

R9. Here, the sun visor mountings are used as access points for the windscreen surround which is susceptible to rust on all models.

R6. The door trims were left in place while a good 'mist' of Wax Seal was created inside the door, before the trims were removed and more fluid injected with the stiff wand.

R8. The Cabrio's rear quarters and B-posts were injected and, in the case of sedan/saloon models, it would be wise to inject the screen surrounds.

You must then go over the vehicle and carefully protect such areas as the insides of Beetle rear lamp units (brush the fluid on), the chrome trim fittings and the luggage bay seal clip, as well as any other areas which could possibly corrode. Remember to place lots of old newspaper on the floor to catch the inevitable drips. *Always* complete all welding and spraying before applying rust inhibitors. They burn easily when fresh and a fire inside an enclosed member could be hard to detect or put out, while silicones used in them could wreak havoc with a paint finish unless every trace is scrupulously removed from the surface of the paint.

4 Finishing Touches

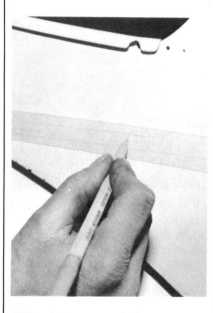

FT1.   It is extremely important to get all the chrome strip lined up perfectly. It's best if you can mark out and drill the primed paintwork before the finish coat goes on, but in our case that wasn't possible. Here the House of Haselock fitter has placed a piece of masking tape along the finished paintwork so that he can write on it without marking the paint and so that he has a reduced risk of damaging the paint with the drill.

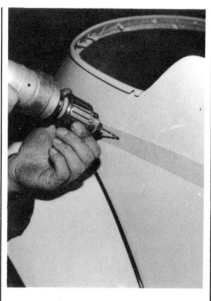

FT2.   After marking the position of each fixing clip, the drill is placed on the marked-out position and then the chuck is turned three or four times by hand; naturally enough, while the finger is kept off the trigger. This starts the drill without there being any risk of damaging the panel, which is what could happen if you used a centre punch. Then just drill right through, carefully at first, so that the drill doesn't slip and, carefully at breakthrough so that you don't damage anything on the other side of the panel.

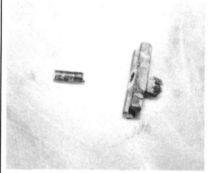

FT3.   Fixing clips come in these two parts . . .

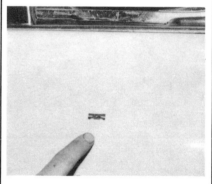

FT4.   . . . The larger part is pushed into the hole you have drilled and then the pin pushed into the centre which spreads the back of the clip and prevents it from coming out.

FT5. Then it is a simple matter of pushing the chrome strip onto the clips but, once again, taking care not to scratch or damage the paintwork. Trim clips and other such fittings are available from Uro Auto Spares but specialist Cabriolet parts are obtainable only through your Volkswagen dealer.

FT6. Uro also supplied new headlamps for this particular car. If you are refitting existing chromework polish it well before fitting it to the car because it is impossible to polish chrome properly once fitted.

FT8. Interior trim and fittings such as the interior lamp (on the Cabrio it is included in the rear view mirror) can be put back together and all wiring connections checked to make sure that they are good.

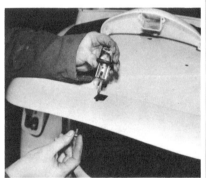

FT10. Other parts of the book show how to remove and refit catches and locks. Now is the time to make sure that they operate properly and that they are well lubricated.

FT7. You should plan to invest in and check on availability of new rubbers well in advance. Now is the time to fit them.

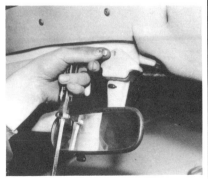

FT9. There are often caps over screws holding interior trim in place; make sure that these go back on.

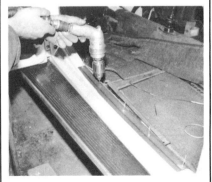

FT11. If you fitted new body rocker/sills you will have to redrill to fit the kickplate. Here as each hole is drilled a pop rivet has been pushed into place to help locate the plate.

FT12. Then a pop rivet gun is used to snap each one tight, holding the kickplate firmly in place.

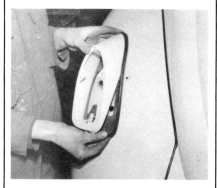

FT13. Uro Auto Spares also supplied new lamp pods and new rubbers for the rear lamps, as shown here.

FT14. Badges take quite a lot of cleaning up but, once again, it is much easier to do them whilst they are off the car.

FT15. After pushing the protruding legs through the holes in the panel, badges are then held in place with clips, rubbers or nuts held on from the back of the panel.

FT16. The 'VW' front badge is held in place on later models with plastic clips pushed into pre-drilled holes. Clean out paint after a respray or they'll be too tight.

FT17. The 'legs' on the badge are a firm push into the clips.

FT18. Rear bumper trim, fitted to some later models, hooks onto one end then clips onto the other and are pulled taut at the clip-end.

FT19. New pedal rubbers are a 'must', the throttle pedal rubber lipping over the sides of the pedal itself.

FT20. Beneath the rear seat, the forked heater channel is covered over with insulator, available from your Volkswagen dealer and held in place here with plastic 'ties'.

FT21. My wife, Shan, cleans the rear seat backrest with STP's 'Son-of-a-Gun' which gives an 'as-new' sheen and is supposed to prevent plastics from age-cracking.

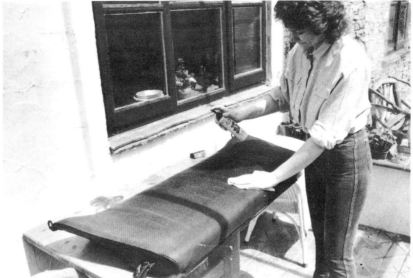

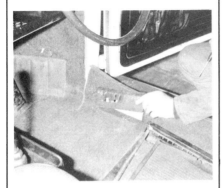

FT22. Heater vents are easily damaged but easily obtained from your Volkswagen dealer.

FT23. Adjust the heater controls for tension and fit new wires if necessary. If the tubes are blocked, see 'Blocked Heater Control Tube Repair' at the end of the 'Interiors' section.

FT24. This can only be done properly with the engine out. New engine bay side trims are supplied overlength and have to be cut to fit the clips and recesses provided, at least on this model.

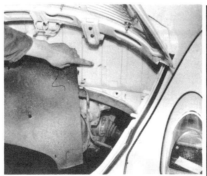

FT25. The rear board pushes onto body-mounted spikes. Turn them straight out . . .

FT26. . . . push the board in place and fold them flat. There are more orthodox clips top and bottom. Use self-tapping screws and large flat washers to prevent the board coming free.

Early Hub Caps

By Rich Kimball of 'Bugs For You', reproduced from 'Dune Buggies + Hot VW's' magazine.

HC1. This is the "nipple' hubcap used on the early caps.

Before we start, how about a short history of the VW hubcap? The first ones had the KDF logo on them. We didn't have one of those to photograph but, did have the logo to show you. Next came the "nipple" cap, similar to the early Porsche cap. It was used up until 1948. In 1949, VW introduced the "big emblem" hubcap, which was used through 1950 (without chrome on the 'Standard' models; painted instead). This cap has been reproduced in both the U.S. and Europe and has been seen on later cars because it is so popular. I have a set on my '52. The "small emblem" baby moon hubcap was used from 1951 through 1965 and there were several small factory variations along the way, plus a myriad of copies have been introduced. In 1966 and 1967, Volkswagen went to a slotted wheel and flat hubcap. These are still available at the dealer, but very expensive. In 1968, the wheels went to four bolt and the cap changed again, for the last time.

The caps of this period (1951 to 1955 — I think) were somewhat unique in that the recessed portion of the VW logo was painted to match the car and the raised portion of the logo had sort of a "brushed" finish. This finish was obtained by beadblasting the logo prior to chroming. This procedure made the logo stick out and helped the paint adhere.

HC2. Here is the KDF logo that appeared on the first caps.

Mirrors

By Rich Kimball of 'Bugs For You'. Reproduced from 'Dune Buggies + Hot VW's' magazine.

Sedan (Saloon) Models

Unlike the outside mirrors, the inside ones were all installed at the factory. Wolfsburg used several different manufacturers and sometimes more than one at the same time, so you can always find some variations. Starting out with the early split windows, there was a non-chrome, stamped steel back oval mirror, referred to by VW restorers as the "Football" mirror. These were used up to 1948 and are very rare. Visors were not used with these mirrors. Visors were introduced along with the deluxe models in late 1949. After the "Football", VW went to the single and double visored, aluminum bracket and mirror back, with a chrome shaft version. (How's that for a description!) These were used in late splits and ovals until the 1958 models. A faithful

reproduction of these units is produced by Vintage VW, in Glendale, California. The visors were plastic and never lasted very long, especially when subjected to the elements.

In 1958, VW switched to a larger chrome bracket and retained the plastic visors for one more year. In 1959, they introduced the padded visors. The mirror itself was mounted off center and became a little larger. These mirrors are becoming scarce among restorers because the brackets were pot metal and as the chrome became corroded and pitted over the years, the pot metal went away faster, leaving small volcanic looking eruptions all over the surface. This makes them impossible to polish and rechrome. That, coupled with the fact that most chromers won't touch pot metal, makes "mint" examples a real prize.

In 1965, the visors separated from the mirror. The visors were now mounted individually, in the corner above the windshield. They attached on the inside to visor clips which are notorious for disintegrating. Reproduction visors and clips, as well as the visors for the earlier edition, are available from Vintage VW and Bugs For You, in Orange, California.

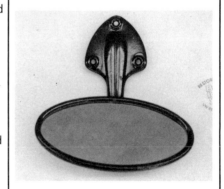

M1. The 1948 Bug was fitted with a rear-view mirror the shape of an (American) football. Hence its nickname the 'football' mirror.

M2. This 'square' mirror was fitted to Bugs from 1949-1951.

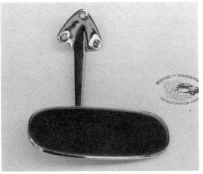

M6. 1965-1967 Bugs wore this little number.

M8. This 1965-1966 Convertible mirror was the same as the one used on later Karmann Ghia convertibles.

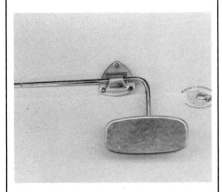

M3. While this, the 'rounded corner mirror', came in from 1952-1957.

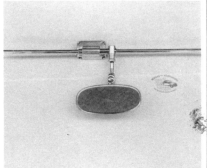

M7. This is the 1957 Convertible mirror and visor arm assembly. Note that the shorter visor is on the passenger side.

M9. Note the black plastic backing to this mirror used only on the 1967 Convertible.

M4. Note the arms for plastic visors on the 1958-59 model.

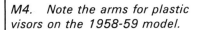

M5. The 1960-1964 mirror accepts padded visors.

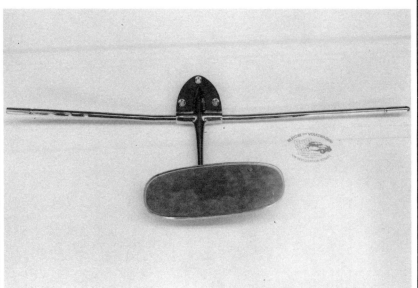

Convertible Inside Mirrors — Expensive and Hard to Find

Interior mirrors on the early cars (pre-1953) are very rare, as are the cars themselves. I heard it said one time that there are probably more Hebmuellers on the road than there are early Karmann convertibles. They only made about 700 of the Hebs, while several times as many Karmanns were produced.

Prior to 1953, the inside mirrors were similar to the 1954 and later version. They were a little "cruder" in design and did not have a passenger visor. The mirrors used from 1954 to early 1959 had a long visor on the left side (same as sedans) and a shorter visor on the right side. The mirror itself had two positions, high and low, because with the top up the mirror had to be low to see out of the small rear window. With the top down, the mirror flipped up so you could see over the collapsed top.

In late 1959, the bracket and mechanics were simplified and visors were now padded and equal in length. The mirror was also made larger. This type was used through 1964.

In 1965, the dome light was moved and incorporated into the mirror bracket. The mirror was again enlarged and stayed in one position (the rear window was also larger and vision was improved). The mirror backing went from polished aluminum to plastic (ugh!) in 1967.

Karmann Ghia convertible mirrors only went through one major change. '56 through '64 mirrors were the same as the hardtop, only the neck was a little longer. In '65, they started using the same bracket with dome light as the bug convertible, with a slightly larger mirror.

If you are restoring a Bug or Ghia and need help restoring your mirror, contact Scott Hendrickson c/o Bugs For You in Orange, CA; Scott is known throughout the industry as the convertible mirror expert of all time, and for a nominal fee he can take your old corroded piece and make it just like new.

5 Interior and Trim

Fitting a Padded Dash

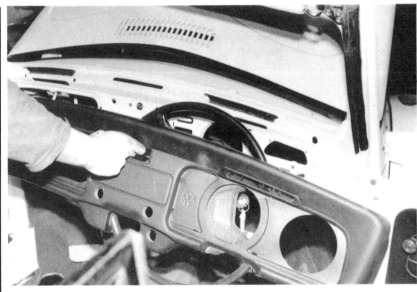

PD1. Fitting a new padded dash to a model where one has already been fitted is simple. They can and do crack with age, although STP's 'Son-of-a-Gun' protector is said to prevent drying out and cracking of existing plastic trim. Here a new Volkswagen dash trim is being offered up.

PD2. If the screen clear vents have been removed, they must be replaced before the dash cover is fitted.

PD3. It's held at the top with cross-head screws which, if no cover has been fitted before, will have to have clearance holes drilled out for them.

PD4. At the bottom, hex-head screws hold the cover in place. The grilles surrounding the speedo are held in place with pushed-over tags bent over, or straightened, from inside the luggage bay.

Fitting Mats and a Sound-Deadening Kit

MSD1. If you have to re-fit all of the mats, it makes sense to fit a complete sound deadening kit. In the UK, the best quality kit is that marketed under the Paddy Hopkirk name (see 'Suppliers' section). All the parts are cut out ready for fitting and suitable adhesive is supplied with the kit. Both the author's Cabrio. and the Haselock's Baja Bug were fitted with these kits.

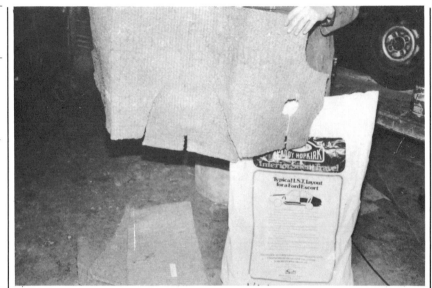

MSD2. After applying the adhesive supplied, the separate section shaped to fit around the pedals was placed on the floor . . .

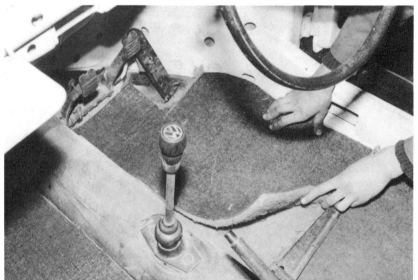

MSD3. . . . followed by that for the under-front-seat area.

MSD4. Here, the complete kit covering the whole 'cockpit' area can be seen, plus there are sections for hidden areas not seen here.

MSD5. Mats were simply placed on top, giving a much more luxurious feel, as well as sound-deadening, and in the rear, more adhesive was applied . . .

MSD6. . . . in the areas where the rear trim was to be glued in place.

MSD7. And again, the outward appearance was completely standard.

MSD8. In the engine bay area there are 'prongs' fitted to the firewall. These are bent outwards, pushed through the sound deadener, and then turned over to hold it in place. With virtually no change to standard spec., the Beetle drum beat was noticeably quieter!

Fitting a Cabriolet Soft-Top

Making and fitting a new Cabriolet soft-top right from scratch can be something of a challenge! But if you're thinking of fitting your own Cabriolet soft-top and the job seems a bit beyond you, take heart! Barry Haselock has come up with a kit to enable the Cabriolet owner to skip all the cutting, sewing and tailoring and just concentrate on fitting the soft-top, headlining or whatever is required.

I should explain here that VW Beetle soft-top makers were nothing if not thorough! The Beetle soft-top consists essentially of three layers: The top layer is what you see from outside the car and looks much like most sports car soft-tops; the headlining, a real life cloth or perforated plastic job, just like those in fixed head cars is visible from the inside while normally invisible is an insulating layer of hair contained within a callico bag and fitted between soft-top cover and headlining.

Earlier cars wore a canvas soft-top with cloth headlining while later Cabrios had a plastic soft-top cover lined with the aforesaid pin-holed plastic.

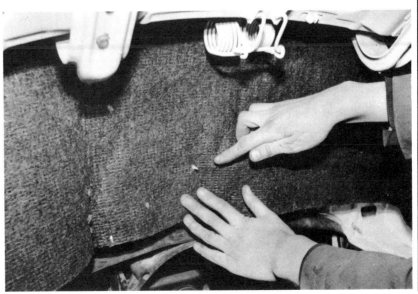

Part 1. Early, cloth soft-tops

ST1. Barry Haselock's trimmer, Roy, holds the 'Cabby's' soft-top frame aloft while he checks that everything operates smoothly and that the frame sits evenly without sticking out more on one side than the other.

ST2. The rearmost soft-top stick's position is free-floating and its correct situation has to be determined by eye, if there isn't another vehicle around to compare it with. All of the soft-top sticks are linked together with two scraps of webbing which Roy has fixed into place here after checking that the rear stick is evenly placed on both sides. The webbing is also tacked to the header and rear rails (made of timber on these earlier cars) and you can see why Roy went to a lot of trouble to ensure that the webbing was fitted sufficiently taut whilst still allowing the soft-top frame to clip down to the windscreen top without too much stress and strain.

ST3. Once satisfied that the sticks were properly fitted, Roy then carefully measured the distance between the header rail and the first stick; the first stick and the second; and so on to the rear of the car. Then he cut out a piece of cloth for the headlining. The length was a little in excess of the distance required from the header rail to the rear of the car while the width covered a distance taken from the crown of the curve in the shape of the soft-top sticks; the curve on each side of the soft-top frame, plus a little for a stitched seam. (If you're lost already, it could be because you're not of the male generation that has done some needlework at school. Tough! You'll have to ask someone who has done some to explain the terms.)

ST4. This is actually the type of cloth cut for the soft-top outer cover, but the principle is exactly the same as for the headlining. A piece of cloth is cut to follow the shape of the door and side window aperture whilst its top edge shadows the edge of the cloth cut for the top section, the one that runs up to the crown of the curve in the soft-top sticks. After tacking all three pieces of cloth into place on the car (that is the top section and the two sides) they are stitched together on a sewing machine. A domestic quality machine should easily cope with headlining material.

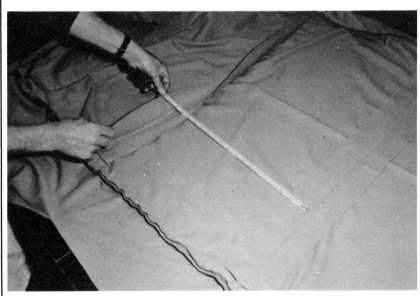

ST5. Strips of headlining cloth about four inches wide and the same length as the width of the top piece are cut out and sewn down to the lower face (when fitted to the car) of the headlining material. Each one (they are known to professionals as listing strips) is fitted so that it falls over a soft-top stick, hence the need for the careful measuring shown in Pic 3. The headlining cloth has to be carefully marked with tailor's chalk — marking out being just as much an important skill to the tailor as it is to the sheet metalworker — and the listing strips sewn precisely into position.

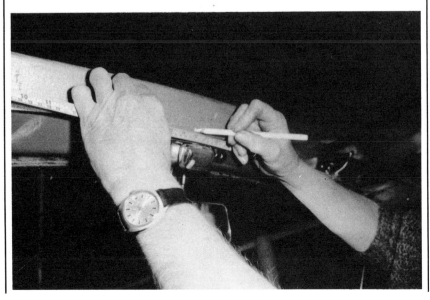

ST6. Now Roy was getting close to fitting the headlining to the car. He measured the header rail, the rail that clamps down to the windscreen top, to find the exact centre and did the same with the front of the headlining.

ST7. Starting with the front soft-top stick, Roy stapled the front listing strip around the stick. It was to be glued in place later on, but Roy preferred a less permanent method of fixing at this early stage in case any adjustment should be required. If you were to fit a Haselock soft-top kit, this would be the stage at which you would have to start work.

ST8. Roy used a few tacks to hold the cloth to the rearmost soft-top stick, the one with a timber strip attached to it.

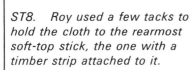

ST9. Working out from the centre, the front of the headlining was tacked to the timber header rail next. Note that Roy has only entered the staples part of the way in case any adjustment should later be required. In fact none was! Later on, once the fit was established, the headlining was wrapped around the bottom of the header rail and glued into place.

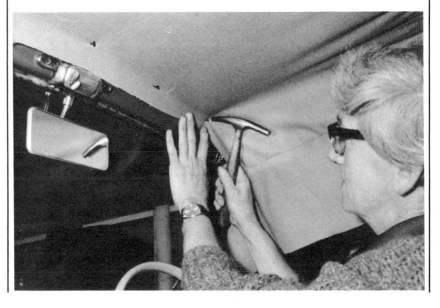

148

ST10. At the rear, a very similar procedure took place, the headlining being tacked to the timber rail. Obviously a totally different procedure is called for here with later Cabriolets because they don't have wooden rails at all.

ST11. The staples can be taken out of the listing strips and they can be glued into place once you're satisfied with the fit. Note how the once-flat sheets of cloth have blended into a smooth, curved, continuous shape.

ST12. From inside the car, Roy marked out the shape of the edge of the soft-top frame, feeling through the headlining and using tailor's chalk.

ST13. Then he started to cut out the material for the soft-top cover.

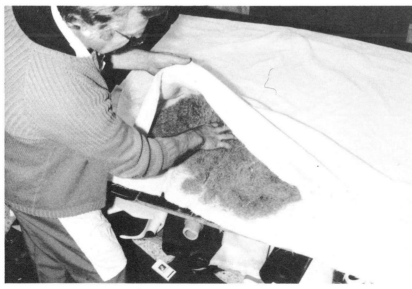

ST14. Roy's partner Rob made a start on the hair lining which gives the Beetle Cabriolet soft-top such a luxurious feel and such excellent insulation properties. He made up calico bags filled with hair. This was once actual horsehair, but since horses have started objecting to having their legs shaved, vegetable, rubberised substitutes are used instead.

ST15. Next, Roy stitched the pieces together with his industrial sewing machine. It is safe to say that domestic models are highly unlikely to be able to cope with this thickness of material, but you can sometimes beg or borrow suitable second-hand industrial machines, or you could leave this part of the work to the experts.

ST16. Then line things up properly to start off with. The hood sticks were correctly positioned with a pair of webbing straps tacked to each of the sticks. The hair bag, made from calico with hair padding inside, has to lie between the headlining and the outer hood skin, so Roy found it necessary to take out the tacks holding the webbing in place, slip the hood bag between headlining and webbing and pin the webbing down on top of the hair filled bag.

ST17. The hair content has to be thinned out at the point where it passes over the sticks so that not only does it not stick up as a bump over each stick, but also so that it is possible to pin through the calico and into each hood stick.

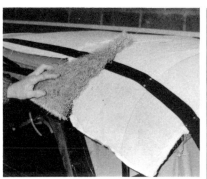

ST18. Roy settled on a type of rubberised matting for the hair bag padding. This has been traditionally used by trimmers for many years and gives greater consistency of thickness than 'loose' hair filling.

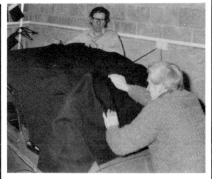

ST19. Having made up the outer hood Roy, assisted here by Barry Haselock, draped the material over the hood framework.

150

ST20. At the front, the centre of the hood was marked with tailor's chalk and aligned with the rear view mirror stem.

ST21. About 3 cm was pulled over the front edge of the header rail and Roy's partner, Rob, is seen here pinning it down.

ST22. After closing the header rail onto the screen top, Roy went to the back of the car and pulled the hood back so that the material was nice and taut. Cloth doesn't have the same amount of stretch as plastic hood material, so Roy had to give the material quite a good pull to obtain the necessary tension.

ST23. Again starting from the centre and working outwards, Roy pinned the hood down, but this time he used tacks which were not driven all the way home. This meant that if he wished to re-adjust the tension or fit — something that he had to do a couple of times before fully satisfied — the tacks could be easily removed and reinserted.

ST24. The fit of the rear quarters is particularly important because it is here that the naturally 'flat' nature of the cloth is most likely to protest at being stretched into a three dimensional curve. Pulling, tensioning and checking was the order of the day when it came to obtaining a good fit here.

ST25. A flap is included on the rear quarter where the hood wraps around the rear pillar. Covered later by a rubber seal, this was pinned down now with tacks, again to help give tension where it matters, but again, in such a way that running adjustments could be made.

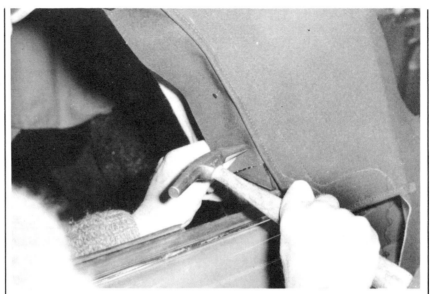

ST26. When the hood is folded down, it stays attached to the frame and the rear screen disappears neatly out of the way. So, it's essential that the hood is pinned onto the rear hood stick. Doing this now helps to keep everything in shape when material is cut out to make room for the rear screen.

ST27. Roy returned to the front of the hood because he wasn't happy with its tension. It was retensioned and . . .

ST28. . . . with the header rail raised by a shade, new tacks were put in to ensure that when the header rail was clamped down, that extra little bit of tension was there. You must try the hood, lifting and lowering it from the screen top at this stage to make sure that: i) there is sufficient tension in the hood when it is closed but, ii) it can be closed without recourse to a block and tackle!

ST29. When Roy was happy with the fit and tension, the front corners were dealt with by carefully pleating the material, one fold at a time, stapling each fold down as it was made and leaving a smooth finish around the top of the header rail.

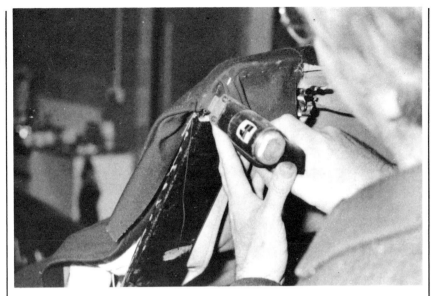

ST30. Then it was belts 'n' braces time as the staple gun was used to fire in a line of staples to supplement the tacks at the rear . . .

ST31. . . . and inside the rear pillar. These are covered later by the window seal rubber..

ST32. If you don't insert the tensioning wire into the sides of the hood, the fit will suffer and the hood will tend to billow upwards when travelling at speed; something from which Karmann hoods should be pretty well immune. The wire runs through a seam on each side of the hood and hooks onto a spring fitted to the frontmost edge of the frame.

ST33. After inserting a needle to prevent his knife from going all the way through, Roy cut a slit in the inner edge of the seam. (This is apparently ready positioned and cut in the House of Haselock kits.)

ST34. The rear end of the wire was passed down the seam and out of the rear end . . .

ST37. After lifting the frame away . . .

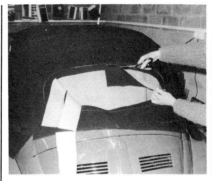

ST38. . . . and cutting a cross in the centre, the surplus material was cut from the hood about 3 cm in from the chalk line.

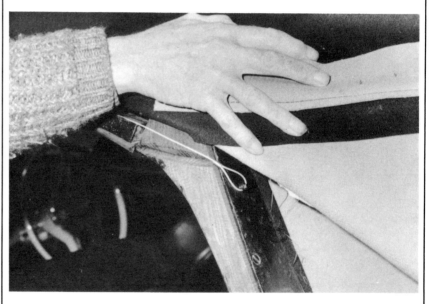

ST35 . . .where the wire was looped and clipped with the clip provided. The wire was pulled against the tension of the spring at the other end and the loop hooked over the screw in the rear frame. You can see a groove in the rear pillar top along which the wire has to lie when it is in place.

ST36. Next Roy, assisted by Barry Haselock carried out the most knee-trembling part of the exercise; cutting out for the rear window. The frame was held in place and marked around its inner edge with tailor's chalk. Needless to say, a great deal of measuring up, checking and double checking went on before the decisive cuts were made!

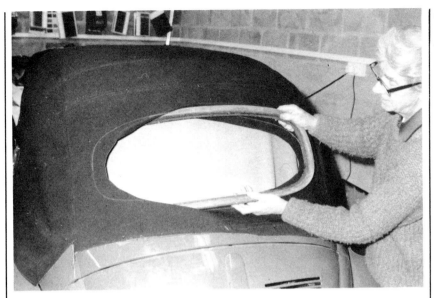

ST39. Then the window frame was slipped into place betwixt hood and headlining.

ST40. Once in position, the hood material was pinned to the frame from the outside. Then the headlining was marked and cut in the same way and then pinned to the frame by folding the spare edge of material over the frame from the inside. Later the rubber sealing strip for the rear screen was fitted in more orthodox manner and the glass let into the rubber.

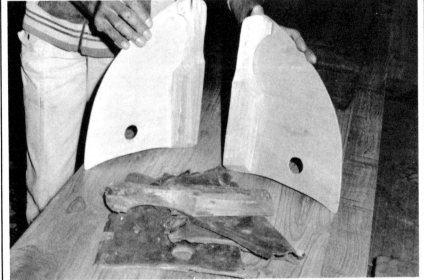

ST41. Inside the car, things didn't look quite so good. Two upholstered 'cheeks' covered the rear quarters, but the car only had one very disintegrated cheek with it. Barry had a replica and a 'handed' replica made from the original and these were re-upholstered by Roy.

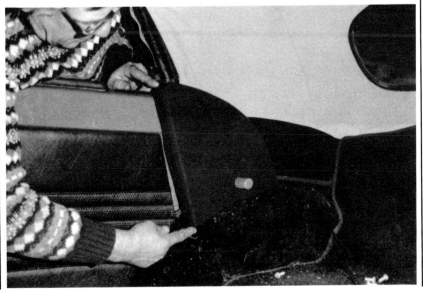

ST42. The new cheeks fitted a treat and finished off that part of the interior well.

ST43. Back to the outside of the hood again. You obviously can't leave the pins and tack heads showing on the outside of the hood. Two ways of covering them up exist, one is to pin chrome mouldings over them and indeed, there were chrome mouldings supplied with this car. Unfortunately, there was no way they were going to fit! I was convinced that they were from a different model and both Roy and Barry felt certain that 'hidem' binding should be used. It was placed across the rear hood stick and along the rear-hood-to-body joint, tidying the joint and covering the tacks all in one go. The ends were finished with nickel plated finishers made for the job.

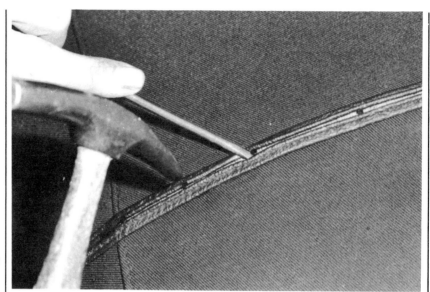

ST44. The finished job looked really impressive! There are, no doubt, one or two minor differences in constructional approach between this and the original — but in any case, there are bound to be differences between the way in which a mass-produced item is made and a one-off, just as there are constructional differences in new and restored bodywork, although the end result can actually be better in some cases!

House of Haselock Cabriolet hood kits should make the fitting of a Cabriolet cloth soft-top possible for the fairly accomplished DIY-er who doesn't like the completely non-original cover-up jobs which are on the market, but can't afford the four-figure sum which he/she may have to pay to have the job carried out professionally.

Incidentally, if you fancy making the complete hood yourself, be sure to use 25 denier cotton to be sure that the stitch holes are filled; otherwise the stitching will be far more likely to leak. A proprietary brand of sealer can be painted on over the stitching to ensure the absence of leaks.

Part 11. Plastic Soft-Top Replacement

The Beetle Cabriolet Plastic Soft-Top is only superficially similar to the one fitted to earlier models made of cloth. Especially different is the way the soft-top fits to the rear of the car. Here's how CTS of Coventry, Haselock's trimmers, set about replacing the later type of soft-top.

PST1. Inside the car the soft-top hinge mechanism is covered by a trim panel held in place with self tapping screws.

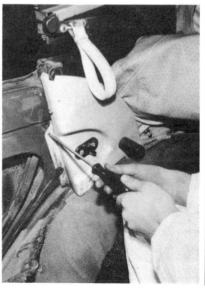

PST2.   Also behind the trim panel are the tensioners for the tensioning cable. These are slackened off with a spanner and pulled out of their locating plate.

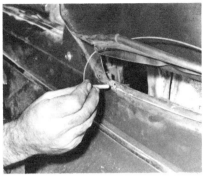

PST4.   The tensioning cable itself passes through the body at the position shown here.

PST6.   Three bolts hold the hinge mechanism to the car itself. Once they are removed . . .

PST3.   This frees the cable that runs around the rear of the soft-top and enables it to be removed from the rear bodywork of the car.

PST5.   The rear of the headlining is clipped to the inside of the car by means of a steel rod which passes through the bottom of the headlining and hooks onto the body clips on the inside of the body.

PST7.   . . . the entire soft-top and frame can be lifted away.

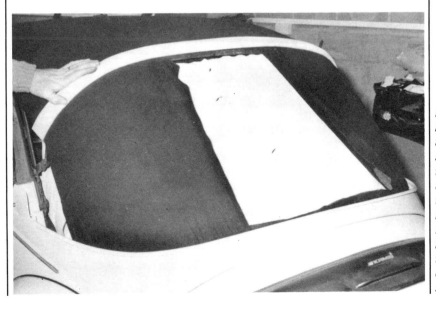

PST8.   The way in which the headlining and hairbag are attached to the hood frame was shown in the previous section and there is very little difference here except for the way the bottom of the headlining hooks onto the bodywork of the car as shown in PST5. Here, CTS trimmer, Roy, has added a strip of foam along the top frame rail to soften the outline once the outer skin of the soft-top is fitted.

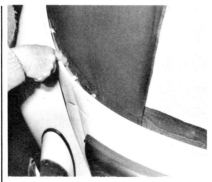

PST9. And here are the clips viewed from outside the car along which the headlining and the hairbag base are fitted.

PST12. At the front, Roy has padded the corners of the header rail with foam then covered it with a piece of plastic bag to allow the envelope in the front corner of the soft-top to slip easily over the header rail.

PST13. After pulling it into place and glueing it down, Roy uses a heat gun to soften the plastic and encourage it to lie smooth and flat.

PST10. Before carrying out any work on the plastic soft-top you must drape it over the car and check that it is the right one. Several different shapes and sizes were made and unless you are starting off with the correct one you will never get it to fit correctly. Best of all, drape the new soft-top over the old one before you even take it off the car. Here Roy is measuring the centre point of the rear of the soft-top and after measuring the centre point of the rear of the vehicle, he can then position it accurately.

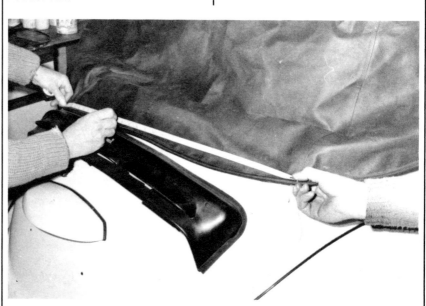

PST11. The wire holding the rear of the soft-top in place is inserted into the flap of material left loose on the bottom of the soft-top by the makers. Then the wire and flap are both pushed upwards into the recess in the rear body. Once the tensioners are put into place and tightened, the rear of the soft-top is gripped immovably.

158

PST14. Then partner, Rob, glues the rest of the front of the soft-top down to the header rail. (Don't forget to insert the foam rubber sealing strip into the rebate on the header rail **before** finally covering the under-part of the header rail.)

PST15. With the whole thing erected and clipped into place Roy and Rob place the wooden and steel window frame in position on the rear of the vehicle and mark out with chalk where they are going to cut out for the rear glass. Note that the wooden part of this frame must be screwed securely to the metal part or its shape will become deformed when tension is put into the hood with the result that you won't be able to get the rear glass to fit properly.

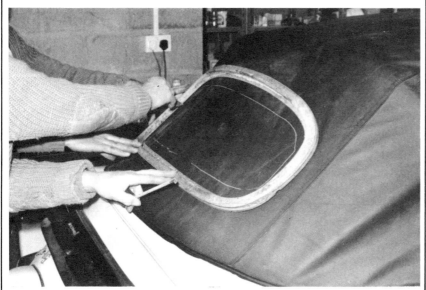

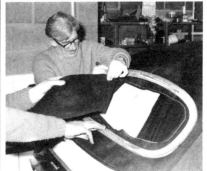

PST16. Roy cuts out surplus material from the outer skin.

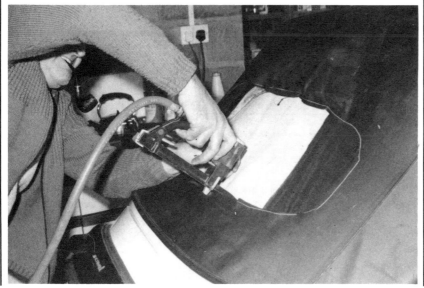

PST17. Then after inserting the wooden frame in between the outer skin and the headlining the outer skin is tacked onto the wooden frame, hidden from view in this shot.

PST18. Here the outer skin is being tacked neatly into place and surplus material trimmed away and now Roy is cutting away the unwanted material from the headlining in the same way. In similar style, this is wrapped around the wooden frame, tacked into place and trimmed back neatly.

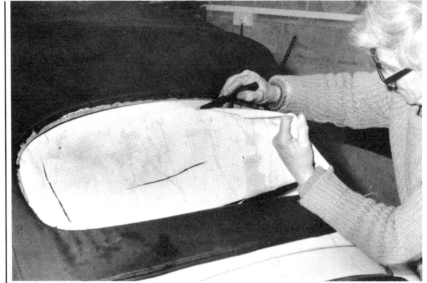

PST19. At some stage, all the sealing rubbers will have to be clipped and glued into place around the frame.

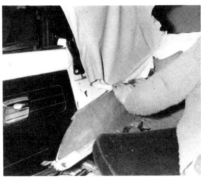

PST21. Inside the car the headlining can be trimmed and fitted around the rear quarters.

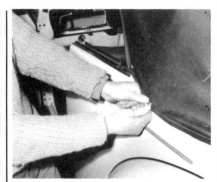

PST23. . . . fitting the clips which hold the rear quarters in place.

PST20. It is important to fit the tensioning wires either side of the hood just as shown in the previous section.

PST22. Rob uses an ordinary hair dryer to soften the plastic of the hood around the rear quarters before pulling it into position . . .

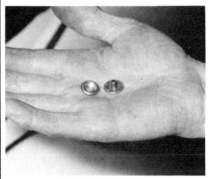

PST24. The clips come in two parts and are best fitted with the correct tool made for compressing them without destroying them.

160

PST25. At the front on the bottom of the header rail Rob fits the chromed locating pins which slot into recesses in the top of the windscreen frame.

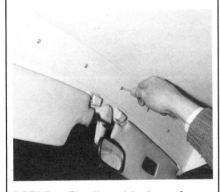

PST25. Finally, with the soft-top erected the trim panel, which fits above the windscreen rail on the inside of the car, can be screwed into place.

*The header rail-to-screen top seal consists of the supplementary seal mentioned in PST14 and a substantial rubber seal which is still available from VW. This is held in place with flat headed upholstery tacks passing through 3 shaped aluminium strips (1 long inner; 2 short, shaped outers) which should be carefully removed when the old soft-top is stripped but can be bought new.

Headliner Replacement

By Rich Kimball of 'Bugs For You'.
Author's note: This is actually a job that is probably beyond a DIY restorer unless he or she has some trimming experience. But the following section outlines what is involved, if you should want to try, or it could be useful to your trimmer if he is not familiar with Volkswagen Beetles.

Volkswagen headliner replacement has been simplified.

The installation simplification results from a new material, a new headliner design and a new installation technique. All told, it adds up to at least an hour's saving in installation time, and a more attractive, trouble-free job.

The modified headliner kit has only two pieces — a one piece headliner that sweeps down over the quarter sections, and a single piece that fits under the rear window.

The design that makes this two-piece liner possible eliminates separate fitting of the top section and the attendant cardboard tabs that are forced into the roof channel along either side. Instead, a single piece curves up from the side windows to give a much cleaner job — one similar to that found in the late model VW's.

It should be emphasized that this new headliner is an almost perfect duplication of that found in Volkswagens built since 1963.

In addition, original Volkswagen fabric, identical to that found in the late model VW's, is used, and is available in a variety of shades.

The material itself did much to make this new VW headliner design possible. It is a vinyl fabric highly resistant to damage and discoloration from moisture and with the stretch and pliability essential to getting the drum-tight fit required on headliners.

After disconnecting the battery and removing the interior light, installation actually starts with the stripping and window removal. (See relevant section of this book for details.)

The rear seat and backrest come out, the backrest being held by two hinge bolts at the bottom. The side panels are removed by snapping them free.

All the old headliner is removed, excepting a section of the lining below the side windows extending about 2 inches back from the door post. Don't worry about the original cardboard tabs inside the roof channel except that over the windshield the tabs should be forced well back into the channel as this is the one place where cardboard tabs will be used for anchoring the new headliner.

All headliner bows are the same length in the Volkswagen, so while they should be salvaged, don't worry about their order of replacement.

The new headliner, with cardboard inserts at the front and the rear window cutout at the back, should have the bows inserted in the pockets before installation begins.

Then, starting with the front, and first centering the headliner as closely as possible, poke the cardboard grips into the channel over the windshield. The bows are slid along the roof channel and the headliner is pulled back against the top edge of the rear window frame.

Stretch the lining back until the rear bow almost touches the channel over the rear window. Use clothespins or spring clamps to hold the headliner firmly in this position while fitting is done inside.

First cut the bow pockets slightly to smooth the curve of the liner, pulling the liner down and out through the side windows as you proceed. More clips and clothespins should be used while this work progresses.

It is generally better to work from the front of the car towards the rear, snipping at the bow pockets and working out wrinkles as you progress.

The most difficult fit is at the rear corner, and here the 3-M adhesive # 1099 should be employed. Coat the top of the fender well under the rear seat liberally and use this to hold the

quarter panel sections as you work the headliner down and back.

As you approach a perfect fit, apply 3-M adhesive around the window frames and remove the clips and clothespins.

It will be quickly discovered that this original VW fabric handles beautifully. It stretches well without losing its strength or resiliency. Don't, however, make the mistake of trying a steamer. It won't work on this material.

At the top of the door posts the headliner is folded so that a fold seam runs diagonally from the corner of the window to the upper corner of the door opening in such a way that it will be secured by the hand strap.

Returning to the headlining over the windshield and doors, you'll need to carefully cut back into the fold running out from the cardboard at each end of the windshield. This will be necessary to remove a wrinkle and hard spot that will appear when the headliner is drawn tight against the clips over each of the doors.

Only after this has been done should the material be wedged into the headliner clips over the doors. Double the material over the doors first to prevent cutting it with your putty knife blade as you force the liner into the clip recess.

The lower section below the rear window is cemented in place, as are the short sections under each of the side windows. Make a fold seam to give an attractive and trouble-free appearance where these panels overlap the headliner.

Before installing the windows, check the job thoroughly, for the material can still be worked free of the adhesive and wrinkles and soft spots removed. Once the windows are in place, it's probably too late to correct any errors.

An experienced trimmer, working alone, will do this job in 2 hours and will turn out a job that is equal in quality to that of the original equipment.

Fronts Seats: Renewing the Covers

RTC1. After removing the seat from the car, take off the domed nut holding the backrest to the base on each side then lever the backrest support arms outwards and free.

RTC2. It's best to remove the outer trim piece by turning the turnbuckle clip and freeing the trim.

RTC3. The trim piece is now just lifted away.

RTC4. Beneath the seat base, a wire passes through the seam on the edge of the cover and is tied-off at each end. Free it . . .

RTC5. . . . then lift up the tabs all the way around, using a screwdriver.

RTC6.   Lift the wired seam off the tabs . . .

RTC7.   . . . press down the springing and lift off the seat cover.

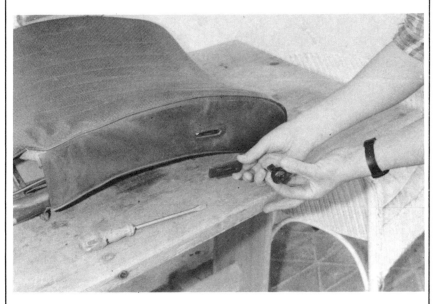

RTC8.   To strip the backrest cover, lever off the knob and trim as shown . . .

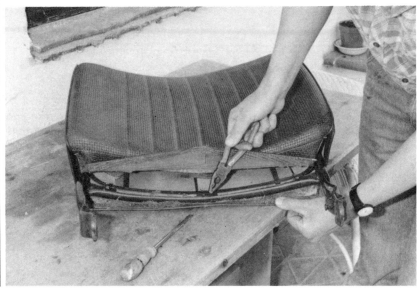

TRC9.   . . . disconnect the wired seams at the base of the backrest from the tags, as before . . .

RTC10. . . . but don't forget the clip holding the trim to the padding beneath . . .

RTC11. . . . after which the backrest trim can be slipped off. ►

Fitting new covers is the reverse of the above procedure. If the wadding has compressed, you may wish to add a thin layer of wadding or foam, in which case drape an opened-up plastic bag over the base or backrest before pulling on the new cover; this helps the cover to slide easily into place.

Blocked Heater Control Tube Repair

BHP1. Right at the end of the ► *job, we encountered a major problem! The heater control cable conduit was blocked! We tried hammering a very thin drift and even drilling with a drill welded to a piece of ⅛ in. rod (these pipes sometimes become solid with rust) but to no avail. We had to establish the exact position of the blockage, cut the tunnel open with a cutting disc on the mini-grinder then cut into the conduit. There was a long strip of cloth jammed inside, shown here being drawn out. How? Why? Who knows? Some of the cloth wouldn't come out and the end pice of conduit was declared unuseable. Here's how the problem was overcome.*

The conduit had been cut with a hacksaw blade at the position shown in the picture. A drill the same size as the conduit was passed along the conduit from the *rear* end, where the heater control wire should emerge from the chassis horn. This gave a rear entry into the chassis. A new piece of copper brake pipe of the correct size was passed into the chassis from the rear and joined to the existing conduit at the front via a piece of plastic pipe and two clips, the two pieces of metal pipe being pushed together until they touched. The heater cable could then be connected up in the normal way and the piece of metal flapped open as shown was MIG welded back into place in the chassis tunnel.

6 Mechanical Components

Beetle and Transporter Engines

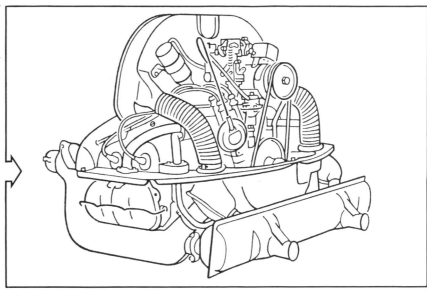

ER1. Air-cooled Volkswagen engines look like virtually no other, mainly because the business end is only the lower third of the engine assembly, electrics, carburation and cooling taking most of the space above the cover plate. (Drawing reproduced by kind permission of Volkswagen.)

All Type 1 (Beetle) and Type 2 (Transporter) air-cooled engines have one tremendous virtue — or a tremendous curse, depending upon what you want to do. They're all very hard to work on whilst fitted into the vehicle, but so easy to remove that engine removal is less of a major operation than for just about any other make of vehicle. On top of that, the engine, once out, is so light to lift (relative to most cast-iron engines — the Beetle engine weighs around 200 lbs) that two people can easily swing it up and onto a bench, or it can be worked on whilst still on the floor. This isn't so good for your back, but its

better than risking pulling the engine off the bench whilst wrestling with some of those tight bolts. If you do work on the floor, place the engine on a large opened-out sheet of cardboard made from a washing machine box or something similar. Remember that dirt is Public Enemy No. 1 of the insides of any engine!

Engine Removal

The engine is held to the gearbox, which is situated ahead of it, by only two studs and two bolts and

the best way for the home mechanic to remove the engine is to pull the engine off the gearbox, supporting it with a trolley jack whilst the rear of the car is held up high on a pair of drive-on car ramps. Don't risk letting the engine fall to the ground because a drop of only a few inches can crack the alloy crankcase quite easily and cause an awful lot of other damage. For that reason, although the engine can be removed by one person, it is best to work with an assistant. Be sure that you have sufficient firm, level ground for the engine to be pulled back on the trolley jack and so that the ramps remain stable.

165

Chock the front wheels securely. A non-cranked 17 mm spanner will be necessary to undo the mounting nuts and studs and a second open-ended 17 mm spanner will also be needed. Drive the car onto the ramps and check the front wheels before starting work.

Beetle Engine Removal

ER2. It may be best to drain the engine oil now, but see 'Engine Strip' for details. Disconnect the battery and, on early models, turn off the fuel tap. Slacken the carburettor air cleaner clamp and take off the air cleaner complete with hoses. Remove the cheese-head screws holding the sealing plates around the pre-heater pipes for the intake manifold. (See photo.) Note that this car is fitted with a non-standard carb. but this makes no difference to the procedure shown here.

ER3. Then lift out each plate; one each side. (Not applicable to very early 1200 models.) Undo, where applicable, the small plate over the crankshaft pulley.

ER4. Take off the pipework and tin-ware from the large cover plate . . .

ER5. . . . and take out the cover plate.

166

ER6. *Disconnect the three generator leads (make a note of where they came from) or take out the wiring plug if there's an alternator fitted. Some alternators also have a separate voltage sensor wire which must be removed and labelled. Don't forget to disconnect the wires from the starter.*

ER7. *Remove the throttle cable from the carburettor. Undo the locking screw which clamps the end of the cable to the link pin on the operating lever. Pull the cable out but do not lose the kink. The cable itself can be pulled through the back of the fan housing as the engine is being withdrawn, but it is best to avoid the risk of its being trapped by pulling it out now. Disconnect the manual choke or undo the connections from the auto-choke and from the solenoid cut-off valve (one each side of the carburettor). Tuck all 'loose' wires and cables well out of the way.*

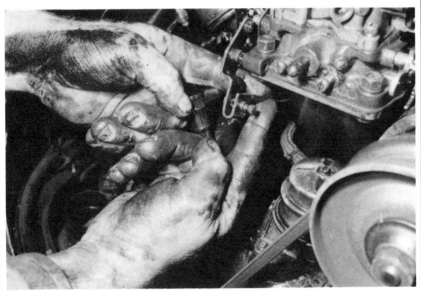

A few Beetles were fitted with fuel injection. See 'Transporter Engine Removal' for information.

ER8. *If you forgot to place the vehicle up on ramps, or if you don't possess any, you can now jack up the rear of the car and support it on axle stands, getting the rear end as high as you can. Make sure that the axle stands are firmly placed, that the front wheels are chocked and remember NEVER to work beneath a car supported only by a jack. Unclip and pull off the heater pipes which fit onto the heat exchangers on either side of the engine. (Photo). Locate the flexible petrol hose at the engine end, pull it off the pipe and clamp or plug it.*

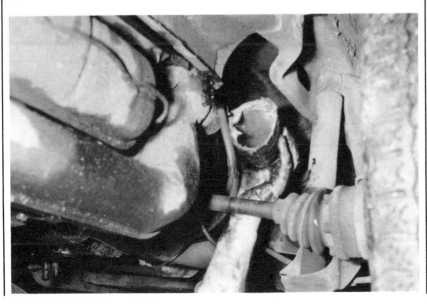

ER9. Disconnect the control wires that run to the heater flaps, one on each side. They are held to the flap control arms by clamps similar to those used on the carburettor. But they're highly likely to be rusted and seized so get hold of a self-grip wrench and releasing fluid before diving beneath. (If you can't tell which the heater controls are, get someone to operate them while you lie there looking.) Heater cable tubes have different appearances on very early models.

It isn't easy to photograph where the two lower mounting nuts are situated (but see

'Transporter Engine Removal' ER20). Imagine a centre line drawn along the bottom of the engine, front to back and establish where this would cross the engine-transmission unit joint. Go about four inches either side of this 'line' then feel about two inches up from the engine-transmission unit joining flange. Use the 17 mm ring spanner to remove the two nuts and washers (if fitted).

Whilst you're still down there, reach up to the left-hand top mounting bolt. (It's a nut on earlier models.) You may wish to use a socket and extension plus a universal joint.

ER10. You really ought to support the engine now with a trolley jack from beneath, the jack head over the oil drain plate. (If you haven't got one, get one now, quick!) Reach around the fan housing, locate the fourth and only remaining bolt and nut (it is also the starter motor top mounting bolt) and undo it. The bolt head (D-shaped) is of a special type which locates onto the transmission — as long as you don't push it back whilst undoing the nut.

ER11. As you see, you can do this single-handed but remember that Phil, shown here working on the author's Cabrio. pre-rebuild, is a trained Volkswagen mechanic. DIY-it in twos! With the jack taking the strain, the engine is tugged back three or four inches backwards and off the studs. It's vital that the engine isn't tilted to avoid damaging the clutch or gearbox first motion shaft, which is very easy to distort.

ER12. The jack is lowered slowly and the engine kept forwards and away from the gearbox shaft. Note that the fan housing and exhaust make excellent points for gripping and steadying. If you're lucky enough to have sufficient clearance, wheel the engine out; if not, as is likely, have someone help you lift the engine and pull the jack out, place 'skids' beneath the engine (shiny magazines are perfect) and slide it out, tilting it if necessary to clear the fan housing.

ER13. Quick clues: Look for oil in the bellhousing to indicate a leaking engine (more likely) or gearbox (less likely) oil seal: you may be able to tell which type of oil it is in there because engine oil is generally clean and gearbox oil is generally dirty; and . . .

ER14. . . . spin the clutch release bearing and listen for signs of roughness indicating unacceptable wear. Be sure that the bearing face is still flat and not grooved. Make notes if replacements are needed.

Transporter Engine Removal

Removal of the Transporter engine is very similar to that of the Beetle with the following additional points to bear in mind.

ER15.   Undo the bolts holding the cover plate to the rear panel. (It's fixed on later models.)

ER16.   Then undo the screws holding it from inside the engine bay.

ER17.   Lift the whole cover plate out.

ER18.   As on the Beetle, the air cleaner must be removed. If it's of the oil-bath type, be careful not to tilt it because spilt oil makes such a mess . . .

ER19.   A support beam gives the later engines extra support. Although there seem to be various styles in the architecture, the principle is the same: Unbolt the beam from the chassis frame — 2 bolts per side — and lower it with the engine, removing it when the unit is on the ground.

ER20.   The lower engine-to-transmission bolts are very similar to those on the Beetle . . .

ER21. ... as are the two upper bolts, reached in the same way, except that sometimes there are bolts screwed into threaded holes in the casing. Just keep and replace whatever comes out!

ER22. The engine pulls off, just as before (see Beetle engine removal) ...

ER23. ... and is then lowered to the ground. Here at Haselock's, there is a hoist to raise the body over the engine. When working at home, remember the extra weight of the Transporter body and ensure that it's raised sufficiently high and safely to allow the engine out.

Pointers

It may be necessary to remove the Transporter's bumper support brackets. Their fixing nuts are likely to be rusted solid and it may require heat, a drill or a hacksaw to remove them.

The Transporter gearbox should be supported with a rope or chain.

North American models with afterburn equipment:

The air pump must be removed from the top of the fan housing. The hose from the activated charcoal filter for the fuel tank should be disconnected.

Automatic models:

a) The ATF filler pipe must be removed. Slacken the 6 mm nuts which secure it to the casing, turn the pipe anti-clockwise and pull it out.

b) Disconnect the vacuum hose from the intake manifold balance pipe.

c) The bolts holding the torque converter to the driveplate must be removed. There is a hole in the lower left-hand side of the converter bellhousing. You can get at these bolts one at a time if you rotate the engine.

d) Remove the transmission fluid dipstick and the dipstick tube grommet on some models.

e) On some models, disconnect the throttle rod at the gearbox lever.

f) Make sure that the torque converter remains on the transmission where there is a possibility that it can be detached.

Later Transporter engines have crept up to the 300 lbs in weight mark. Handling them is more difficult and it can help to have three people involved.

Fuel Injection engines: Disconnect the control unit wiring plug, the right-hand wiring plug at the front bulkhead double relay (Transporter), the resistor multi-plugs and the deceleration valve hose. On vehicles for California, disconnect the wire for the oxygen sensor.

ER24. Removal of as much tin ware as possible is recommended on 1972-'79 Transporters because it gives more room in which to work and manoeuvre the engine and it increases visibility.

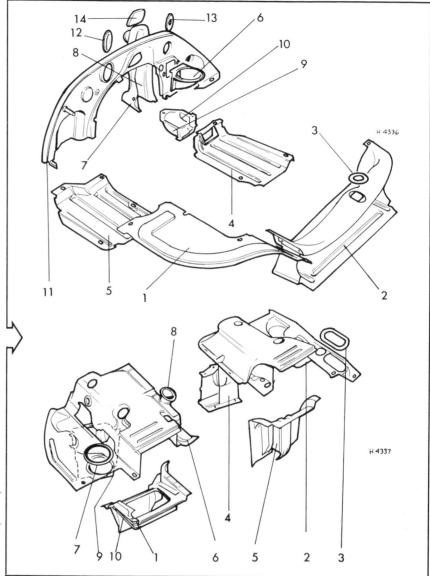

Engine Strip

Even though there were around 24 different stages of Beetle engine development over the years, all the engines were put together in the same basic way. So, although this sequence, showing the dismantling of a 1600 engine is actually relevant to all the engines it couldn't possibly show every variation and complication that took place. For fine details, however, you would need to look in which ever one of the eight Haynes manuals on the Volkswagen Beetle and Transporter ranges is relevant to your vehicle.

One of the best and simplest pieces of advice I ever saw on stripping an engine was in Robert Persig's exhilarating book with a crazy title, 'Zen and the Art of Motorcycle Maintenance'. He suggests having a note pad by your side and noting down every point that catches your attention as the components come apart, whether it seems important at the time or not. At the end of it all, your grubby paper will be a goldmine of information that's special to your engine and full of the sort of detail that is relevant to you and that no manual or restoration guide could possibly include. It will have stuff in it that seems so obvious at the time the unit comes apart, but that seems almost designed to be forgotten in the welter of small-scale information that passes through your head during such jobs.

ES1. As the previous section showed, the engine can be removed complete with most of its ancillaries. Removal of these parts takes up a large part of the total dismantling time.

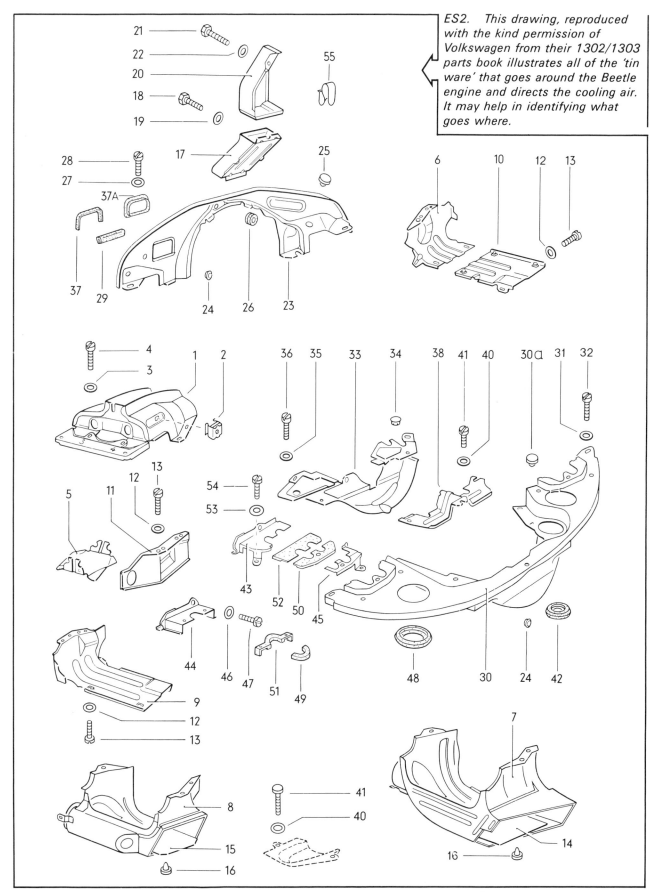

ES2. This drawing, reproduced with the kind permission of Volkswagen from their 1302/1303 parts book illustrates all of the 'tin ware' that goes around the Beetle engine and directs the cooling air. It may help in identifying what goes where.

ES3. If your engine suddenly starts running hot, as mine was doing when I bought it, you could do worse than check the air intake at the front (rear?) of the fan housing. This one had a pancake air filter element pulled into it!

ES5. At House of Haselock where this engine was stripped, the unit was placed onto engineer Barry Haselock's own design of engine stand.

ES7. When the crankcase is dry, he takes the plate and filter away to be washed in petrol.

ES4. One sign of wear in a Volkswagen air-cooled engine is crankshaft end-float. You can carry out a crude check by levering the crankshaft pulley back and forth.

ES6. Haselock's engine rebuild expert is a highly experienced gentleman by the name of Albert. Here, Albert slackens the filter plate screws to drain out the rest of the engine oil – there's no drain plug on this model.

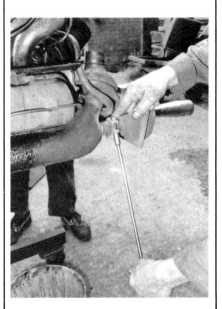

ES8. Albert slackens the lower silencer box clamp from the heat exchanger . . .

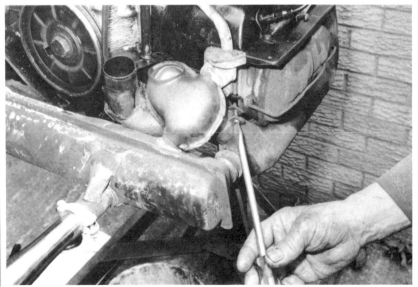

ES9. . . . and from the upper heat exchanger clamp.

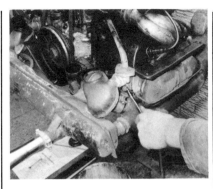

ES10. Then the nut and washer are taken from the upper exhaust mounting . . .

ES12. . . . and the whole exhaust system is lifted away as an undismantled assembly. Of course, if any of it is faulty, you'll have to slot in the required bits to repair it.

ES14. And more tin ware, too. This is ES2 No. 9 held to the crankcase . . .

ES11. . . . the inlet tract pre-heat pipe is undone . . .

ES13. The heat riser pipes, connected to the air cleaner, are disconnected and removed.

ES15. . . . and to the heat exchanger by cheese-head screws.

ES16. This is piece No. 11 disconnected from beneath the engine. Obviously these parts often vary slightly in shape, so don't panic if your engine's tin ware doesn't exactly match this. Although if there are pieces actually missing, cooling will suffer and so will engine life-expectancy.

ES17.   On the other side of the fan housing, the nuts holding piece No. 20 were removed.

ES20.   . . . the generator pulley is locked with a screwdriver and the nut undone, enabling the generator belt to be taken off, Barry Haselock jnr. here lending a hand.

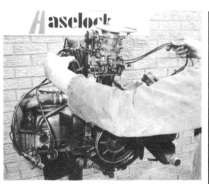

ES23.   If the distributor and plug leads weren't taken off before removing the engine, take them off now.

ES18.   Then No. 17 was slotted off without totally unscrewing the retaining bolt.

ES21.   The generator is disconnected from the generator pedestal.

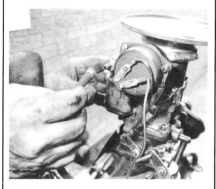

ES24.   Fully disconnect the carburettor from any petrol pipes, remove them and take off the carburettor. (Note that, as quite often happens, this engine has been fitted with a non-standard carb.)

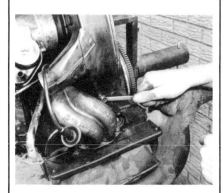

ES19.   The main fan housing was tackled next. Bolts on the side . . .

ES22.   And this allows the fan housing, generator and coil still attached, to be lifted away as a piece.

ES25.   In order to remove the inlet tracts and manifolds, you have to undo the inner clips then the outer clips . . .

ES26. . . . then slide the rubber connectors inboard along the inlet tract.

ES27. The manifold can then be unbolted from the heads and lifted off.

ES28. You're getting closer to taking off another piece of tinware but Barry hasn't taken it off yet because he'll later remove it with piece No. 6 still attached – take out the screws holding it in place.

ES29. Take off the nuts holding the heat exchangers in place.

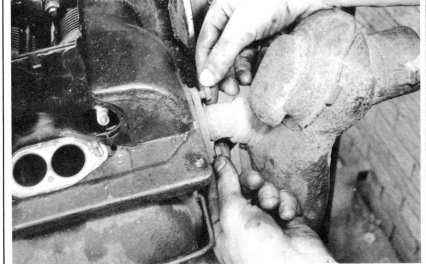

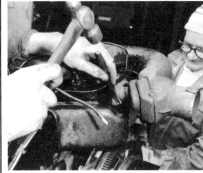

ES30. Sometimes these nuts are absolutely solid with rust. Rather than risk shearing the studs, Barry chooses to place a sharp chisel on the thinnest part of the nut and to cut it off, two or three firm blows being all it takes.

ES31. The heat exchanger and tinware described in ES28. are taken off together.

ES32. Albert unbolts the fuel pump body and lifts it off . . .

ES33. . . . followed by the bakelite flange and pump operating rod. Albert says that the bakelite flange is often tight in the block but to try to lever it out would ruin it. Leave it in place until the crankcase is split then carefully tap it free from the inside. In fact he recommends that on post-'67 engines, the flange is not removed at all because the thinner material used from that date makes it likely to break or distort — recognise later flanges by the 5 mm studs used to hold the fuel pump in place, whereas older engines used 6 mm studs.

ES34. Unbolt the generator pedestal (it doubles as the oil filler neck and it's fixed on early models) and lift it away, not forgetting to unbolt the oil breather pipe separately.

ES35. One more bolt and off comes the distributor . . .

ES36. . . . followed by the oil cooler.

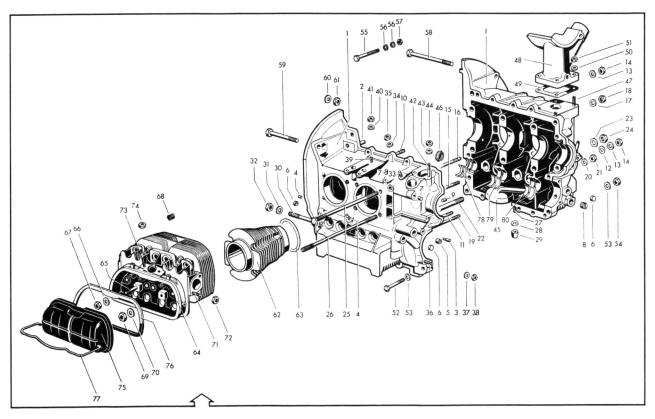

ES37. At long last, you've got to where you'd often START an engine strip with a conventional engine! These are the 'static' engine parts.

46	Oil filler cap
47	Stud
48	Dynamo mounting bracket
49	Sealing gasket
50	Corrugated washer
51	Nut
52	Mounting bolt
53	Corrugated washer
54	Nut
55	Mounting bolt
56	Corrugated washer
57	Nut
58	Mounting bolt
59	Mounting bolt
60	Corrugated washer

61	Nut
62	Cylinder
63	Cylinder gasket
64	Cylinder head
65	Stud
66	Corrugated washer
67	Nut
68	Threaded insert for spark plug
69	Nut
70	Plain washer
71	Stud
72	Nut
73	Stud
74	Nut
75	Rocker cover

76	Rocker cover gasket
77	Securing clip
78	Camshaft bearing shell
79	Camshaft bearing shell
80	Camshaft bearing shell

ES38. Take off the rocker cover. The tappet adjusters often seize up so slacken them to allow cleaning fluid into the threads when the engine is cleaned.

1	Crankcase
2	Dowel
3	End plug
4	End plug
5	End plug
6	End plug
7	End plug
8	Screwed plug
9	Dowel for main bearing
10	Stud
11	Stud
12	Sealing washer
13	Spring washer
14	Nut
15	Stud
16	Stud
17	Washer (corrugated)
18	Nut
19	Stud
20	Washer (corrugated)
21	Nut
22	Stud

23	Plain washer
24	Nut
25	Stud
26	Stud
27	Stud
28	Sealing washer
29	Domed nut
30	Stud
31	Corrugated washer
32	Nut
33	Stud
34	Corrugated washer
35	Nut
36	Stud
37	Washer
38	Nut
39	Stud
40	Corrugated washer
41	Nut
42	Stud
43	Corrugated washer
44	Nut
45	Oil filler neck

ES39. Remove the rocker gear and pull out the push rods. Number them so that they can be replaced in the correct relative positions if they are re-used and mark them for top and bottom. A good way of storing them is to push them through holes in a piece of card with their positions marked on the card. (This is important to avoid rapid initial wear as 'strange' components bed themselves in.)

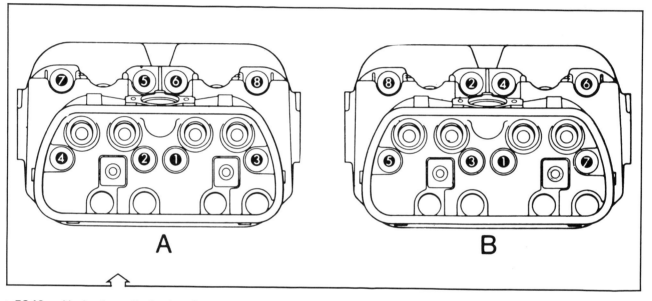

ES40. Undo the cylinder head stud nuts in the REVERSE order to the tightening sequence shown here. With a lightweight aluminium cylinder head of this type, this is especially important. Release each nut a little at a time until each one is slack and then take them right off.

(a) up to 7 lb ft (1 mkg)

(b) up to 23 lb ft (3.2 mkg)

ES41. Remember that these studs hold the barrels as well as the heads and that the pushrod tubes are clamped between heads and crankcase.

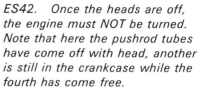

ES42. Once the heads are off, the engine must NOT be turned. Note that here the pushrod tubes have come off with head, another is still in the crankcase while the fourth has come free.

ES43. This illustrates one of the most common problems especially with later units: the cylinder head is cracked between the valve opening and the spark plug. You could have this welded by a specialist, but the usual remedy is to replace the head.

ES44. Unclip the deflector plate and the pushrod tubes and measure the pushrod tubes from their shoulders where they butt up against the crankcase and head — if any of them measure less than 181 mm (7.1 inches) they should be replaced or they will leak oil when refitted.

ES45. Now the barrels can be removed — it helps to free them if they are lightly tapped with a soft faced hammer, but take great care not to damage the cooling fins.

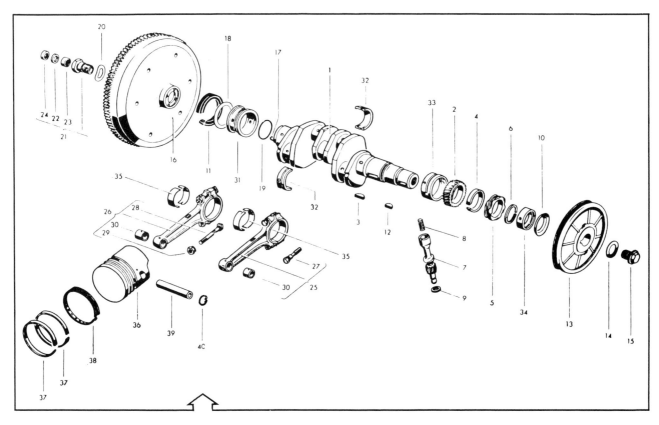

ES46. This drawing shows most of the main 'moving' components within the engine.

1	Crankshaft	12	Key for pulley	22	Sealing washer	33
2	Crankshaft gear	13	Crankshaft pulley	23	Needle roller	34
3	Woodruff key	14	Washer		bearing	35
4	Spacer	15	Bolt	24	Collar	
5	Distributor drive	16	Flywheel	25	Con rod	36
6	Securing ring	17	Dowel	26	Con rod	37
7	Distributor drive	18	Spacer	27	Con rod screw	38
	shaft	19	Locking washer	28	Con rod screw	39
8	Spring	20	Locking washer	29	Nut	40
9	Washer	21	Hollow bolt with	30	Small end bush	
10	Oil baffle washer		needle roller	31	Main bearing	
11	Oil seal		bearing	32	Bearing shell	

33 Main bearing
34 Bearing shell
35 Big end bearing
   shell
36 Piston
37 Piston ring
38 Scraper ring
39 Gudgeon pin
40 Circlip

ES47. Use long-nosed or circlip pliers to remove the gudgeon pin circlip.

ES48. Push out the gudgeon pin and take the piston from the connecting rod.

ES49. Take out the bolt holding the crankshaft pulley wheel in place. If there are holes in the pulley, push a large screwdriver through one of them and lock it against the crankcase: if there are not, it may be necessary to make up a simple clamp to bolt to the flywheel end of the engine, locking the starter ring solid. If the pulley sticks to the crank, apply plenty of releasing fluid and apply gentle heat only towards the centre of the pulley.

Haselock's DIY tip: The VW spark plug spanner is just the right length to 'jam' between flywheel teeth and the exhaust where it leaves the cylinder head. Put it in there and remove the crankshaft pulley nut and the flywheel mounting nut before stripping the engine.

ES50. Take off the bolt and washer and remove the pulley, but be careful not to buckle the pulley as it is knocked or levered off.

ES51. After the pulley, more tinware can be removed. The flywheel can also be taken off at this stage – it takes quite a lot of turning force – but Haselock's leave it until later because the engine stand gets in the way.

But note: A far, far easier way to get it undone is to follow the Haselock tips at ES49.

ES52. The oil pump is housed behind this plate on the end of the camshaft.

ES53. The gears themselves can easily be taken out at this stage – tag them so that you know which way round to replace.

ES54. The mounting studs are removed by the double-nut trick: Run two nuts onto the stud, lock them tightly together then attempt to unscrew the bottom nut. But since it's locked onto the top nut, the stud should unscrew instead. The pump body will still be gripped by the two halves of the crankcase so wait until they have been split before removing.

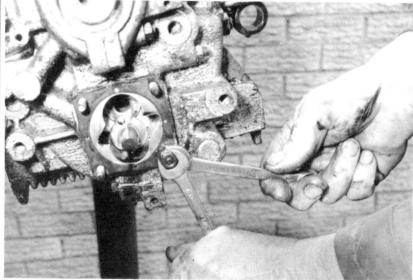

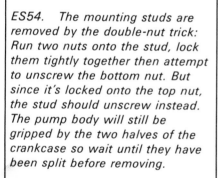

ES55. Barry undoes the stud nuts and the nuts and bolts holding the two halves of the crankcase together.

ES56. Don't forget that some involve nuts and bolts and you will need two spanners to stop the bolt from turning.

ES57. Before attempting to do the splits, remove all the washers because otherwise they could bind on the studs or they could fall off and get lost.

ES58.   Tap each of the four corners with a hammer and wooden block . . .

ES59.   . . . to free the two halves of the crankcase all round.

ES60.   As you lift the upper half, four of the cam followers will drop harmlessly into the crankcase. Try to note where they came from and label them for correct replacement. DON'T try splitting the crankcase with the split vertical because the crank and camshafts will fall about causing damage. If you haven't got an engine stand, devise some other means of supporting the unit at this stage.

ES61.   The camshaft has been lifted out here – you can see the split bearings still in place and then the remaining cam followers can be removed.

ES62.   The con-rod and big-end caps can be undone and the con-rods removed. It is easier to remove the con-rods in this way, but if the crankcase is not to be split, take out the con-rods like so . . .

ES63. Remove the big-end nuts, then push the big-end apart with a long screwdriver.

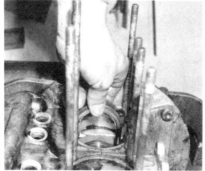

ES64. Pull off the big-end and remove the con-rod through the other side of the crankcase.

ES65. Now the crank complete with flywheel and camshaft drive gear can be lifted out. If you can lock the crank and remove the flywheel before splitting the crankcase, the retaining bolt will actually be easier to remove. It is held on with an enormous figure of 217 lbf/ft so it will require a large extension tube to shift it. Be certain to mark the position of the flywheel on the crank so that it can be re-fitted in exactly the same place.

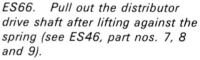

ES66. Pull out the distributor drive shaft after lifting against the spring (see ES46, part nos. 7, 8 and 9).

ES67. Don't lose the pair of shims on the end of the shaft.

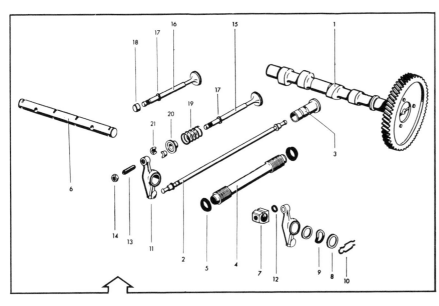

ES68. *This is the arrangement of the camshaft and valve gear.*

1	Camshaft and gear assembly	11	Rocker arm
2	Pushrod	12	Sealing ring
3	Tappet	13	Tappet adjusting screw
4	Pushrod tube	14	Locknut
5	Pushrod tube seal	15	Inlet valve
6	Rocker shaft	16	Exhaust valve
7	Shaft support bracket	17	Oil seal
8	Thrust washer	18	Valve cap
9	Corrugated washer	19	Valve spring
10	Securing clip	20	Valve spring seat
		21	Valve cotter halves

Stripdown pointers

The oil pressure relief valve, if faulty, can cause all sorts of problems with this type of engine. Models up to 1969 (and all 1200s) had one valve situated in the underside (outside) of the crankcase to the left of the oil pump at the rear. Once the slotted retaining screw has been removed with a large screwdriver, the piston beneath and spring should drop out. The piston is a free sliding fit, but if it is seized, it may be necessary to drill and tap a hole in the piston and pull it out. A scored piston should always be replaced and the spring under a load of 7.75 kg (17 lbs) should be 23.6 mm (0.9 ins.). Some pistons have a groove in them and these should not be used in the 1200 engines except in hot climates.

On later engines, there are two valves, one towards the front the other towards the rear of the crankcase. Always replace the washer or washers beneath the retaining screw head because they are otherwise prone to leakage.

If you only wish to remove the cylinder heads and not the barrels, take care not to pull the barrels off with the heads.

Your best advice now it to thoroughly clean every part and then decide which parts will require replacement or reconditioning. Price the parts through your usual supplier but not until checking everything over against Volkswagen's own tolerances or by asking a specialist such as Haselock's or a Volkswagen dealer (V.A.G. or Audi-Volkswagen dealer in Britain) to carry out these checks for you. This will obviously cost a little but you will have the benefit of experienced advice, and the work will be done by someone with all the correct equipment.

Repair, Replace or Recondition?

With the engine in bits, you'll want to know what to repair or replace and while experience is a useful factor in knowing how much wear is too much wear, you're advised to replace parts when in any doubt, with an engine that takes as much stripping and rebuilding as this one! The following paragraphs will give you an idea of what to look for.

Oil cooler

If it leaks, replace it. If it's clogged up, clean it. But the only way of fully checking its operation is to have it pressure tested by a Volkswagen dealer or someone with the correct test equipment. But you're best advice is not to risk ruining your new engine for the sake of a faulty oil cooler; fit a new one.

Oil pressure relief valve

Can be stripped and examined with the engine in the car. See stripdown text for details.

Oil pump

You should always replace the oil pump when reconditioning an engine. However, signs of wear are:

Bad scoring in the cover plate. Light scoring, which can be removed with grinding paste is acceptable.

If the driving spindle rocks in the body, the inside of the pump body will be worn.

Put a straight edge across the opened end of the pump body and measure the clearance between the straight edge and the gears with a set of feeler gauges. (Make sure there is no gasket left on the pump body!) If the wear is above 0.1 mm (0.004 in.) the pump body will most likely be worn.

Cylinder heads

With the valves taken out, check each head carefully for cracks. New replacements are very

expensive unless you shop around, but second-hand ones are often available from specialists like Haselock's.

Slightly pitted valve seats can be ground in, but the cost of having them refaced by a specialist is small and guarantees the correct angle on the valve. Badly pitted valves may have to be scrapped.

Bad pitting in the valve seats can be cut out inexpensively by a specialist or it may be possible to let in new valve seat inserts if the pitting is too far gone – but this can be more expensive than new heads!

Rock the valves in the valve guides: Any appreciable wear and the guide should be replaced or the heads exchanged.

Rocker gear

There should be no play between the rocker arm and the shaft. In practice, performance and noise are not affected by moderate wear, however.

Cylinders

There are rough and ready means of measuring bore wear, but I cannot recommend other than the use of an internal micrometer or dial gauge. The vast majority of home mechanics will therefore have to leave this to a specialist. Bore ovality will become apparent as will differences between the unworn bore top and that lower down. Acceptable tolerances differ between engines, however, and this information will be found in your workshop manual and will almost certainly be on hand at your specialist shop.

Pistons

Side clearance in the piston ring grooves should not exceed 0.12 mm (0.0047 in.) for the top ring and 0.1 mm (0.004 in.) for the other two.

If the bores are worn, the pistons will have to be replaced as a matter of course.

Connecting Rods and Bearings

Have your specialist check your con-rods for out-of-true if you suspect them of being bent.

Weigh the con-rods. They should all be within 10 grams of each other. Metal can be removed from the shoulders near the big-end of the wider parts where the bearing cap mates up to it.

The small-end (gudgeon pin) should be a push fit at 70 degrees Farenheit with no lateral rocking. new bushes may be necessary if new pins show any signs of rocking, but their replacement requires the use of a special reamer – go to your Volkswagen dealer or specialist.

It would be wise to renew big-end bearings as a matter of course. They should be matt grey in colour, any wear allowing the backing metal to show through.

Camshaft and Tappets

The camshaft lobes and tappet faces should be free from pitting. Slight wear can be polished out, but severe wear will require replacement. If the wearing surface of the tappet is flat – it should be convex – replace.

The gear wheel should be tightly riveted to the camshaft and the teeth unbroken.

Flywheel and Starter Ring

If any of the locating dowels are loose in either crank or flywheel, new dowels or, if the flywheel holes are ovaled, a new flywheel will be needed. See text.

If the starter ring is badly chewed up, it is not possible to fit a new ring onto the flywheel. It is OK to have up to 2 mm machined off on the clutch side however, and then to de-burr the teeth.

Crankshaft

Once again, the best way of checking is to use a micrometer on each journal and to compare

the figure read-off with the manufacturer's recommendations.

Before splitting the crankcase, crankshaft end-float should be measured with a dial guage — usually a job for a specialist.

The bronze worm gear which drives the distributor drive spindle: Replace if there's any ridging or 'feathering' or variations in the thickness of each spiral tooth.

Crankcase

The crankcase must be free from cracks or other severe damage.

The mating edges must be in perfect, leak-proof condition.

In a severely worn engine, the main bearings can have worn to the extent that the crank has 'hammered' the crankcase. If this is so the crankcase will have to be scrapped.

If the stud threads have become stripped, they can be repaired by your Volkswagen dealer or specialist or by a machine shop used to handling aluminium parts, by inserting a 'helicoil' insert after machining the block.

Exchange Engines

Many enthusiasts gain a great deal of satisfaction from doing all their own engine repairs and from having the knowledge that everything has been done 'their' way. Parts are readily available from Volkswagen dealers to 'original' spec. or from Volkswagen specialists such as Haselock's, from whom they may be considerably cheaper to buy. The reconditioning and specialist checks can then be carried out by a firm of specialist engine reconditioners.

However, from the purely economic point of view, it costs no more to go for an 'exchange' engine than to buy all the parts individually and pay for the reconditioning to be carried out. Haselock's fitted an exchange engine from Uro Autospares into my Beetle, this having the

advantage of saving time and the risk that the crankcase may be scrap while not incurring any greater cost. However, for those highly involved people who want to fully do their own thing . . .

Engine Re-assembly

It pays to remember that here you're dealing with an unconventional engine, the like of which, except in Porsche motor cars, can't be found in common use anywhere else. So, even if you're an experienced mechanic, don't switch onto mechanical auto-pilot, but take each stage carefully as it comes and don't try to rush anything. A wrecked Volkswagen engine is an expensive proposition and one with internal problems caused by your own mistake would be time consuming to dismantle all over again – but then you already know that by now! Take Teutonic care with your engine re-assembly, work with scrupulous cleanliness and a feeling for what you are doing (what ever you do, if you start feeling resentment for the time the whole thing takes, leave the job until the feeling subsides; otherwise you're even more likely to end up with problems on this type of engine than on most). Read each of the re-assembly note

given here and the engineering information on things like torque figures in your Haynes manual very carefully. Look over them to gain a view of the way the job seems likely to go before commencing work, dig out the notes you took whilst dismantling the engine, and follow the assembly notes at each stage of the job. Then you'll see that there is nothing there other than a series of tasks, each of which is quite practicable, so that, given care, you'll be successful!

Have all the gaskets you will need close to hand, clean all the tools you will be using so that no grit can be transferred from them and have an oil can filled with fresh oil ready to lubricate all bearings and seals as they go back together.

Don't forget that, as I said earlier, the number of different engine types built from 1947-on makes it quite impossible to show every modification and type here. Do be sure to work with this book for guidance and your manual for specific data.

ER1.   Here the reground crank along with the end main bearing (a circular, not a split bearing), the camshaft gear, a spacer and the distributor drive are ready for re-assembly. The crank has been blown through with an air line and all of the oil ways checked for blockages.

ER2.   AFTER fitting the No. 3 main bearing – it's the larger of the two one piece shells – and remembering to fit it with the small dowel peg hole (which is not central) towards the flywheel end of the crankshaft – the camshaft drive gear can be fitted. This is fitted with the chamfered edge-first. Here the House of Haselock way of fitting the gear is shown – it is placed on a fire brick and gently heated to expand it . . .

ER3.   The crank nose, the crank keyway and the inside of the camshaft drive gear should have been cleaned up and any burrs or roughness scraped off with great care. The crank will have been supported vertically in the vice (with protected vice jaws) and, after picking up the gear, it can be pushed right home . . .

ER4. . . . but quickly, without giving it time to cool and contract. Whatever you do, don't heat the gear excessively because you could damage it. The Haynes manual shows the gear being tapped on with a drift (but one which is kept away from the gear teeth) but it is then absolutely essential that the gear is tapped on perfectly square. If you use the Haselock's approach, you should still finish off by drifting the gear just to make sure that it is tight up against the bearing and that that is against the crank shoulder.

ER6. . . . followed by the distributor drive gear which is fitted in the same way as the camshaft drive, after being mildly heated to expand it.

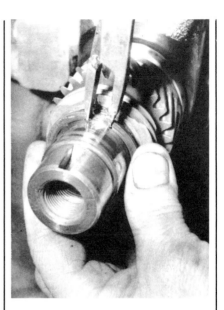

ER8. Next a spring clip, or securing ring is fitted to the groove in the crank.

ER5. Next the spacer is slipped on . . .

ER7. Here a protective spacer has been temporarily placed over the parts assembled so far and Albert is drifting them fully home.

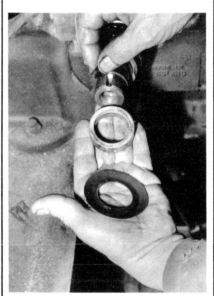

ER9. Next, the Woodruff key shown between Albert's finger and thumb, and the smaller bearing and oil thrower are made ready to fit.

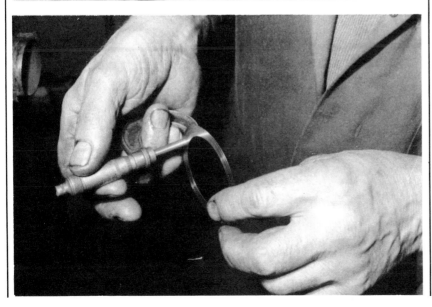

ER10. The bearing is now fitted, again making sure that the offset dowel peg hole is towards the flywheel end of the crankshaft. (Don't confuse this with the circular groove machined in the outside of this bearing!) The oil thrower pushes on with the concave side outwards . . .

Albert's tip:- before fitting the Nos. 1, 3 or 4 bearings to the crank (only No. 2 is split), place them into the crankcase, lining up the dowel peg holes. Draw a pencil line on the outer face of the bearing against the edge of the crankcase so that when the bearings are fitted with the crank, they can be rotated so that they drop easily into place without the struggle of lining dowel holes up.

ER11. . . . and the Woodruff key is pushed back into the keyway.

ER12. Olympic games? Audi ad.? No, these are the shims that go behind the flywheel on the crank to give the correct endfloat.

ER13. In order to check that the thicknesses are what you want, you will of course, need a micrometer. The sizes will originally have been visible upon them, but that may not now be the case. Fresh ones are available in the sizes: 0.24 mm, 0.3 mm, 0.32 mm, 0.34 mm, 0.36 mm, 0.38 mm but the original ones are likely to give the correct endfloat again — assuming that it was right last time the engine was assembled!

ER14. After fitting the shims, Albert likes to fit the flywheel and to torque it up now. Remember to fit a new 'O' ring to the inside of the flywheel before fitting it, and also check the fit of the locating dowels. If any are slack, the flywheel could do what its name suggests it might, with disastrous consequences! So renew any slack ones! Torque the flywheel up to 75 lbf/ft for now, that being the figure that will enable you to check the endfloat accurately. Final tightening can come later.

ER15. NOTE! Some recommend that you fit the connecting rods to the crank at this stage, others that they are fitted with the crank in place. The disadvantage of the former approach is that the con-rods have to be fed through the bores when fitting the crankcase halves together, while with the latter approach, there's the problem of fitting the big-end caps through the same bores. Really, it's much better to fit the con-rods now. Fit the split bearing shell to the lower crankcase half, lubricate enthusiastically all of the bearings and lower the crankshaft into place.

ER16. Place the camshaft shells into their journals in the crankcase and also push the tappets (cam followers) in.

ER17. Turn the crank so that the punch mark, on the inner face of the camshaft drive gear is at '3 o'clock' on the camshaft side.

ER18. Then the camshaft, complete with camshaft gear, is lowered onto the half-shells (after lubricating them heavily), the similar, although larger, punch mark in the camshaft gear lying adjacent to that on the crankshaft gear.

ER19.   Now a smear of good quality, non-setting jointing paste should be spread evenly over all the jointing faces of the crankcase, taking care to keep it away from the oilways and taking special care to cover the base of the studs properly.

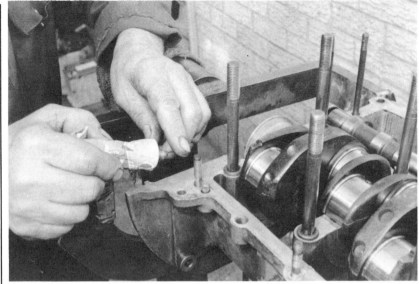

ER20.   This should include the area where the oil pump housing fits, then the housing can be put in place and more compound smeared onto its upper face. Also fit the camshaft sealing plug, coated with sealing compound and with its recess facing inwards, although on some later ones, it faced outwards: Check your manual or your strip-down notes if in doubt.

ER21.   Now the crankcase upper half is lowered into position (bearing in mind that the engine is being re-assembled on its side and the two halves become a left- and a right-hand half after assembly).

ER22.   If the engine uses crank case bolt seals (earlier ones do not), fit new ones. Fit the washers and the crankcase stud nuts. First tighten the six large nuts to a torque of only 11 lbf/ft then the smaller nuts to the same torque.

ER23.   Don't forget this small nut near the lower large stud clamping round No. 1 main bearing. Tighten to its full torque of 14 lbf/ft.

ER24. ... and don't forget those with a nut and bolt rather than studs. N.B. Early engines had only one side of nut and these should be tightened to 22lbf/ft.

Different Beetle and Transporter engines require their crankcase bolts to be tightened to different torque figures.
Refer to your manual for details.

ER25. A new oil seal must be fitted to the end of the crank behind the crankshaft pulley. This one is being tapped in with very great care so that it goes in perfectly square.

ER26. But it is very easy to twist and damage it and if you can get hold of a special tool such as the one that Haselock's use (here it is shown tightened up on the end of the crank, pushing the new seal home, the old held in the foreground) so much the better.

Engine Rebuild Pointers

If you have 'lost' the positions of con-rods on crankshaft:

Lay the crankshaft down, flywheel flange pointing away from you.

No. 1 con-rod is on the right nearest the flywheel end and

No. 2 is also on the right. No. 3 is nearest the flywheel end on the left and No. 4 is in front of it.

The number on each con-rod and cap must face downwards. On the other side (obviously facing upwards) is a forging mark. If new rods are fitted, check with your supplier which way round they go.

Earlier rods with fixed bolts in the caps should not be mingled with later ones with 'loose' bolts passing through the caps.

Rotate the engine after fitting each new bearing shell to check for tightness, which is most likely caused by dirt trapped between shell and cap or a ring of carbon on the inner face of the cap. Tap

the shoulder of each rod with a light hammer after tightening to relieve the stress in each one.

If the oil pump suction pipe is loose, it must be carefully peened into place with the ball end of an engineer's hammer.

Before fitting the cam followers to the 'upper' half of the crankcase, place a dab of grease behind the lip of each one to help it to stay in position as the crankcase half is fitted.

New piston rings are best fitted from the top of the piston, starting with the bottom ring. The blade of a feeler gauge will help to slide it over the grooves, but remember that rings are extremely

brittle and break very easily indeed. Some rings are marked 'top', other 'oben' (German for top) and some may be marked in Spanish ('superficie'?). Space the ring gaps around.

A gudgeon pin will slide very much more easily if the piston is first heated in hot water. Do NOT play a flame on it!

New pistons will have 'flywheel' marked on the top of the crown or an arrow indicating which side of the piston is to face the flywheel.

Note that the flat fins on each pair of cylinders face each other.

Because the cylinders are placed onto the pistons, the ring compressor used must be able to be split and taken from around the piston.

Ensure that each cylinder gasket is properly in place before tightening down. Tie each one down with string or wire as it is fitted so that you can rotate the engine without dislodging it.

Valves: Remember that the close coils of the valve springs go against the head. Later engines have an oil deflection ring round the valve stem which must be fitted before the spring cap. Spring collets can be difficult to replace. Pick up and insert them with a dab of grease on the end of a screwdriver.

Pull on the ends of the pushrod tubes before refitting them so that there is some 'compressability' in the concertina ends. Fit a new sealing ring over each end.

The steel deflector plates cannot be fitted after putting the heads and tubes in position. Fit them beforehand and ensure that they are fitted to the correct side, their shape following that of the cooling fins. Bend out the clips to make sure that they fit tightly.

Some, but not all engines have a copper/asbestos ring gasket between the cylinder and head. If one came off, fit a new one. The cylinder head stubs must clear the cylinders' cooling fins with a small gap. Later engines without head/cylinder gaskets can be placed in location with each other with a smear of fine grinding paste between the two (before fitting the cylinders to the pistons, of course). The cylinder is twisted against the head to ensure a gas-tight seal — but don't overdo it and do make sure that you wash off all traces of grinding past. Imagine what it would do to your new piston rings and bearings!

It helps to have an extra pair of hands to fit up the pushrods as the heads are pushed into place. They are easiest to fit with the engine turned so that the cylinders are upright.

Remember to place a new seal over each rocker shaft stud before fitting the rocker gear. On later models, the support blocks were chamfered and slotted. The chamfers should face outwards and the slots upwards.

The flywheel should be replaced to the correct figure of 217 lbf/ft otherwise vibration can loosen it (but too high a figure could induce stresses). A rough (but probably near-enough) way of doing so is: Use a four-foot overall length of lever, stand on an accurate pair of scales and pull on the end of the lever until just 55 lbs is 'removed' from your weight. So, 55 lbs x 4 ft = 220 lbf/ft which is near enough.

The order in which the ancillaries can be refitted (assuming that they haven't been fitted so far) so that nothing gets in the way of later component fitting is as follows:

Lower rear cover plate
Crankshaft pulley wheel
Oil cooler
Upper cylinder cover plates
Heat exchangers (but not tightened down)
Inlet manifold (not tightened down)
Generator pedestal (some are not removable)
Fan housing (not yet tightened down)
Fan/generator assembly
Silencer assembly (connect up with heat exchangers and inlet manifold)
Fuel pump
Carburettor
Distributor

Attach the thermostat bellows (where fitted) to the pull rod and adjust the setting before fitting the lower right-hand duct plate.

Refitting the Engine

RTE1. Haselocks built up the author's engine, supplied by URO Autospares, with 'Stage 1' tuning parts such as Bosch .009 distributor and a UVA — supplied more efficient exhaust system.

1) Refit the starter motor to the transmission (if removed) before replacing the engine.

2) Check that all the engine-to-transmission mounting nuts/bolts run freely.

3) Put the accelerator guide tube in position through the fan housing and ensure that the cable can't become trapped or kinked.

4) Lift the engine dead level so that it doesn't foul. As soon as it is lined up with the clutch, feed the accelerator cable through the guide tube.

5) Move the engine forwards and 'waggle' it fully into place and tighten the nuts/bolts. Whatever you do, DON'T use the mounting bolts to pull the two halves of the engine/transmission together because one of the casings could easily crack and it could bend the gearbox input shaft.

6) From beneath, connect the fuel line; heater hoses; heater flap control wires; starter cables; adjust the clutch pedal free play. 'Top end' connections are made as the reverse of those described when the engine was taken out.

7) When the engine is ready to run – DON'T. First, remove the sparking plugs, ensure that the battery is fully charged and turn the engine over for some time to circulate the oil through all of the bearings and bearing surfaces until the oil warns light goes out. If it doesn't, you've got a problem that needs further investigation. When the engine is fired, look into the engine bay to ensure that everything seems OK and that there's no inverted oil gusher (oil leaks) beneath the engine.

8) You'll need a full engine tune to obtain the best performance after disturbing so many parts and to ensure that no damage is done through running with faulty timing or mixture.

RTE2.   It is far, far easier to 'waggle' the engine into place (see paragraph 5 above) with the standard exhaust fitted.

Gearbox Removal

Safety

Don't release the gearbox from its mountings without having an adequate support to take its fairly considerable weight and have a helper working with you when lowering it to the ground. When trying gearchange selection adjustments, be careful when driving, pulling out and overtaking until you Mechanical Components are sure that there is no inherent tendency to jump out of gear under acceleration.

Tool Box

You'll need a full complement of standard workshop tools with metric sized spanners and you'll also need a number of special, one-off or improvised tools, according to which job you are carrying out and on which model. The text and captions give details of what's wanted.

Overhauling the Volkswagen gearbox is not covered here for a couple of reasons: First, the unit is a strong one which doesn't often give problems; and second, its overhaul is the sort of job that is not often contemplated by the average home mechanic. But for those really determined to have a go, the Haynes manual for your model of Beetle or Transporter covers the job admirably. Should you come across severe problems with your gearbox, it is undoubtedly true to say that the least expensive way out is to buy an exchange gearbox complete with a guarantee, or even to buy a second-hand unit. For some reason which I have never fully understood, it always seems more expensive to buy the parts to overhaul your own 'box than to have a specialist gearbox restorer do it for you. Curious! Then when you add in the fact that the Volkswagen gearbox is more complex that most (it's said that, if you haven't rebuilt a gearbox before, you shouldn't start on a Volkswagen!) you begin to realise how appealing exchange gearboxes can be. Exchange 'boxes to original specification are, of course, available through your Volkswagen dealer or less expensive units are available through specialists such as House of Haselock. You pays your money and you takes your pick . . .

This series of pictures actually shows a Transporter

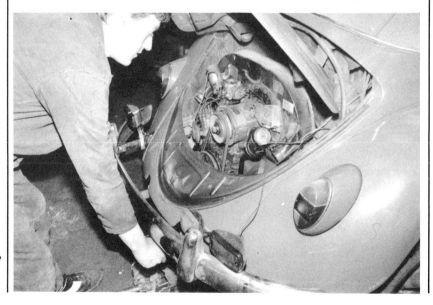

gearbox with later-type transmission being removed at Haselock's. Beetle gearbox removal, both early and late type, involves some differences in approach and these are described in the pointers at the end of the section.

The engine must always be removed before any of the Beetle or Transporter gearboxes can be removed. The starter motor, if still in place, should also be taken off.

GB1.   High up on the side of the casing at the engine end, the clutch cable is removed from the operating mechanism.

GB2.   Viewed from way down low, the gearchange mechanism is unbolted from the rear of the gearbox.

GB3.   The bolts holding the drive shaft to the differential unit are undone and both drive shafts disconnected.

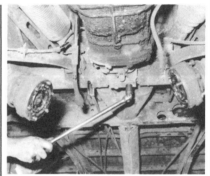

GB4.   At the rear, the 'box is bolted to the frame . . .

GB5.   . . . and at the front it is also bolted in place at the top of the casing. The unit is being supported by an assistant at this stage.

GB6. As it comes free, a great deal of weight can seem to be released unless you are prepared for it, although the gearbox is not significantly heavier than most, bearing in mind that it incorporates the differential unit. It takes two to lower it, however.

Don't forget to always refill the unit with fresh oil. This is easiest to do from above before the engine is replaced.

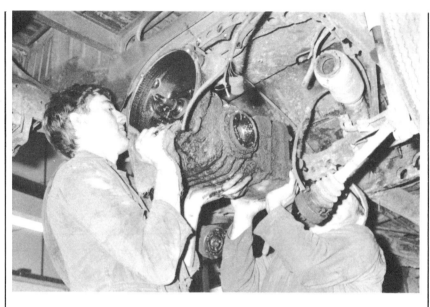

Beetle Gearbox Removal – Double-jointed Driveshafts

Lift up the back seat and remove the tunnel cover, held in place by a single bolt. Beneath it is a square headed screw holding the gearchange rod to the gearchange lever. Undo the locking wire and undo the bolt until the coupling is free.

When reconnecting the gearshift to the shift operating rod, make sure that the point of the locking screw engages in the dimple in the shaft. Re-lock the screw with wire. If gear selection is not quite to your satisfaction, or there's any jumping out of gear, make adjustments to the gear lever mounting.

The gear lever is held by two bolts to the floor and the mounting holes are elongated. If the bolts are slackened and the assembly is moved forwards, selection of 2nd and 4th gears will be more positive; moving it rearwards helps selection of 1st and 3rd. Aim to find the central position which will give positive selection on all forward gears, but remember that this won't cure a fault in the gearbox itself!

Swing-arm Suspension

There are two types of gearbox unit, the one prior to 1961 being made from a split casting while after that date, the casting was one-piece. The removal procedure is the same for both types and is more complex than for the later type of suspension.

Take off the shroud over the handbrake lever and disconnect the cable ends. Take off the circlip in the groove at one end of the handbrake lever pivot pin and drift it out. Move the handbrake rearwards a touch and it can be lifted out. DON'T press the ratchet release button now because the ratchet mechanism will fall out.

From beneath the car, pull the two handbrake cables from the transmission casing tubes.

Disconnect the gearchange coupling as described above for later models.

On the top of each axle tube, there's a hydraulic hose bracket. Take off the hoses.

On the flange nearest the top nut and bolt, which holds the axle to the spring plate, will be seen a 'V' notch in the casting. Make another notch exactly in line with it, using a chisel, in the edge of the adjacent spring plate. It's essential that the axle tube is positioned exactly when it's refitted.

Disconnect the lower ends of the shock absorbers/dampers.

Disconnect the clutch cable. (See GB1. above.)

Undo the nuts and bolts holding the axle tubes to the spring suspension plates so that they can be moved out and down on each side.

Now the gearbox can be unbolted front and rear and removed as described above.

When reconnecting, remember that the rear hydraulic system will need bleeding and the notches in the axle bearing housings and the spring plates will have to be correctly lined up.

Gearchange selection can be made more positive in the way described above.

Rear Suspension & Driveshafts

Safety

You'll have to work on a car suspended off the ground so take care to use axle stands on a firm surface and with front wheel well chocked. Always tighten fixing nuts to the correct settings and always fit new split pins where split pins are used.

Tool Box

As well as the usual complement of workshop tools, you'll need some special, one-off or home made tools. They're described in the text.

The Beetle (all models) and Transporter (from 1968) were fitted with just two types of rear suspension. Early cars and the more 'down market' models, such as the Beetle 1200 were fitted with a type of rear suspension where the axle tubes also carried the weight of the wheels; this being known as the 'swing axle' type of suspension. Later Beetles and Transporters from 1968 used a vastly superior type of suspension using trailing arms and double-universally-jointed drive shafts taking the power to the back wheels.

Trailing Arm Suspension

RSD1. These drawings reproduced with kind permission of Volkswagen from their 1302/1303 parts book, shows the trailing arm suspension at the top and the arrangement of the drive shafts beneath as used on the Beetle.

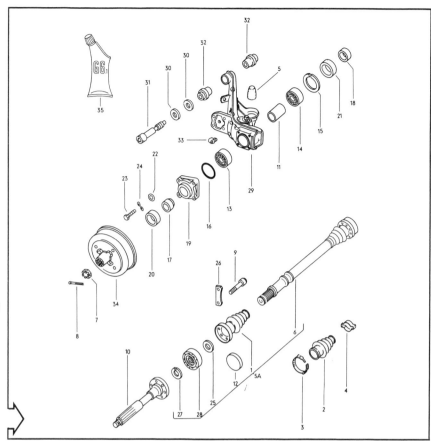

RSD2. The Transporter drive shaft arrangement is absolutely identical and the principle of the trailing arm suspension is very similar, but the parts themselves, having more work to do, are different as this drawing (reproduced by kind permission of Volkswagen) shows.

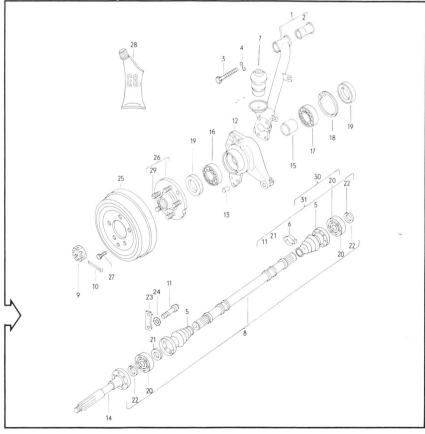

RSD3. These drive shafts are seen on a Transporter. They've been detached at the gearbox end already and indeed, in this shot, the gearbox has been taken out, although that isn't something connected with working on the drive shafts.

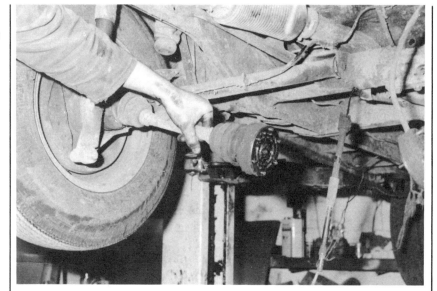

RSD4. Before attempting to disconnect the drive shaft couplings, carefully clean out the screw heads which are invariably filled with road dirt.

RSD5. The correct tool to use is the splined tool made for the job. You can just get away with a hexagonal wrench provided that it is a very good fit, but if you round off the internal splines, you'll have great difficulty in undoing the screws, so you'd be strongly advised to use the correct tool.

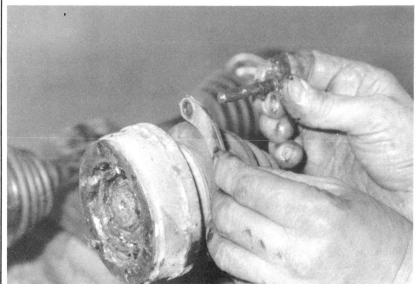

RSD6. Hang on to the screws, the spring washers and the lock plates (RSD1. part No. 26) when removing the drive shafts.

RSD7. With both ends disconnected and the driveshaft on the bench, you can take off the rubber boot by tapping back the metal cover to which it's attached (RSD1. part No. 1); it isn't necessary to renew the boot unless it is split.

RSD8. Then after removing the circlip (RSD1. part No. 27) . . .

RSD9. . . . the joint (RSD1. part No. 28) can be pulled off, or the joint placed over opened vice jaws and the shaft tapped out.

RSD10. Hang on to the concave washer from behind the joint. (RSD1. part No. 27)

RSD11. Although the manual claims that the rubber boot doesn't need removing, in practice House of Haselock's find that it is prone to leakage if disturbed. So undo the clip (RSD1. part No. 4), pull off the boot, clean up the shaft where the boot sits tightly on it and fit a new clip.

RSD12. This was the drive shaft from the author's Cabriolet and was fitted with new parts from Uro Autospares. They supply a new boot and metal plate and this was pushed on first.

RSD13. Then using a socket as a drift, the new joint was tapped into place after first fitting the concave washer (RSD1. part No. 25).

RSD14. The worn out parts from one side compared with the overhauled drive shaft from the other. On my car, the old drive shafts showed no sign of wear until they were stripped down, but then they were found to be so full of rust that they were urgently in need of replacement. New ones must be thoroughly packed with fresh grease — and the need to seal the ends of the rubber boot can't be over-emphasised.

Rear Suspension

Before undoing the bolts holding the spring plates to the diagonal arm, it is important to mark both the arm and plates with a chisel so that the rear wheel geometry is not lost.

The bushes (RSD1. part Nos. 32) can be renewed and the pivot bolt (RSD1. part No. 31) must be retightened to 87 lbf/ft.

If the suspension arm (RSD1.

Wheel bearings and Oil Seal

Take out the split pin from the axle shaft nut and undo the nut (RSD1. part No. 7 & 8). It will be very tight and you will need the handbrake hard on.

Place the car on axle stands and remove the drive shaft (RSD1. part No. 6) as described above. Pull off the brake drum with the wheel still attached using it as an aid to pulling off the drum.

Take out the four screws holding the bearing cover in place (RSD1. part No. 19) and remove the O-ring (16) and brake plate complete with brake shoes (not shown). Hang this up out of the way without putting strain on the hydraulic hose. Use a soft faced mallet to knock the wheel shaft out (RSD1. part No. 10) and remove the inner spacer (18). Take

out the oil seal (21) using a tyre lever.

Remove the circlip (RSD1. part No. 15) from behind the oil seal and then knock out the ball bearing (14) from the other side using a suitable drift.

Remove the spacer sleeve (11) and the inner race of the roller bearing (RSD1. part No. 13). The outer race will have to be drifted out from the arm (RSD1. part No. 29).

Put things back together as the reverse of removal, but bear in mind to:

Fit the oil seal with the lip facing inwards.

Pack grease into the hub centre and ball bearing then put the spacer on the shaft so that the chamfered edge marries up with the radius on the shaft flange.

Fit the spacer sleeve over the wheel shaft, grease the outer race of the roller bearing and drive it into position in the housing.

Use a length of tube and a hammer to fit the inner race over the shaft.

Grease all oil seals, O-rings and bearings thoroughly.

Tighten the four bearing cover bolts to 43 lbf/ft and the axle shaft nut is tightened to 253 lbf/ft (trailing arm suspension type only). In practice, few DIY-ers have a torque wrench capable of reaching this figure, but if the

casellated nut is fitted exactly as before, it should be correct. To check, use a four-foot long extension (total length of nut to hand grip) and stand on an accurate pair of bathroom scales. Press down until you become 64 lbs 'lighter' on the scales, after which you will have exerted 64 lbs x 4 ft which = 256 lbf/ft which is near enough. Fit a new split pin and spread the ends.

Swing Axle Models

RSD15. These are the suspension components and axle shaft of the swing axle suspension models.

1	Axle shaft nut	13	Bearing housing
2	Brake drum	14	Bump stop bracket
3	Bearing retainer	15	Bump stop
4	Oil thrower	16	Gaiter
5	Oil seal	17	Axle tube retainer
6	Spacer (outer)	18	Axle tube
7	'O' ring	19	Axle shaft
8	Shim washer	20	Gasket
9	'O' ring	21	Retainer plate
10	Bearing	22	Support bush
11	Spacer (inner)	23	Spring plate
12	Pin (locating bearing housing to tube)	24	Torsion bar
		25	Damper

It is rare to have to renew an axle shaft and for that reason, the job is not covered here. The Haynes manual on the model of Beetle concerned shows how to carry out the job, however, should it need doing.

If the oil seal boot (RSD15. part No. 16) splits, it can be renewed without dismantling the suspension because it is in two halves. It MUST be renewed as soon as a split is discovered because the axle tubes share the transmission oil and that can leak away. Drain off at least 2-3 pints of transmission oil before taking off the old boot. Remember to thoroughly clean up the surfaces against which the boot is pressed so that it seals properly.

Before renewing an oil seal or wheel bearing, the rear axle shaft nut (RSD15. part No. 1) has to be undone. You'll need a long-handled extension, a 36 mm socket, the handbrake on, and the wheel on a hard 'grippy' surface to stop it turning. Also undo the wheel nuts while you're at it.

Lift the car onto axle stands, slacken the brake adjuster and after taking off the axle shaft nut

split pin followed by the nut itself, pull the brake drum off the shaft. It helps to leave the wheel on and to pull with that. In severely stuck cases, it may be necessary to get hold of a puller. Although not shown in RSD15. the brake backplate is held on by the same four bolts that hold the oil seal retainer (RSD15. part No. 3) in place. Undo the bolts, hang the backplate complete with brakes out of the way (don't strain the hydraulic hose) and take off the bearing cover.

If all you're suffering is an oil leak, renew the gasket and O-rings (RSD15. part Nos. 20, 9 and 7 respectively). Then drift the oil seal (RSD15. part No. 5) out of the housing without damaging the housing and tap in a new one.

If the bearings are grumbling and groaning, take off the shim (RSD15. part No. 8) and pull off the bearing with a fine pronged puller. Or, since no-one actually seems to own a fined pronged puller . . . Place the axle shaft nut back on, castellated sections first, hold a piece of hard wood over the nut/shaft and hit it hard, one with a heavy hammer. Pull it back

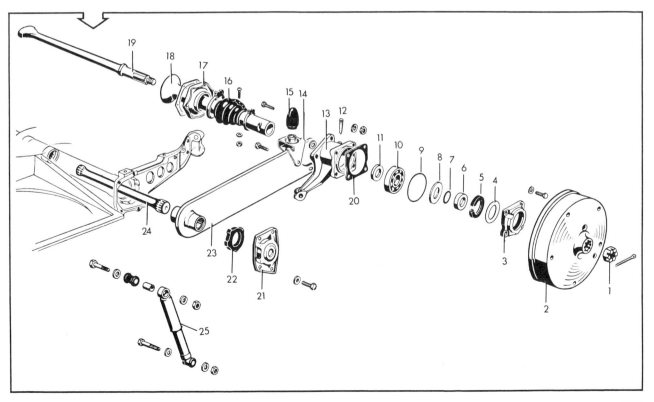

out and the shaft should have moved down inside the bearing sufficiently to get a pair of levers, one either side of the bearing, to lever it off. Hit the shaft inwards JUST far enough to get your levers in place; any further could damage the differential. Renew the oil seal, gasket and O-rings and spacers as shown in the diagram.

The four bearing retainer bolts are tightened to 43 lbf/ft and the axle shaft nut is tightened to 217 lbf/ft (swing axle-type only). In practice, few DIY-ers have a torque wrench capable of reaching this figure, but if the casellated nut is fitted exactly as before, it should be correct. To check, use a four-foot long extension (total length from nut to hand grip) and stand on an accurate pair of bathroom scales. Press down until you become 55 lbs 'lighter' on the scales, after which you will have exerted 55 lbs x 4 ft which = 220 lbf/ft which is near enough. Fit a new split pin and spread the ends.

Transporter

RSD16. Transporter rear wheel shaft and bearings from 1968 August 1970.

1	Split pin	10	Bolt
2	Nut	11	Spring washer
3	Bolt	12	Bolt
4	Brake drum	13	Lock washer
5	Wheel hub	14	Dowel pin
6	Grease seal	15	Bearing housing
7	Circlip	16	Spacer sleeve
8	Roller bearing	17	Ball bearing
9	Backplate assembly	18	Wheel shaft

RSD17. Transporter rear wheel shaft and bearings from August 1970-on.

1	Split pin	9	Dowel pin
2	Nut	10	Bearing housing
3	Brake drum and hub	11	Spacer ring
4	Back plate assembly	12	Grease seal
5	Bolt	13	Circlip
6	Spring washer	14	Roller bearing
7	Bolt	15	Spacer sleeve
8	Lock washer	16	Ball bearing
		17	Wheel shaft

1600 rear suspension parts are not interchangeable with 1700/1800 parts and neither of them are interchangeable with Beetle parts.

Replacement of wheel bearings is similar to that described for later Beetles except that three screws hold the backplate to the bearing housing flange and the handbrake cable and hydraulic brake line must, unfortunately, be removed before the back plate can be taken off.

On pre-August 1970 models, both bearings are retained by circlips. They should be renewed when bearings are renewed.

When the bearings are replaced, the spacer between them should also be replaced.

It is very easy to distort the later types of roller bearing if they are not driven on absolutely squarely. The later type roller bearing has a rounded edge to one side of the cage and this side goes inwards.

Use sealing compound between the back plate and the bearing housing so that water can't worm its way in.

On early types, don't forget the spacer sleeve in the outer oil seal. The chamfered bore of the spacer faces inwards.

The lips of the oil seals face inwards.

The axle shaft nut has to be tightened to 250 lbf/ft. See advice

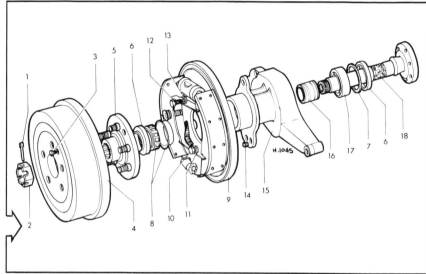

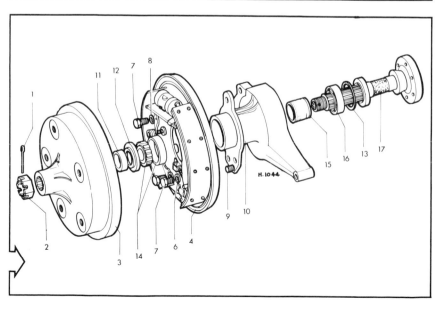

on Beetle axle shaft nut fitting. Fit new split pins and spread the ends.

RSD18. Cross-section of rear bearing and hub assembly.

Early type	Later type
1 Outer spacer	1 Outer spacer
2 Large 'O' ring seal	2 Large 'O' ring seal
3 Small 'O' ring seal	3 Small 'O' ring seal
4 Bearing	4 Bearing
5 Inner spacer	5 Inner spacer
6 Axle shaft	6 Axle shaft
7 Thrust washer	7 Thrust washer
8 Bearing housing	8 Bearing housing
9 Oil seal	9 Oil deflector disc
10 Oil slinger and tube	10 Shaft nut
11 Brake drum	11 Brake drum

end of the rear axle on split screen vans contains two hefty cog type gears and *four* bearings on each side, so rear wheel bearing replacement can be quite a performance. This article explains the procedure for tackling the job. Obviously bearings should be bought new but if you are unlucky enough to have any other damaged parts such as the reduction box casing or the gears you will have to search for a secondhand replacement. The reduction boxes are different on 1200 cc vans from 1500 cc models. The main distinguishing feature is that the 1200 cc boxes have a 36 mm rear hub nut whereas the 1500 cc have a 46 mm nut. The lower outer bearing is also different but basic replacement procedure is the same.

It is a good idea to tackle

support on a chassis stand and chock the other wheels. Release the handbrake and remove the wheel. Then, after slackening off the brake adjusters, remove the rear hub/brake drum. This will reveal the drive shaft and brake shoes. Remove brake shoes, locating pins and springs and handbrake cable. Undo the four bolts which hold the bearing plate and seal housing on to the reduction box casing and the bolt holding and rear brake cylinder. On the rear of the reduction box casing there should be a brake pipe support bracket with a rubber grommet. Undo this bracket (13 mm spanner) and there should be sufficient length of brake pipe to allow the backplate to be carefully eased off over the drive shaft (slightly straightening the brake pipe). If this is the case you will avoid having to bleed the

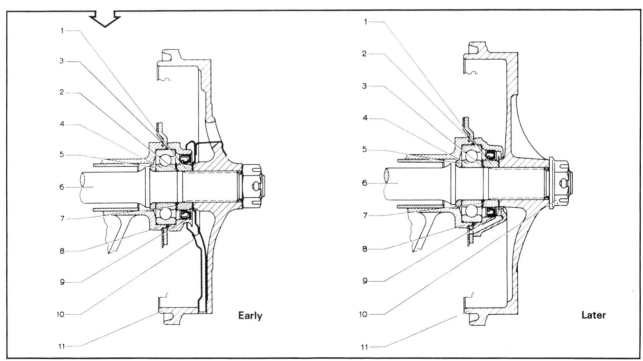

Early

Later

Servicing Transporter ('Split-Screen') Reduction Boxes

(Produced by the Split-Screen Van Club.)

The reduction boxes at the

both wheels at the same time while you are in your overalls and have the tools to hand.

With the van on the ground, handbrake on and in second gear loosen all wheel nuts and both rear hub nuts (R.H. threads, 36/46 mm). Jack up the van on the side to be tackled first,

brakes, otherwise you will have to disconnect the brake pipe and bleed the brakes when the job is complete. Let the back plate drop to the floor out of the way of the reduction box.

Drain the hypoid oil out of the box. This will tend also to drain the gearbox, but as the van

is jacked up at an angle not too much oil will be lost. Remove the 8 mm bolts (13 mm ring spanner/socket) around the reduction box casing. Tap the top of the casing above the driveshaft lightly with a hammer until it has come apart enough to get a large screwdriver either side of the top and prize off the outer half of the casing to reveal the gears and bearings.

While you have the box dismantled it is best to check all the bearings and replace any which are suspect as this is not the sort of job you want to tackle regularly. (The top two bearings are the same as those for the Beetle driveshaft.)

Top Outer Bearing

This is removed by taking off the circlip and prizing the bearing off with two screwdrivers against the top gear.

Top Inner Bearing

This is the most difficult bearing to renew and its replacement is not always necessary. Once the outer bearing has been removed the top gear can also be taken off and you will see the top bearing. John Muir says that hitting the end of the driveshaft (with gear removed) will hopefully jar the bearing out of its housing enabling you to grip the outer track with a mole wrench. Have you ever tried gripping a hard bearing track with hard mole wrench jaws? I have and it is no go!! My alternative method is to use two T-bar extractor bolts. These will take about an hour to make but are well worth it.

The idea is to file or grind the heads of two bolts so that they are T-shaped to fit in between the ball bearings. To do this the bearing cage has to be broken to allow the T-shaped heads to turn. The bolts need to be approx. 3½ ins long with at least 1½ ins threaded. (Bolt dia 5/16'' or 8 mm). The T-shaped head has to be ⅛'' wide and approx. ⅜''

long. This head goes into the bearing with the long part in line with the steel balls and is then turned so that this part goes into the ball groove. The bolt then will not pull out of the bearing. Then drill two holes in a flat plate so that it can be fitted over the ends of the two bolts. Tightening nuts on the bolts will then usually start to pull the bearing out of the driveshaft casing.

Bottom Outer Bearing

This is held to the bottom shaft by a circlip. Once the circlip has been removed it can be prised off in the same way as the top bearing. The outer track of this bearing will have come off with the outer half of the case and should be tapped out using a drift in the slots provided.

Bottom Inner Bearing

On 1200 cc boxes the bottom shaft is a push fit into the inner bearing and both it and the bearing can be prized off.

On 1500 cc boxes things are more complicated as the bearing is held by a nut at the rear and access to this is gained through a plate on the back of the reduction box. To get to this the reduction box must be disconnected from the torsion bar spring plate (4 bolts). When the box is loose it can be pulled clear of the plate and lowered towards the floor. Scrape off the dust and crud to find a round tin plate. Don't despair, it's there right enough, probably under about 20 years of rust!! These plates seem to be impossible to get hold of so you will have to re-use the old one. I removed it by drilling two ⅛ in holes close together on the top of the plate, knocking a large screwdriver in and levering the plate out. Afterwards these holes were blocked up with solder. An alternative method, if you have access to a welder, is to weld a short bolt to the back of the plate. Tapping this from side to side will ease the plate out. The

bolt can then be cut off and any remains filed flat. Behind this tin plate is a large nut (approx. 2¼'' across the flats) held with a lock tab. This nut is R.H. thread and can be undone by holding the large gear on the front. Tap out the driveshaft, leaving the bearing in its housing. Then remove the large circlip at the front and tap out the bearing from the rear.

Put everything back together in the reverse order. There should be no special difficulty. New gaskets for the casing are hard to come by (although they can be specially ordered from VW) so you may have to make new ones. In an emergency, silicone gasket sealer can be used in its place. The reduction box should be filled with half a pint of EP 90 oil. The gearbox oil level should also be checked. When the van is back on the ground tighten the rear hub nut to 217 lbf/ft (a lot of pressure on a long bar but see earlier sections for details of how to approximate this figure) and fit a new split pin with ends turned over.

This job may sound very complicated but it can be done in 2 or 3 hours using no special tools other than a 2¼'' socket, 36/46 mm socket and ¾'' drive bar for the rear hub nut and internal and external circlip pliers.

Front Suspension Overhaul

The front suspension fitted to both Beetles (with the early-type suspension) and Transporters was very similar except that for the Transporter, things were scaled up in size. Part of the Volkswagen's reputation for strength comes from the construction of its front suspension. The car's traditional front suspension consisted of two torsion bars mounted across the car, one above the other. Each one runs in a tube and is clamped to the centre of the tube. (See FS1. above.) The outer ends fit into the

tubular ends of the torsion arms which support the wheels via the kingpin carrier and stub axle. Up to 1965 the torsion bars supported the link on pins running in plain bushes and the steering pivot was a kingpin running in plain bushes. After 1965, the function of link pins and kingpins was taken over by balljoints, two each side. These tubular ends of the torsion arms are pivoted on the axle tubes by fitting on needle rollers and plain bushes into the axle tubes.

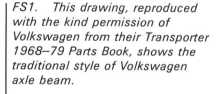

FS1. This drawing, reproduced with the kind permission of Volkswagen from their Transporter 1968–79 Parts Book, shows the traditional style of Volkswagen axle beam.

FS2. Here Haselock's have taken off the brake backplate from the earliest suspension type to show the kingpin-type of suspension where the steering knuckle is supported on a kingpin. Here you're looking from the front with the torsion arms reaching towards the back of the car.

FS3. Here the Transporter balljoint style of supporting the knuckle joints is shown. The Beetle's is very similar, but note the slight differences between disc and drum brake types. Again, you're looking from the same sort of angle as in FS2.

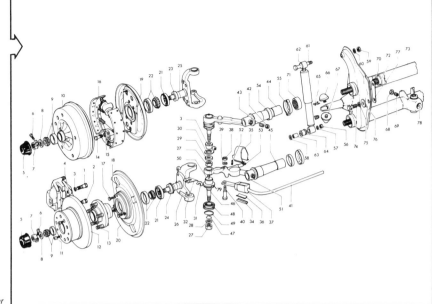

1 Caliper bolt
2 Shouldered bolt
3 Spring washer
4 Caliper
5 Hub cap
6 Bearing nut clamp screw
7 Bearing clamp nut
8 Thrust washer
9 Taper roller bearing, outer
10 Brake drum
11 Socket head screw
12 Brake disc
13 Wheel hub
14 Backplate bolt
15 Spring washer
16 Front brake
17 Bolt
18 Spring washer
19 Backplate
20 Splash shield
21 Seal
22 Taper roller bearing, inner
23 Spacer ring, drum brakes
24 Spacer ring, disc brakes
25 Steering knuckle, drum brakes
26 Steering knuckle, disc brakes
27 Self locking nut
28 Washer
29 Washer
30 Brake hose clamp-drum brakes
31 Lock plate
32 Brake hose clamp-disc brakes
33 Eccentric bush
34 Retaining clip
35 Clamp
36 Plate
37 Stabilizer mounting
38 Nut

39 Lock washer
40 Bolt
41 Stabilizer
42 Nut
43 Set screw
44 Torsion arm, upper
45 Torsion arm, lower
46 Ball joint
47 Ball joint retaining ring
48 Boot
49 Ball joint retaining ring
50 Plug
51 Sealing washer
52 Pin
53 Shock absorber pin
54 Seal
55 Seal retainer
56 Nut
57 Lock washer
58 Lock washer
59 Nut
60 Lock washer
61 Bolt
62 Shock absorber
63 Sleeve for bush
64 Bush
65 Retaining plate
66 Bump stop buffer, upper
67 Bump stop buffer, lower
68 Nut
69 Set screw
70 Torsion bar
71 Needle bearing
72 Metal bush
73 Axle beam
74 Bolt
75 Spring washer
76 Lock washer
77 Packing plates 5 mm
78 Grease nipple
79 Eccentric bush for camber adjustment

FS4. This is the Beetle's balljoint front suspension showing that while the form is different — in other words some of the bits are shaped differently — the substance, or the way it works, is the same.

1 Damper
2 Upper suspension ball joint
3 Eccentric bush
4 Steering knuckle and stub axle
5 Upper torsion arm
6 Lower torsion arm
7 Lower suspension ball joint
8 Grease nipple
9 Screw and locknut
10 Stabilizer bar
11 Stabilizer bar clamps
12 Oil seal
13 Inner wheel bearing
14 Brake drum and hub
15 Outer wheel bearing
16 Thrust washer
17 Bearing clamp nut
18 Clamp screw
19 Bearing dust cover
20 Seals
21 Needle roller bearings for torsion arms
22 Bushes for torsion arms
23 Torsion bars
24 Front axle assembly

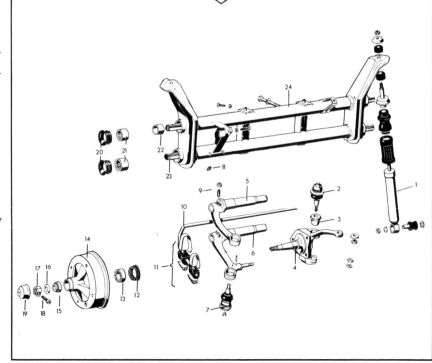

208

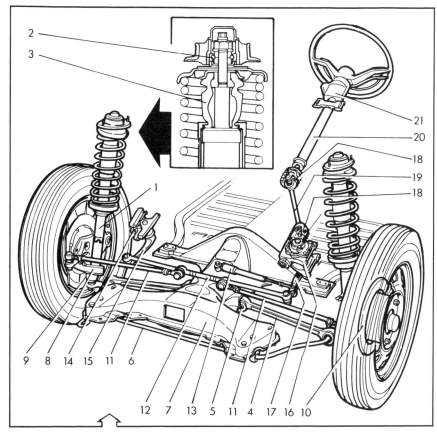

Slacken the nut on the end of the pinch-bolt in the torsion bar arm. When it is free tap the end of the pinch-bolt to make sure it is free and then remove the nut and take out the bolt. The link pin may then be drifted out of the torsion arm and kingpin carrier.

FS6. If the link pins and/or bushes are badly worn then they should be renewed. Wear can also occur on the shim washers preventing full adjustment from taking place. At the same time assess whether the kingpins and bushes are worn. If the link pin bushes are worn it will probably be necessary to renew the king pin bushes. Check them for wear.

FS5. In 1972, a sensational change took place in the Super Beetle's (then the 1302 & 1303's) front suspension. In order to gain more luggage space, MacPherson strut front suspension was fitted, doing away with the torsion bars and instead using coil springs over dampers, the whole thing becoming much simpler to work on in many ways.

1	Suspension strut
2	Detail of strut upper bearing
3	Rubber buffer
4	Track control arm
5	Track control arm eccentric pin for camber adjustment
6	Stabilizer bar
7	Frame head
8	Steering knuckle
9	Suspension ball joint
10	Brake disc
11	Tie rod
12	Centre tie rod
13	Steering damper
14	Idler arm mounting bracket
15	Idler arm
16	Steering gear
17	Drop arm
18	Universal joint
19	Steering column shaft lower section
20	Steering column tube
21	Steering column switch

Torsion Bar Front Suspension – Kingpin Type

The stub axle assembly is held to the two torsion arm eyes by link pins which run in steel bushes in the link pin carrier. The outer eye of the pin is flanged and the inner end is clamped into the split eye of the torsion arm by a pinch-bolt. The bolt locks into a groove in the pin. However, this groove spirals part way round the pin so that if the pin is rotated axial tension can be applied to take up any play which may develop between the torsion arm and the kingpin carrier. The inner end of the pin has two flats machined onto it to enable it to be turned with a spanner. Compare this description with the drawings shown here and the photographs and captions, but rest assured that, if it still doesn't make complete sense, it will when you actually get into and start working on it!

With the front of the car raised off the ground and supported on an axle stand, take

FS7. Whether the old or new pins and bushes are being fitted, this method of ensuring the correct shimming should be followed. This involves measuring the offset of the torsion arm (i.e. the amount one 'sticks our' more than the other). This has to be done to within ½ a millimetre, which is possible with a good measuring eye and a good steel rule. Here Haselock 'Number Two Son' Stuart Haselock is holding the rule tight across the eye of the lower torsion bar (ensuring that it is clean and not damaged). The top torsion bar is set back from it and he is measuring how far back from the rule the top torsion bar eye is lying. It should be 7 mm and if it is less than 5 mm or more than 9 mm, one of the torsion bars is faulty and you'll have to get the car to a Volkswagen agent for checking. Make a note of the offset and work out what shims you will need from one of the tables that follow. Note that up to 1960, there were ten shims fitted while after that, eight shims plus a dust washer were used.

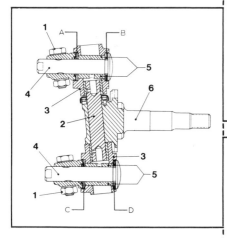

FS8. Take a look at the following tables and fit the shims in the numbers shown and at the points indicated by the letters A to D in this drawing of the kingpin, the kingpin carrier and stub axle.

A,B,C,D – location of shims. 1 – clamp bolts. 2 – kingpin. 3 – kingpin carrier. 4 – torsion arm link pins. 5 – torsion arm link pin bushes. 6 – stub axle.

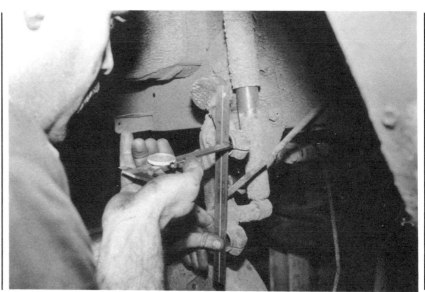

Table 1. Ten-shims models up to 1960

Transmission offset in mm.	No. of washers fitted to pins at:			
	A	B	C	D
	(UPPER SHIMS)		(LOWER SHIMS)	
5	3	7	7	3
5.5	3	6	7	3
6	4	6	6	4
6.5	5	5	6	4
7	5	5	5	5
7.5	6	4	5	5
8	6	4	4	6
8.5	7	3	4	6
9	7	3	3	7

Table 2. Eight-shims models 1960-on

Transmission offset in mm.	No. of washers fitted to pins at:			
	A	B	C	D
	(UPPER SHIMS)		(LOWER SHIMS)	
5.5	2	6	5	3
6	2	6	4	4
6.5	3	5	4	4
7	3	5	3	5
7.5	4	4	3	5
8	4	4	2	6
8.5	5	3	2	6

FS9. Assemble the correct number of shims under the head of the upper link pin, push it through the link and put the remainder of the shims on the other side, using the numbers given in the tables. The old pin can be seen discarded on Haselock's bench. Don't forget the dust washer on the eight-shim type. Do the same with the lower pin and then offer the pins up to the torsion arm eyes. Make sure you have the thing the right way up! You'll have to put a jack under the lower arm to raise it against the springing.

Make sure that everything is really clean and well greased.

The dust washers should be lined up so that the projection fits into the gap of the eye of the torsion arm. Then rotate the pins until it is possible to put the pinch-bolts back.

Note that the correct setting of the link pins is really important! If you overtighten them, the suspension will be stiff and the shims will wear out rapidly. But if they're too slack, things will slop around. Get it right thus: Tighten the link pin fully with a spanner, then back it off by ⅛th revolution. Tighten again until resistance can just be felt.

If the pin is rotated as far as it will go and play still exists between link and torsion arm, the shims and the bearing surfaces are worn. You may get away with just fitting new shims but DON'T just add shims to those already there because the steering geometry will be thrown out. When the pin setting is OK, tighten the pinch-bolt nut to 32 lbf/ft.

NOTE THAT THESE PINS SHOULD BE REGULARLY ADJUSTED! For this you follow the adjustment instructions given (do it every 6,000 miles of if you notice play) but there's no need to remove the backplate or hub. If you find that regular maintenance has not occurred, you'll have to strip the assembly, clean it up and lubricate it properly. Otherwise the addition of grease might just make a nice grinding paste in there!

What to do about Renewing Link Pin and Kingpin Bushes

Refer to the drawing FS8. and the pictures FS6. and FS9. See where the bushes are in the drawing, find them on your car, discover whether there's sufficient play there (wheel off ground; car supported on axle stand, NOT the jack) to affect steering. If so, they must be renewed.

After taking off the link pins as already described and taking off the track rod (use a joint splitter and/or strike both sides of the joint simultaneously with a pair of hammers to 'spring' the taper), press out the link pin bushes. You'll need a large vice or press and a stout piece of steel tube. If you try to drift them out, you may distort the link. The king pin, stub axle and kingpin bushes can be drifted and tapped out but be careful not to damage bores in which bushes fit.

The fitting of new bushes is a specialist operation involving the use of a special pilot reamer to ensure absolutely perfect alignment of top and bottom bushes. This can't be carried out in the DIY workshop, but a specialist such as House of Haselock regularly carries out such work or they can supply a complete kingpin assembly (removed from the link pins) on a mail order exchange basis. This then leaves you to set up the kingpin assembly to the link pins, shimming it properly as described earlier.

Balljoints (1965-on) Overhaul

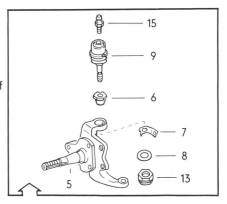

FS10. (Thanks to Volkswagen for allowing the reproduction of this drawing.) This shows the stub axle (part No. 5) (actually from a Transporter, so others may look slightly different) plus the top balljoint (9) and the eccentric bush for adjusting front suspension angles. Also, not shown here, is the bottom joint which fits into an identical taper in the lower part of the sub axle. Also see FS3. for more drawing details.

FS11. The top half of the balljoint (FS10. part No. 9) fits into the torsion arm. (FS4. parts No. 5 & 6). It is virtually impossible to remove without a high pressure press, but once again you will have to go to a specialist or, exchange torsion arms are available from House of Haselock on a mail order exchange basis. This leaves you to remove and replace the torsion arms as shown in the following section.

FS12. First off, you have to remove the damper from the front axle frame (see FS4.). Note that the steering tie-rod should also be detached from the stub axle or it will be placed under great strain by the torsion bars when the damper is released. If the top nut won't unscrew from the stud, the hexagon on the buffer stud must be held with a 42 mm thin open-ended spanner. Or the piston rod can just be unscrewed from the buffer stud now. But note that the Transporter damper (FS3.) is bolted on differently at the top.

FS13. Then the stabiliser bar clamp (FS4. part No. 11) which holds the stabiliser bar (10) to the lower torsion arm (6) is removed. You slide the clip (held in the right-hand here) off the bottom of the clamp and remove the clamp.

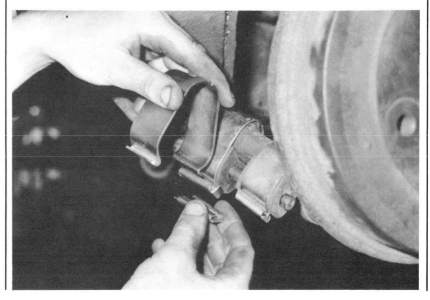

First free the balljoints from the stub axle, but don't bother trying to take them out; the pressure of the torsion bars will be

trying to pinch the torsion arms inwards. The balljoints are a taper fit into the stub axle and tend not to want to come out! Be positive! Use a balljoint releasing tool (there are many different styles and types on the market and at accessory stores), apply pressure with the releasing tool and if the joint doesn't spring free (it probably won't!), try striking one side of the eye in which the taper sits with a hammer. Then strike both sides simultaneously – with really well timed blows – using a pair of hammers.

FS14. Slacken the locknut (FS4. part No. 9) with a spanner . . .

FS15. . . . then use an Allen key to remove the screw (also FS4. part No. 9) holding the link arm to the axle.

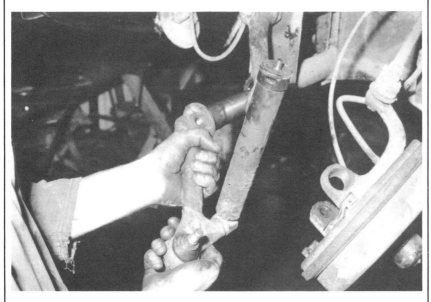

FS16. Because the link arms are free to turn and are not pressed inwards by the force of the torsion bar springs any more, the stub axle assembly can be taken out. (If you remember, the balljoints holding it in place have already been freed.) Here the bottom torsion arm complete with damper is being just pulled out of the axle.

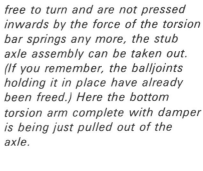

FS17. And here, out comes the top torsion arm. But remember that before either can be removed, the locating screw taken out with the Allen key, must be taken right out.

213

FS18. The exchange torsion arms, having arrived complete with their new balljoints pressed into place, can be fitted to the car, pushing them into the axle and locating them with the Allen keyed screw. It's best if the lock nut is taken right off, the screw tightened (whilst being properly located) and then the lock nut fitted and tightened. The stub axle assembly, which won't have been removed from the steering, is swivelled into position with the bottom torsion arm and the balljoint pushed in and the new lock nut and washer fitted by hand.

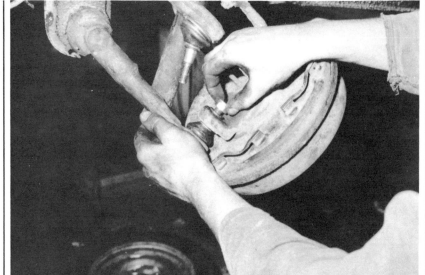

FS19. The eccentric bush, which adjusts the car's camber angle (if you want it set up, take it to your Volkswagen dealer) is first pushed into the eye and turned so that the positioning notch in the edge faces directly forwards.

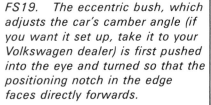

FS20. If you're feeling powerful, you can lift the top arm into place, but it packs quite a spring and it may be better to use a scissors jack placed between the two arms.

FS21. Tighten both lock nuts with a spanner and the balljoints are in place!

FS22. Refit the stabiliser bar clamps and clips, noting that the tapered slot end goes towards the wheel and that the lugs which bend down on the clips point towards the centre of the car when being fitted. You may need to fit new clamps and rubbers: buy at the same time as the rest of the parts you need. Grease the axle well.

The torsion bars, if broken, can be replaced after slackening the locating pin locknut in the middle of the bar and removing the pin (FS1. above part No. 14). The bar can then be pulled out most easily if one of the arms is left in place. Make sure that the new one is the correct one for your car since there were several different specifications.

New inner bushes (FS1. part No. 12) and needle roller bearings (11) can only be fitted by a Volkswagen dealer or specialist with the correct equipment.

MacPherson Strut Front Suspension

FS23. On the left, (with strut insert part No. 12) is shown the MacPherson strut suspension arrangement for the 1302 models, while on the right (with strut insert part No. 28) is the arrangement for 1303 Beetles. This drawing reproduced with kind permission of Volkswagen. Beneath shows how the anti-roll bar attaches to the body (through bush, part No. 4 and clip part No. 9) and how it attaches to the front suspension arm (track control arm).

Take a look at the section on removing the body from the chassis, where the strut top of the author's 1302 Beetle is shown being detached and replaced. There Haselock's are fitting a new Uro Autospares strut assembly complete.

Whether the spring or the damper is faulty, it is probably worth replacing the complete

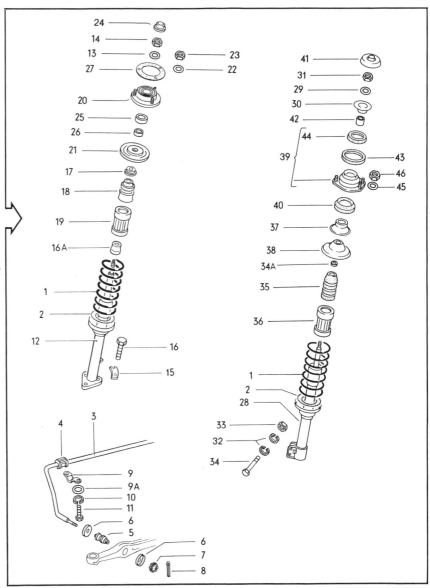

assembly because you'll have to remove the whole thing from the car in any case in order to work on it.

Remove the brake disc or backplate and hang it up without straining the hydraulic line. You don't have to dismantle the front brakes.

Remove the three nuts holding the top of the strut to the wing valence in the luggage bay. (FS23. 20-23, 1302 Beetle; part of 39, 45 and 46, 1303 Beetle.)

Remove the three bolts (1302) or pinch-plate arrangement (1303) holding the bottom of the strut in place.

FS24. With the bottom of the strut released from the balljoint (and bear in mind that the stub axle fits between the strut base and the balljoint and, on the 1302, is held in place by the same three 13 mm bolts), lever the suspension (track control) arm (15) down against the force of the stabiliser/anti-roll bar (9) and this allows the strut (and the stub axle by the way) to come free. The stub axle on the 1303 is constructed slightly differently to take account of the pinch-plate arrangement.

Fit a new unit with the same colour-code spring as the old one. It is dangerous to attempt to release the spring from the unit without the proper compressor tool — another reason for replacing the whole unit when it fails!

1   Bolt
2   Spring washer
3   Clip
4   Rubber mounting
5   Split pin
6   Castellated nut
7   Washer
8   Rubber bush
9   Stabilizer bar 19.5
     mm dia
10 Self-locking nut
11 Self-locking nut
12 Eccentric washer
13 Eccentric bolt
14 Rubber bush
15 Track control arm
16 Ball joint
17 Frame head

Strut Balljoint Renewal

1302 only. Remove the strut as already described and take the balljoint from the suspension (track control) arm using the technique described under suspension balljoint replacement — torsion bar suspension.

1303. The balljoint is pressed into the suspension (track control) arm and has to be pressed out and a new one pressed in by a specialist or Volkswagen dealer with a mandrel press.

N.B: ALL TYPES. The axle nut is held on with a very high torque figure. See 'Rear Suspension'; brake drum removal for details of how to remove and replace. Always use and bend over a new split-pin of the correct size when reassembling.

Braking System

There is a mind boggling number of changes to the brakes fitted to Beetles and Transporter, so much so that every type used couldn't possibly be covered here in full detail. However, that's no bad thing because it leaves room to deal with the restoration of the braking system while information on the 'specifics' of repair can be left to the Haynes manuals. Earlier Beetles' braking systems are not actually covered by the Haynes manuals, but Rich Kimball of 'Bugs For You' has for sale reprints of the October 1952 to 1955 Volkswagen workshop manual.

The other area that is not covered in this section is the one on rebuilding master and wheel cylinders and brake calipers. The reasoning is two-fold: Firstly, if you're restoring your Volkswagen's brakes to the standard shown here, where House of Haselock are shown rebuilt a 1302S's braking system, you'll want all new components; and the second is that the condition of brakes is so important to life and limb that I'd recommend the use of new components rather than rebuilt ones in any case. Of course, there may be times when it just isn't possible to do any other than rebuild the existing cylinders, in which case the Haynes manuals come, once again, to the rescue.

When rebuilding brakes, I always deviate from original spec. in two ways. First, I fit copper brake pipes in place of the original steel. Copper won't ever corrode dangerously, even in hidden places where steel can deteriorate and, under extreme circumstances, burst without warning. The brake

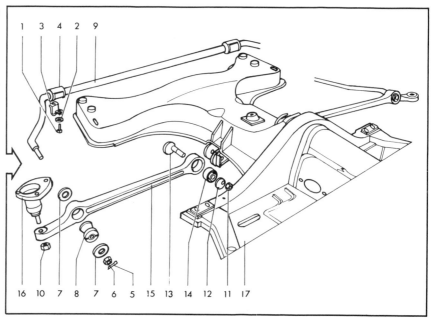

pipes used here were made by Automech and come ready to fit, cut to length and with the correct threaded 'ends' and pipe flares already in place. The second alteration is to use silicone based brake fluid. Whereas standard brake fluid absorbs moisture from the air and so ought to be changed completely every few years, silicone brake fluid does not. Consequently, although its more expensive than normal fluid, silicone will never cause the brakes to fail under panic braking because of 'vapour lock' (the moisture in the system boils and the vapour gives the same effect as air in the system – no brakes!) and in addition, internal corrosion of master and wheel cylinders is also cut right back, making them longer lived. And as Automech again point out, there's another big plus for the owners of restored cars. Conventional brake fluid is a pretty effective paint stripper, which is why the area around most master and clutch cylinders is pretty scruffy. Silicone fluid doesn't harm paint, so there's no worry about spilling the odd drop when the master cylinder is being topped up.

Let's take a brief look at the types of brake system that Volkswagens have used. The Beetle started off with cable brakes and indeed, they were used on the 'basic' 1200 models for some years, even up to 1962. (Very few of these models reached Britain or the USA, incidentally.) On the other hand, hydraulic brakes started to be fitted in 1950. All 1200 and 1300 models used drum brakes all round throughout their lives, but 1500s started using disc brakes at the front and from 1967, (but not on 1200 models, it would seem) a tandem master cylinder was used so that, should a circuit fail, the other one would still operate. Transporters used drum brakes all round until August 1970, but then disc brakes were fitted at the front and the rear drum was made detachable from the hub, which ran against traditional Volkswagen practice.

Servo assisted brakes became an option from 1971-on. All 1700, 1800 and 2-litre Transporters were fitted with disc brakes of course and virtually all American market vehicles were fitted with self-adjusting rear brakes, as well as those Transporters exported to many other markets.

Handbrakes have been cable operated all through in the normal way. Except that on early cars with cable operated foot brakes, the handbrakes also worked on all four wheels.

Although this section deals with the restoration of a 1302's braking system at Haselock's, there are diagrams and notes to explain how to locate and fit the relevant parts for all other models.

Safety

Some of us have a 'thing' about asbestos dust. The type of asbestos used in brake shoes is the most dangerous sort around, but its dangers don't make themselves immediately apparent. You should be aware of those dangers though, and handle them intelligently. Wear a particle mask when removing a brake drum and NEVER blow loosed dust about. After removing the drum, spray a mixture of washing up liquid and water around the shoes, backplate and drum to kill the dust and wipe it up with a rag as well as wiping brake dust off the garage floor. Dispose of the rag in a sealed plastic bag. Don't sand or file brake shoes. Don't drive the car with wet brake shoes – 'cos they won't work! Never work beneath a car supported on a jack;

always use axle stands on firm ground and chock the wheels still on the ground.

DIY-ers are strongly recommended to have a trained mechanic check over work carried out on brakes before taking to the road. There's little that is more important to be got right, for safety's sake.

Remember that the following pictures are of a 1303S with notes and drawings on variations at the end of each section.

The Business End

B1.   Undo the hub nut after removing and discarding the old split pin (see chapter on Rear Suspension & Driveshaft Overhaul and take note of the correct torque figures shown in the manual for your model of vehicle when retightening).

B2.   Pull the brake drum off. If it won't come, re-fit the road wheel and use that to gain extra 'pull'.

B3.   This is the 1302 rear brake shoes, handbrake and mechanical assembly reproduced with kind permission from the Volkswagen 1302/1303 parts book.

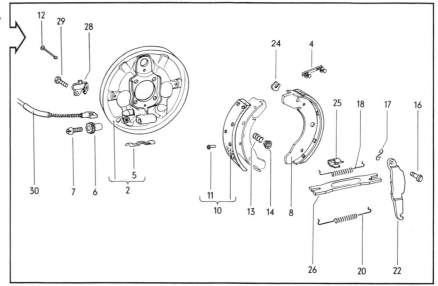

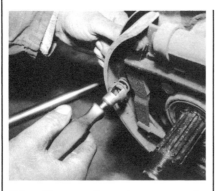

B4.   The steady spring, cup and pin (B3, parts No. 12, 13 & 14) are removed by pushing in the cup and twisting to free it. You don't need this special tool.

B6.   Unhook the bottom spring, disengage the ends of the two shoes from the adjusters and the two shoes complete with handbrake lever and plate (but not connected to the springs as shown here) can be lifted out.

B8.   Here the wheel is on (even though the body isn't) but the point is being made that the brake pipe has to be unscrewed (or does it? — see later) and the wheel cylinder bolt undone from behind the backplate.

B5.   Unhook the handbrake cable from the operating lever.

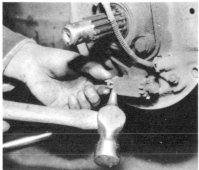

B7.   The adjuster wheel and screw can be taken out together, but you'll probably find that they need a little friendly persuasion.

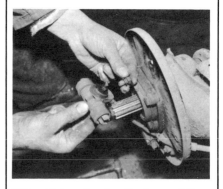

B9.   This wheel cylinder and the pipework were destined for Haselock's bin, so to save time, the old pipe was cut.

218

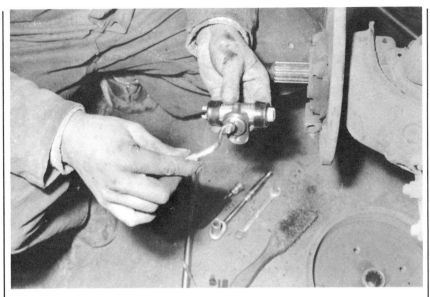

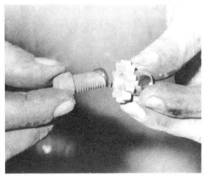

B10. This new Uro Autospares wheel cylinder was fitted with its bleed nipple before placing the wheel cylinder on the backplate.

B11. The adjusters were cleaned up and freed. Haselock's like to put a smear of lithium 'brake grease' (not normal grease which could melt and get on the brakes) onto the threads and the wheel shank or you could use a 'Copper-eeze' type of copper-based lubricant.

B12. New Uro brake shoes were fitted and new handbrake cables threaded down the cable tubes before being located as shown on the handbrake operating lever.

B13. From the same mighty source came new brake drums. They were wiped down with solvent before fitting to remove the protective coating on them. Good re-usable drums should be 'glaze busted' with abrasive paper on the rubbing surfaces.

B14. After fitting the new drum, placing the wheel on and tightening the hub nut to the correct torque, a new split pin must always be fitted. Bend it sideways rather than around the end of the axle: The pin head won't disappear into the castellations, making it easier to get out next time.

The same rear brake assembly was fitted in very similar form to all Beetle rear brake set-ups apart from that shown below.

B15. This front rear assembly was fitted to 1303 models. Note the single adjuster at the top. (Drawing reproduced with kind permission, Volkswagen.)

B16. And this shows the location and components of the wheel cylinder. (Drawing reproduced with kind permission, Volkswagen.)

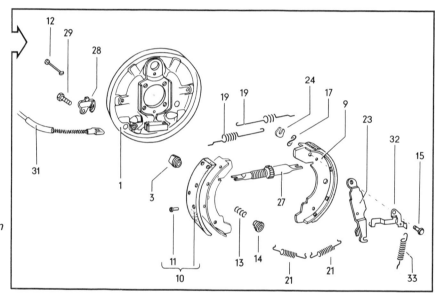

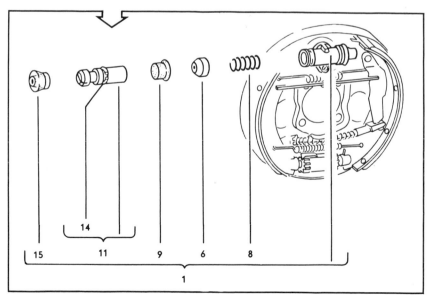

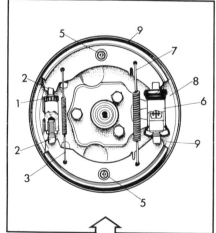

B17. This is the front brake assembly going back to 'way back when' (hydraulic brakes only).

To remove mechanical brake shoes, remove the expander and operating link, remove the cotter pin and take off the leaf spring for the brake shoes, swing down the tops of the shoes as one and withdraw them from the locating pins.

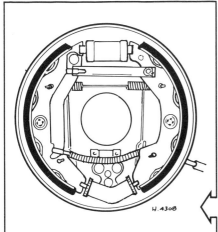

B18.   Transporter models with non-detachable drums are essentially the same as those already shown for the Beetle. This is the later-type with detachable drums, held on with two set screws to the wheel hub.

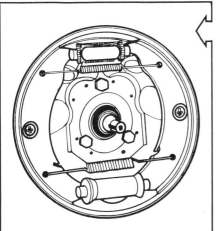

B19.   This is the 1302 front drum brake assembly. (Always, when fitting new brake shoes, ensure that the angled ends are correctly situated and located.)

GENERAL: Always back off brake shoe adjusters before attempting to remove brake drums. Otherwise, you have to fight against the shoes fouling on the edges of the drums. Beetles with mechanical brakes have a screwdriver-slot adjuster towards the top of the wheel, accessed through a hole in the drum; later cars also have a hole in the drum but there's a knurled wheel (see photographs) which has to be turned with a screwdriver. The 1303 has a single knurled wheel at the top, all others have two wheels.

B20.   While here is the disc brake assembly as fitted to the 1302S. Later models had slight modifications as did the Transporter disc brakes. I don't recommend rebuilding the calipers or skimming worn discs (unless the amount to be taken off is very light indeed). Thinner discs are less efficient and the risk of faulty calipers not worth the risk. All new Uro-supplied components were fitted in the Haselock restoration featured in this book.

1	Pad retaining pin (see note)	13 Caliper outer housing
2	Spreader spring (see note)	14 Seal
3	Friction pad	15 Caliper inner housing
4	Piston retaining plate	16 Brake disc
5	Clamp ring	
6	Seal	
7	Piston	
8	Rubber seal	*Note: Arrow shows*
9	Dust cap	*forward rotation of*
10	Bleeder valve	*disc. Later models*
11	Hexagon nut	*have modified*
12	Cheese head screw	*spreader springs and only 1 retaining pin*

16   12   13   3   2   4   5   6   7   8   14   15   11   1   10   9

Pipework, Pedals and Master Cylinder

B21.   The pedal layout for left-hand drive Beetles shown here differs from . . .

1 Clutch pedal	11 Accelerator pedal
2 Pedal shaft	roller
3 Bush	12 Accelerator
4 Locating pin	connecting lever
5 Brake pedal	13 Clip
6 Master cylinder	14 Accelerator pedal
pushrod	lever pin
7 Pushrod lock plate	15 Mounting bracket
9 Bush	16 Circlip
10 Mounting tube	17 Stop plate

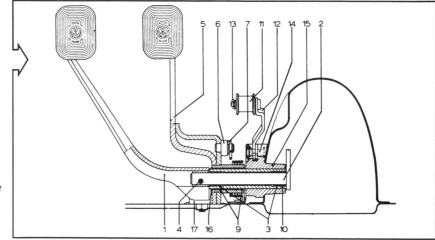

B22.   . . . that for right-hand drive cars, where the throttle operating lever pass over to the same side as that for left-hand drivers. Restoration could well involve the replacement of worn bushing in either type of pedal cluster and especially the left-hand drive cars where the clutch pedal wears the bushing more quickly. Note the locating pin (B21, 4).

1 Clutch pedal	12 Accelerator
2 Bush	connecting lever
3 Brake pedal	13 Circlip
4 Pushrod lock plate	14 Bush
5 Master cylinder	15 Washer
pushrod	16 Mounting bracket
6 Brake pedal return	17 Stop plate
spring	18 Cross shaft
7 Bush	19 Mounting bracket
8 Accelerator pedal	20 Cover plate
11 Accelerator pedal	21 Cover plate guide
shaft	

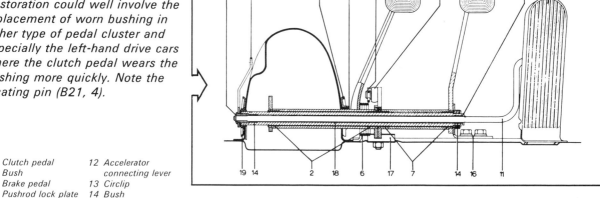

The clutch cable hooks onto a lug which is part of the pedal assembly inside the tunnel. When withdrawing the pedal assembly, keep the clutch pedal as upright as possible so that the clutch cable, disconnected at the other end, can be pulled out with it. Otherwise, if the pedal is allowed to flop down, the cable can come loose and come adrift inside the tunnel.

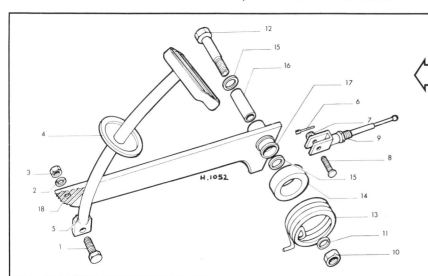

B23.   The brake pedal cluster on early R.H.D. 1600 Transporters and all L.H.D. models is very different from that of the Beetle. It is very important that the spring holds the pedal against the stop or the servo will give trouble.

1	Bolt	10	Nut
2	Lock washer	11	Lock washer
3	Nut	12	Bolt
4	Seal	13	Return spring
5	Brake pedal	14	Plastic ring
6	Split pin	15	Seal
7	Washer	16	Mounting tube
8	Pin	17	Bush
9	Push rod	18	Brake pedal lever

B24.   Some versions of R.H.D. models had this brake and clutch pedal cluster. The clutch pedal rotates freely on the shaft, but the brake pedal is clamped to the shaft. The brake pedal lever is clamped and keyed to the other end of the shaft.

1 Split pin	14 Lock washer
2 Washer	15 Brake pedal lever
3 Clevis pin	16 Seal
4 Push rod	17 Clutch pedal
5 Master cylinder cap	18 Bush
	19 Seal
6 Pin and clip	20 Thrust washer
7 Return spring	21 Woodruff key
8 Nut	22 Shaft
9 Lock washer	23 Brake pedal
10 Bolt	24 Return spring
11 Push rod	25 Seal
12 Seal	26 Bush
13 Clamp screw	

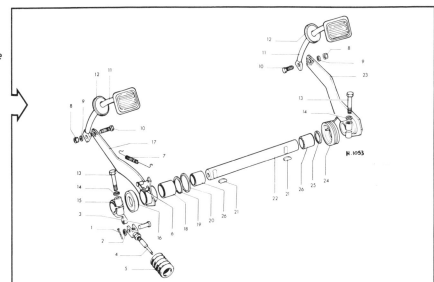

B25.   This is the author's car at Haselock's, showing where the left-hand drive pedal cluster sits, bolted down to the floor.

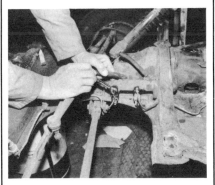

B26.   In order to remove the master cylinder, the pipework is disconnected (if leaks are a problem – they obviously weren't here – place plenty of rags beneath . . .

B27.   . . . and disconnect the reservoir supply pipes. Either plug these pipes or have a container ready to collect the contents of the reservoir.

B28.   Then take out the two bolts holding the master cylinder to the header frame.

223

B29. When re-fitting the master cylinder (and here a new Uro-supplied master cylinder was fitted after the car's conversion to right-hand drive — see relevant section for details), remember to insert the brake pedal pushrod. It is really important that the rod is screwed in or out (after undoing the locknut) to give 1 mm clearance before the ball end of the pushrod contacts the bottom of the recess in the piston. It is important with dual-circuit brakes that the pedal stop is set far enough back so that if one brake circuit fails the pedal can move far enough to operate the other circuit before the panel gets in the way.

The principle in removing and replacing all Beetle master cylinders is the same. But note the earliest master cylinders had an integral fluid reservoir and that the clearance between pushrod and piston on those models should also be 1 mm, otherwise the bypass port which feeds in fluid from the reservoir will not be clear of the main rubber cup. Adjust the pushrod to between 2.09 and 2.05 mm in length and adjust the pedal stop plate to give the clearance you need.

Transporter master cylinders are removed after taking off the front undertray covering the steering mechanism. The fluid reservoir is removed (don't forget to have a container ready to catch the fluid), the piston rod is disconnected at the clevis pin, the hydraulic pipes are undone and the cylinder unbolted and taken away. When re-fitting, the ball end of the pushrod MUST have 1 mm clearance before it contacts the bottom of the recess in the piston. On models up to Chassis No. 219238131, the piston rod length of 106 mm should NOT be altered and the adjustment should be made on the brake pedal stop. (The 1 mm clearance on the cylinder represents 4-6 mm movement at the top of the brake pedal.) From Chassis No. 2102000001-on, the adjustment can be made on the piston rod itself after undoing the locknut. Later re-tighten.

B30. The old brake lines are unscrewed from the wheel cylinders in the same way that they came off the master cylinder. The pipe quite often shears off as the union is undone. If you need to have a single piece of pipe made up, take the old length with you, check that the garage has the correct metric thread pipe union available (in an emergency, you may be able to use your old one if it's in good condition).

B31. The rear T-piece is bolted to the rear floorpan.

B32.   Where a rigid section of pipe meets a flexible hose, grip the flexible hose hexagon with a spanner whilst undoing the pipe union.

B33.   Then pull out the clip which holds them both to the frame or suspension arm. You'll probably need to soak them with releasing fluid and to pull the clip off with pliers.

B34.   The Automec copper brake pipe used as replacement was easy to bend into shape and new flexible hoses from Uro Autospares were also fitted as a matter of course. Always take great care not to screw the new unions in cross threaded, especially if you use steel pipe which tends to pull the union into any angle except the one you want it to go in. For that reason, don't clip the pipe down until the union threads are at least well under way.

Bleed the system after breaking into it. If you don't there will be air in the pipes and air, unlike brake fluid, compresses instead of pushing the wheel cylinders — and thus the brake shoes or disc pads. If you've only carried out work on one 'limb' of the system, you may only have to bleed that bit of it. Otherwise it will all have to be bled.

Get yourself plenty of fresh fluid (Automech's silicone fluid if the whole system has been replaced or drained), a clean glass or plastic container and brake bleeding tube — a piece of pipe with an end to push over the bleed nipple found on each of the wheel cylinders and a non-return valve on the other end. The latter device stops it being so essential to keep the end of the tube submerged — although I still do!

Clean off the bleed nipple (or pull off the protective cap), put 25 mm (1 in.) of fluid in the container, connect one end of the pipe to the bleed nipple and the other in the fluid in the jar. Fill the brake fluid reservoir with fluid and NOTE WELL that it is not allowed to run out of fluid during the whole job, or you will pull air back into the system and have to start all over again.

Slacken the bleed nipple with the pipe on it by half a turn. Now have a helper pump the brake pedal until fluid starts to come from the pipe. Watch the fluid level! Tighten the bleed nipple, go to the next one and do the same, then do the same to each bleed nipple in turn. Now go to the furthest bleed nipple from the reservoir. Slacken the bleed nipple and have the helper pump down once on the pedal smartly, saying 'down' once the pedal is there. Tighten the bleed nipple and allow the pedal back up. ('Up', says your helper, so that you know where you are.) Slacken the bleed screw, pump 'down', tighten, return and so on over and over again until the stream of bubbles coming through the pipe is replaced by clear, bubble-free fluid. (Keep checking that reservoir level!) Then go to the next bleed nipple and the next and last until all are done. Try the brake pedal. Have you got a 'good pedal' as they say, or does it feel 'spongy' and go too close to the floorboards? (Are the brakes adjusted properly first?) Be prepared to bleed each wheel cylinder several times until everything is satisfactory, particularly if you're starting with an empty system.

Don't re-use fluid. And if you must use 'old-fashioned' brake fluid, change it every two years or 30,000 miles, which ever comes first.

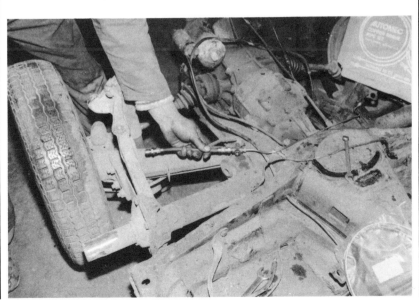

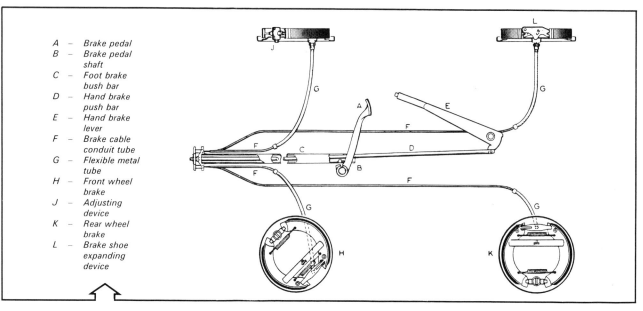

A — Brake pedal
B — Brake pedal shaft
C — Foot brake bush bar
D — Hand brake push bar
E — Hand brake lever
F — Brake cable conduit tube
G — Flexible metal tube
H — Front wheel brake
J — Adjusting device
K — Rear wheel brake
L — Brake shoe expanding device

Cable Brakes

B.35.   Here you can see the weird and wonderful way a Volkswagen's mechanical brakes operate. Both the footbrake push bar (C) and the handbrake push bar (D) push forwards to the front of the car where, in between the letters 'F' on the diagram, a bar pushes taut all four brake cables. The handbrake cable tubes pass through conduit tubes in the tubular backbone of the frame. Where the cables run in the open, they're protected by flexible tube covered by protective hoses. There's one adjusting device at each backplate for adjusting the brake shoes. This diagram comes from a manual sold by Rich Kimball of 'Bugs For You' and is reproduced with the kind permission of Volkswagen.

Volkswagen recommended removing the push bars from the front of the car after lifting the front hood or bonnet, when it will be seen in the lower part of the front panel.
1)   Lift the front of the car (onto axle stands), release hand brake and remove spare wheel.
2)   Remove front shock absorbers.
3)   Remove frame head cover.

4)   Remove stop light switch.
5)   Remove cotter pin plate and cover at brake cable junction head.
6)   Unhook brake cables.
7)   Use a piece of wire to unhook the return spring of the footbrake pushbar and attach it to the locknut of the torsion bar centre anchor.
8)   Withdraw both push bars through the front of the body.

You should check the whole thing for wear, although if Rich Kimball can't help with spares, it may be necessary to have parts made or built up. On the other hand, Volkswagen used these parts until the early 'sixties, so you may be lucky. Refit by:
9)   Greasing all the components well.
10)   Place the handbrake push bar in the opening of the frame head and push the slotted end along the right-hand side (viewed from the rear of the car) of the frame tunnel until the ball of the handbrake lever engages in the slot of the push bar. When the push bar can no longer be turned, this is an indication that the ball is properly engaged.
11)   When fitting the footbrake push bar ensure that the nose of the brake pedal shaft engages in the slot and the handbrake push bar engages in the hole of the footbrake push bar. The correct assembly can best be controlled

by an assistant moving the foot pedal and the handbrake lever. Connect the push bar return spring.
12)   Adjust correct play of 1 mm between the handbrake push bar and the footbrake push bar by turning the adjusting screw.

Remove and Re-fit Brake Cables

1)   Remove the brake drum as described in the appropriate section. At the rear, the oil deflector will also have to be removed.
2)   Lever off the operating link and expander using a screwdriver.
3)   Remove the pin that connects the brake cable to the operating link and withdraw the cable from the back plate through the adjusting sleeve.
4)   Remove the frame head cover, cotter pin, plate and cover at the brake cable junction head.
5)   Remove the stop light switch.
6)   Unhook the brake cable for the front wheel. Pull up the handbrake lever and withdraw the cable from the conduit tube towards the rear.
7)   Fit new ones as the reverse of the above, but remember to grease well, and adjust the front wheel bearings, stop light switch and brakes.

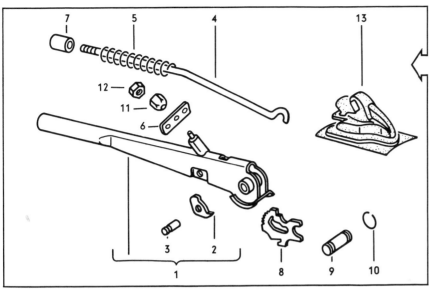

The Handbrake/Parking Brake Mechanism

B36.   What can go wrong with the handbrake mechanism? The button (part No. 7) could come loose and require glueing back on; the gaiter (part No. 13) can split; the pivot pin (part No. 9) can wear and require replacement and the ratchet and pawl (parts Nos. 8 and 2) can wear. You may be able to restore the latter with careful filing or they may have to be replaced, or the handbrake may not hold at all. The same can happen if the pivot pin allows the lever to slop about so that the handbrake misses the pawl. Again, the remedy is clear.

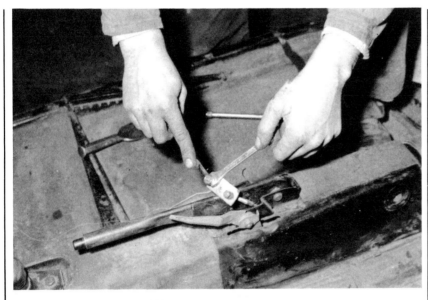

B37.   Haselock's fitted new Uro brake cables to this car. First the locknuts were slackened and the adjusting nuts removed, freeing the cables at the end.

B38.   Then the cables were unhooked from the operating levers on the shoes. You also have to undo the bolt holding the outer sleeve clip (held here in the left hand) to the brake backplate at the point where the cable passes through. Disengage the whole clip assembly, draw the cable out from the backplate and pull the cables out of the tubes leading towards the handbrake lever.

B39.   Before you can reconnect the threaded ends of the cables, the handbrake lever has to be removed. Take off one of the circlips (B35. part No. 10), pull out the pin (part No. 9) and pull the cables through. You may need to hook them up with a piece of wire.

Put the cable through the backplate and work the sleeve clamp through the hole in the backplate so that the spring and washer are on the inside of the slotted bracket of the clamp. Replace the bolt into the back of the backplate and tighten it. Make sure that the spring and washer are properly fitted between the eye of the cable and the outer sleeve. Early models have conduit tube at the backplate which must be removed.

Just check that the cables haven't become crossed, insert the threaded ends into the handbrake lever mounting plate (B35. part No. 6) and re-fit the handbrake lever.

The handbrake should pull the rear brakes fully tight after three 'clicks' of the ratchet. Adjust the rear shoes correctly first then tension the cables by means of the adjusters at the handbrake so that you've got an equal pull — most important should the handbrake ever have to be used as an emergency brake.

Early Beetles still used a version of the mechanical brake handbrake system even though the footbrake was hydraulic. Their handbrake goes to a push bar at

the front of the car; removal and adjustment are carried out beneath the frame head cover, beneath the front of the front hood/bonnet.

B40.   The Transporter handbrake device operates on an 'umbrella handle' system. When the handle is pulled, the lever (part No. 20) pulls the connecting rod (21) beneath the floor. At the other end of this rod is the pair of cables as described for the Beetle. They link to the rear brakes in much the same way. The handbrake should

be fully 'on' after six clicks of the ratchet and the equalizer bar where the cables are connected to the mechanism (not shown here) should be at right angles to the connecting rod (21).

This is the only example of unworthy engineering I have yet come across from Volkswagen. On R.H.D. models, the cable can foul the servo. It's therefore threaded through a tube on the servo shoulder and this plastic tube should be replaced with new cables. Will it need replacement before the cable? Check it!

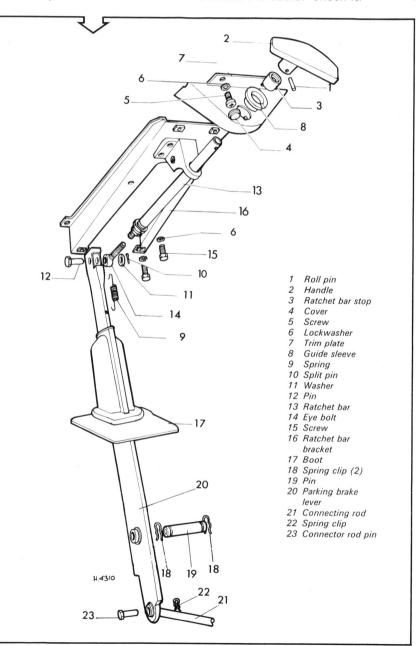

1 Roll pin
2 Handle
3 Ratchet bar stop
4 Cover
5 Screw
6 Lockwasher
7 Trim plate
8 Guide sleeve
9 Spring
10 Split pin
11 Washer
12 Pin
13 Ratchet bar
14 Eye bolt
15 Screw
16 Ratchet bar
   bracket
17 Boot
18 Spring clip (2)
19 Pin
20 Parking brake
   lever
21 Connecting rod
22 Spring clip
23 Connector rod pin

H.4310

Steering Gear Overhaul

There are basically four kinds of steering gear fitted to the vehicles covered here. All of them are operated by a steering box except the latest 1303 which is fitted with a steering rack. The simplest way to tackle them is to take them chronologically and then cover the Transporter.

Safety

Never work under a car supported on a jack; use a firmly supported of axle stands. Where tab washers are used, always lever them tight against the nut of bolt head after re-tightening and fit new ones if necessary. Replace all locknuts or lock washers and always use a new split pin where a split pin is fitted.

Models with Torsion Bar Suspension

The steering box is a worm and roller type gear; from the drop arm a single track rod runs straight to the stub axle of each front wheel. Simple!

SG1.   From the steering box, movement to the front wheels travels through the drag link (23) which pushes the track rods (19 & 21). These are connected to the stub axles and turn the wheels one way or the other.

1	Top cover-steering box
2	Roller shaft
3	Steering gear housing
4	Steering shaft coupling (lower)
5	Coupling disc
6	Steering shaft coupling (upper)
7	Column tube
8	Column support bracket
9	Locking sleeve
10	Steering shaft
11	Steering wheel retainer nut
12	Steering wheel
13	Turn signal sleeve
14	Special washer
15	Thrust ring
16	Column/shaft bearing
17	Track rod end (outer)
18	Track rod clamp
19	Track rod (long)
20	Steering damper
21	Track rod (short)
22	Track rod end (outer)
23	Drag link
24	Steering gear mounting clamp
25	Seal
26	Worm shaft
27	Adjusting nut
28	Locknut
29	Worm shaft bearing (lower)
30	Worm shaft bearing (upper)

Play in the steering takes place in two main areas: The worm shaft bearings and between the worm and roller.

Set the wheels to straight ahead and move the steering wheel from side to side. The amount of free play before the wheel starts to move shouldn't exceed 25 mm (1 in.) in either direction. Double check by supporting the wheels off the ground on axle stands and see if there's endfloat (up and down movement) in the steering column shaft at the steering wheel. (SG1. 4 & 6). If there is adjust the play by turning the steering to one side as far as it will go. At the lower part of the steering box there's an adjuster plug (SG1. 27).

Undo the locknut (28) and

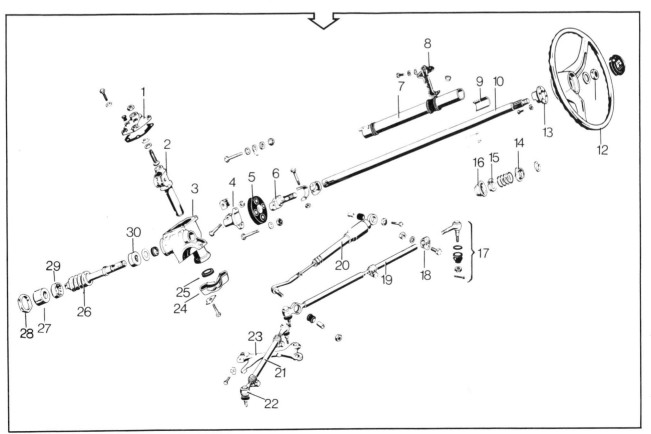

229

turn the adjuster plug gradually just far enough to get rid of the endfloat. Tighten the locknut then check the steering, lock to lock: There must be no tight spots at all. If there are even though there's still some endfloat, there is too much wear within the box and it must be replaced with an exchange or a good second hand unit.

If there's still too much play at the steering wheel, there's another adjustment you can try. With the wheels still off the ground, turn the steering wheel away from straight ahead by a 90 degree turn of the wheel. The roller shaft (SG1. 2) can be adjusted through a hole in the back of the spare wheel well. Slacken the lock nut then turn the adjuster anti-clockwise about one turn. Then turn it clockwise until you feel it just make the roller contact the worm. Tighten the locknut then check the steering wheel free play. If there's still free play in one direction but not the other, adjust the worm and roller with the wheel turned in that direction by ¼-turn. Don't overtighten the worm and roller.

Safety

Before using the car in earnest again, drive carefully to your local garage and have the toe-in checked. Then road test the car. If the steering doesn't self-centre after cornering, the roller shaft adjustment must be slackened off. Remember that there may be no self-centring action to the steering during this stage – drive mindfully to the garage or workshop, being prepared to return the steering to straight-ahead manually after cornering. Corner slowly and with care.

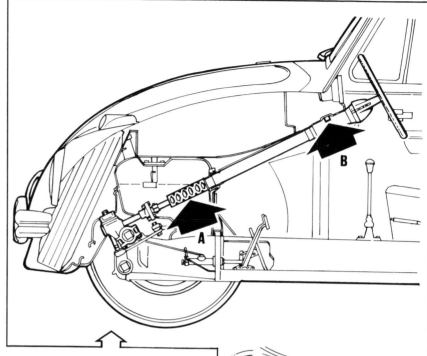

SG2. *These drawings show the collapsible steering column fitted to later cars. The top column mountings at B involve the use of plastic rivets designed to shear off in a crash, while the lattice section (A) is designed to compress. The detailed drawing shows the horn cable connection at A, the column clamp screw at B and the tube support ring (C).*

Steering Track Rods and Joints (Refer to SG1.)

Never try to straighten bent track rods, only replace. NOTE that on the left-hand end of each rod, there's a left-hand thread (anti-clockwise to tighten) while on the right-hand end, the threads are right-hand (conventional: clockwise to tighten).

To remove the balljoint (track rod end) from its socket at either end, after removing the split pin and nut, use a balljoint splitter (available from accessory shops) and also if necessary strike both sides of the eye at once with a pair of hammers to 'spring' the tapered joint free.

To remove each track rod end from its track rod: It screws out but is also split and clamped to prevent movement. Some clamps are by U-bolt, others are held by a taper tightened by a hexagon. Both types must be released before the track rod end can be screwed off, bearing in mind what has been said about left- and right-hand threads. New track rod ends must, of course, be for the correct end.

If you're working on the end with the steering damper attached, it will have to be removed if the whole rod is being taken off. In any case, work it in and out and check that it 'damps'; if not replace it to get rid of the kick-back you were no doubt sometimes getting through the steering wheel.

Make sure, if a complete rod is being replaced, that it is the

right way round – left-hand threads to the left. Remember to fit new split pins after tightening the taper pins.

IMPORTANT. Right after doing the job, drive down to your local garage and have the track set. To be sure that the car is handling at least safely (it'll still probably be scrubbing tyres), use a couple of sticks to measure the distance between the wheel rims at the '3 o'clock' position. Measure again at the '9'o'clock' position. The wheels measured at the front should 'toe-in' (be closer) by ⅛ in. compared with the measurement at the rear of the rims. But still have the track checked properly right away: This is just a rough and ready way of doing it.

MacPherson Strut Suspension & Steering Box

Steering adjustments are carried out just as for the torsion bar suspension models. The adjuster plug on right-hand drive models is on the upper side while on L.H.D. models it is on the lower side.

Take a look at the layout of the front suspension and steering in drawing FS5. There you'll see that in order to take advantage of the extra luggage space gained by changing the suspension, the steering box had to be used with an 'idler'. The steering box drop arm (FS5. part No. 17) and the idler arm (15) are connected by the centre tie-rod (12). So, when you turn the steering wheel, the steering box's drop arm moves the idler arm by the same amount because the centre tie-rod links them together. But the actual wheel movement is imparted by the two tie-rods (11) which are connected to the centre tie-rod and to the arm on the stub axle. As usual on Volkswagen steering systems, there's a damper (13) to take out kickback.

SG3.   This drawing shows the mechanical layout of the (left-hand drive) 1302 and 1302S steering gear including the track rod ends which are clamped at one end and held tight by a lock nut at the other.

1 Split pin
2 Castellated nut
3 Sealing ring
4 Retaining ring
5 Boot
6 Nut
7 Spring washer
8 Bolt

9   Tie rod clamp
10 Tie rod end
11 Nut
12 Taper ring
13 Tie rod end
14 Tie rod
15 Tie rod
16 Cap
17 Seal
18 Centre tie rod
19 Bolt
20 Lockwasher
21 Bolt
22 Lockwasher
23 Steering damper
24 Sleeve
25 Bush
26 Nut
27 Drop arm
28 Bolt
29 Washer
30 Steering gear
31 Self-locking nut
32 Washer
33 Idler arm
34 Idler arm shaft
35 Bolt
36 Nut
37 Bolt
38 Washer
39 Bracket
40 Rubber bush

The joints at each end of the central tie rod are rubber bushed pins. The whole tie-rod has to be replaced when you find wear there.

Note that track rod ends have a left-hand thread for the left side of each track rod and a right-hand thread for the right end. Note also that 1302 track rod ends are not interchangeable with other types.

Follow the advice given on having wheel alignment checked in the section on torsion bar suspension-type steering and take note of the 'safety' comments there.

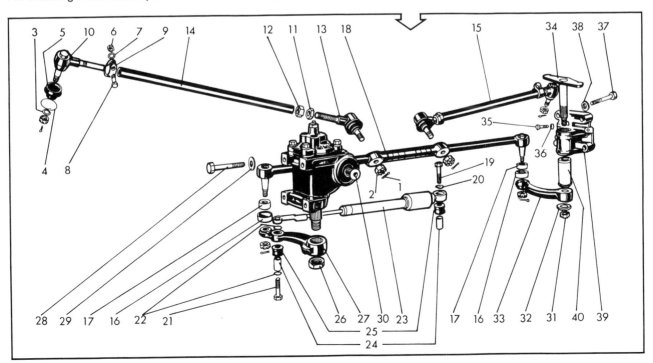

SG4. Before starting to remove any of the steering joints, take out the split pin. Always fit new split pins when re-assembling.

SG5. If these shots look a little different, it's because this Beetle has been tipped by Haselock's onto its side. Here the damper retaining nut is being taken off.

SG6. Viewed from above the spare wheel tray, this shot shows where the damper is actually located — although it's actually the other side of the tray, of course.

SG7. The balljoints fit into the arms in a taper and these can be very hard to free. Use a joint splitter (the type shown is just one type of many) and give both sides of the eye a simultaneous crack with a pair of hammers.

SG8. Remember that this car is on its side and in addition, the wing/fender has been removed for other purposes. The steering box and idler are both removed by taking out the bolts from the side panel after disconnecting the track rod ends as already described.

SG9. After taking out the bolts, the idler can be simply lifted away.

SG12. Then the steering box (here with the lower column shaft still attached) can be taken off.

SG13. Should you want to remove the steering column upper section, remove the top universal joint as shown, disconnect the wiring and undo the two bolts shown here before pulling the column out of the support bracket.

SG10. The steering box is, of course, also held to the steering column. Here, with the fuel tank removed, the rubber gaiter around the top universal joint is being peeled back.

SG11. The locating pin has to be taken right out – it slots into a recess machined out of the column shaft – before the universal joint is pulled off the splines. If you haven't had to remove the fuel tank, as Haselock's had done with this car, it may be easier instead to take off the lower universal joint in the same way.

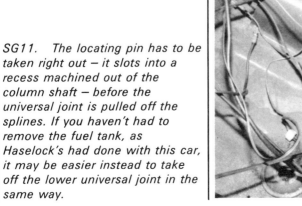

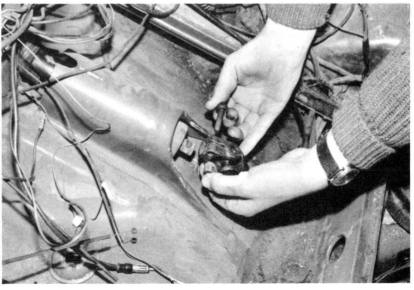

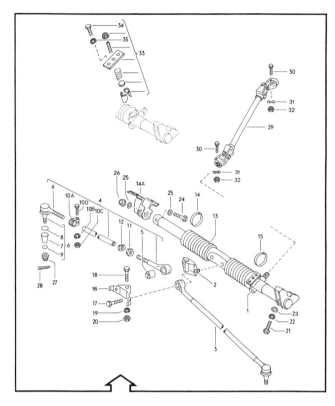

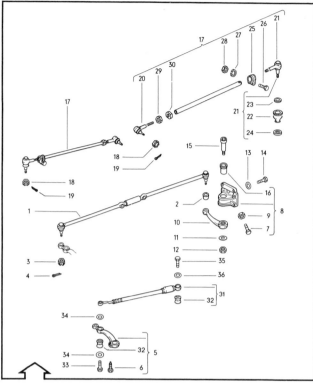

MacPherson Strut Suspension & Steering Rack

SG14. This drawing, shown here with kind permission of Volkswagen, shows the general arrangement of the 1303 steering rack and track rods. Parts No. 24, 25 and 26 bolt the rack to the body mounting bracket (14A) which is held, in turn, to the body with bolts and washers as shown (21, 22, 23). Only the outer ends of the track rods involve the use of taper joints.

Transporter

The adjustments to the Beetle steering box already described can be carried out to the Transporter box, but with the following differences. Up to 1972, VW used a 'worm and peg' type of box where the only adjustment is at the adjuster screw in the end plate. First check that the cover bolts and mounting bolts are all tight and that the swing lever is not a loose fit in the bushes in the gear case. In this case a replacement box is the only answer.

SG15. This drawing reproduced with kind permission from Volkswagen's Transporter parts book, shows the general arrangement of the steering gear, less the steering box.

Up to '72, adjustment is carried out by tightening the screw (after backing off the lock nut) a shade at a time until the 'feel' of the steering wheel shows just a little resistance, but not too tight. Then tighten the locknut, check that everything is OK from lock to lock, road test and be prepared to re-adjust as necessary.

From August '72-on: Check for excess play by turning the steering wheel to 'straight ahead' then see how much free play there is. It shouldn't exceed 15 mm either way.

If adjustment is needed, separate the drag link (SG15., part No. 1) from the steering box. Look at the part of the box where the column shaft enters and you'll see a pointer. Line this up with a raised lug and you've got the exact 'straight ahead' position. Now turn the steering wheel exactly half a turn (180 degrees) either way.

Slacken the adjuster screw locknut, back off the adjuster screw a little way, then screw in while rocking the steering box drop arm until there's no backlash. Tighten the locknut and check the straight-ahead free play again with the wheels on the ground and steering connected up. You can tighten the adjuster a little more if there's still excess free play there, but DON'T go so far that the steering starts to become stiff, have tight spots or doesn't self-centre after cornering. Too much wear and the box will have to be replaced.

To remove the steering box, you have to take the undertray from beneath the front of the vehicle. Separate the drag link from the drop arm, pull the drop arm off the steering shaft with a puller, remove the steering column coupling after taking out the bolt and unbolt the steering box from the body.

When refitting, make sure the notch on the drop arm lines up with the notch on the shaft. The drop arm must be pulled on with the securing nut, NOT hammered on.

7 Electrical Components

6 volt to 12 volt Conversion

Some owners of cars with 6 volt electrics refuse point blank to consider changing to 12 volt electrics because it means changing the original specification of the car. They're entitled entirely to their view and after all, it's a free world — more or less! However, my view is that where you can make mild modifications that add to the basic safety of a car you should; after all, how can the safety of people be valued less than total originality of a motor car? The sort of things I've got in mind are tyres, brakes (although all of the Volkswagen's brakes are up to the business if looked after properly) and lighting. And the only way you can obtain acceptable lighting in a 6 volt Beetle is to throw out the six-volt system altogether. The House of Haselock 'Sparky' shows how it's done in the Haselock workshop.

SV2. Here the old, removed generator is held up by Sparky to show the two terminals taking the very short cables from the generator to the regulator which is fitted straight onto the generator body.

SV3. 12-volt regulators were fitted away from the engine bay, beneath the rear seat. You can make life easier for yourself by fitting it to the fan housing, the fire wall (bulkhead) or place it in the Volkswagen position if you wish.

SV1. You'll have to fit a 12-volt generator (a dynamo or an alternator) and you may need a generator tower, depending upon the model. Check before attempting to fit.

SV4. Now make the generator-to-regulator connections, using heavy duty wiring, and extend the wires running from the old regulator to reach the new one. Ensure that the correct wires go to the correct terminals, making reference to how they went previously. If you get lost, refer to the wiring diagram in your Haynes manual.

SV5. Haselock's fit a 12-volt Bosch coil . . .

SV6. . . . and, still in the engine bay, fit a 12-volt automatic choke, if that's the type you've got fitted. Some carbs. used an electromagnetic pilot jet and on those cars, the 12-volt component swap must also be made.

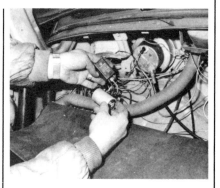

SV7. The flasher unit will have to be changed and you may wish to change the headlight dipping relay although, like so many things on a Volkswagen, they're built so well that you can get away with using the 6-volt relay, even though its total life-expectancy can't be as long.

SV8. On the other hand, the headlamp bulbs must be changed. (Take a look at the condition of the headlamp backs while you're in the area and if they're at all corroded, renew them.

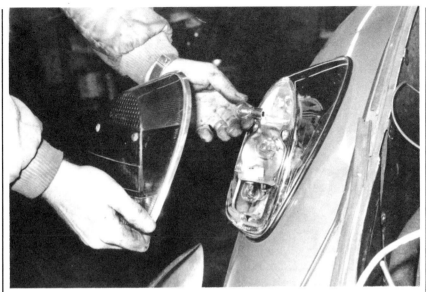

SV9.   All the other bulbs in the car must also be changed (otherwise, they would glow rather brightly before they blew!) incuding licence plate, parking (side-lamps), interior, instrument and warning, turn, tail and brake lights.

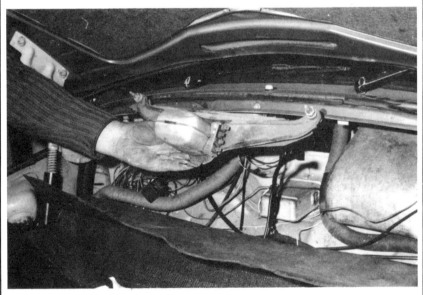

SV10.   You'll need a 12-volt windshield/screen wiper motor, either a good second-hand unit, which is what Haselock's are fitting here, or new. Some say you need a 12-volt horn, but in fact the 6-volt unit seems to work and to last perfectly well, although I suppose, as I said before, that its life expectancy can't be as high. The 12 volt wiper motor will probably have to be transferred to the 6 volt mechanism, otherwise it may not fit your car.

SV11.   You may wish to change your starter solenoid (although some say you can easily get away with the 6-volt unit), but the 6-volt starter is likely to do the job perfectly well. You won't believe how well the engine will start turning over when you twist the key! But if you want to fit a 12-volt starter, you'll have to fit the '12-volt' 132 tooth flywheel. Also, you'll have to grind about $^1/_{10}$ inch off the inside of the bell housing (the flywheel is larger), fit a modified starter bush for the smaller diameter armature and machine out the flywheel to fit onto the '6-volt' crankshaft.

SV12. Last, but not least, you'll have to change the battery. If the terminals are situated differently, you might have to make modifiations to the cables. It's best if you buy one that will go in easily!

Headlamps – Preventing Dimness

Beetle lamps are not the very best in the world, but they become even worse unless certain maintenance steps are taken. You can easily loose 2 volts through dirty contacts, which is bad enough on a 12-volt system, but with only 6-volts to start off with, your headlamps wouldn't embarrass a glow-worm! Take some very fine sand paper (don't use emery cloth – the stuff used for sanding metal – it's electrically conductive) and start with the battery terminals. Clean the battery posts, the insides of the terminals and the body end of the 'ground' or 'earth' wire. Next, do the same with all of the contacts in the headlamps and on the bulbs themselves and make sure that the spring contacts are a good fit. Now check the condition of all the

wires where they join the fuse box and the lamp units. Frayed, corroded ends should be cut off and new connections made with bright shiny metal. In fact, the cleanliness of the contacts and the soundness of the wiring are the two things to check carefully to claw back those two lost volts. You can help protect the battery terminals against the sort of furring up that you often get, by washing the old gunge off withhot water, drying the terminal thoroughly then coating the whole battery post and terminal liberally with petroleum jelly.

Generator (Dynamo) & Starter Motor

GSM1. These two drawings show the generator/dynamo and the starter motor components. Where you encounter a severe fault, it may be best to fit new or reconditioned units to the car and in the case of my restored Cabriolet, Haselock's fitted reconditioned Uro Autospares units, part-exchanging them for the old ones. The part numbers below refer to this drawing.

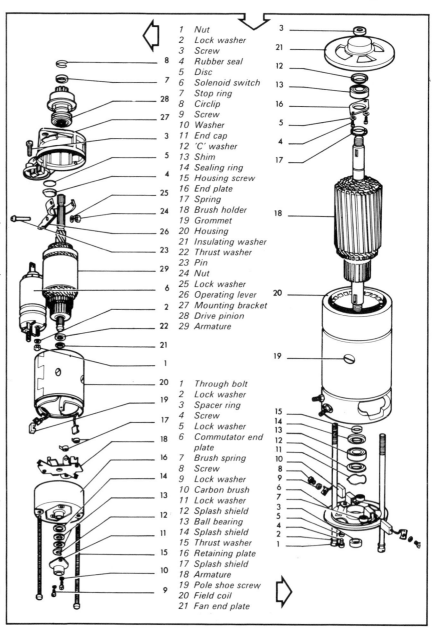

1 Nut
2 Lock washer
3 Screw
4 Rubber seal
5 Disc
6 Solenoid switch
7 Stop ring
8 Circlip
9 Screw
10 Washer
11 End cap
12 'C' washer
13 Shim
14 Sealing ring
15 Housing screw
16 End plate
17 Spring
18 Brush holder
19 Grommet
20 Housing
21 Insulating washer
22 Thrust washer
23 Pin
24 Nut
25 Lock washer
26 Operating lever
27 Mounting bracket
28 Drive pinion
29 Armature

1 Through bolt
2 Lock washer
3 Spacer ring
4 Screw
5 Lock washer
6 Commutator end plate
7 Brush spring
8 Screw
9 Lock washer
10 Carbon brush
11 Lock washer
12 Splash shield
13 Ball bearing
14 Splash shield
15 Thrust washer
16 Retaining plate
17 Splash shield
18 Armature
19 Pole shoe screw
20 Field coil
21 Fan end plate

To simply renew the brushes, you can remove the end cover, hook out the two carbon brushes (10), then undo and *carefully* remove the screws (8) that hold the leads. Try not to drop the lock washers, either. If the brushes are badly worn down, clean the face of the armature (18) with a petrol dampened rag. If that is badly scored, you'll need Plan B (below); if not, wipe it clean, and fit new brushes, making certain that the clips hold the brushes down and that the holders don't allow the brushes to slop about.

Plan B! Either give up now and get an exchange generator, or strip yours to see what you can do. You can try holding the armature upright in the vice (fitted with protective jaws) and toing-and-froing a strip of sandpaper around it to clean it. Then the segments between the copper can be cut back with a piece of hacksaw blade. Ideally, the armature should be skimmed in a lathe, and so you may decide to simply exchange the old unit if there's a problem that new brushes alone won't solve.

A starter is easy to remove, but not so easy to strip. A fault may be in the solenoid (6) which is simple to detach by undoing the nut connecting the strap between the solenoid and the starter and then the two screws holding the solenoid to the end frame. Unhook the solenoid from the operating lever (26). If only the solenoid is at fault, it can be replaced as a unit. When refitting ensure that the plunger hooked end is securely placed over the operating lever.

New brushes can be fitted after removing the end plate. Note that two of them are removed by undoing the screws, but two of them are soldered on. If anything more than new brushes are required, it may be best to go for a reconditioned unit.

Again, ensure that the brushes move freely but not sloppily and that the clip holds them firmly in place.

Another check to make on the starter: The pinion drive should only turn easily one way inside the clutch. If it turns both ways, the whole starter needs renewing.

Horn

If the horn stops working, take an independent feed to it direct. If it still doesn't work, the contacts inside the body are probably worn. Now, there's an adjustment screw on the back of the horn, but you'd be advised to leave that well alone until after you've checked the contacts. Alternatively, if you want to fiddle with it to see if you can get other than a half-choked sound out of the horn, mark its original position then turn the screw a little one way and then the other. If things are no better, put the adjuster back to its original position, split the horn body (some have small nuts and bolts; others have rivets which have to be drilled out and replaced later), clean the contacts carefully with fine sand paper, re-assemble the beast and try it again, re-adjusting the screw as described. If things are still no better, throw it as far as you can, buy a new one and blame the author for wasting your time!

HN1. *This is the steering wheel and horn ring layout on the 1302. If there's nothing wrong with the horn when you take a direct feed to it, ensure that the fuse hasn't blown and that the contacts at the horn are good, then suspect the horn push button. Place a test lamp across the horn wires at the horn end and 'blow' the horn with the ignition on. If the lamp doesn't light, suspect the push button. Strip it and check and clean the contacts.*

1 Horn cap	20 Column switch
2 Rubber plug	21 Clamping screw
3 Steering wheel	24 Screw
4 Nut (27 mm spanner)	25 Retainer
5 Spring washer	26 Lock cylinder
6 Circlip	27 Steering lock
7 Screw	28 Ignition/starter switch
8 Toothed washer	29 Screw
11 Turn signal switc screw	30 Clip
13 Turn signal switch	31 Slip ring and cancelling cam
15 Circlip	32 Insulating cap
16 Bearing	33 Steering column
19 Contact ring and insulation	

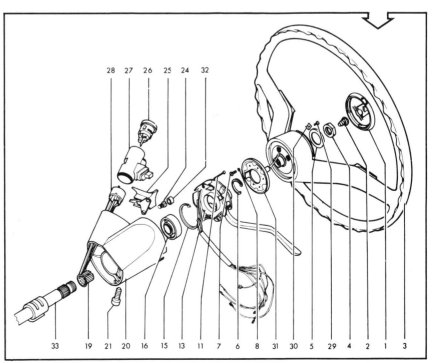

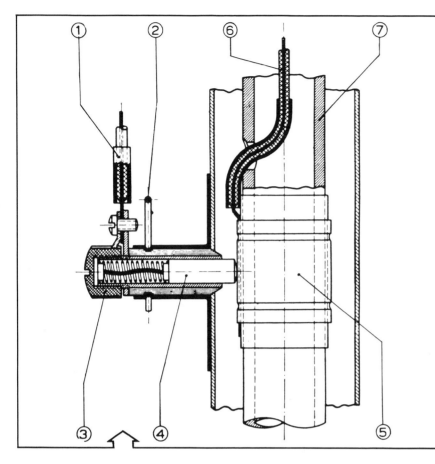

WM2. Take out the glovebox and the fresh air vent, disconnect the cables from the motor and undo the bolt that holds the motor and frame in place.

HN2. On early models, check that the connections (1 & 6) are still in place, that the ring (5) isn't dirty and that the brush (4) isn't worn out. Replace it by removing the spring clip, pulling out the brush holder with the brush and fitting a new brush and spring.

1	Cable from horn (live – insulated from earth)	4	Brush and spring
		5	Contact ring
2	Spring clip	6	Cable to steering wheel horn push
3	Brush retainer cap	7	Steering column

Wiper Motor Removal/Replacement

WM1. Disconnect the battery earth lead, take off the wiper arms and remove the nuts and seals from around the spindles.

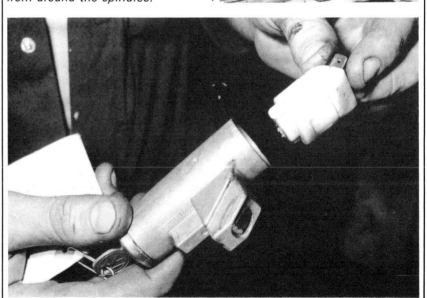

Starter Switch

SS1. A faulty starter switch on later models (HN1. part No. 28) can be replaced by taking off the steering lock and lock cylinder complete, after removing the single Allen screw holding it in place and clipping off the wiring clips.

Replacement is the reverse of this, but remember to put the spring washer between motor shaft and frame and the coil spring between the connecting rod and the frame. The spindles must be at right angles; and don't overtighten the spindle nuts.

Fitting a Radio, Cassette Player, Speakers and an Antenna/Aerial

Car audio can look complicated, but don't get hung up on tweeters and woofers, wow and flutter, crossover networks and physiological volume control. Just remember that all car radios consist of is a receiver, an aerial and a speaker. Then, when you've read all the brochures and had to go hide in bed to suck your thumb and stroke your favourite blanket, cling to that fact; it may help you to keep a grip on things!

Valve Sets

Early units, right up to the early 1960s, used valves that had to run at around 200 volts DC. To supply the appropriate HT voltage they used a separate box, usually called a 'vibrator' at the time, but now more likely to be called by its proper name of 'synchronous vibrator unit'. By the 1960s, valve technology had improved to the point where 12 volt valves were available and some sets were 'hybrids' using a mixture of transistors and valves. Radios of this type were invariably held in place by their tuning and volume control spindles, with an extra bracket at the rear for good measure. Fitting one of these units to a Beetle of an appropriate age should present no problems at all unless a hole has been cut in the dash to accept differently spaced spindles or, horror of horrors, a front fitted radio which demands a rectangular hole in the dash. Oddly spaced holes are usually covered by the radio face plate while the only way around a gaping hole is to make up a mounting plate or have the dash repaired. Vibrator units can be mounted in a cool place in the luggage bay area, but a word of warning: Because of the high voltage, high tension current inside the radio, don't try fiddling with its inside components with the thing switched on unless you really know what you are doing.

Early aerials and speakers are not much different in principle from their modern-day counterparts.

Modern Sets

Some owners of more modern Beetles may wish to fit audio equipment into their cars for the much more prosaic reason of wanting to listen to the radio, or a favourite tape. Then, the far more efficient and pleasant-to-listen-to modern radios and radio/cassette players come into their own. While it can't be denied that some of the more sophisticated units are a little more time consuming to fit, you don't need to be a skilled electrician to do it; however you do need to understand a few basic principles and to follow the instructions!

Speakers

Philips Car Audio sent expert Peter Monk to talk me through the fitting process as it applies to a Beetle. Peter always starts by fitting the speakers first because they are the items that can be most difficult to site. In many ways, they are all too often the weakest link in the audio chain and should be selected with at least as much care as is given to choosing the set itself. (Listening to superb stereo equipment through sub-standard speakers has been likened to gazing at the Mona Lisa through frosted glass!) It is theoretically essential that the impedance of the speaker, measured in ohms, agrees with that of the set although in most cases manufacturers allow a range of impedances for their sets ranging from 4 to 8 ohms.

The physical size of the speaker is less important than those in a home hi-fi set up because there isn't room inside a car to allow the bass notes to develop in the same way. Siting and fitting are far more important! The speaker must be fitted on a baffle which insulates the front of the speaker from the back because then not only will the baffle vibrate with the speaker and give extra depth of sound, but also the air, pushed forwards and back by the cone in the speaker as it rapidly vibrates, will then be unable to short-circuit into the air movements taking place in the opposite direction at the back of the speaker. A free standing speaker can give a volume equivalent to a power output of 1/2 watt, but can then give as much as 10 watts when fitted into a sealed box! In most cases, there isn't much choice of baffle, the trim pad on the car door or the rear parcel shelf being all that is available. Metal does not make a good baffle, however, as it resonates and vibrates producing a harsh sound. In general, the rear parcel shelf is a poor place to fit a speaker or speakers. In later Beetles, those with headrests, a lot of sound is swallowed by the upholstery and, if the speaker lies horizontally, most of the treble notes will pass through the rear screen leaving only the booming bass notes in the car. Stereo speakers are best mounted in the doors or rear side trims of these cars. Footwell mounted speakers are excellent for those with ears up their trouser legs while one stereo speaker in the front and one in the rear will suit those who drive while gossiping and looking mainly in the direction of the passenger. Normal folk should go for side-to-side stereo speakers mounted in a place from where most of the sound will 'get through'.

The ideal power capacity of the speakers selected will be just slightly over the output rating of the radio or radio/cassette. If the unit gives 8 watts per channel, 15 watt speakers would be acceptable, but 50 watt speakers would be 'underdriven', as they say, and lose clarity.

Peter Monk showed me how to fit Philips speakers into a Beetle door. You have to be careful to find a part of the door which is free of other protrusions and it is surprising how difficult this can be, even though top quality speakers such as these are designed to give maximum output from the minimum physical depth. 'Our' cars, being fitted with vents (quarter lights), are a better prospect than most other vehicles because there is usually a 'free' area beneath the ventilator. On top of that, modern Beetles will have some sort of provision in the shape of the door frame to allow speaker fitting, the 1972 Beetle Cabriolet featured here having holes in the door frame. You must watch out for the intrusion of that stiff door stay, however! You don't actually notice it while the door is open and Philips have come across cases where poor owners have fitted speakers in blissful ignorance only to smash one of them to smithereens the first time the door is slammed shut. Also, beware the length of the speaker mounting screws; don't use screws so long that they foul on the window winder mechanism.

Philips, like most manufacturers, supply a template on the speaker box which can be cut out and taped to the door or other trim in the place where the speaker is to be fitted. Template and trim can all be cut out together with a craft knife giving the correct shape to house the speaker. Spiral nuts are slipped over the edges of the trim panel and the self-tapping screws supplied passed through the speaker body and into the nuts. Some door mounted speakers have their own grilles; others have to be fitted and then have a separate grille screwed over the top. If you can't stand the thought of cutting into your car's trim panels, there are speakers such as the Philips EN 8241 which are designed to be free standing in their own pods and with a high power output specially designed to give a strong stereo effect. You can screw them down or even fit them with Velcro and they really do give the best of both worlds for the car owner who doesn't want to make any permanent changes to the interior of the car.

Unless stereo speaker wires are correctly connected, the speakers can counteract one another, the cone of one 'pushing' air while the other is 'pulling' air, reducing both volume and stereo effect. Speaker wires are always colour coded. Decide which one you are going to term 'positive' and look for a + or a dot on one of the two terminals on the speaker. Connect the similarly coded wire to the same terminal on the other speaker, too.

Once the speaker is fitted and connected to a door, you have the problem of feeding the wiring through to the body of the car. It should go without saying that grommets must be used to prevent raw metal edges chafing the wires where they pass through the door frame and the hinge pillar. (And DO remember to pop the grommets on at the appropriate time because they won't go on with all the wiring in place no matter how much cursing you do!) The speaker wiring holes should also be drilled so that they are NOT in alignment, which enables the wire to fold neatly out of the way when the door is closed. If the wire sticks out of the door gap on the inside or, worse still, the outside of the door when it is shut, put a twist in it until it agrees to stay hidden. Passing the wire through the hinge pillar can be a bit of a chinese puzzle. Push glasshouse wire, which is both flexible and insulated, through the hinge pillar hole from the inside, twist the speaker cable round the end of it and pull through into the footwell or bulkhead. Later Beetles have a large interior light switch on the door pillar which can be easily unscrewed to give ease of access into the hinge pillar; others may have rustproofing holes already drilled which can be utilised.

Polarity and voltage

If you are fitting equipment which is contemporary to your car, there should be no real problem, but if you attempt to fit some older equipment to an older car — which you may wish to do in order to keep the character of the accessory in tune with the age of the Beetle — you may have difficulties if the radio you have chosen is positive ground (earth) while the Beetle you're connecting it to is negative ground. Antenna (aerials) have to be 'grounded' ('earthed') to the car's bodywork in order to screen them from interference and, since the aerial connects to the body of the radio, you can't readily avoid grounding the radio set. You could insulate the radio from the car and fit a screen mounted aerial, the sort that is simply stuck on to the inside of the screen, but they are far less efficient than body mounted aerials and give greatly inferior reception.

In order to fit a radio built for positive ground/earth-radio to a car built with negative ground or earth, you are left with two options other than wrecking the set within seconds of connecting it up the 'wrong way round'. You can either convert the car to positive ground/earth, or you can have the radio itself converted. The former option may seem a terrible thing to do to your Beetle but in fact it can actually be less dramatic to carry out than the latter and it is of course reversible at any time. Things like lights, indicators and wipers (in most cases) work equally well no matter which way they are connected and even equipment such as electric windscreen washers, heater motors, ammeters and 'difficult' (in

most cases) wiper units will work after the terminal positions have been simply reversed. However, alternators need a specialist's attention to be converted if they can be converted at all, while clocks, air horn and electronic tachometers either cannot be converted at all or can only be converted after some difficulty. The ignition coil, incidentally, will appear to work perfectly well connected up the wrong way round, but there will in fact be a loss of efficiency. Assuming that there is no problem with accessories all you have to do is change the battery leads over and turn the battery round, then re-harmonise the generator/dynamo. Connect up the battery leads in their new positions, but ensure that the fan belt is on the generator/dynamo to stop it acting as a motor and running itself to destruction. Take a wire, which should previously have been connected up to the positive terminal on the battery, and brush it a couple of times on the small terminal on the generator/dynamo, the one known as the field terminal, creating a good fat spark. This reverses the field in the generator/dynamo and allows it to work perfectly in its new role. You absolutely must place a label on the vehicle in a prominent place stating that it has been converted to prevent major connecting-up problems in the future. Expert advice should always be sought if you are in any doubt.

The other alternative is to have the set itself converted by a specialist, although conversion is unlikely to be cheap.

If your Beetle is one of the many with 6 volt electrics, you may be able to buy a 6-to-12 volt radio converter from a parts specialist. If not, you can again have the set adapted by a radio specialist although, once again, at a price!

Fitting the unit

All modern radios and mountings in cars conform to DIN mounting standards. Deutscher Industrie Normenausschus were German national standards which have become international norms, accepted by all the leading radio makers (most of which, incidentally, are Japanese with the European exception of firms like Philips and Blaupunkt. Even the Radiomobile name has been bought by the Japanese!). Today's cars invariably have a mounting slot covered by a plate or small storage slot into which the radio can fit. Spindle mounted radios are fitted after clipping a special mounting plate to the mouth of the aperture while slot-in type radios are preceded by a special cage which holds the radio in place.

All radios should be fitted with a separate fuse, the Philips radios I saw being fitted having a built-in fuse which is best of all because there is no unprotected wire at all. Those units with digital tuning and a memory, such as the Philips AC760, must be connected up to a permanent power supply and not through the ignition or the memory will be lost every time the ignition is turned off. I can't see the point of wiring a transistorised set through the ignition at all because it effectively prevents you from listening to the radio whilst sitting for any length of time with the engine turned off. On the other hand, valve sets take a great deal more power to run and are best used when the generator is putting plenty back into the battery!

Fortunately, older radios made to fit the 7in. x 2in. slot can be refitted to a slot opened out for a DIN-sized radio so there's no need to worry about causing irreversible damage to a slot of that size.

Whichever type of set-up you want, it should be possible to fit it yourself. But once the thing is in, one problem remains; how do you USE the TLCD or the Opto-Electronic Tape Transport Monitor? I think I'll have to go and stroke my blanket again.

Thanks are especially due to

Philips Car Audio for their assistance and to audio specialist Peter Monk of Marpet Car Audio, advising on behalf of Philips.

CR1.   If you haven't got an antenna/aerial fitted, take out the plug in the body and clean part of the hole to bare metal so that the fitting can make electrical contact. Protect against rust with a generous smear of petroleum jelly.

CR2.   Feed the wire towards the radio mounting, and tighten the antenna clamp down. Angle the antenna/aerial back because FM reception will be improved that way. Excess antenna/aerial wire should never be coiled.

CR3. Take off part of the door trim (see 'Door Stripdown' for details) and locate the cut-out in later doors where the speaker can be fitted or a suitable site where there's no speaker provision already there. Use the template provided with the speaker to cut out a hole for the speaker, but be sure to use a craft knife that is really sharp.

CR4. If necessary, drill a hole in the door pillar and another in the door, but position them so that they don't line up. This allows the wire to tuck itself in. If it tends to stick out between door and wing/fender, put a twist in it. Use an interior light switch opening to gain access to your drilled hole, if there's one fitted.

CR5. Now feed the speaker wire through into the luggage bay.

CR6. The heater can unit will have to come out (See 'Stripdown' section for details) because then you can feed the wire through to the rear of the radio. You'll also need to check that the depth of the radio isn't too great for the limited amount of space available here.

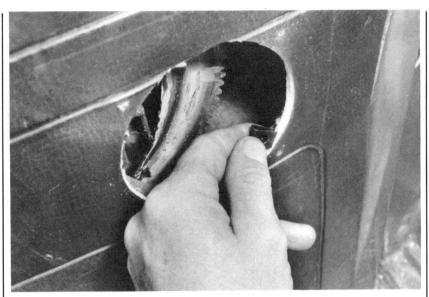

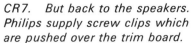

CR7. But back to the speakers. Philips supply screw clips which are pushed over the trim board.

CR8. After piercing the board, the speaker can be fitted and the screws inserted. But if you have cloth trim, don't use a power drill because you could easily 'ladder' the cloth and ruin it.

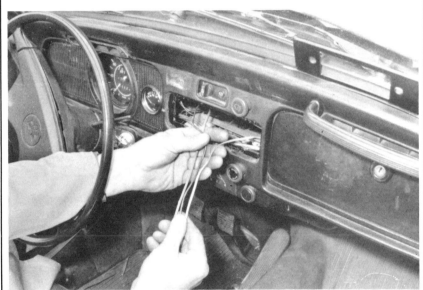

CR9. Prepare the radio aperture by feeding through the speaker and power wires. Use a test lamp to discover whether the feed wire you have chosen works with or without the ignition and remember that where a radio doesn't have a built-in fuse (all of Philips radios do, it seems) you MUST include one in the line.

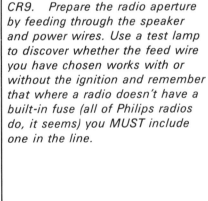

CR10. Lay out the radio fitting kit so that you can see where everything goes. This is the Philips kit with spindle mounting plate which clips into the standard aperture.

CR11. Offer up the radio and fit the wires to the terminals. There are special speaker wire clips supplied with this radio and these have to be fitted to the wires (the CORRECT wires) before clipping in to the set.

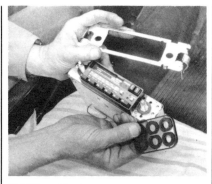

CR12. Fit the mounting kit and then the radio. There should be spacers supplied with the kit to pack the radio spindles so that not too much of the spindles show.

CR13. Tune the radio to a weak station, low down on the frequency scale and turn the antenna/aerial trimmer until you achieve maximum volume.

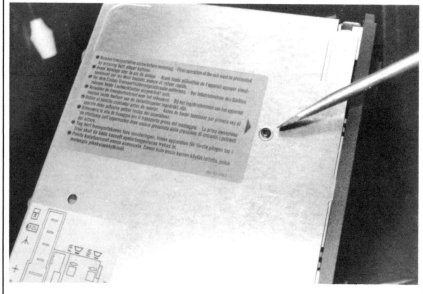

CR14. Many radios have their trimmer mounted in the body, in which case it may be necessary to tune the trimmer before inserting the radio. The location of the trimmer will be described in the fitting instructions.

CR15. Another common type of fitting system is the 'cage' type where a complete 'cage' is fitted into the mounting slot and the radio then pushes in, automatically clipping into place. It's then impossible to remove without the 'keys' supplied; theoretically, that's a great anti-theft device, but it's not so great if the frustrated thief starts carving the dash about in a desperate attempt to force the radio out!

8 Modifications

Left-hand to Right-hand Drive Beetle Conversion (or vice versa)

Quite a number of Beetles are taken into Britain from the European mainland and, of course, they all have left-hand drive. Some owners are happy to drive them as they are; others hate not being able to see to overtake safely. So, for them, here's how House of Haselock converted a 1302LS Cabriolet. There will be differences between this and other models, particularly those with differing steering layouts, but the basic principles are shown here. If anyone in North America or Continental Europe should somehow import a right-hand drive car and want to go the other way, why not?

But first, a major word of warning! The skills required to carry out this work are not in themselves above average (although the work is time consuming), but the need for everything to be soundly done and for everything to be well fitted and to line-up exactly as it ought to, is paramount and so the work must be done by someone who is totally competent in these areas and with a high sense of engineering accuracy. If you have the slightest doubt as to your skills in this area, don't do it but leave the work to a specialist.

DC1.   First job was to strip out the wiring loom from behind the dash and to remove all of the instruments. Needless to say, the battery had been disconnected. All of the wires were carefully tagged with pieces of masking tape on which their locations were carefully written and a sketch was made to back this up. They're nothing if not thorough at Haselocks!

DC2.   Getting straight on with it, the position of the steering column hole was measured with meticulous accuracy from a non-converted right-hand drive car and the position marked under the dash.

DC3. Barry Haselock used a tank cutter set to the right size to bore the steering column hole.

DC6. The steering column support tunnel won't be any good to you on the wrong side! Haselocks took one from a scrap car, cutting it away, scuttle panel and all.

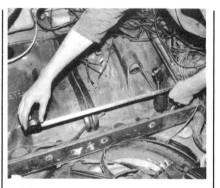

DC9. Once again, the tunnel positioning has to be done with great precision, but it is a good idea to carry out a rough-and-ready double check too, just to confirm that you are in the right part of the car!

DC4. The column was taken off the other side. (See section on 'Steering' for details.)

DC7. Then the mini-grinder was used to grind through each of the spot welds, through the unwanted lower panel, leaving a sound, complete tunnel.

DC10. The lower part of the tunnel has a flat which can't now be welded into place unless you drill a few holes in the scuttle panel and plug-weld from beneath.

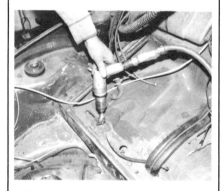

DC5. The fuel tank had been taken out and the position where the lower part of the steering column disappeared through the floor beneath the fuel tank was very accurately marked and bored.

DC8. If you don't have access to a scrap car, you could cut out the existing tunnel, drilling out the spot welds as shown in some of the 'Bodywork' sections of this book.

DC11. Later, the tunnel can be seam welded around its edge, but for now it could be pop-riveted in place.

DC12. There's also a dash support-cum-steering column mounting plate which can also be transferred from another car.

DC14. Use the replacement as a template and cut out the old dash, leaving a small area or overlap.

DC15. Once again, because the steering column is mounted there, the dash has to be positioned with great accuracy. It can be held initially, until it is welded in, with clamps and/or pop-rivets or screws.

DC13. One of the hardest parts of the operation could be in finding a replacement dash for your car. This was a second-hand dash (and why not?), but if you wished to, you could buy a new panel from Volkswagen. Do remember to get hold of the dash trim panels (at the time of writing, some of these were no longer available from Volkswagen) and cut out the new dash to include the mounting holes and recess for the steering column mounting. If you use a second-hand dash, include the steering column mounting.

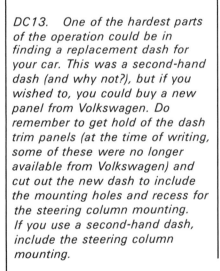

DC16. Along the bottom of the replacement dash, holes were drilled by Ghenti, the Haselock panel beater, so that it could be plug welded by the MIG welder. Later, when ground off, these would be virtually invisible but still very strong.

DC17.	The edges of the dash were seam welded by Ghenti then ground flush. On this car, a new plastic dash cover was obtained through the Volkswagen main dealer so the welds here were covered. Even if they're not, it should be perfectly possible to present a smooth, unblemished surface with very careful use of filler, provided that the work is as neatly and tidily done as Ghenti is capable of doing it.

DC18.	The steering systems on the Beetle are all described in the section on 'Steering'. But the conversion was made easy here because although there is a separate steering box and idler, they fit the same mounting points and are interchangeable.

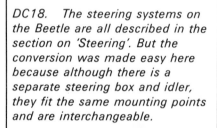

DC19.	Here the car is on its side as the steering box (or idler) is removed from the inner wing/fender area. The steering arms were retained and the steering damper was swapped around so that it faced the other way, but still retaining the same central mounting.

DC20.	Easily the hardest part of the whole job was changing the foot pedals over. Here the old pedal cluster is being unbolted. (By this time the car was stripped of its bodywork — you wouldn't otherwise see so clearly what is going on.)

DC21. Another pedal cluster was obtained from a right-hand drive car, checked to see that the bushings were all sound, and fitted up. (See section on 'Brakes'.) Note that the redundant hole in the frame head has been covered over with a specially cut out plate and gasket.

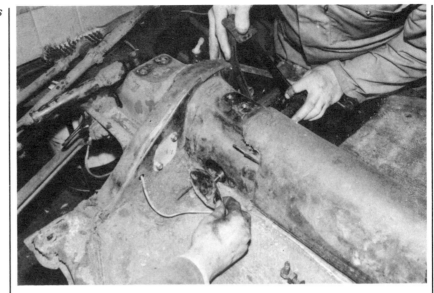

DC22. Of course, a mounting hole had first to be cut into the other side of the central tunnel. The tunnel was covered with masking tape and a card template cut out.

DC24. Exactly the same meticulous system was used to establish the position of the new holes in the frame head.

DC25. Here the new master cylinder supplied by Uro Autoparts was fitted — it would be crazy not to overhaul the system having got it to this stage . . .

DC23. Then after the position was marked onto the tunnel and the mounting holes centre punched for accuracy, the mounting holes were drilled and the large central hole cut out. A series of holes were drilled close together around the edge, the hole was chiselled out and carefully filed to shape.

DC26. . . . followed by the pedal cluster as described in detail in the section on 'Brakes'.

DC27. There has to be provision for bolting the pedal cluster to the floor . . .

DC28. . . . and the throttle pedal too. In both cases, Volkswagen had left indentations in the floor pressings which obviously serve for both types of market. But don't just rely on those indentations; measure up accurately too.

Apart from the steering column hole beneath the dash, which could be filled with a grommet or welded up, there is no need for there to be any visible evidence that the car has been converted, especially since the moved steering column tunnel is hidden beneath the fuel tank. After all, they were only made out of pieces of metal to start off with, so what's wrong with re-arranging those pieces of metal — provided that the work is done with scrupulous thoroughness and complete accuracy?

Improving Your Split-Screen Transporter Heater (text provided by the Split Screen Van Club)

The heater blower Motor

I obtained this from a 412 Variant together with the associated dual cut-out connector and mounting bracket. The blower is found on the left-hand side of the engine compartment. The blower of a Type 4 saloon could be used although the twin outputs are less convenient. Remember that these blowers are 12v — perhaps an alternative 6v motor could be found for earlier 'Splits'. I fitted the blower to the left-hand side of my engine compartment, suspended by its bracket, with the input nozzle pointed towards the rear, having ensured that the non-return flap was vertical.

The air ducts

I made these using an old 5 litre oil can as raw material. A strip of the metal was formed into a tube 6ins. long with a diameter the same as that of the inside of the cardboard hose which connects the fan housing to the heat exchanger. The seam was soldered. A second tube of only 4ins. length was made and this

was grafted on to the first at an angle of 45 degrees. I now had a pipe junction which looked something like a motorway exit sign! It was not difficult to produce a neat and airtight job using copious amounts of solder. Two of these ducts were needed.

Connecting up

First of all the old cardboard tubes were removed from the fan housing. The two new ducts were pressed down into the tops of the primary heat exchangers with the 'motorway exits' pointing upwards towards the fan housing. Two short lengths of card hose connected the fan housing to the legs of the ducts. Two long lengths of card hose, supported by nylon cable straps were necessary connecting the tops of the ducts to the blower output.

Controls

A dashboard switch provided a switched, ignition controlled, supply to a relay which in turn supplied power to the blower which draws up to 7 amps. I protected the supply with an 8 amp fuse in an ex-Beetle fuse holder.

In action

The system now supplied a constant flow of hot air. Demisting is far more effective and the cab more comfortable. The only disadvantage to date has been a tendency for the ignition lamp to glow *very slightly* on those wintry mornings when I have the headlights, wipers and the blower on together and the engine is at idle.

Additional Improvements

In addition to the blower I have insulated the heat exchangers using the insulated covers fitted to the Type 3 units. These are slightly longer than the Type 1 or 2 units so the covers need trimming. The steel protection

plates on the underside and rear of the Type 3 exchangers have also been fitted. Insulating jackets removed from the later model Type 2 were fitted to the long, fore and aft heater duct below the floor. These are needed, especially at the front end where the heat loss is at its greatest.

The system is at least three times as efficient as previously!

Transporter Spare Wheel Carrier

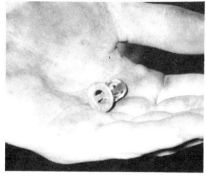

TSW1.   After taking off the 'VW' badge at the front of the Transporter, Stuart Haselock took out the captive nuts from the Haselock fixing kit.

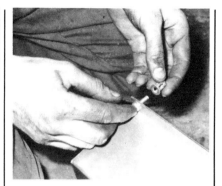

TSW2.   Here's how they work: They're pushed into holes drilled into the front of the body, then when the spare wheel carrier is bolted up tight, the nuts expand and grip in place.

TSW3.   Stuart had held the carrier precisely in position, marked the holes and drilled them to match the captive nuts taking care to avoid any of the wiring and other 'plumbing' in there — see Transporter Front Panel Replacement section.

TSW4.   He'd started the screws through the carrier and into the captive nuts. The nuts may bottom on the inner skin, but they shorten as well as spread when tightened. If they still seem to bottom, tap them in against the inner skin with a hammer, but make sure you're not mistakenly trapping any inner wiring.

TSW5. *Then it's just a matter of bolting on the spare wheel, freeing up a lot of very useful space inside the load bay. A cover with 'VW' insignia sets the whole thing off really well.*

Split-Screen Transporter Parts Swaps

(text produced by the Split-Screen Van Club)

Engines & Gearboxes & Exhausts

Many people have written to the Club enquiring about suitable engines/gearboxes for their vans and about the interchangeability of these units with other models. This is an attempt at a comprehensive run-down of this subject.

Original engines

The engines fitted to these vans paralleled their Beetle counterparts.

Up to 1954	1200cc 25bhp
1954–1959	1200cc 30bhp
1960–1961	1200cc 34bhp (non fresh-air)
1961–1964	1200cc 34bhp (fresh-air)
1965–1967	1500cc

The 1300cc unit was never used in these vans. 1967 models had 12v electrics.

Possible replacements

Vans fitted with 1200cc engines, despite their lower gear ratios, are rather underpowered. Unless you want to keep your van original it is not difficult to uprate this as any Beetle or van engine up to 1600cc can be fitted although brakes must be uprated to a suitable extent and 'chassis' components must be in first-class order.

Differences between engines

The 25bhp, 30bhp and early 34bhp engines all have non fresh-air heating. The design of the crankcase of the 25/30bhp units is entirely different from the later 1200cc engines, the most easily distinguishable feature being the integral dynamo pillar. The exhaust on these engines is not interchangeable with the 34bhp non fresh-air exhaust.

From 1962 the 34bhp 1200cc engine was fitted with fresh-air heat exchangers and looks similar to all other upright air-cooled VW engines. However, the stroke is shorter which means the distance between the exhaust ports on the cylinder heads is also shorter. This in turn means that the exhaust and top engine tin are narrower. The inlet manifold is also of a different design. These differences do not present a problem with secondhand replacements as these are generally complete with all ancillaries. Recon. engines are usually supplied 'short' so if you are fitting a larger replacement for a 1200 there will be some complications.

Exhausts

There is no problem in obtaining a van exhaust for a 13/15/1600cc engine. They are all interchangeable and all the same as the exhausts fitted to the later 1600cc engines (apart from the tail pipe which is curly rather than right angles). 1200 van exhausts for the 34bhp fresh-air engines are also still available. The earlier 1200cc engines van exhausts are scarce. Of course, a Beetle exhaust can be used with the tail pipes stuck through holes cut in the bumper! This is not an ideal solution because either the bumper or the tail pipes have to be removed before the engine can be taken out.

Clutches

1200 and 1300cc engines use a 180mm clutch whereas the 1500/1600cc engines use a 200mm clutch. This difference in size only affects the pressure and centre plates. The thrust bearing is the same on all Split-Screen Vans. It does mean, though, that if you are uprating from 1200cc to 1500 or 1600cc you will have to buy a new clutch. Although the 1200 (180mm) flywheel could be fitted to the larger engine it would not be advisable to use the smaller diameter clutch. (Of course it is also possible to fit a larger clutch to a 1200/1300cc engine by changing the flywheel.)

Flywheels

Apart from the difference in clutch size there is also the difference between 6v (109 teeth) and 12v (132 teeth). If you buy a 12v engine to fit into a 6v vehicle the flywheels can easily be changed round. It is not so simple if you want to fit a 6v engine to a 12v vehicle. The end of the 6v crankshaft is of a slightly larger diameter than the 12v shaft so the flywheel will need to be ground out to fit over the shaft.

6 or 12v?

This is covered in depth in the 'Electrics' section of this book and although it relates to the Beetle, most of it applies equally to the Type 2.

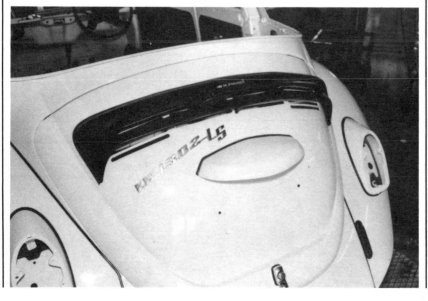

Fitting a Spoiler and Engine Vent Cover

Spoiler

S&VC1.   A Kamei front spoiler was used here simply because it's the best around. It bolts to the lower edge of the front bumper with four bolts passing through both the bumper and the spoiler with a good thick rubber washer between each of them. To stop the bottom of it flapping around it also screws to the front wing. Here the House of Haselock fitter is drilling a hole in the front of the spoiler and into the front wing ready to take . . .

S&VC2.   . . . a large self-tapping screw which passes right through the spoiler and locates in the front wing. Again, there is a thick rubber washer to fit between them to cut out any vibration or chafing.

Vent Cover

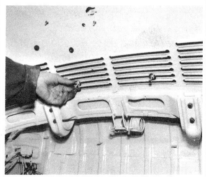

S&VC3.   The Kamei rear lid cover is held in place with bolts which pass through the slats in the grid itself.

S&VC4.   It stops water gathering in the engine tray and is an attractive addition to the car.

If either of these are to be painted see the Prep. & Paint Section for details.

Interior Trim Accessories

TA1. Kamei also produce this excellent oddments tray which fits into the space around and to the front of the gear lever. Where else would you keep your rubbish?

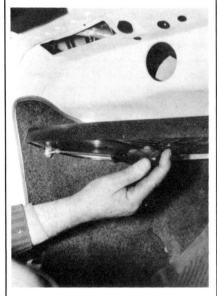

TA2. And there's also a Kamei parcel shelf which clamps beneath the dash, although it's not recommended here if you've got big-ish feet since they tend to catch when braking.

FRS2. First, strip down the seat base as shown under the section on 'Front Seats: Renewing The Covers' under 'Interior Trim'. The sprung base is held to the frame with tabs of metal . . .

FRS3. . . . which are bent back then cut off, after the springing has been taken away.

Fitting Replacement Seats

FRS1. Cobra make an excellent range of replacement car seats in the UK, such as this one shown here with its own headrest. Cobra also sell their own range of fitting kits but this section shows how to adapt the existing seat bases. The process is suitable for most replacement seat types.

FRS4.   The tilt mechanism is removed by cutting through the cross tube, level with the outsides of the frame. You can now weld a couple of cross-pieces onto the frame to match up with your Cobra seat, or whatever make you have selected (make sure they fit!), screw the seat to the frame and slide the fully adjustable frame back into place in the car.

Front Auxiliary Lamps

Beetle headlamps are not noted for their excellence but you can't uprate them to quartz halogen spec. The best way of overcoming the problem is to fit auxiliary dipping lamps (check that they're legal in your area) giving twin dip and high beams.

FAL1.   The Cibie Oscars shown here are acknowledged to be about the best you can get. See section on spraying for information on spraying the shells to match the car body colour. Brackets were made up to fit the bumper brackets and the shells bolted down using Cosmic (sold in the UK) locking spotlamp fittings.

FAL2.   The wires were connected up to the headlamp circuit, but if your auxiliary lamps are to be switcheable, you would be best advised to wire them in via a relay to avoid placing too much load on the switch and long wiring runs. The lamps were set up on headlamp beam setter to ensure correct settings. Their appearance set off the front of the car wonderfully well and performance is terrific!

Wheels and Tyres

There are almost as many tyre manufacturers as there are wheel manufacturers, or so it seems. But the choice is an important one because the cars safety, handling, the correct speedometer setting and engine revs. to say nothing of the car's looks, all rely to an extent on wheels and tyres. I selected Pirelli P4 tyres because of their international reputation for superb grip and good wearing properties, and Cyclone wheels because they seemed to offer the very best combination of looks, durability and easy-to-clean properties. Wheels with too many nooks and crannies can be an absolute pain to keep clean in dirty weather!

Another consideration will be the rolling circumference of the wheels and tyres chosen. If you go down from 15 in. wheels, the standard Beetle size, you'll have to increase the tyre size to 185 (i.e. 185 mm width) to gain extra tyre 'height' and put back most of the missing rolling circumference. Naturally enough, Pirelli are experts on the subject and will be delighted to answer queries about which are the best sizes of tyre to select for your car.

W&T1. These Cyclone wheels foul the disc brake callipers on this model of Beetle unless front wheel spacers are used. But that makes fitting the wheels extremely difficult! Here's how I overcame the problem: I went to my local Mercedes dealer and bought a pair of wheel bolts from a G-Wagen cross country vehicle which are the same thread but much longer than Beetle bolts. The head was cut off each.

W&T2. These dummy studs were screwed into the hub, one in each of two opposing bolt holes. The wheel spacer was placed over them.

W&T3. Then the wheel was fitted, the dummy studs again acting as guides and supports, and then the two vacant bolt holes were used to insert two 'proper' wheel bolts. Once they were in place, the dummy studs were screwed out and the other two 'proper' wheel bolts fitted.

W&T4. Cyclone can supply, as well as the correct chromed wheel bolts which are of very high quality finish, lockable bolts which only unlock with the correct 'key' — an excellent way of protecting some very fine and expensive but very vulnerable wheels and tyres from theft.

Fitting An Anti-Theft Device

Although it's virtually impossible to make any car totally theftproof, the trick is to make it *difficult* to steal, so that the potential thief will go elsewhere. After all, there are plenty of other cars in the car park and if yours looks as though it will be risky to steal, the thief will almost certainly leave it alone. One of the simplest ways of thief-proofing a car is to fit a concealed switch in an extended version of one of the low tension wires to the distributor and, indeed, the Sparkrite electronic ignition includes a switch to unable you to switch the ignition 'off'. However, by the time these systems work,

the thief is in your car and could have helped himself to the audio system or vandalised the interior.

Other systems work by 'arming' the cars electrical system so that any change in the current output — for instance, by opening a door and turning on the courtesy light, will cause the alarm to sound. Most are key operated which means that the bodywork has to be cut into and, again, the thief is unlikely to know about the system until he has started on your car. An attractive alternative is the Sparkrite AT-100 system shown here.

AT1. The system is operated by a 'switch' fitted to the windscreen of the car from the inside. A self-adhesive pad holds it in place and the wires from the 'switch' run down the side of the dash or through a vent. The 'key' is an infra-red sender unit which is small enough to double as a key fob and fits on your key ring. The windscreen-mounted unit flashes subtly to itself, giving a clear warning to would-be thieves.

AT2. A control box to which the wiring from horn, lamps and courtesy lights is taken fits in the luggage bay. The Sparkrite kit includes extra switches so that you can protect the engine cover and fuel filler flap, too, if you wish. The battery itself is also connected to pick up any other power drain, such as from the turning of the ignition key.

AT3. Haselocks like to fit the alarm horn in the luggage bay, preventing a thief from disconnecting the wiring and neutralising the horn. The Sparkrite AT-100 is easy to use and to fit in accordance with the clear instructions enclosed and the infra-red key is coded to each individual car.

BUD2. They fit beneath the Beetle bumper and have to protrude a touch so that the great curve of the bumper doesn't affect the beam.

Fitting a Back-up Device

BUD1. VW Campers and Transporters, Cabriolets and early cars with small rear windows are all difficult or even dangerous to back-up because visibility to the rear is so restricted. One answer is to fit a warning device that uses ultrasonics to detect rear obstructions. The Range Master, marketed by Sandalloy in the UK does just that with the two sensors which are screwed or bolted to the rear bumper, as shown.

BUD3. A 'black box' is fitted somewhere suitable — here beneath the engine bay trim, although behind the rear seat would be fine — into which the devices wires are connected with the DIN plugs already fitted.

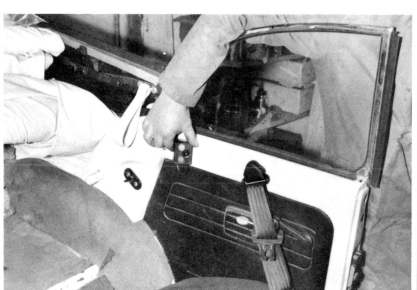

BUD4. Last, the indicator unit is fitted in the driver's line of vision when reversing and again the connecting cable connected to the 'black box' after drilling a suitable hole through the rear fire wall. The indicator glows orange and 'beeps' intermittently when the vehicle is three feet away from an obstacle then glows red and 'beeps' continuously when the vehicle is half that distance closer. If you're worried about children or pets or even damaging your vehicle when parking, the Range Master is a great reassurance.

⑨ Buggies, Bajas and Specials

This section is based around showing you how to fit a Baja kit to a Beetle, using a kit supplied by UVA Ltd (See 'Suppliers' section). The kit was fitted at House of Haselock (see 'Suppliers' also, for address) where virtually all of the work shown in this book was carried out. Remember that you will invariably have to carry out repairs as well as to simply fit the kit . . .

Tool Box

You'll need a hacksaw, electric drill and a file, a mini grinder, sharp bolster chisel and hammer, rule and scriber, pop rivets and a gun and a face mask (See 'Safety').

Safety

Apart from the usual hazards associated with carrying out bodywork repairs, and especially that of the risk of cuts from sharp cut metal edges, the main risk here is with fibreglass. Avoid inhaling dust from drilled, cut or filed fibreglass as the strands can be injurious to your lungs. If you use polyester resin, take note of the manufacturer's safety instructions, especially with regard to the catalyst.

You start by removing the luggage bay lid as shown in the relevant section of this book, as well as the engine cover, remembering to disconnect the license plate/number plate light lead for re-use. Unbolt and remove both running boards and retain the bolts for re-use if you intend fitting a side bar kit. Remove lights, bumpers, trim and other fittings as shown in the stripdown part of the bodywork repair section.

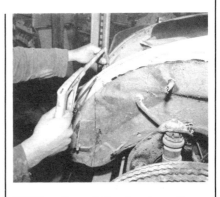

BBS2.   Cut off the front section taking off the superfluous bracket shown here . . .

BBS1.   After removing all four wings, make reference to the shape of the replacement nose piece and mark out the inner wing/fender panel accordingly.

BBS3.   . . . and take the complete front section away after cutting across the rear of the spare wheel well.

BBS4. Here the House of Haselock welder repairs the spare wheel well, basically as shown in the repair section of this book, but shaped to fit the more restricted shape of the kit's front end.

BBS5. The inner panels then had to be extended to match the Baja's front panel. An alternative would have been to have cut the inner panel at this point and to grind off the old, unwanted bracket.

BBS6. The new section was offered up and pop-riveted in place.

BBS7. Then the luggage bay lid (Baja variety) was fitted to the hinges. UVA recommend that you either take off the lid spring altogether and add a stay, or weaken the spring to take account of the fibreglass lid being so much lighter than the steel one.

BBS8. Almost plan view from the House of Haselock balcony shows the lid being used to check the fit of the front panel before many pop-rivets are added to the few used to hold it in position. The luggage bay lid must close on and touch the new nose panel and the existing side panels at the same time.

BBS9. Now you can see the inner wing/fender cleaned up and de-rusted, the line of pop-rivets holding the front panel in place and the markings and drilled holes in the front panel where the new front wing/fender has been offered up for marking out. None of these things are pre-drilled!

BBS10. For 'rear' read 'front' where the procedure is similar except that the cut out is left open apart from a top cover and the cut off steel matches the edges of the rear wings/fenders. See later pictures.

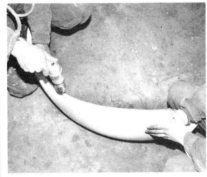

BBS12. . . . transfer this measurement to the wing/fender flange and drill it out.

BBS13. When offering up and fitting the new rear wing/fender, ensure that its edge and the rear panel cut-off point match.

BBS11. In order to drill the mounting bolt holes in the correct positions in the wing/fenders, mark the body panel with pencil lines at the positions of the holes, hold the new wing/fender into place and copy the positions of the pencil lines onto it. Draw a pencil line around the edge of the wing/fender on the car body, measure the correct distance in from the line to the centre of the hole in the bodywork . . .

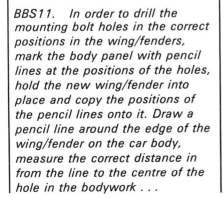

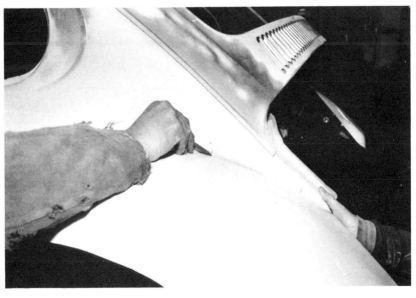

BBS14. Then the rear replacements can be bolted on in the normal way, ensuring that new, large flat washers are used to spread the load.

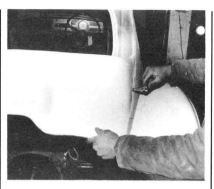

BBS15. In similar fashion, the rear lid is drilled and bolted into place.

BBS16. Apart from the marking out and drilling shown in BBS9. fitting the front wings follows the same pattern.

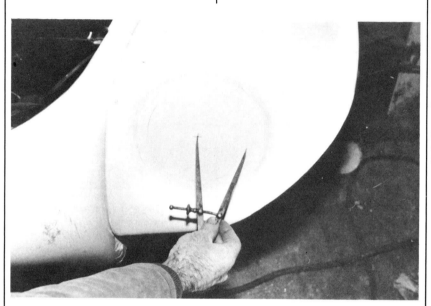

BBS17. You could use second-hand 7in. headlamps or new Cibie quartz halogen lamps, according to the depth of your pocket. Measure the centre of the mounting position, scribe a circle (kid sister's school compass or a piece of 1/8th welding wire with both ends sharpened and bent in the middle would do) . . .

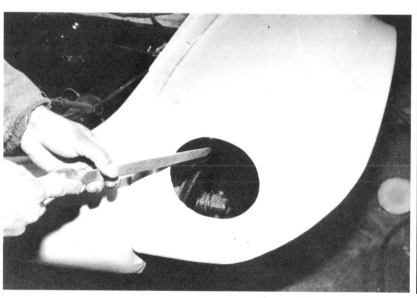

BBS18. Drill around the inner side of the line . . .

BBS19. . . . knock out the surplus and file smooth.

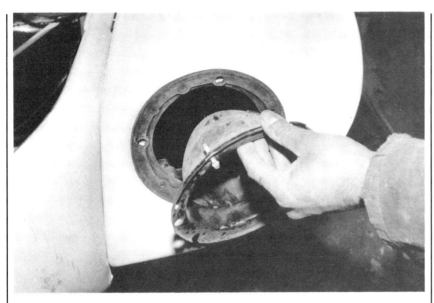

BBS20. Then the new lamp can be simply fitted into place.

Finishing, fitting-up and painting are virtually the same as for a standard restored Beetle. In fact, the Baja Bug respray is shown in part of the 'Prep. and Paint' section.

The verdict? With the original wheels, the car appeared ridiculous, but really wide wheels gave it a meaty appearance. The kit itself was, in the words of Barry Haselock, 'a pain to fit' since nothing seemed to go together very well. For instance, the luggage bay lid was not a brilliant fit and the headlamp blanks were sloping back, so the mountings had to be specially built to stop the beams pointing up high. On the other hand, it looked really good, especially when the joints were blended in with filler and rubbed down and the quality of the fibreglass seemed strong. Fitting a kit is actually more expensive than replacing old panels with new and, in any case, if outer panels have deteriorated, you'll have to carry out restoration repairs to the (undoubtedly) equally rotten inner stuff, but if you just fancy the looks of a Baja kit, fitting one isn't too tough!

BBS21. You can actually turn your rusty Beetle into a completely new car using one of the many body kits on the market. This is the UVA Montage which comes equipped with a host of extras, it seems, including air conditioning if you want it.

BBS22. It's based on the Type 1 'swing-axle' Beetle, but apparently many owners fit uprated chassis and engine specs to these cars; with a 2.2 VW engine, the makers claim 0–60 in 7 secs. and a top speed of 127 mph!

BBS23. At the other end of the sophistication scale (except in engineering terms) come UVA's range of Beetle-based dune buggies and racers.

BBS24. They're as tough as they look and they put out some 'go' to enable them to achieve this sort of lift off! As with their other models, these are mostly DIY built using the parts supplied.

10 Tuning the Beetle

This section appeared originally as a series of articles in 'VW Motoring', the VW owners' magazine. It was written by leading Beetle tuning expert Alan Arnold, Managing Director of UVA Ltd, foremost suppliers in the UK of Beetle tuning parts (see 'Suppliers' section for address). It was compiled and edited for 'VW Motoring' by Peter Dickinson.

Safety

None of the modifications shown here, apart from 'mild' engine improvements to 1500 and 1600cc cars, are recommended by the author of this book for road use since they do not comply with the manufacturer's original design specifications. Any structural work should be checked by a competent, qualified mechanic.

When the word 'tuning is mentioned, most people's thoughts immediately turn to engines with multiple carburettors, hot camshafts and the like. During the course of this section, however, we will use the term to cover all aspects of modifying the Beetle from the ground up. After all, it's no use having a fire breathing monster of a car if it's going to collide with the scenery at the first bend!

From the logical point of view, the car has to handle and stop at least as well as it goes, both for driveability and from the safety aspect. So, before getting down to details, we will have a general look around the suspension and brakes to see what can be done . . .

Suspension and Brakes

There are three basic models of Beetle referred to here:

	Models	Years	Front Suspension	Rear Suspension
A.	12/13/15/1600	1967–1978	Torsion bar	Swing axle
B.	1302/1302S	1970–1972	MacPherson strut	Double CV
C.	1303/1303S	1973–1977	MacPherson strut	Double CV

The optimum chassis uses the torsion bar front suspension from the Beetles in group A and the rear suspension from the Beetles in groups B and C. The ideal way to achieve this is to buy a Beetle 1302/1303 chassis, have the MacPherson strut frame head cut off and replaced by a Beetle torsion bar front frame head. The Beetle front beam will then bolt straight to it. Oddly enough, this chassis package is the original set-up found on 1968–1970 American model Beetles and can also be found on European automatic Beetles.

Before we go into depth on how to improve the handling further let's just examine what we have in terms of chassis concept. Starting with the suspension at the back end: this is a fully independent trailing arm arrangement where the driveshaft is a non-suspension-stressed member (unlike the swing-axle Beetle system where the drive shaft is part of the suspension to chassis connection).

The VW's torsion bar front suspension is a sound design and can be adjusted to fine-tune it. For tarmac use, go for the later balljoint beam found on Beetles after 1967; while the pre '67 beams are better for off-road applications because the link/kingpin design allows for greater suspension travel without bottoming-out the top and bottom swivels. The 11½" diameter disc brakes found on the 1500cc Beetle are ample for stopping higher horsepower cars as proven by Manta cars in the USA who used this front set up on their 350 cu in mid-engined V8 Mirage street race car.

Height adjustment

The ride height is determined by the centre mount of both top and bottom beams. The torsion leaves traverse from the left suspension arm through the fixed centre mount and connect up to the right hand arm. This system is identical on both top and bottom tubes. Sway-a-Way produce an adjustable centre mount which replaces the fixed centre by way of hacksawing out the old mount and welding in the front end adjuster.

Steering

When you are running with wider wheels and tyres any discrepancies in the steering geometry are magnified, especially when you raise or lower the car. So a few simple steps will ensure you don't experience the dreaded 'bump steer'.

The Beetle's steering box is clamped around the top transverse tube of the front beam assembly. With a lowered car, loosen the mounting clamps and rotate the steering box so that the steering arms are brought to the horizontal. With horizontal steering arms (when the chassis is fully loaded with its body, fuel tank, spare wheel etc.) the arc in which they move during suspension movement minimises their tendency to shorten geometrically – confused? Well, don't worry, just get 'em horizontal.

If you are going for a real 'pan scraper' you may experience problems in twisting the steering box enough to get into the horizontal plane. The answer here is to move the outer steering balljoints from the mounting above the steering arm to below it. Because the balljoints are a taper fit, your local machine shop will come in handy to machine up a fitting to achieve this. The steering arms are now lower and *level*. Don't forget to set the toe-in to 1/16". Also, remember that excessive lowering will require shorter shock absorbers.

Bushings

The side load imparted into the front beam when cornering hard is very high; these side loads are transmitted into the torsion leaves allowing the wheels to change camber. The expedient is simplicity itself.

Remove the four outer needle roller bearings into which each of the four suspension arms fit and replace them with urethane front end grommets. These urethane bushings have a flange, allowing the suspension arms to bear against this as opposed to bearing directly into the torsion leaves. The bushes also give a better bearing surface in which the suspension arms may pivot.

Front shock absorbers

Fit adjustables; they allow you to tune the ride comfort and handling to suit yourself and are a bolt on fit.

Front anti roll bar (sway bar)

A stiffer front anti roll bar helps control body roll and improves tyre adhesion under hard cornering. The stiffer bar is a direct replacement for the standard one and uses the original fixing brackets but with urethane mounts to improve handling further.

Front beam location

The beam is bolted to the chassis with four bolts which are fairly close to the centre of the chassis. Front suspension stiffeners attach to the extremities of the beam and locate it to the outer edges of the chassis floor pan. These stiffeners in effect widen the mounting base of the front beam which stops the beam flexing under hard cornering or braking.

Adjustment

One of the many unique and useful advantages the VW chassis offers is adjustability, so that you can fine-tune it to your particular requirements and get it *spot-on*.

Pay particular attention to the concentric top swivel mounting, atop each front upright. This little gizmo allows you to adjust the front wheel camber and castor. Set this up to 0–½° negative camber and keep the little pointer, on the concentric top nut, towards the rear of chassis. This move will make sure that you have as much castor as is practical on the front. This extra castor helps maintain straight line direction as opposed to the car wandering from side to side on the road.

Steering damper

The stock unit has proven to be ideal providing it is not worn out.

Front brakes

As mentioned previously, the 1500cc Beetle front beam has disc brakes as standard. If your beam does not have discs, don't worry, a complete front disc brake conversion kit is available which includes new discs, stub axles, bearings, seals, hoses and the latest large calipers which give even better braking.

That about covers the front end but one final word which goes for all the work you are undertaking: make sure all the remaining standard parts are in good condition, as any worn parts will not allow the special suspension parts to work to their optimum.

Turning to the rear of the car we will go through it in the same way, starting with

Rear height adjustment

Unlike the front suspension's ten torsion leaves per tube the rear torsion bar has a solid sprung bar each side with different spline ratios at each end of it. These splines allow you to pull the spring plate off the torsion bar and reposition it around the splined bar's circumference, to raise or lower the car's ride height. In

practice, this operation becomes a hit or miss method because each torsion bar inevitably wears differently. With trial and error (and, in particular, patience) you can eventually get the setting equal and to your chosen ride height.

Because of this hassle, adjustable spring plates are available. They are designed to replace the original spring plate and offer two main advantages. Firstly, they enable you to adjust the car's ride height independently each side so that the car can be set up perfectly level regardless of the torsion bars' inaccuracies. Secondly, it offers a stronger spring plate than stock which gives better suspension location and improved handling.

Rear bushings

The spring plates rotate in rubber bushings which are clamped in place by the torsion bar's outer bearing housing. The bushes not only act as bearings for the rotating torsion bar but also locate the forward and rearward movement of the suspension. Their compliance is too soft for sports car handling so they are replaced with urethane bushes.

There are five different sizes and styles of bushes used by VW so a little homework with a ruler is necessary to identify which type is fitted. Basically there are three sizes with four locating lugs on each of them (known as the knobby type grommets) 1¾" ID, 1⅞" ID, 2" ID, and two sizes with no lugs (known as round type grommets) 1¾" ID and 1⅞" ID. The knobby type grommets are normally on the outside of the spring plates and the round type on the inner side. If you are using adjustable spring plates then the size of the bushes is relevant only to these spring plates, 2" knobby outer and 1⅞" round inner.

The spring plate is attached to the main A-arm of the rear suspension and this A-arm has its own inner pivoting location bush.

Replace this rubber bush also with a urethane kit.

Rear suspension lowering

Volkswagen, in their design wisdom, built into their double jointed rear suspension a percentage of negative camber which increases as the suspension is compressed. The idea of this negative camber is to help keep the wheel upright (for better tyre-to-ground contact) when the suspension is compressed and the body is rolling about the chassis pivot point in a hard cornering situation.

When you attempt to lower the back end by several inches to match your pan-scraping front end, this negative camber becomes more apparent and excessive, especially when viewed from the rear of the car. Your super double jointed rear suspension starts to resemble the earlier Beetle swing axle type. A solution is at hand.

You will need the assistance of a hammer and a sharp cold chisel. Carefully break the welds that hold the shock absorber towers and bump stop mounts to each of the suspension A-arms. Remove these two mounts from each A-arm and keep them in place relevant to their respective handlings, i.e. keep the left-hand side parts left and the right-hand side parts right, right? — good.

Now swap over the A-arms only, flip the left one over to the right-hand side and the right one over to the left-hand side. So far what you should have done is turn each A-arm upside down and swapped left to right. Now have each shock absorber tower rewelded on to its new A-arm by a top-class welder in exactly the same position as before relevant to the chassis and the top shock absorber mount.

If you are going really low do not reaffix the bump stop mounts, but use a different method like urethane bump stops to increase your travel. If a medium ride height is envisaged, cut the original metal mount down to

bring it closer to the A-arm and also cut the rubber bump stop down to approximately 1" in height.

Rear shock absorbers

Fit adjustables; these will allow you to determine your own ride comfort and will even cater for the heavily lowered rear end.

Rear anti roll bar

There is a kit which bolts on to the chassis frame horns and picks up on the lower shock tower mounts. The kit has a ¾" sway bar and urethane mounts and can be adjusted to introduce suspension jacking for the circuit racer. The advantages are reduced body roll and improved tyre adhesion.

Adjustment

The rear suspension should be adjusted similarly to the front end with 1/16" toe-in. Make sure this is equal on both sides, i.e. firstly, each wheel should be parallel with the front end and then set to 1/32" toe-in on each side making 1/16" in total. This adjustment is achieved by loosening the three bolts that attach the spring plates to the A-arms; the bolt holes are elongated for forward and rearward adjustment. Rear wheel camber is not adjustable, your only other adjustment is the ride height.

Rear brakes

The standard rear drum brakes are OK for medium performance engines, but if you are going for an all-out power house then change the rear drum brakes to discs. Rear disc brake conversions are available and include a mechanical hand brake (to keep within the law) and the latest hydraulic sliding calipers to give excellent braking capacity. Tuning houses can also supply the 11½" diameter front and rear discs drilled to improve brake cooling and efficiency.

General chassis information

One of the annoying design ideas in the Beetle floor pan is the use of bolts to hold the road wheels in place. These can cause aggravation when struggling to locate a wide wheel. A stud and nut conversion can be fitted, the studs screwing permanently into the drum so that you are rewarded with a conventional four-stud hub where the wheels are held in place with domed chrome nuts. (Or, see the author's suggested method of locating wheels or wheels and spacers whilst retaining the existing fitting method, under 'Fitting Wider Wheels'.)

The transmission is held in the chassis by rubber mounts and there are no conventional engine mounts as the engine hangs on to the back of the transmission. This system is an excellent idea and works very well. Its drawback, however, is the same as with any rubber mounted power plant; spirited acceleration makes for excessive engine and transmission movement. The answer is to replace the rubber mounts with urethane (vote for urethane — urethane rules — OK!). This material gets everywhere and is a great help in stopping the motor from trying to jump out of the chassis.

The alternative is to use solid mounts but they transmit engine vibrations into the chassis and make for uncomfortable long distance driving. If your car is already built then the quick expedient is to install an insulated trans-strap kit which keeps the transmission and engine in place whilst lead footing. This method won't require removal of the engine.

The other advantage of urethane transmission mounts is that they make for easy installation of water cooled engine conversions. Even a V8 Rover/Buick engine can be hung onto the VW transmission by way of one of UVA's engine adaptor

kits, and no other mounts are required.

Wheels & tyres

Choose your tyres wisely. The size of wheels and tyres will be determined by the kit design. An ideal size combination, if your kit will permit, is 7" x 14" fronts with 245/50 x 14" tyres and 8" x 15" rears with 275/50 x 15" tyres. Your choice of rubber wear should be a good brand radial. On narrow rims your choice is broad, on wider rims stick with BF Goodrich or Pirelli. Good quality radial tyres will take advantage of your suspension mods — cheapies will not.

If you need wheel spacers to fill out the wheel arches of your chosen dream machine, go for the solid long stud type which are safer and easier to use. Alternatively, use a good quality wheel adaptor if Jaguar/Chevy 4¾" pcd bolt pattern wheels are to be used.

If you are stuck with the Beetle swing axle rear end, don't despair. The above chassis tuning information can be used to tweak your Beetle pan to good effect. Just remember to mention you have swing axles when ordering the parts.

Adjustable Front Suspension

The first alternative is the Select-A-Drop, which is welded on to one of the two suspension beams, lowering just one beam and increasing the tension on the other, making for rather a rough ride.

The second alternative is a bolt-on Select-A-Drop. This does not require any cutting or welding but it does introduce stiffness into the suspension in the same way as the standard variety. In effect, it acts as a large clamp compressing the suspension between the steering arms and the chassis.

Again, the lower you go, the harder the ride.

The essence of any lowering device is the ability for it to be adjusted, so that the desired ride-height can be obtained once everything has settled. This adjustability is of particular value when a total 'body-off' rebuild is being undertaken, such as when building a kit car, because the final ride height cannot be ascertained until all the components have been fitted, including the occupants (and a full tank of petrol). There is then often some further settling after a few weeks of use as the various bits and pieces bed themselves in.

The most successful method of lowering the front end is to install Sway-A-Way front-end adjusters. These can be used for either lowering or raising the front end. It is worth mentioning at this point that each device available for adjusting front suspension height varies between the link/king-pin type and the balljoint type. If you are not sure which type of front suspension you have on your car, the link-pin front ends were used on VWs up to 1965 and the balljoint front ends were fitted to models from 1966 onwards.

The Sway-A-Way front end adjusters offer approximately 4" of front end adjustment. You can install just one of these front end adjusters into the top beam only, but this will give you two disadvantages.

The lowering adjustment will be limited because the tension will increase on the non-adjusted bottom beam. This will, in turn, give you a harsher ride. The best method is to put in two front end adjusters, one in each of both the top and bottom beams.

To install these the front beam has to be removed from the car and completely disassembled. This will entail undoing the four front bolts that hold the front beam to the chassis, undoing the additional two top bolts under the fuel tank, and removing the steering tie-rods and the steering shaft. Once the beam is out of the

car the steering box should be removed, the anti-roll bar removed, then remove the hub/stub axle assembly from the suspension arms, slacken the lock nuts and remove the Allen headed bolts from the four suspension arms, and withdraw these arms from the beam. Finally, slacken and remove the two Allen headed bolts from the centre of each beam and slide out the suspension leaves from both these beams.

Now clean the beam off and check for any rust damage. Because the installation of the Sway-A-Way adjuster requires welding, any minor rust damage can be repaired at the same time.

The first step is to mark a 3″ line lengthwise (horizontally) along the top tube through the centre of the set-screw hole which originally secured the front suspension leaves. This 3″ line should be 1½″ each side of the centre hole. Now mark a vertical line, 3″ long, around the circumference of the tube, again centrally through the centre fixing hole. Make a third line 3″ long and parallel with the first line, 9/16″ above this first line (you should have drawn an 'H' lying on its side). Now mark your cutting lines round the circumference of the tube an inch to the left and an inch to the right of the centre line. This means you will be cutting a 2″ section out of the centre. (The above details apply to balljoint axles only, although the fitting method for link/king-pin axles is similar. Full instructions are supplied with each kit.)

The cutting operation is best accomplished with a tube cutter. If a tube cutter is not available then utilise a worm drive clamp (jubilee clamp). Undo the clamp completely, open it out and put it over the tube and re-tighten it against your cutting line. The clamp will assist in giving you a cutting guide to make sure you cut through the tube squarely with a hacksaw.

Once this centre section has been removed, clean the edges with a file or angle-grinder. Before

installation of the adjusters you can set up for the direction or directions of adjustment you prefer; for example, if you want only downward adjustment (lowering) you should set the block and its set-screw as far back from the bracket as possible. If you require upward adjustment (raising) set the block and screw as close to the bracket as possible. Setting the block and screw in the middle of its movement will allow you both upward and downward adjustment. See illustration T10.

Once the adjuster has been placed in your desired position, installation can begin. As mentioned earlier, the procedure does vary slightly according to whether you are installing a link/king-pin unit or a balljoint unit. With a link-pin front end place the whole adjuster unit in the tube with the spring mount disc (No. 9) as shown in the illustration No. 1. The line you have already marked on the beam should pass through the centre of the new socket set-screw (No. 8). The adjuster unit should be so placed that the sleeve assembly (No. 4) and the socket set-screw (No. 2a) open towards the front of the car. The adjuster block (No. 3) and its tapered set-screw (No. 8) should be on top. Tack-weld the unit in place.

With a balljoint front end, place the adjuster unit in the tube with the ½″ set-screw (No. 6) not yet installed. It is important at this point to make sure the spring mounting disc (No. 5) is turned as shown in the illustration (Figure B). The second 3″ parallel line you marked on the beam (i.e. the top line) should pass through the centre of the new socket set-screw (No. 2). The unit should be placed so that the sleeve assembly (No. 4) and the socket set-screw (No. 2a) open towards the front of the car. The adjuster block (No. 3) and its socket set-screw (No. 2) should be on top. Tack weld the adjuster in place.

Once you have got to this point and before final welding

takes place, it is advisable to make sure the adjuster is straight, set parallel in the beam. The easy test here is to reinsert the leaf springs. They should be centred at both ends of the beam. If they are not, you have not installed the adjusters correctly. Once you have confirmed the correctness of the installation of the adjusters, you can now completely weld it into place. Now repeat this same procedure on the bottom torsion bar.

To reiterate our previous comments, you can achieve a measure of adjustment by installing only one adjuster. However, you will be creating a stiff ride because you are making one set of torsion leaf springs work against the other. Fitting adjusters to both beams makes everything work together more harmoniously.

If yours is a link-pin front end you can replace the leaves in the beam, loosely mount the adjuster screw (No. 8) and re-install the beam on to the car.

The balljoint front end requires a little more work. Firstly, replace the leaf springs and remove the socket set-screw (No. 2). Then attach a torsion arm or a spanner to the springs and rotate them until the lower set-screw hole (No. 6a) is visible through the slot in the main adjuster body. Make sure the torsion leaves are central then insert the small set-screw (No. 6). Now rotate the springs back to their original position and re-insert the big socket set-screw, block and lock nuts (Nos. 1, 2 & 3). You can now reassemble the rest of the front suspension and re-install the beam on to your Bug.

The adjustment procedure is quite easy. Loosen the lock nuts (No. 1), turn the adjusting set-screw (No. 2a) to achieve your desired ride height and then re-tighten the lock nuts. This adjustment should be carried out simultaneously when two front end adjusters are installed.

The set-screws should be torqued to 13lbf ft and the lock

nuts to 55lbf ft. If difficulty is experienced replacing the torsion leaves, gently chamfer the leading edge of the torsion leaves and place a rubber band round this leading edge to hold the leaves closely together. These two tips will help guide the torsion leaves into the centre mount.

Wherever possible, adjust the steering box mounting to keep the steering connecting tie rods in a near horizontal level when the car is running at the desired ride height. You should also set the front camber to ½° of negative and the front toe-in to 1/16″. It's as easy as that.

When lowering the front end more than 2″ it is advisable to fit shorter shock absorbers to prevent bottoming-out the standard units.

Front suspension Round-Up

The soundness of design of the Beetle's suspension is illustrated by the fact that it is used (or, some may say, abused) in such events as desert racing in California, and has also been found in some very rapid road and racing cars, including the Formula Vee single-seat racers. Obviously, the two extremes require different methods of setting-up, and occasionally some radical alterations, but it is still basically Dr Porsche's design.

Having lowered (or raised) the car, any discrepancies in the steering gear are going to be magnified, especially when wider wheels and tyres are fitted. The phenomenon to be particularly avoided is 'bump steer', which occurs, especially with radically lowered front suspension, when one front wheel is forced upwards by a bump. The steering track rods may well be running at peculiar angles, and the action of the wheel rising has the effect of shortening the steering arm, which gives a nasty pull on the steering wheel via the steering box.

The ideal solution is to bring the steering arms to the horizontal position, to minimise the effects of bumps on the steering. The first step is to move the outer steering balljoints from their positions on top of the suspension arms to a position under the arm. A kit is available to facilitate this, the only additional work required being to drill a 15mm hole through the arm.

If the arms are still not horizontal, the thing to do then is to rotate the steering box on the beam until the arms *are* level. It goes without saying that the steering box should be correctly adjusted, and that there should be no excessive play in the steering and suspension balljoints (or king/link-pins). The front wheel alignment should be set to 1/16″ toe-in.

A spot of negative camber gives better turn-in performance when cornering hard, and also improves straight-line stability. If you have fitted, or you are contemplating fitting urethane bushes in place of the front suspension torsion arm bearings as already discussed, negative camber can be introduced by a little judicious cutting and filing of the outer ends of the top beam only.

With just the top torsion arms and torsion leaves removed from the beam, take ⅓″ from the end of the top tube. Reassemble the beam, and with the assembly held perfectly horizontal and the pointer on the top concentric adjuster facing forward there should be approximately 1½° negative camber, measured at the hub assembly outer face. If not, take a little more off the tube to achieve the desired angle. Repeat the operation for the other side, making sure that both sides are equal (although minor discrepancies can be taken up by the top concentric adjusters).

Having moved the top arms inwards, the indentations in the torsion leaves are not going to mate with the holes in the arms. Turn the leaves through 180° and make new indentations using a centre punch and a ½″ drill. Make sure that the leaves are properly clamped before drilling. Again, after doing any work on the front suspension and steering, have the front wheel alignment checked and reset if necessary.

As far as the shock absorbers are concerned, the adjustable variety should be fitted so that the handling and ride can be set up to individual preference. If you have gone really low, it will probably be necessary to fit shorter shock absorbers to avoid bottoming the normal length ones. Going up may require longer shock absorbers so that the full suspension travel is not compromised, the decision either way largely depends on how far the car is to be raised or lowered.

Before leaving the front suspension, let's have a look at some of the more esoteric alterations that can be made to the poor old Bug.

For example, mounting the steering box in the centre of the beam, rather than to one side or the other, does give the advantage of equal-length steering arms and some reduction of the bump-steer problem, but is really only a practical proposition for single-seat rails or radically altered Bajas. On the other hand, rack-and-pinion steering is practicable, if a trifle expensive, and will give more feel to the steering due to its more direct aciton.

Coil-over shock absorbers are a good bet for those who have gone up in the world and have raised their Beetles. In effect an additional coil spring wrapped around a shock absorber, these will give more 'bounce' to the suspension and will enhance the off-road capability of the vehicle.

Finally, what must surely be the ultimate front-end is the inboard suspension set-up for the strutted (1302/1303) Beetles, which gives a very low profile suitable for use with some of the very low fronted kit cars.

To convert to this layout, the lower track control arm is retained, while the strut itself is cut down

to form the upright upon which the hub is carried. A top wishbone is added mounted onto a frame built onto the floorpan, and a very short coil-over-shock unit is attached at its top end to the upper wishbone, with the lower end mounted to the middle of the floorpan. Steering is rack-and-pinion, as on the standard 1303 set-up. This system is obviously not suitable for off-road use, but will provide the best handling for the strutted floorpan, especially as it is allied to the double-jointed rear end. The cost? it's gulp-making!

Rear Suspension

Going through the rear suspension in the same way as the front, we start by examining the springing medium. At the back, instead of torsion leaves making up one 'bar', each side at the rear has a single round bar splined at each end, with different spline ratios at each end. It is possible to remove the spring plates, which hold the torsion bar in place at the outer end, and twist the bars to raise or lower the ride-height, or, as they inevitably wear at different rates, to bring the car back on to even keel.

This, however, requires time and endless patience for the trial and error method which is necessary. To overcome this, and to provide a means of altering ride-height, the answer is to fit adjustable spring plates. These are available for both swing-axle and double-jointed Beetles — just specify!

There is an added advantage, in that these spring plates allow the fitting of either swing axle or double-jointed torsion bars to either type of suspension. For instance, the 21¾'' swing-axle torsion bar would be more suitable for off-road use, as it is stiffer than the longer (26-9/16'') double-jointed variety which is softer and more suitable for road use.

To fit the spring plates, first

jack up the rear of the car and make sure that the car is supported *firmly*. Undo the four 14mm bolts holding the spring plate cap, and then the four 19mm nuts and bolts holding the spring plate to the suspension arm. Lever the spring plate out of its housing and off the bottom stop, *taking extreme car*, as the spring plate is under tension, pre-loaded onto that stop. As it pulls out, it flies down extremely rapidly and can cause injury. Before completely removing the spring plate, mark its position on the torsion housing which will give a datum (starting) point for the reassembly sequence.

To help the final removal of the spring plate, raise and tie up the suspension to its highest point. This will allow the spring plate to fall out from between the suspension arm and the mounting point on the body.

At this point, as these spring plates are being fitted to improve handling, it is beneficial to install urethane bushes in place of the standard rubber suspension bushes. It may, in fact, be a necessity as there is a possibility that the bushes required for the new set-up will differ in size from the original ones.

Reassembly, as all the best manuals say, is the reverse of the dismantling procedure. Grease the torsion bar splines, and the bushes, install them and line the new adjustable spring plate up with the original mark. If you wish to lower the car, set the adjuster to its maximum height before fitting; if raising, set the adjuster to the minimum setting. There is approximately three inches of adjustment available from the base setting.

Getting the spring plate home on to its splines may require the assistance of a copper headed mallet. Once the spring plate housing is reached, the spring plate has to be pre-loaded on to the housing bottom shoulder. The best way to do this is to use a trolley jack and chain, looping the chain under the jack and over the suspension casting at the shock

absorber top mount, linking the chain in a complete loop by using a clasp or nut and bolt. The end of the spring plate can then be jacked up to raise it into position above the housing shoulder, and then drifted fully home with the copper mallet.

When reassembling the rest of the suspension, difficulties may be experienced with lining up the spring plate cover. Use two bolts longer than standard, and draw the cover on with the two longer bolts placed diagonally opposite each other. Put the two standard bolts in the other two holes and tighten them, remove the longer ones and replace those with the other two standard bolts.

The elongated slots in the spring plate are for toe-in adjustment, which should be set to 1/16'' toe-in. The best way to achieve this is to go to a tyre specialist who will have up-to-date optical equipment and can get the setting absolutely spot-on, but try to get the wheels roughly parallel before moving the car.

Standard torsion bars and shock absorbers are intended for the standard Beetle, to give a comfortable ride and fair handling, with a front anti-roll bar to reduce body roll. Adding weight by loading on equipment or lightening by fitting a fibre-glass body is going to alter the compromise and change the ride and handling of the car, which is where the foregoing articles come in.

If you like and feel safe with the end result, fine. If, however, you have a four-wheeled jelly, or you are riding on rocks, go out and get advice from a tuning specialist to help get the car fully sorted. Apart from the car itself, a comfortable and/or good handling car is safer, as the driver is more relaxed and does not have to struggle with the car.

There is also a financial aspect. Trial and error with springs and shock absorbers takes time and can cost a lot of money, but a trip to the local One Who Knows can probably get it right first time,

as his experience is wide enough to have an answer for most situations, and he may have ways of getting round problems that no-one else has thought of.

After modifications and before use, the car should be checked by a qualified engineer.

Brake Modifications

So far we have concentrated on making the Beetle go round corners and soak up the bumps. The next stage in the proceedings is to examine the system and decide how far to go with the brakes, arguably the most important safety-related part of any car.

One way to decide what is needed is to equate stopping power to the proposed engine power, and then go one stage further to give an additional margin of safety. It may be considered better to go for the ultimate stopping set-up, thus covering all but the most extreme of eventualities. It is not wise to skimp in any way in this department, so budget for the best in brakes and, if necessary, save a little elsewhere — otherwise the consequences can be disastrous.

Now that all the suspension mods have been done, the time has come to work outwards a little and get the brakes properly sorted. The first thing to do is to look at the alternatives.

The air-cooled range of VWs have had a variety of braking systems fitted during the years of production. The obvious two main differences are the drum and disc brake variations, but there is in fact a higher level of swopping around possible. Have a look at the chart which clearly identifies the different combinations on the various models. The early 205mm pcd (5-stud) Beetles are not swoppable, but the later 130mm pcd (4-stud) models are.

In the early days of Beetle tuning the Done Thing was to fit the brake drums, linings and accoutrements from the Porsche 356, which was, more or less, a simple bolt-on job. The obvious modern Beetle conversion is to replace the front drums with the disc set-up from the 1500cc Beetle.

The advantages of disc brakes as opposed to drums are twofold. Firstly, they are not inclined to grab at low speeds, which the drum variety is likely to do. (This can be great fun in wet weather conditions.) The other advantage is that a disc brake dissipates heat far more easily than a drum, and consequently gives better braking at high speed. This is particularly relevant where a front spoiler is fitted to a Beetle, or where all-enveloping bodywork has been fitted, reducing the flow of cooling air over the front brakes.

The only less beneficial factor associated with the 1500 brakes is that the brake calipers and pads are relatively small. The very late 1303S Beetles have much bigger calipers and pads. However, a kit is available, comprising new stub axles, discs, bearings, hoses, fittings and the later larger calipers, which will give good, powerful braking for any torsion-bar Beetle.

Turning our attention to the rear, the standard Beetle drum brakes can be replaced with the larger 1600cc Type 3 brakes. This does require a little bit of parts swapping and spacing, but the larger brakes will improve the rear end stopping power. The other thing you have to be careful of is that the Type 3 rear drums will increase the rear track slightly, so watch your tyre-to-wing contact.

The better rear braking alternative is to fit a rear disc-brake conversion. This consists of special discs, hubs, calipers, mountings, hoses, seals, fixtures and fittings plus the special 'fist' calipers that hook up to the standard hand brake so that the original hand brake mechanism operates correctly. The braking capability of the 11" front and rear disc brake set-up is phenomenal. The final icing on the cake for the disc brake set-up is to cross drill the discs. This has the advantage of dissipating heat better, making sure that the disc pad faces do not glaze and minimises the wet weather water build up that can occur between pad and disc face.

The front to rear braking balance ratio is all important. To get the optimum braking efficiency the front to rear ratio needs to be set correctly. The simple way to achieve this is to fit an adjustable balance brake pedal assembly. This assembly allows the front to rear ratio, via a simple adjustable bolt, to be altered. The system also incorporates two individual master cylinders. This offers dual-line safety, in that if one hydraulic system fails, the other half is still fully operative.

Excluding the obvious brake swapping, the other items that can affect brake balance are weight changes. For example, changing engines to a heavier or lighter version, changing the body, changing the position of driver or occupants and fitting different sized wheels and tyres, can all change the required front/rear braking ratio.

Fitting servos to VWs will not improve their braking efficiency. The servo is designed to make the effort of braking easier; you physically cannot improve the actual braking efficiency of the standard design. Fitting a servo to a VW usually necessitates the insertion of two servos, because most Beetles and campers have a dual hydraulic braking system as standard. Because the two systems are hydraulically separate, the servos equally have to be individual to each system. The other point you have to bear in mind with a servo installation is it has to be plumbed in to the inlet manifold so that a constant vacuum is generated to activate the servo.

If you are in a position where you have to replace one of the brake pipes because it can be seen to be corroded, Murphy's

Law states that the remainder of the pipes will be on their way out. Play safe and replace all the standard brake pipes with the copper variety that utilise brass unions and fittings. They will not corrode and will give you a lifetime margin of safety.

Beetle/Variant Brake Variations

Model	Year	Front	Rear
1200/1300	1965–67	Dr 230 x 40mm	Dr 230 x 30mm
1200/1300	1968 on	Dr 230 x 40mm	Dr 230 x 40mm
1500	1967–70	Dc 50 x 58mm	Dr 230 x 40mm
1302/1303	1970–77	Dr 248 x 40 mm	Dr 230 x 40mm
1302S	1970–6/71	Dc 50 x 58mm	Dr 230 x 40mm
1302S	7/71–1972	Dc 55.5 x 53mm	Dr 230 x 40mm
1303S	1973 on	Dc 63 x 52mm	Dr 230 x 40mm
Type 3	1965–71	Dc 55.5 x 53mm	Dr 248 x 46mm
Type 3	1971 on	Dc 61.5 x 56.5mm (larger caliper mount)	Dr 248 x 46mm

Dr – Drum brakes   Dc – Disc brakes

Drum/Disc Conversions

The relative merits of disc and drum brakes having been discussed, we are now going to examine the braking system more closely and, using the Variations chart, mix and match various components to effect improvements. The fitting of disc conversions, the ultimate in fade-free stopping, is also covered.

As far as the front brakes are concerned, there is no point in playing around with the standard drums, as no major improvement can be obtained. The first step, therefore, is to change to the disc brake set-up found on the 1500 and GT Beetles.

Basically, what are needed from the donor beam are the stub axles, bearings, discs and caliper assemblies. While everything is to hand all the components can be cleaned and checked for wear, and any bits requiring replacement can be renewed and fitted as the work progresses.

Remove the drums, speedo cable, linings, hydraulics and backplates from the existing beam. At this point any worn

components in the suspension and steering (balljoints, track-rod ends and the like) can be renewed as necessary.

Now do the same dismantling job again, this time on the donor disc beam. At this point we make no excuses for reiterating our point to *check everything that is being fitted back to the car* and replace any bits that are suspect. Obviously, the best way to do things is to use all new parts, but reconditioned exchange calipers are as good as new, and if using the existing discs make sure that there is no appreciable wear on the disc faces, and that there are no cracks and no run-out (distortion) is apparent.

Putting it all back together again is a reverse of the dismantling procedure, using care to make sure that everything is correctly tightened and working. The last job, after connecting up the flexible hoses, is to bleed the brakes — for the cost of the fluid, it is worth refilling with fresh fluid to avoid getting any water or other impurities into the system, and to finish the job properly.

An alternative method of doing the swop is simply to exchange the entire disc beam for the drum axle — after checking everything is out, of course. This makes it all more accessible, as the work can all be carried out on the bench, but getting the beam in and out is usually a two-man job, owing to the weight of the assembly!

Ideally, the way to go about things is to do all the front end work at the same time, completing the suspension mods and the brake conversion at the same time. That way, the beam only has to come out of the car once (what do you mean, you've only just bolted it in?).

At the back there is a wider latitude of choice. With a mild to medium sort of engine, the standard drums will suffice — just make sure they work OK. A more adventurous engine means improving the brakes, which is where the Type 3 drum set-up comes in.

The swop is similar to the disc/drum exchange at the front, the only difference being that the brakes come from a different model rather than an uprated version of the same car. That aside, the Type 3 drums and associated hardware fit in exactly the same way as the Beetle drums, so the change is simply a bolt-on job.

Points to watch are as follows. In the same way as at the front, *make absolutely sure that everything is in good condition*. Use new wheel cylinders and hoses when fitting the brakes, and make sure that there are no cracks or deep score-marks in the drums. The other point is that, as the Type 3 drums are wider than the Beetle ones, tyre-to-wing contact may be made, especially if very wide wheels and tyres are used.

For those who have designs on something really tremendous in the tail, the only way to go is an all-disc set-up. Rear disc conversion kits contain everything to do the job, apart from hydraulic fluid and a set of spanners! Having acquired your kit, and raised the car and removed the wheels, the first thing to do is to remove and discard the rear brake drums, the brake backplates complete with cylinders, adjusters and brake shoes, and the metal brake pipe from the backplate to the flexible pipe. With all that out of the way, now is a good time to clean and check that the wheel

bearings and seals are in good order.

In place of the old brake backplate, fit the caliper mount bracket with the caliper mounting boss rearmost. Replace the bearing seals and gaskets and bolt the bearing carrier back on with the original bolts, sandwiching the caliper mounting bracket in the same way as with the drum backplate.

Now fit the disc and hub assembly onto the splines and lock in position with the brake drum locknut (as if refitting the original drum). Torque the nut up to 185 lbf ft.

Bolt the caliper in place, making sure that the handbrake fitting is at the lowest part of the caliper. Now make sure that the piston and caliper are fully back in their housing, and fit the two disc pads into the caliper, ensuring that the raised section in the back of the pad is in line with the slot in the piston. Then fit the caliper retaining pins. The pads have electrical contacts fitted, which are pad wear indicators. These can either be cut off and discarded or hooked up to a dashboard warning light. If it is decided to use these, only use one on the piston side of each caliper.

Fit the copper brake pipe with its UNF thread end into the caliper, and the metric thread end into the flexible pipe on the axle, making sure that it cannot chafe on the body, wheel or suspension. Cut the handbrake cable return spring to an uncompressed length of 3", feed it through the caliper stop and hook it on to the lever on the caliper, with the outer cable centred in the caliper stop. Now start again on the other side!

Once everything is fitted, all that has to be done is to adjust the handbrake and bleed the brakes.

Having fitted the heavy hardware, it's time to think about the ancillary bits and pieces, and check the rest of the system equipment for wear.

If, while working on the brakes, any brake pipes have been found to be corroded, the chances are that all the pipes need to be looked at fairly critically. Replace the whole set with copper pipes – apart from having nice new pipes, they are almost a 'fit and forget' item as they are practically corrosion-proof. They polish up nicely, too.

Dual-circuitry is a Good Thing to have, too, giving a greater margin of safety in the event of any failure, and not difficult to arrange. The later Beetle master cylinders will fit the existing Beetle pedals (assuming that the original system is single circuit), or there is the option of fitting one of the aftermarket pedal assemblies. It is wise to check the existing master cylinder seals and piston, reconditioning as necessary, and change the hydraulic fluid (which should be done periodically anyway unless you use the highly-recommended silicone type).

Don't forget the handbrake! Again, the best thing to do is to replace the cables, as the existing ones are almost certain to have stretched, and even possibly frayed. Make sure that cable runs are clean and well lubricated, and that any other moving parts are, in fact, moving!

Probably of interest only to a few of the off-road fraternity, but included here anyway, is a mention of fiddle brakes. They have been seen for years on the sort of cars used for trialling, and their use on off-roaders is the same – to help cornering on loose or slippery surfaces.

Without going into details, there are two levers (although an alternative type uses a single push/pull lever) with cable or hydraulic hook-ups to each individual rear wheel. The idea is to lock up the inside rear wheel on the turn and give a squirt of power to the outside rear wheel, pushing the car around the sharpest of corners. A specialised piece of equipment for a specialist purpose, but mentioned here to give a more complete picture of available modifications.

Gearbox Modifications

The time has now come to give careful consideration to engine application, if this has not already been thought out. It may seem peculiar to open the gearbox instalments of this series by referring to engines, but it is something of a nuisance to have to dismantle engine and gearbox (having once fitted them) if the 'box is not strong enough for the job or a wrong choice of gear and/or final-drive ratios has been made.

Suspension and brakes will already have been modified to suit the builder's choice of use – the same criteria apply to gearbox choice. This instalment will look generally at gearbox installations and strengthening for high power outputs.

Identification

There are two main types of transaxle fitted to the Beetle. The swing-axle type has fixed drive shafts attached to the trans-axle where only the inner end has a pivoting joint. These run through from 1961 – 1977 and are found on 1200, 1300 and 1500cc Beetles. The other type (and more popular for competition use) is the type that uses independent drive shafts with joints on both ends. This box was fitted to 1967-onwards 1500cc automatic Beetles, 1302 and S Beetles 1970 – '72, 1303 and S Beetles 1972 – '77, and the Type 3 1600cc from 1967 onwards.

The other change which is general across the gearbox range affects the clutch and clutch release bearing area. Up to 1970 the clutch release bearing was held into the clutch release fork by two round dowels and its mating clutch cover assembly had a thrust bearing pad fixed to it. 1971-on gearboxes have a simpler clutch bearing which slides up and down its own guide tube which surrounds the gearbox first motion

(input) shaft. The 1971-onwards clutch cover assembly doesn't have a clutch release bearing pad affixed to it. These are interchangeable by swapping the clutch forks and corresponding bearing and cover assemblies.

To simplify matters, we refer to the pre-'70 gearboxes as early and '71-onwards as late, whilst the fixed drive shaft gearboxes will be referred to as swing-axle and the double jointed drive shaft as the IRS model. To help visually identify between early and late gearboxes, a general guide is that the early boxes have two drain plugs, one beneath the gear cluster casing and the other beneath the differential section of the casing, whilst the later boxes only have one drain plug under the differential case.

Mid-engine units

The Beetle transaxle is also an ideal unit for mid-engined installation and providing the gearbox is in good condition it can cope with 150bhp in standard form. It is preferable to use the IRS gearbox for mid-engined application. All the engines that UVA manufacture adaptor kits for rotate in a clockwise direction (as does the Beetle), which means a 15 minute modification is required to the transaxle.

Because you are turning the transaxle from facing backwards to facing forwards, the crown wheel on the pinion needs to be swapped over to maintain forward motion. Remove both output driveshaft side covers and swap tham, complete with differential, to their opposite sides and bolt them back up. This simple operation reverts the gearbox to a forward drive (because nobody wants four reverse gears and only one forward gear). It is preferable, at this stage, to confirm that you have the correct pinion to crown wheel mesh.

It is also worth mentioning that a Haynes Beetle workshop manual should be by your side at all times to help you on assembly

and make sure you don't end up with spare parts at the end of the job!

The backlash between crown wheel and pinion should be .005″ – .020″. The pre-load on the differential bearing is easily measured by loosening the bolts on the differential side cover so that it can spring away from the case. You can then measure the gap between the side cover and the main casing with a feeler gauge, setting this up as per workshop manual tolerances.

Now that the gearbox has been reversed, the gearshift will be back to front. What is needed is a mid-engined gearshift kit which bolts on the gear selector output shaft and reverts the gear selector 'H' pattern back to normal for either central or side gearshifting.

If a cable clutch operation is difficult to install after reversing the box, convert the system to hydraulic by using a bolt-on hydraulic slave cylinder which can be coupled to either your own hydraulic pedal assembly or one of the after market items.

Transaxle strengthening

If the transaxle is going to be subject to hard abuse on tarmac and/or high bhp figures then fit the following components. A super duty differential side cover, the type of which depends on transaxle, model and year. These side covers maintain a constant mesh between the crown wheel and the pinion, stopping the tendency for high performance engines to ride the crown wheel up the helix angle of the pinion. This is caused by flexing of the standard side cover.

Third and fourth gears are a press-fit on their syncro hub carrier. These need pressing off this hub and refixing in a stronger manner to prevent the gear spinning on its syncro hub. The satisfactory method is to re-assemble with Loctite but if you prefer a belt and braces method, then MIG weld four ½″ welds on

the face of the gear and its syncro hub, stitching them together. These welds then need to be faced off to retain the original machined face. Earlier gearboxes had third and fourth gears fixed to their shafts by key ways. The later gearboxes had only third gear affixed this way. Replace these Woodruff keys with heavy duty items. Third and fourth gears also have a spring which keeps them apart. This spring should be replaced with a spacer and washer kit. This modification reduces the shock load through the gears.

Racing application

The standard VW differential planetary cluster uses two spider gears. It is preferable to fit four, which naturally doubles the differential's transmission abuse capacity. Super duty carriers are the best way to go, but a less expensive and halfway measure is to fit a four-spider gear section only.

Assembly

Setting up the gears and differential, as mentioned previously, is easy with commonsense and following the workshop manual procedure. The only area where you will need professional guidance and/or an assembly jig is the setting of the gear selectors. UVA for example, can supply the tool or can perform this operation for you. Alternatively, you can make your own gear selector tool by using an old VW transaxle case with a 4″ square cut out of its side allowing you to set the gears and selectors up as if in its assembly form. Good quality gaskets are worth reinstalling when a major box strip down is intended.

Clutches

Always use the 200mm clutch as fitted to the 1500cc/1600cc Beetles as a minimum. For engines producing up to 100bhp use heavy-duty clutch cover

assemblies. For 100+bhp and/or racing applications use a racing diaphragm clutch cover, and if hard and fast gear shifting is envisaged, opt for the rigid clutch disc as opposed to the sprung version. If there will be a lot of clutch slippage envisaged in your chosen competition application, use a Feramic clutch disc. Also use the heavy duty clutch throw-out bearing, particularly in racing applications.

Two further useful components to remember are the heavy duty throw-out arm and bush kit which can take the arduous abuse of racing, and the clutch release bearing retaining springs. These inexpensive little springs are a boon for all early transaxles where the standard springs have a tendency to jump out.

Remember, the VW transaxle is a remarkable piece of equipment and providing the correct parts are fitted and the box is in good condition, well in excess of 200 brake horsepower can be fed through it.

Gear & Final Drive Ratios

Over the years of Beetle production quite a few changes have been made to the ratios of gears and final drives (differentials), and one or two variations in the case itself.

Prior to 1961 the transmission casing was split vertically into two halves, and syncromesh was fitted on second, third and fourth gears only (early cars and the standard models had 'crash' boxes – no synchro!). There are by now few of these boxes left, so they will not figure in these discussions.

The other main external difference is the fitting of the double-jointed driveshafts to the 1302/1303 range and automatic Beetles, the rest having swing-axle rear suspension. Although the internal ratios are the same, and the two types look similar apart from the driveshaft fitting, swopping is not a practical proposition, as the time and expense involved would far outweigh any advantage gained.

Reference to the chart will show that, with one or two exceptions, the ratios in the gear clusters right through the Beetle range are the same, the main difference in the boxes being the final drive ratio. The 4.375:1 differential is fitted to the 1200/1300 range, and the 4.125:1 generally through the 1500/1600 gearboxes, *whether swing axle or double-jointed driveshafts are fitted.*

The 4.125:1 differential gives slightly higher ratios through the gearbox, and allows the more powerful 1500 and 1600 engines to pull higher speeds in the gears as well as a little more top speed. Don't get the idea, though, that fitting the 3.875:1 diff will make a standard car go faster still. Theoretically, that ratio fitted in the 1500/1600 box would give another 10mph or so, but in practice the car would run out of breath at the 'normal' top speed, if not sooner. In addition, while higher maxima could theoretically be achieved in the lower gears, acceleration times would suffer as the car would be overgeared and find the higher ratios more difficult to pull.

A highly tuned engine, on the other hand, may need a higher diff ratio, as with the extra torque and/or higher revs available it may be found that the car is undergeared, giving too low a maximum speed for racing applications and uneconomical cruising. Ideally, a high-speed road or race car requires a high-ratio differential and close-ratio first, second and third gears to improve mid-range acceleration.

The ideal gearbox for kit cars is the 1303/GT gearbox (with the 3.875:1 differential). The lighter weight of these vehicles enables even the standard engines (apart from the 1200/1300 engines) to pull the slightly higher gearing more easily, conferring a little more top speed.

Off-road use, however, requires a different approach. Top speeds are lower, and the nature of the terrain, especially in short-course racing with very steep gradients and almost non-existent straights, requires low ratios both for hillclimbing ability and for the rapid acquisition of speed on the sprint sections.

One way to obtain a set of low ratios is to fit a Type 2 gearbox. The earlier swing-axle equipped boxes were much the same as those fitted to contemporary Beetles, but with the addition of reduction gears at the hubs (giving an incidental benefit of additional ground clearance), while the later vehicles were fitted with double-jointed driveshafts and low ratio differentials without the reduction gears. The Type 2 gearbox can be incorporated into an off-road rail fairly easily at the building stage, but fitting into a Beetle is considerably more involved.

New mountings for the gearbox (which is wider and heavier than the Beetle item) require making up and welding very carefully into place, and shorter driveshafts are needed to fit within the existing suspension. This gearbox swop is not really a cost-effective exercise; in this case the serious off-roader is better advised to open up the gearbox and use the Bugpack ratios available (see chart). For off-road racing third and fourth gears need to be brought closer to first and second, and a lower final drive ratio fitted. The Bugpack ratios are designed for this use, and enable the gearbox to be tailored to suit the use intended.

It is possible to ring the changes with gear and final drive ratios in the transmission, but apart from the above special case it is far easier and less expensive to swop whole units, a more practicable and cost-effective solution. If it is considered necessary or desirable to open up

and delve into the transmission, however, don't forget that some special tools and equipment may be needed, as well as some very careful setting up once the job is completed. It may be better to have this kind of work done for you — asking someone to reassemble a gearbox from a kit of parts in two carrier bags and a cardboard box does not add to personal popularity!

Once the gearbox is sorted, the final effect on overall gearing comes from the size of tyre fitted. The main effect on the gearing comes obviously from the rear wheels — the front will be looked at later.

The overall diameter of the standard wheel/tyre combination is 25½ inches, and any great deviation from this size will affect the gearing. To give an example, one reason why the racing rails and Bajas run low-ratio gears and differentials is to overcome the rise in gearing when using rear tyres up to 32″ tall! The tyres used for off-road racing are all tall, due to the heavy tread and the high profile construction, and therefore raise the gearing.

For street use there is a little more flexibility, as tyre height can be altered to suit the car by using different profiles while maintaining the wheel rim width, and tyre section, or by changing wheel diameter. A full list of tyre sizes, heights and recommended rim widths is available from UVA to guide buyers in their choice. Remember, though, that 25½″ is the standard wheel/tyre size, and larger or smaller diameter means higher or lower gearing.

Another point to remember is not to over-tyre the car. A really hot street-racing Bug may require all the rubber it can get on the road, but a mildly tuned and restrained example might look a little ridiculous if shod in the same way. Wider tyres mean more drag, both aerodynamically and through frictional losses, so if the tyres are too wide it can actually slow the car. Wide tyres are also more

prone to aquaplane in very wet conditions, so a little moderation should be used when considering what to buy.

The only other item to require attention if deviating from the standard tyre diameter is the speedometer, which is driven by the left-hand front wheel. An accurate speedometer is a legal requirement, so to help avoid the attention of the local constabulary either the original unit will have to be recalibrated, or an aftermarket speedometer (such as the VDO unit) fitted, calibrated to suit whatever tyre size is fitted.

safety's sake, the necessary route for tuning a car, and deal with the handling and stopping before anything else. Having done that, and also looked at the gearbox for good measure, the logical approach leads us to the powerplant.

Before going into tuning too deeply, make sure first that the basic engine is up to scratch. It is surprising how much power can be restored when the engine is carefully serviced, and all the normal service adjustments made. In fact, a weekend spent doing servicing, adjusting and lubricating

Beetle Gear and Final Drive Ratios

Fitting	Reverse	First	Second	Third	Fourth	Ring & Pinion	Overall in Fourth
Up to 1960	4.63:1	3.60:1	1.88:1	1.22:1	0.79:1	4.375:1	3.45:1
1961–1965	3.88:1	3.80:1	2.06:1	1.32:1	0.89:1	4.375:1*	3.89:1
1966 on[1]	3.88:1	3.80:1	2.06:1	1.26:1	0.89:1	4.375:1	3.89:1
1967–1977[2]	3.88:1	3.80:1	2.06:1	1.26:1	0.89:1	4.125:1	3.67:1
1973–1977[3]	3.79:1	3.78:1	2.06:1	1.26:1†	0.93:1†	3.875:1	3.60:1
1971–1977 (Ghia)	3.79:1	3.78:1	2.06:1	1.26:1	0.93:1	3.875:1	3.60:1
1975 on & Brazil	3.79:1	3.78:1	2.06:1	1.36:1	1.04:1	4.620:1	4.80:1

Bugpack ratios
(use standard first and second)

Bugpack ratios	–	–	–	1.42:1	1.04:1	4.86:1	5.05:1
designed	–	–	–	1.48:1	1.13:1	4.86:1	5.49:1
mainly for off-	–	–	–	1.58:1	1.22:1	4.86:1	5.93:1
road & drag	–	–	–	1.70:1	1.32:1	4.86:1	6.41:1
racing	–	–	–	–	1.46:1	4.86:1	7.10:1

1) All 1200/1300 swing-axle and double-joint types.
2) All 1500/1600 swing-axle and double-joint types, except below.
3) 1303S & GT Beetles.
* If you expect to abuse a 4.375:1 ring and pinion, use the later gear set with the 8-bolt ring gear.
† These gears have very fine teeth, and although quieter will not withstand much abuse. Coarser-toothed gears for these late transaxles are available from UVA.

A complete list of gearbox and final drive ratios is available from UVA Co. Ltd.

The Powerplant

Way back we stated that we were going to take the logical and, for

work all round the car can make an economical improvement in performance — and that's *before* money is spent in earnest!

Our starting point is the 1584cc 50bhp (DIN) dual-port

engine. This has the obvious advantage of being the largest capacity Type 1 engine, and has an improved internal lubrication system which is better able to handle mild increases in power before more attention has to be paid to lubrication. It also features the more efficient dual-port cylinder heads.

The dual-port type of cylinder head is preferred because the inlet flow properties are better than the single-port design. Briefly, instead of one port feeding two cylinders (single-port head), there are two inlet ports, one to each cylinder. (Both types of cylinder head have exhaust ports individual to each cylinder.) Each cylinder can potentially be filled more efficiently with the fuel/air mixture required for combustion, leading to an increased power output.

If your existing engine is a 1200 (30 or 34bhp), 1300 (40 or 44bhp), or 1500cc (44bhp), the easiest and most cost-efficient way to boost your power is simply to change engines to a larger size. It is also possible to increase the capacity of the 1300 and 1500 engines by changing barrels and pistons to the 1600 size. A pair of dual-port heads (if not already fitted) and the appropriate inlet manifolding and carburetter should then bring the power level up to around 50bhp. Note that 1300 heads will require machining to accept the larger 1600 barrels. The 1500/1600 clutch is really the only size to consider when tuning and swopping engines unless outputs of over 85 bhp are aimed for in whch case, see an earlier section for detais.

There was a change in the clutch operating mechanism in late 1970, and this should be considered when engine swopping or ordering performance clutch parts. This change was to the clutch release bearing, which in turn altered the clutch release fork and the cover plate assembly. The centre (driven) plate remained the same.

Beetles up to late 1970 had a release bearing with two round dowels (one each side) to attach it to the clutch fork, the cover assembly having a corresponding thrust pad fitted. 1971-on models had a bearing carrier tube around the clutch shaft and no pad on the cover plate. All these components are interchangeable.

Apart from the release bearing, if you're delving into the bellhousing of a 6-volt Beetle, there is some more work needed. Gentle application of a grinding wheel is required here and there to provide clearance for the larger 1600-type flywheel. One way to find out where is to fit the engine, turn it a couple of times, remove it and see where the marks are (usually round the rubber mounting bosses).

Use of the larger flywheel also means converting the car to 12-volt electrics (if not already done). The number of teeth on the 12-volt flywheel/starter motor combination differs from the 6V application, so a 6V starter will not mesh correctly with a 12V flywheel. What is needed for this part of the job is a special replacement bush, which fits into the bellhousing in place of the original part and carries the pinion end of the starter motor shaft. These bushes are available from many VW parts stores (Bugpack part no. B3557).

Author's note: The following chart gives some idea of the parts available for high-performance tuning of the Beetle engine. However, since the upper reaches of engine performance are beyond the scope of this book, only Stages 1 – 3 are dealt with here. For further information, contact UVA Ltd. or your local tuning specialist. It cannot be over-stressed that any engine modifications beyond those discussed in the following section should not be carried out to 1500 or 1600 models without suitable chassis (i.e. braking and suspension) modifications and for safety reasons, increasing the performance of smaller engined cars beyond their design capacity cannot be recommended for road use.

Engine Stages 1, 2 and 3

This section relates only to the 50bhp 1600cc dual-port engine since, compared with the performance of the unit, smaller engines are hardly worth tuning!

Engine tuning equates to two important factors: the size of your budget and your ability. If you are expecting 200bhp out of your Beetle engine for £200, forget it. Likewise, if the extent of your 'hands on' ability is oil and plug changes, think twice before you tackle a full-race engine build. Both these problems are resolvable; the first one means you have to allocate a larger budget if you want more performance, and as for the second one, your skills can be improved by studying and reading about the subject before you tackle it. A good book to read is 'How to Hot Rod Volkswagen Engines'. The other important book to have to hand is a Haynes VW workshop manual, which gives all the basic information and specifications you will need.

The first areas we are going to cover when tuning the VW engine are the Stages 1, 2 and 3 on our chart which do not necessitate the engine being removed or dismantled. Note that engine tuning is only beneficial on an engine that is in sound condition. Tuning cannot overcome any mechanical defects which are already in the motor, so always check and correct the basic adjustments on the engine and the components you are not replacing, i.e. carburetters and air filter, the ignition coil, points, condenser, HT leads and spark plugs and finally, the valve tappets. Also make sure you use a good quality engine oil.

Beetle Performance Parts Chart

Tuning Stage	1	2	3	4	5	6	7	8	9	10
Estimated DIN bhp	55	60	70	75	85	100	110	120	140+	Race
Performance Exhaust	√	√	√	√	√	√	√	√	√	√
Air cleaner	√									
Adj. main jet	√									
Twin carburetters		√	√	√	√					
Bosch .009 distributor		√	√	√	√	√	√	√	√	√
Hi-ratio rockers			√						√	√
Power pulley & belt			√	√						
Oil pressure boost kit			√	√						
Performance cam & lifters				√	√	√	√	√	√	√
Big bore barrels/pistons					√	√	√	√	√	√
Twin dual carburetters						√	√	√	√	√
Engine balance							√	√	√	√
Windage tray							√	√	√	
Stroker crankshaft								√	√	√
Alloy fan housing							√	0 √	√	√
Cylinder cooling tin							√	√	√	√
Hi-performance cyl. heads									√	√
Rocker swivel feet				√	√	√	√	√	√	√
Hi-perf. ignition leads				√	√	√	√	√	√	√
Hi-perf. coil				√	√	√	√	√	√	√
Remote oil cooler					√	√	√	√	√	√
Hi-perf. oil pump					√	√	√	√	√	√
Eng. oil breather system						√	√	√	√	√
Oil suction kit						√	√	√	√	
Electric fuel pump									√	√
Fuel regulator									√	√
Lightened flywheel							√	√	√	√
Dry-sump lubrication										
Case-savers thread inserts					√	√	√	√	√	√
Hi-performance pushrods			√				√	√	√	√
8-dowel crank drilling (tool)							√	√	√	√
Large gland nut/washer							√	√	√	√
Hi-perf. rocker shaft							√	√	√	√
Chr-moly stud kit										√
Hi-perf. pushrod tubes					√	√	√	√	√	√

Stage 1

Stage 1 is the simplest tuning stage and starts with the most fundamental of performance improvers, which is to replace the standard exhaust system with a tuned version. Over 45 different styles of exhaust are available for this engine which can accommodate most requirements, even VW-powered motorcycles.

Exhaust system choice is critical for several basic reasons. Firstly, what is going to be done with your Beetle? Is it going to stay stock-bodied, be turned into a Baja, or one of the many kit cars available? Assuming that it is going to stay stock-bodies, the choice required is an exhaust system which exits below the rear body valance panel. It should also be borne in mind that, when choosing an exhaust system, one should be purchased that has the primary pipe lengths (the ones that go from the cylinder head to the silencer collector flange) of an equal length. The reasons for this, to put it in simple terms, is so that each cylinder has the same exhaust draw length.

Whilst dual Buggy-type exhaust systems may look preferable on a Beach Buggy, the two individual systems cannot give the same improved performance as a 4-into-1 exhaust system produces because the 4-into-1 system allows each cylinder's exhaust gases to help evacuate its fellow cylinders.

The above exhaust information is relevant to every stage of engine tuning and, in fact, the more power your engine produces, the more important the

correct system choice becomes. Next time you see UVA's off-road racing Fugitive, take a close look at the exhaust system. All the four equal-length exhaust pipes are gently and carefully brought together into a single collector pipe exiting upwards into a single 1¾" open tail pipe.

Right, that's enough about exhaust systems. We assume you have made your choice and fitted a system which still retains the exhaust heat exchangers, because our stock-bodies Beetle is going to be used all year round.

Now that the exhaust gases are being more effectively extracted from the engine, the flow of the air/fuel mixture into the engine should be improved to gain full benefit for this particular tune-up, so attention is turned to the carburetter. Check the carburetter to make sure that it's not worn. The main area of wear is on the spindle butterfly shaft. Replace the standard air cleaner with a good quality sports variety, which will not only improve the engine compartment visually, but will also allow more air flow through the carburetter.

The final change in Stage 1 is to replace the standard fuel main-jet in the carburetter with an adjustable version. The logic here is obvious, with improved air flow into the carburetter and out of the engine via the exhaust, we must assure ourselves that we obtain the correct air/fuel mixture. The adjustable main jet allows tuning of the carburetter to obtain this optimum ratio. This is the only area that, if you don't feel confident about, we would suggest you have the carburetter set up by an expert, preferably with a rolling-road facility.

Stage 2

The Stage 2 tuning requires a little more work to get a little more performance. Starting with the same basic criteria (to get better air/fuel flow through the engine), the exhaust is changed for a performance item but, instead of

tweaking the standard carburetter, this unit is dumped in favour of either two single-choke carburetters (one sited over each of the cylinder heads) or one dual progressive twin-choke carburetter.

The twin carburetters are more expensive than the dual progressive variety, and are slightly better on performance, but involve a little bit more work in tuning them. The dual progressive twin-choke version has the added advantage, for the economy minded, of using just one of its two chokes when cruising, whilst the second choke opens when accelerating hard.

A good progressive twin-choke carburetter kit (like all carburetter kits) should contain all the parts you require to complete the installation, including the dual inlet manifold. Don't be fooled by the salesman who tells you that you can fit a dual carburetter with an adaptor to your existing inlet manifold. Logic dictates that you cannot get the air/fuel flow of a twin carburetter through a manifold designed for a standard single carburetter.

When fitting the dual progressive twin-choke carburetter, which is positioned in the same place as the original, make sure that the two heat risers that run from the exhaust system up to the inlet manifold are retained. If you don't, you will experience carburetter icing.

The final modification on Stage 2 is to replace the standard vacuum advance distributor for a mechanical advance distributor. The favourite here is the Bosch .009. The advantages of fitting this distributor are the improved ignition advance characteristics it gives, which suit the engine tuning carried out. A good 'ballpark' ignition setting with this distributor is 28° of advance at 3,000rpm.

Stage 3

Stage 3 tuning is a further advance on Stage 2. Already replaced are the exhaust,

carburetter and distributor. Next attention is turned to the rocker assembly, by removing the standard 1.1:1 units and replace them with 1.5:1 high-ratio rockers.

This is achieved by simply unbolting and removing the stock rocker assembly and pushrods, replacing the stock pushrods with high-performance cupped-type, replacing the rocker assembly with the high-ratio version and re-adjusting the tappets in the normal way.

These rockers work by moving the centre picot closer to the pushrod, which increases the ratio from 1.1:1 to 1.5:1. This, in turn, opens the valves in the cylinder-head to a greater extent, allowing more air/fuel mixture to enter the cylinders. More fuel means a bigger push on the piston, which means more power.

The next step is to replace the standard crankshaft pulley with a power pulley, which is smaller in diameter than the standard pulley. The kit contains a corresponding smaller fan belt. Basically, this conversion achieves a reduction in the speed at which the generator and fan rotate in proportion to the engine revolutions which, in turn, reduces the drag (power absorption) on the engine. This particular modification is ideally suited to the UK but is not such a good idea in very hot climates. It is also kept as a tuning aid for the lower horsepower tuning stages because, as we start getting into the 100+bhp power outputs, the extra heat generated in the engine needs to be removed as efficiently as possible.

The final modification for Stage 3 is to pay some attention to the lubrication system. The oil pressure relief springs and pistons (either one or two depending on the engine size and year of manufacture) can be found on the underside of the engine. These should be replaced with an oil pressure boost kit, which will improve the oil pressure and lubrication in the engine. It can also be a good thing for tired stock engines.

Thanks are due to Robin Wager, Editor and Publisher of 'VW Motoring' magazine for permission to use these articles and especially to Alan Arnold of UVA Ltd. (see 'Suppliers' section for details) who is responsible for the information contained in them.

T1. The UVA Fugitive shows what off-roading, and an advanced level of tuning, can be all about.

T2. The bare bones of a balljoint front beam, this with a centre-mount steering box.

T3. This beautifully prepared Beetle 1302/1303 floorpan includes an 'ultimate' inboard front suspension.

T4. Adjustable rear spring plates of the CVJ-type suspension.

T5. Although usually fitted to kit cars, this dual-circuit brake/throttle pedal assembly can be fitted to Beetles.

T6. A cross-drilled disc brake conversion available from UVA Ltd. and referred to in the text.

T7. Quite apart from the power aspect, this engine would enhance the appearance of any Baja or Buggy.

T8. Uprated clutches are mentioned in the text but this is the Feramic racing assembly for very highly tuned applications.

T9. This is one of the urethane bushes recommended by Alan Arnold.

T10. These are the two types of Sway-A-Way adjusters, one for ball-joint beams (upper right) and one for link-pin beams (lower left). Since the ball-joint type is a little more complex and requires more work, the illustration shows the spring disc in two different positions (A&B). In position A, the ½ in. set screw (No. 6) is shown before it is tightened down to secure the torsion springs in place.

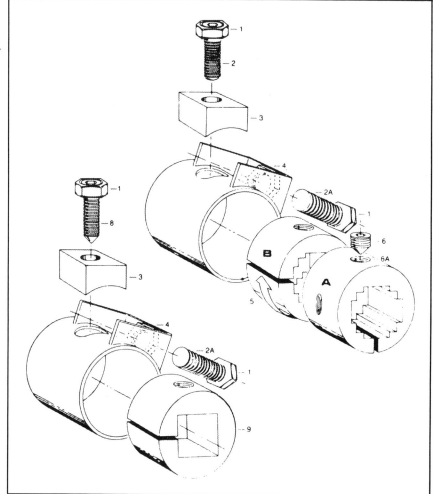

T11. These are the marks necessary before cutting the beam. As the top line is only required for ball-joint beams it is shown dotted.

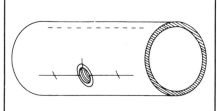

T12. A 'blown' or supercharged engine is not beyond the bounds of possibility but reliability can suffer unless the engine is strengthened.

T13.   This is a UVA-supplied mechanical advance Bosch .009 distributor, highly recommended if other simple tuning is carried out.

T14.   The ideal 'tuned' exhaust system has a single outlet with 4-into-1 equal length primary pipes.

T15.   Electronic ignition, such as this Sparkrite unit, gives a stronger spark and is ideal for the relatively low-revving Beetle. Points are retained, but used only as a switch so that burned points become a thing of the past while efficiency is increased.

T16. K & N make an air filter that fits in place of the stock unit . . .

T17. . . . and another that replaces the element in the existing car (later models with non-oil bath air cleaners). Both types last for 100,000 miles without replacement and allow the engine to 'breathe' cleanly but freely, releasing more power!

APPENDICES

1 Workshop Procedures

Professional motor mechanics are trained in safe working procedures. However enthusiastic you may be about getting on with the job in hand, do take the time to ensure that your safety is not put at risk. A moment's lack of attention can result in an accident, as can failure to observe certain elementary precautions.

There will always be new ways of having accidents, and the following points do not pretend to be a comprehensive list of all dangers; they are intended rather to make you aware of the risks and to encourage a safety-conscious approach to all work you carry out on your vehicle.

Be sure to consult the suppliers of any materials and equipment you may use and to obtain and read carefully operating and health and safety instructions that they may supply.

Essential DOs and DON'Ts

DON'T rely on a single jack when working underneath the vehicle. Always use reliable additional means of support, such as axle stands, securely placed under a part of the vehicle that you know will not give way.
DON'T attempt to loosen or tighten high-torque nuts (e.g. wheel hub nuts) while the vehicle is on a jack; it may be pulled off.
DON'T start the engine without first ascertaining that the transmission is in neutral (or 'Park' where applicable) and the parking brake applied.
DON'T attempt to drain oil until you are sure it has cooled sufficiently to avoid scalding you.
DON'T grasp any part of the engine, exhaust or catalytic converter without first ascertaining that it is sufficiently cool to avoid burning you.
DON'T inhale brake lining dust – it is injurious to health.
DON'T allow any spilt oil or grease to remain on the floor – wipe it up straightaway, before someone slips on it.
DON'T use ill-fitting spanners or other tools which may slip and cause injury.
DON'T attempt to lift a heavy component which may be beyond your capability – get assistance.
DON'T rush to finish a job, or take unverified short cuts.
DON'T allow children or animals in or around an unattended vehicle.
DO wear eye protection when using power tools such as drill, sander, bench grinder etc., and when working under the vehicle.
DO use a barrier cream on your hands prior to undertaking dirty jobs – it will protect your skin from infection as well as making the dirt easier to remove afterwards; but make sure your hands aren't left slippery.
DO keep loose clothing (cuffs, tie etc.) and long hair well out of the way of moving mechanical parts.
DO remove rings, wristwatch etc., before working on the vehicle – especially the electrical system.
DO ensure that any lifting tackle used has a safe working load rating adequate for the job.
DO keep your work area tidy – it is only too easy to fall over articles left lying around.
DO get someone to check periodically that all is well, when working alone on the vehicle.
DO carry out work in a logical sequence and check that everything is correctly assembled and tightened afterwards.
DO remember that your vehicle's safety affects that of yourself and others. If in doubt on any point, get specialist advice.
IF, in spite of following these precautions, you are unfortunate enough to injure yourself, seek medical attention as soon as possible.

Fire

Remember at all times that petrol (gasoline) is highly flammable. Never smoke, or have any kind of

naked flame around, when working on the vehicle. But the risk does not end there — a spark caused by an electrical short-circuit, by two metal surfaces contacting each other, or even by static electricity built up in your body under certain conditions can ignite petrol vapour, which in a confined space is highly explosive.

Always disconnect the battery earth (ground) terminal before working on any part of the fuel system, and never risk spilling fuel on to a hot engine or exhaust.

It is recommended that a fire extinguisher of a type suitable for fuel and electrical fires is kept handy in the garage or workplace at all times. Never try to extinguish a fuel or electrical fire with water.

Fumes

Certain fumes are highly toxic and can quickly cause unconsciousness and even death if inhaled to any extent. Petrol (gasoline) vapour comes into this category, as do the vapours from certain solvents such as trichloroethylene and those from many adhesives. Any draining or pouring of such volatile fluids should be done in a well ventilated area.

When using cleaning fluids and solvents, read the instructions carefully. Never use any materials from unmarked containers — they may give off poisonous vapours.

Never run the engine of a motor vehicle in an enclosed space such as a garage. Exhaust fumes contain carbon monoxide which is extremely poisonous; if you need to run the engine, always do so in the open air or at least have the rear of the vehicle outside the workplace.

If you are fortunate enough to have the use of an inspection pit never drain or pour petrol, and never run the engine, while the vehicle is standing over it; the fumes, being heavier than air, will concentrate in the pit with possibly lethal results.

The battery

Never cause a spark, or allow a naked light, near the vehicle battery. It will normally be giving off a certain amount of hydrogen gas, which is highly explosive.

Always disconnect the battery earth (ground) terminal before working on the fuel or electrical systems.

If possible, loosen the filler plugs or cover when charging the battery from an external source. Do not charge at an excessive rate or the battery may burst.

Take care when topping up and when carrying the battery. The acid electrolyte, even when diluted, is very corrosive and should not be allowed to contact the eyes or skin.

If you ever need to prepare electrolyte yourself, always add the acid slowly to the water, and never the other way round. Protect against splashes by wearing rubber gloves and goggles.

Mains electricity

When using an electric power tool, inspection light etc. which works from the mains, always ensure that the appliance is correctly connected to its plug and that, where necessary, it is properly earthed (grounded). Do not use such appliances in damp conditions and, again, beware of creating a spark or applying excessive heat in the vicinity of fuel or fuel vapour.

Ignition HT voltage

A severe electric shock can result from touching certain parts of the ignition system, such as the HT leads, when the engine is running or being cranked, particularly if components are damp or the insulation is defective. Where an electronic ignition system is fitted, the HT voltage is much higher and could prove fatal.

Compressed gas cylinders

There are serious hazards associated with the storage and handling of gas cylinders and fittings, and standard precautions should be strictly observed in dealing with them. Ensure that cylinders are stored in safe conditions, properly maintained and always handled with special care and make constant efforts to eliminate the possibilities of leakage, fire and explosion.

The cylinder gases that are commonly used are oxygen, acetylene and liquid petroleum gas (LPG). Safety requirements for all three gases are:

Cylinders must be stored in a fire resistant, dry and well ventilated space, away from any source of heat or ignition and protected from ice, snow or direct sunlight. Valves of cylinders in store must always be kept uppermost and closed, even when the cylinder is empty.

Cylinders should be handled with care and only by personnel who are reliable, adequately informed and fully aware of all associated hazards. Damaged or leaking cylinders should be immediately taken outside into the open air, and the supplier and fire authorities should be notified immediately. No one should approach a gas cylinder store with a naked light or cigarette. Care should be taken to avoid striking or dropping cylinders, or knocking them together.

Cylinders should never be used as rollers.

One cylinder should never be filled from another.

Every care must be taken to avoid accidental damage to cylinder valves.

Valves must be operated without haste, never fully opened hard back against the back stop (so that other users know the valve is

open) and never wrenched shut but turned just securely enough to stop the gas.

Before removing or loosening any outlet connections, caps or plugs, a check should be made that the valves are closed.

When changing cylinders, close all valves and appliance taps, and extinguish naked flames, including pilot jets, before disconnecting them.

When reconnecting ensure that all connections and washers are clean and in good condition and do not overtighten them.

Immediately a cylinder becomes empty, close its valve.

Safety requirements for acetylene: Cylinders must always be stored and used in the upright position. If a cylinder becomes heated accidentally or becomes hot because of excessive backfiring, immediately shut the valve, detach the regulator, take the cylinder out of doors well away from the building, immerse it in or continuously spray it with water, open the valve and allow the gas to escape until the cylinder is empty.

Safety requirements for oxygen: No oil or grease should be used on valves or fittings. Cylinders with convex bases should be used in a stand or held securely to a wall.

Safety requirements for LPG: The store must be kept free of combustible material, corrosive material and cylinders of oxygen.

Dangerous liquids and gases

Because of flammable gas given off by batteries when on charge, care should be taken to avoid sparking by switching off the power supply before charger leads are connected or disconnected. Battery terminals should be shielded, since a battery contains energy and a spark can be caused by any conductor which touches

its terminals or exposed connecting straps.

When internal combustion engines are operated inside buildings the exhaust fumes must be properly discharged to the open air. Petroleum spirit or mixture must be contained in metal cans which should be kept in a store. In any area where battery charging or the testing of fuel injection systems is carried out there must be good ventilation and no sources of ignition. Inspection pits often present serious hazards. They should be of adequate length to allow safe access and exit while a car is in position. If there is an inspection pit, petrol may enter it. Since petrol vapour is heavier than air it will remain there and be a hazard if there is any source of ignition. All sources of ignition must therefore be excluded. Special care should be taken when any type of lifting equipment is used. Lifting jacks are for raising vehicles; they should never be used as supports while work is in progress. Jacks must be replaced by adequate rigid supports before any work is begun on the vehicle. Risk of injury while working on running engines, eg, adjusting the timing, can arise if the operator touches a high voltage lead and pulls his hand away on to a projection or revolving part.

Work with plastics

Work with plastic materials brings additional hazards into workshops. Many of the materials used (polymers, resins, adhesives and materials acting as catalysts and accelerators) readily produce very dangerous situations in the form of poisonous fumes, skin irritants, risk of fire and explosions.

Jacks and axle stands

Any jack is made for lifting the car, not for supporting it. NEVER

even consider working under your car using only a jack to support the weight of the car. Jacks are for lifting; axle stands are available from many discount stores and all auto parts stores. These stands are absolutely essential if you plan to work under your car. Simple triangular stands (fixed or adjustable) will suit almost all of your working situations. Drive-on ramps are very limiting because of their design and size.

When jacking the car from the front, leave the gearbox in neutral and the brake off until you have placed the axle stands under the frame. Then put the car into gear and/or engage the handbrake and lower the jack. Obviously DO NOT put the car in gear if you plan to turn over the engine! Leaving the brake on or leaving the car in gear while jacking the front of the car will necessarily cause the jack to tip. This is unavoidable when jacking the car on one side and the use of the handbrake in this case is recommended.

If the car is older and if it shows signs of weakening at the jack tubes while using the factory jack, it is best to purchase a good scissors jack or pneumatic jack (depending on your budget).

Workshop safety — summary

1) Always have a fire extinguisher at arm's length whenever welding or when working on the fuel system — under the car, or under the bonnet.
2) NEVER use a torch near the petrol tank.
3) Keep your inspection lamp FAR AWAY from any source of dripping petrol (gasoline), for example while removing the fuel pump.
4) NEVER use petrol (gasoline) to clean parts. Use paraffin (kerosene) or white (mineral) spirits.
5) NO SMOKING!

If you do have a fire, DON'T PANIC. Use the extinguisher effectively by directing it at the base of the fire.

2 Tools and Working Facilities

Introduction

A selection of good tools is a fundamental requirement for anyone contemplating the maintenance and repair of a motor vehicle. For the owner who does not possess any, their purchase will prove a considerable expense, offsetting some of the savings made by doing-it-yourself. However, provided that the tools purchased are of good quality, they will last for many years and prove an extremely worthwhile investment.

To help the average owner to decide which tools are needed to carry out the various mechanical tasks detailed in this book, we have compiled three lists of tools under the following headings: Maintenance and minor repair, Repair and overhaul, and Special. The newcomer should start off with the 'Maintenance and minor repair' tool kit and confine himself to the simpler jobs around the vehicle. Then, as his confidence and experience grows, he can undertake more difficult tasks, buying extra tools as, and when, they are needed. In this way a 'Maintenance and minor repair' tool kit can be built up into a 'Repair and overhaul' tool kit over a considerable period of time without any major cash outlays. The experienced do-it-yourselfer

will have a tool kit good enough for most repairs and overhaul procedures and will add tools from the 'Special' category when he feels the expense is justified by the amount of use these tools will be put to.

Maintenance and minor repair tool kit

The tools given in this list should be considered as a minimum requirement if routine maintenance, servicing and minor repair operations are to be undertaken. We recommend the purchase of combination spanners (ring one end, open-ended the other); although more expensive than open-ended ones, they do give the advantage of both types of spanner.

Combination spanners – as full a range of metric sizes as you can afford.
Adjustable spanner – 9 inch
Engine sump/gearbox/rear axle drain plug hexagonal key (where applicable)
Spark plug spanner (with rubber insert)
Spark plug gap adjustment tool
Set of feeler gauges
Brake adjuster spanner (where applicable)
Brake bleed nipple spanner

Screwdriver – 4 in. long x ¼ in. dia. (plain)
Screwdriver – 4 in. long x ¼ in. dia. (crosshead)
Combination pliers – 6 inch
Hacksaw, junior
Tyre pump
Tyre pressure gauge
Grease gun
Oil can
Fine emery cloth (1 sheet)
Wire brush (small)
Funnel (medium size)

Repair and overhaul tool kit

These tools are virtually essential for anyone undertaking any major repairs to a motor vehicle, and are additional to those given in the Basic list. Included in this list is a comprehensive set of sockets. Although these are expensive they will be found invaluable as they are so versatile – particularly if various drives are included in the set. We recommend the ½ square-drive type, as this can be used with most proprietary torque wrenches. If you cannot afford a socket set, even bought piecemeal, then inexpensive tubular box spanners are a useful alternative. Note that cheap socket sets are made of carbon steel which will give way and break

293

when tightening or undoing some of the high-torque bolts found on Volkswagens. Chrome vanadium steel or some other high-grade steel should be selected. 'Metrinch' socket sets, available in most countries, will fit both Metric and AF size nuts.

The tools in this list will occasionally need to be supplemented by tools from the Special list.

Sockets (or box spanners)
Reversible ratchet drive (for use with sockets)
Extension piece, 10 inch (for use with sockets)
Universal joint (for use with sockets)
Torque wrench (for use with sockets)
'Mole' wrench – 8 inch
Ball pein hammer
Soft-faced hammer, plastic or rubber
Screwdriver – 6 in. long x ⁵/₁₆ in. dia. (plain)
Screwdriver – 2 in. long x ⁵/₁₆ in. square (plain)
Screwdriver – 1½ in. long x ¼ in. dia. (crosshead)
Screwdriver – 3 in. long x ⅛ in. dia. (electrician's)
Pliers – electrician's side cutters
Pliers – needle noses
Pliers – circlip (internal and external)
Cold chisel – ½ inch
Scriber
Scraper (This can be made by flattening and sharpening one end of a piece of copper pipe)
Centre punch
Pin punch
Hacksaw
Valve grinding tool
Steel rule/straightedge
Allen keys
Selection of files
Wire brush (large)
Axle stands
Jack (strong scissor or hydraulic type)

Special tools

The tools in this list are those which are not used regularly, are expensive to buy, or which need to be used in accordance with their manufacturer's instructions. Unless relatively difficult mechanical jobs are undertaken frequently, it will not be economic to buy many of these tools. Where this is the case, you could consider clubbing together with friends (or a motorists' club) to make a joint purchase, or borrowing the tools against a deposit from a local garage or tool hire specialist.

The following list contains only those tools and instruments freely available to the public and not those special tools produced by the vehicle manufacturer specially for its dealer network.

Valve spring compressor
Piston ring compressor
Ball joint separator
Universal hub/bearing puller
Impact screwdriver
Micrometer and/or vernier gauge
Carburettor flow balancing device (where applicable)
Dial gauge
Stroboscopic timing light
Dwell angle meter/tachometer
Universal electrical multi-meter
Cylinder compression gauge
Lifting tackle
Trolley jack
Light with extension lead

Buying tools

For practically all tools, a tool factor is the best source since he will have a very comprehensive range compared with the average garage or accessory shop. Having said that, accessory shops often offer excellent quality goods at discount prices, so it pays to shop around.

Remember, you don't have to buy the most expensive items on the shelf, but it is always advisable to steer clear of the very cheap tools. There are plenty of good tools around, at reasonable prices, so ask the proprietor or manager of the shop for advice before making a purchase. Avoid carbon-steel spanners, because they are inherently weaker than those of the chrome-vanadium or other high-quality steel alloy variety.

Care and maintenance of tools

Having purchased a reasonable tool kit, it is necessary to keep the tools in a clean and serviceable condition. After use, always wipe off any dirt, grease and metal particles using a clean, dry cloth, before putting the tools away. Never leave them lying around after they have been used. A simple tool rack on the garage or workshop wall, for items such as screwdrivers and pliers is a good idea. Store all normal spanners and sockets in a metal box. Any measuring instruments, gauges, meters etc., must be carefully stored where they cannot be damaged or become rusty.

Take a little care when the tools ae used. Hammer heads inevitably become marked and screwdrivers lose the keen edge on their blades from time-to-time. A little timely attention with emery cloth or a file will soon restore items like this to a good serviceable finish.

Working facilities

Not to be forgotten when discussing tools, is the workshop itself. If anything more than routine maintenance is to be carried out, some form of suitable working area becomes essential.

It is appreciated that many an owner mechanic is forced by circumstance to remove an engine or similar item, without the benefit of a garage or workshop. Having done this, any repairs should always be done under the cover of a roof.

Wherever possible, any

dismantling should be done on a clean flat workbench or table at a suitable working height.

Any workbench needs a vice: one with a jaw opening of 4 in. (100mm) is suitable for most jobs. As mentioned previously, some clean, dry storage space is also required for tools, as well as the lubricants, cleaning fluids, touch-up paints and so on which soon become necessary.

Another item which may be required, and which has a much more general usage, is an electric drill with a chuck capacity of at least $5/16$ in. (8mm). This, together with a good range of twist drills, is virtually essential for fitting accessories such as wing mirrors and reversing lights.

Last, but not least, always keep a supply of old newspapers and clean, lint-free rags available, and try to keep any working areas as clean as possible.

Spanner jaw gap comparison table

Jaw gap (in)	Spanner size
0.625	$5/8$ in. AF
0.629	16 mm AF

Jaw gap (in)	Spanner size
0.669	17 mm AF
0.687	$11/16$ in. AF
0.708	18 mm AF
0.710	$3/8$ in. Whitworth/$7/16$ in. BSF
0.748	19 mm AF
0.750	$3/4$ in. AF
0.812	$13/16$ in. AF
0.820	$7/16$ in. Whitworth/$1/2$ in. BSF
0.866	22 mm AF
0.875	$7/8$ in. AF
0.920	$1/2$ in. Whitworth/$9/16$ in. BSF
0.937	$15/16$ in. AF
0.944	24 mm AF
1.000	1 in. AF
1.010	$9/16$ in. Whitworth/$5/8$ in. BSF
1.023	26 mm AF
1.062	$11/16$ in. AF/27 mm AF
1.100	$5/8$ in. Whitworth/$11/16$ in. BSF
1.125	$11/8$ in. AF
1.181	30 mm AF
1.200	$11/16$ in. Whitworth/$3/4$ in. BSF
1.250	$11/4$ in. AF
1.259	32 mm AF
1.300	$3/4$ in. Whitworth/$7/8$ in. BSF
1.312	$15/16$ in. AF

Jaw gap (in)	Spanner size
1.390	$13/16$ in. Whitworth/$15/16$ in. BSF
1.417	36 mm AF
1.437	$17/16$ in. AF
1.480	$7/8$ in. Whitworth/1 in. BSF
1.500	$11/2$ in. AF
1.574	40 mm; AF/$15/16$ in. Whitworth
1.614	41 mm AF
1.625	$15/8$ in. AF
1.670	1 in. Whitworth/$11/8$ in. BSF
1.687	$111/16$ in. AF
1.811	46 mm AF
1.812	$113/16$ in. AF
1.860	$11/8$ in. Whitworth/$11/4$ in. BSF
1.875	$17/8$ in. AF
1.968	50 mm AF
2.000	2 in. AF
2.050	$11/4$ in. Whitworth/$13/8$ in. BSF
2.165	55 mm AF
2.362	60 mm AF

3 Specifications

These are some of the technical specifications of the Beetle as they appeared at some of the main change points.

Type 1 from 1945 to 1953

Engine	4-cylinder horizontally opposed air-cooled 1131cc, 75mm bore x 64mm stroke Compression ratio 5.8:1 25bhp at 3,300rpm 1 Solex 26VF carb. until 1948, then Solex 26VFIS to October 1952, then Solex 28PC1
Transmission Fine-drive	4.43:1 ratio, spiral bevel
Suspension	Independent all round Front: transverse laminated torsion bars with trailing arms Rear: single transverse torsion bar; swing axle with radius arms Single-acting hydraulic shock absorbers all round until April 1951 when double-acting
Wheels & Tyres	Steel disc wheels, five bolt mounted with 5.00 x 16in tyres until Sept. 1952, then 5.60 x 15
Steering	Worm and nut
Brakes	Mechanical, cable operated drum brakes but hydraulic brakes fitted to Export model from April 1950
Dimensions	Wheelbase, 7ft 10½in Front track, 4ft 3in Rear track, 4ft 1¼in Length 13ft 4in Height 5ft 1in, reduced to 4ft 11in from October 1952 Unladen weight 1596lbs

1200 from 1954 to 1960

As Type 1, except for:

Engine

77mm bore x 64mm stroke, 1192cc
Compression ratio 6.6:1
30bhp at 3,400rpm

Transmission

Final drive ratio 4.4:1

Suspension

Front anti-roll bar on Export and Cabrio. from August 1959

Dimensions

Unladen weight 1602lbs, Cabriolet 1758lbs

1200 from 1960 to 1978

As above except for:

Engine

Compression ratio 7:1
Solex PICT carb. until November 1963, then Solex 28 PICT-1
to July 1970, then Solex 30 PICT 3
34bhp (DIN) at 3,600rpm

Transmission

Final drive ratio: 4.375:1

Steering

Worm and roller

Wheels

4-bolt mounting from August 1967

Dimensions

4ft 5½in rear track from August 1967
Unladen weight 1669lbs

1300 from 1965 to 1975

As 1200 except for:

Engine

77mm bore x 69mm stroke, 1285cc
Compression ratio 7.3:1 but 7.5:1 from August 1970
Solex 30 PICT-1 carb. to Feb 1968, 30 PICT-2 to Aug 1970,
30 PICT-3 to June 1971, then 31 PICT-1
40bhp at 4,000rpm but 44bhp (DIN) at 4,100rpm from Aug
1970

Dimensions

Front track 4ft 3¼in
Rear track 4ft 1in but 4ft 5½in from Aug 1966
Length 13ft 4½in
Width 5ft 0¾in
Height 4ft 11¼in
Unladen weight, Cabriolet, 1669lbs

1500 from 1966 to 1970

As 1300 except for:

Engine

83mm bore x 69mm stroke, 1493cc
Compression ratio 7.5:1
Solex 30 PICT-1 carb. to Aug 1967 then 30 PICT-1
44bhp (DIN) at 4,000rpm

Transmission

Final drive ratio 4.125:1
Semi-automatic final drive ratio 4.125:1

Suspension

Semi-automatic: Semi-trailing arm rear suspension with
double-jointed drive shafts

Brakes

Discs at front

Dimensions

Front track 4ft 3¼in
Rear track 4ft 5in
Length 13ft 4½in
Width 5ft 0in
Height 4ft 11in
Unladen weight 1758lbs, Cabrio. 1848lbs

1302, 1302S from 1970 to 1972

Engine

As 1971 1300 for 1302
1302S: 85mm bore x 69mm stroke
Compression ratio 7.5:1
Solex 30 PICT-3 carb. to June 1971, then 34 PICT-3
50bhp (DIN) at 4,000rpm

Transmission

1302S: Final drive ratio 4.375:1

Suspension

Front suspension by coil spring and MacPherson strut
Rear suspension as 1500 semi-automatic

Wheels and tyres

4½J rims with 5.60 x 15 tyres

Dimensions

Wheelbase 7ft 11¾in
Front track 4ft 6¼in
Rear track 4ft 5¼in
Length 13ft 4½in
Width 5ft 2½in
Height 4ft 11¾in
Unladen weight 1915lbs, Cabrio. 2027lbs

1303, 1303S from 1972 to 1975

As 1302, 1302S except for:

Dimensions

Front track 4ft 6¾in
Rear track 4ft 5in
Length 13ft 7in
Unladen weight 1893lbs, Cabrio. 2050lbs

4 Production Modifications

Vast numbers of production modifications have been made to the Beetle and its stablemates over the years and there are far too many to show here in complete detail. However, the most significant ones are shown below. Very many of the parts are interchangeable between early and later model Beetles, so there is rarely a problem with keeping an early car on the road and there are increasing numbers of specialists supplying and even manufacturing early parts on both sides of the Atlantic. In fact the supply situation for even the oldest parts is said to be total in the U.S. — provided you are willing to pay high prices for them.

The following section is broken down into two sections for the various models of Beetle and Transporter. They are: Type 1 Beetle Saloon and Cabriolet (1945–1981); and Type 2 Camper/ Transporter (1949–1979). It is important to note that specifications and production changes for early Beetles were not consistent.

Also note that prior to 1955 all Volkswagens were built according to calendar year. On August 1 1955, however, a 'model year' system was established. (See notes under '1955'). DON'T CONFUSE MODEL YEARS WITH 'REAL' DATES!

Production changes took place at different times in different markets. As a result, the following list may only be regarded as a guide.

Production modifications

Beetle Saloon & Cabriolet

KdF-Wagen and pre-production Prototypes

1932 Type 12
3 only built for Zundapp, 2 saloons and 1 cabriolet

1934 Type 32
3 only built for NSU, all saloons

1935 Type 60 'Beetle' prototypes
1 saloon (V1), 1 cabriolet (V2)

1936 Type 60
3 saloons, VW3

1937 Type 60
30 saloons, VW30

1938 Type 60
44 saloons, VW38

1939 Type 60
50 saloons, VW39

1940–45 Wartime production
Type 1 saloons (built to 'prove'

production equipment), 630; Kubelwagen, 50,000; Kommandeurwagen (4 WD saloon) 650+; Schwimmwagen 14,000+; Kubel/KdF saloon, c700

1945 Type 1 Saloon
Blue/grey standard colour but military colours available plus black, maroon (for Russian cars — only a handful built), blue (for RAF cars) and dark grey (for U.S. Army cars). No chromework. VW logo on nipple-type hub caps, which were chromed for special and export cars. Wire screen wiper arms. 1131cc Schwimmwagen-type engine. Carburettors built at Wolfsberg with the aid of Voigtlander, the camera manufacturers. Memscheid single-acting shock absorbers.

Instrumentation still basically KdF-Wagen through with VW monogram. Straight gear lever; some cars still with DAF badge on gearknob. Upholstery of sprung metal frame, horsehair padding, woolcloth covers. Leathercloth covered hardboard door trims.

1946
Rear lights with push-on lens. Luggage compartment behind rear seats partly formed.

1947
Nipple-type hub caps discontinued and larger VW emblem used. 'Pope's nose' combined

numberplate and stop lamp fitted from middle of year. Rear lights with round pressed-in lens. Copy of Solex 26 VFJ carburettor, marked 'HUF' fitted.

1948
Plain black gearknob replaces those with DAF monogram.
January. Rear footwell introduced to increase passenger footroom.
April. Grease nipple fitted on pedal shaft.
October. Accelerator pedal roller increased in size, driver's seat position made more comfortable. Single reinforcing rib beneath rear glass replaced three ribs previously used.

1949
June. Crankcase breathing improved with new oil filler, phosphorus content of cylinders increased.
July. 'Export' model introduced with extra chromework, wing stoneguards, choice of colours, grooved bumpers, painted horn grilles in front wings, round in shape. Adjustable front seats, arm rests front and rear, ivory-coloured instrument panel and operating knobs, black faced speedo, optional extra clock, two-spoke steering wheel in white.
April. Heater control operated with rotating locking knob.
May. Body No. 85393377537. Luggage compartment opening changed from external handle to internal control. VW badge on luggage compartment lid with fluted trim. Narrow 'cow catcher' over-riders deleted for more conventional type.
June. Ashtrays fitted front and rear. Horn fitted out of sight beneath wing on Export model. Pancake air filter discontinued for T-shaped unit. Rear lights with chrome surround proud of the casing. Starting handle hole discontinued. Licence number plate indentation deleted.
August. Double-acting Fichtel & Sachs or Boge shock absorbers fitted.
New type-numbering system introduced:

Type 11A Basic left-hand-drive saloon
Type 11B Basic right-hand-drive saloon
Type 11C Export left-hand-drive saloon
Type 11D Export right-hand-drive saloon
Type 14A Hebmuller Cabriolet l-h-d only
Type 15A Karmann Cabriolet l-h-d
Type 15B Karmann Cabriolet r-h-d

Transmission case now of magnesium-aluminium alloy. License plate indentation on rear deck dropped. Solex carburetter introduced as standard equipment. Starting crank hole dropped. Noise muffler added to heating duct, heat riser mixture control added.

1950
January. Lower torsion bar received extra leaf. Front torsion bars changed from 4 to 5 leaf construction.
February. Transporter model introduced (Production began en-masse March). Type 2 designation. 1132cc standard Beetle engine, stepped-down transmission, Kubelwagen-style.
April. Optional fitted sunroof and (Export cars only): optional opening rear windows, ventilator cut-outs in door windows, plated horn grilles. Hydraulic brakes in place of cable operated on Export model.
May. Thermostat to prevent cold weather over-cooling. Pistons with offset gudgeon pins used.
June. Ventilation flap fitted to front quarters.
December. Chassis No. 1220471. Cable brakes replaced by hydraulic type.
New Type numbering system introduced:

Type 11E Basic l-h-d saloon
Type 11F Basic r-h-d saloon
Type 11G Export l-h-d saloon
Type 11H Export r-h-d saloon

Later, a completely modified numbering system took over:

Type 101 Basic l-h-d chassis
Type 102 Basic r-h-d chassis
Type 103 Export l-h-d chassis
Type 104 Export r-h-d chassis
Type 111 Basic l-h-d saloon
Type 112 Basic r-h-d saloon
Type 113 Export l-h-d saloon
Type 114 Export r-h-d saloon
Type 115 Basic l-h-d saloon with sunroof
Type 116 Basic r-h-d saloon with sunroof
Type 117 Export l-h-d saloon with steel sunroof
Type 118 Export r-h-d saloon with steel sunroof
Type 151 Karmann Cabriolet l-h-d
Type 152 Karmann Cabriolet r-h-d

1951
First chassis No. 220472 'Wolfsberg Castle' badge featured on the Export model luggage compartment lid. Opening rear windows deleted. Chrome plated screen surround fitted. Vent flaps added to front-quarter body panels.
January. Magnesium alloy crankcase (material known as 'Elektron').
March. Camshaft gear built from synthetic fibre.
May. Double valve springs replaced by single. Double acting telescopic dampers fitted to rear suspension.

1952
September. 'Pope's nose' numberplate/stop lamp discontinued. Ventilation flap deleted from front quarters. Vent window (¼-light) added. Heating controlled by rotary knob; formerly pull knob. Now with 2 brake and tail-lights. Grooved bumpers replaced by new, stronger shape, round horn grilles supplanted by oval shape, quarter lights (ventilators) fitted to doors, rounded rear view mirror in place of angular one, 15in. wheels in place of 16in. with rim section up from 3in. to 4J. Still unventilated, 5-bolt fixing, at same time as 6-leaf front torsion bars and longer shock absorbers fitted: suspension travel increased from 105 to 135mm. External T-handle to engine compartment lid in place of

loop-type and oval rear lights with stop lamp lens on upper surface in place of central, single brake and stop light. 'Juke Box' dashboard styling with speedo. in front of driver with oblong grille in middle of facia. Lid on glove compartment and Wolfsberg crest on steering wheel. Indicator switch moved from dash to steering column. Seats improved and window winder mechanism made faster to use. (3½ instead of 10½ turns.) Wire screen wiper arms replaced by flat arms with wider sweep, self-parking. Rear brake wheel cylinders increased in length, reduced in bore. 5.60 x 15in. tyres replace 5.00 x 16in. Front torsion bars increased to 6 leaf and with increased travel. Synchromesh fitted to top 3 gears on Export model. Rear torsion bar diameter reduced.
October. Solex 28 PCI carb. fitted with accelerator pump.

1953
March. 'Split' rear window reshaped to oval pattern. 'Export' cars now with aluminium alloy body trim. Brake fluid reservoir relocated behind spare wheel instead of at master cylinder as formerly.
Front torsion bars changed to 8 leaves. Crankshaft, flywheel and clutch assy. balanced. Lower 4th gear. Heating outlets for rear passengers discontinued. Quarter lights (vents) now lock. Brake fluid reservoir moved from master cylinder to behind spare tyre.

1954
January. Engine capacity raised from 1131cc to 1192cc and compression ratio increased from 5.8:1 to 6.1:1. Horsepower up from 30 to 36bhp. Larger inlet valves and vacuum advance added to distributor. Oil bath air cleaner fitted. Heads with more cooling fins. Engine running-in requirement dropped. Double filament bulbs fitted to rear lamps, stop lamps now showing red instead of orange. Top 'window' in tail light dropped. Automatic 3-way courtesy light added to export

models. Starter no longer button on dash of export models; now incorporated in ignition switch.

1955
Bumper over-rider 'bows' added and semaphore indicators replaced by flashing indicators low on wings on US models. Model year system replaces calendar year dating system, starting August, i.e. 1956 model year Beetles started leaving production lines after August 1955.
August. Rear lights raised 2in. up rear wings. Single exhaust replaced by twin chromed pipes on Export cars and black enamel on basic cars. Sunroof material changed from canvas to PVC. Seats with adjustable backrest angle. Engine compression ratio raised to 6.6:1.

1956
Engine camshaft gear changed from fibre to alloy.
March. Transporter production transferred to new Hanover plant. Gear lever moved forwards and cranked. Body slightly widened and front seats made 1¼in. wider.
October. Oil pump size increased.
December. Adjustable door striker plates fitted.

1957
Engine with larger oil passages. Tubeless tyres fitted. Front heater outlets moved back to within 5in. of door.
August. Chassis No. 1600440. New dashboard layout. New, enlarged rear window and enlarged windscreen. Smaller air intakes, simplified engine cover shape and dish-shaped lens to no. plate light. Wider front brakes.
October. Damp resistant soundproofing fitted in engine bay. Heater outlets moved nearer the doors.

1958
Instrument panel redesigned. Grille immediately in front of driver with vertical instead of horizontal slats surrounding speedo. Roller accelerator pedal replaced by oblong pedal.

1959
Larger rear-view mirror. Export Beetles fitted with anti-roll bars at front, rear torsion bars shortened and made thinner and rear-axle pivot point lowered giving much better handling, but necessitating tipping power unit forwards by 2 degrees. Frame strengthened.
July. Stronger clutch springs and fan belt fitted.

1960
Push-button type door handles in place of pull-out type. Dished steering wheel with half ring horn push. Contoured seat backs.

Note
March. Hydraulic steering damper fitted and front torsion bar bushes replaced by needle rollers.
August. 1200 Beetle given larger luggage bay with redesigned fuel tank (giving 65% more luggage space) and screen washers as standard. Flashing indicators on front wing tops and non-repeat ign./starter switch. De-luxe 1200 with increased bhp engine (up from 30 to 34bhp DIN), new all-synchro. gearbox, auto. choke carb. redesigned crankshaft and new cylinder spacing, hydraulic steering damper, grab handle and padded sun visor for passenger. Flashing indicators replace arm type.
August (for following model year). Engine undergoes major redesign. Stronger crank, rotating cup tappets, reworked combustion chambers, 7:1 compression ratio, Solex PICT carb. distributor with vacuum advance only. 13% more power, giving 34bhp. Gearbox redesigned giving 1st gear synchro. New engine identifiable by: bolt-on instead of cast-in dynamo support; fuel pump moved from side to top of crankcase, plug leads no longer in tubes. Foot rest for front passenger.

1961
Transparent brake fluid reservoir. Non-repeat starter switch. Beetle-inspired 1500 model introduced (Type 3) in 2-door and Karmann Ghia forms. Cooling fan mounted

on end of crankshaft.
April. 1200 Beetle De-luxe with crankcase vent. via air cleaner.
August. Check straps on doors, 2-colour 3-piece inc. stop, tail and indicator lamps in rear lamp clusters, safety belt anchorage points built in. Worm-and-roller steering box replaces earlier worm-and-nut type, with 'maintenance free' adjustable track rods.
De-luxe. Fuel gauge mounted alongside speedo and reserve fuel tap deleted. Slides over heater outlets. Counterbalanced luggage bay lid. Enlarged fan housing.

1962
Windscreen washers now compressed air operated. Seat belt mounts fitted. Variant 2-door station wagon version of 1500 (Type 3) introduced.
August. Cabriolet rear window enlarged. Leatherette headlining. Basic saloon now with crankcase ventilation.
October. New emblem without coat of arms. (Poss. De-luxe only.)
December. Fresh air heater as standard

1963
Folding handle for sunroof. Foam insulated floor. Nylon window guides.
August. Horn ring replaced by twin thumb buttons on steering wheel, wider rear licence no. plate light, metal sunroof replaces fabric on Type 114 sunroof models. Aerated vinyl replaces leatherette seat upholstery on DeLuxe.
Transporter wheel size changed from 15in. to 14in. dia. and 1493cc commercial engine introduced.
Type 3 1500S introduced with 2-carb high-compression engine.

1964
Basic 1200 model receives hydraulic in place of cable operated brakes.
August. The first two digits indicate Type No., the third is Model Year where '5' = 1965 model year (produced from August 1964) and so on while the rest are

chassis numbers. Series Numbers have an even third digit for r-h-d cars and an odd third digit for l-h-d cars. Sunshine roof versions have a '/M560' suffix on some cars from October 1973 and on all cars from August 1968. All windows much larger and windscreen now slightly curved. Larger spring-mounted wipers. Heater control: screw knob deleted, levers between front seats substituted. Engine cover release now push button in place of T-handle. Front seats rounder and thinner. Additional Beetle production plant built at Emden on North Sea coast.

1965
January 1965: 1964 modifications introduced to U.K. market.
July. Production of right-hand-drive 1200, 1300, 1300A halts.
August. Basic model redesignated as 1200A with non-chrome bumpers — Germany only although available U.K. to special order. 1200 motif on engine cover.
August. 1300 De-luxe model introduced. New 1285cc engine. Identified by 19 instead of 14 fin heads. Slotted wheels with flat hub caps. Emergency blinkers in USA, multi-use steering column stalk, 41.5bhp engine. Horn push ring and black steering wheel. Extra demisting vent.
July. Balljointed suspension with 10-leaf torsion bars and dampers with supplementary rubber springs. Reinforced rear brake drum.

1966
August. 1500cc 53bhp 1500 model introduced in Germany. Engine based on 1500 Transporter engine. Front disc brakes and 1500 emblem on engine cover. Cabriolet included. Locking buttons on doors, 12-volt electrics. Volkswagen name plate on engine cover. Sunroof model and Cabriolet imported to U.K. Z-bar spring on rear suspension and reduced dia. rear torsion bar. Wider rear track. Shorter engine lid with vertical no. plate provision.
July. Last 1300 Cabriolet

imported. Wider rear track, re-shaped rear lid to allow vertical number plate. Recessed interior door handles.
July/August. 1200A discontinued in Germany. 1300A introduced as replacement, with 1300 badge on engine cover and black dished steering wheel. Not available in U.K.
July. Kingpin and stub axle layout discarded for Type 3 type balljoint system. Higher 3rd gear ratio. Increased flywheel dia. 4-bolt wheels in place of earlier 5-bolt for 1300 and 1500 only. 'Fastback' TL 1500 (Type 3) introduced: Now 12-volt. U.S. Beetles with vertical, slightly recessed headlamps, dual brakes, back-up (reverse) lights.

1967
January. 1200 model introduced in Germany, superseding 1300A. Similar to 1300 but less chrome trim and without over-riders. Rubber mats fitted. Reserve fuel tank but no fuel gauge. 41.5bhp engine 1192cc.
August. 1200 model modified in Germany. Vertical slightly recessed headlamps in place of sloping, external fuel tank filler, shorter gear lever and handbrake. Collapsible steering column with ign. switch on column. External fuel filler cap. 1300 modified as for 1200 but also with vertical headlamps, higher, larger bumpers without over-riders (known as 'Europa bars') and larger rear lights with integral back-up (reversing) lights, dual circuit brakes, fresh air ventilation, 2-speed wipers, fuel gauge in speedo. and 12-volt electrics necessitating new starter ring gear, thus new flywheel: limiting engine interchangeability. 4-bolt wheels in place of 5-bolt. 1500 Beetle modified as for 1300 De-luxe (in Germany) but also with new carb. and with semi-auto gearbox option.
August. Emission control equipment in USA. Federal safety sticker on door post. Semi-automatic gear box introduced. Hi-back seats.

1968

1200 model exported to U.K. with lockable filler cap and luggage compartment release, improved seats and ventilation.

August. 1300 model modified as 1200. U.K. models of 1500 Beetle with 1200-type mods. plus steering lock. 1302S model introduced (known as 'Super Beetle') with 1493cc engine. As 1200 Beetle with steering wheel lock.

November. Greatly improved semi-trailing arm rear suspension in place of swing-arm system. Rear window defroster on up-market models, with steering lock and fuel filler flap lock. Front lid release in glove compartment. Dipping rear view mirror. Warm air outlets moved rearwards, remote heater knobs on door columns. 'Stepped down' transmission discontinued on Transporter models. Beetle-derived 411 (Type 4) introduced with 1679cc engine, later superseded by 412 with 1795cc and fuel injection option.

1969

Cabriolet now available in U.K. only to special order.

september. 1300 De-luxe semi-auto. available in U.K. special order only.

October. Dual-circuit brakes fitted to 1200 and 1200L, as fitted to 1300. 914 'VW-Porsche' sports car entered production. Only the 1600 engine option offered on U.S. market. 1600 'Super Beetle' introduced into U.S. market to help compensate for loss of power in 'de-toxing' engines. 10ths of mile appear on mileage odometers.

1970

1302 Beetle model introduced with distinctive, bulbous front end, MacPherson strut suspension replacing front torsion bars and spare wheel recessed into the floor instead of carried vertically, allowing a larger luggage bay. Semi-trailing arm rear suspension. Rubber bumper inserts. 'L' suffix added to model number indicated Beetle with high spec. range of

option extras. 'S' suffix indicated additional performance spec. 1302 model normally fitted with 1300cc engine but . . .

January. 1302S (known as 'Super Beetle') also with extra air intake on engine compartment lid. Semi-automatic transmission available on these models. 1200 and 1300 Beetles still available.

July. 1500 'Super Beetle sun roof model discontinued in U.K.

August. 1500 'Super Beetle' saloon discontinued in U.K.

September. 1600 1302S 'Super Beetle' model introduced in U.K. as 1300 but 1584cc engine with twin-port heads, modified suspension, front disc brakes and more luggage space. Semi-auto. option. 2-speed wipers, hazard flashers, repositioned pedals, straight gear lever in place of cranked. Also Cabriolet (man. and auto.) 1302LS to special order.

September. 1200 Beetle. Towing eyes front and rear, larger screen washer bottle. Sunroof versions only to special order.

September. 1300 De-luxe. Through flow ventilation. Front and rear towing eyes. Sunroof only to special order. Modified engine with twin-port heads and anti-pollution carb. distributor settings. Improved drum brakes. Headlamp switch wired to ignition. Remote heater knobs discontinued from door pillar. Lock on glove compartment door. Smaller head restraints. Buzzer sounds (US) when door opened with key in ignition, side reflectors (US) in rear light housing. 1600 Transporter with 1302S engine.

1971

'Top range' models. Through-flow ventilation with outlets behind side windows. Headlamps go off with ignition (US). Super Beetle with fan-powered ventilation, carpets.

October. 1200 Beetle. Rear window widened by 1½in. Fuel tank filler car screw threaded. Computer diagnosis plug on left of engine bay. 1300 De-luxe modified as 1200 but also with padded steering wheel, steering

column mounted wash-wipe lever, 4 instead of 2 vents on engine bay lid, parcel shelf. Also 1302S and 1302LS Cabriolet modified as for 1300 plus larger disc brakes and padded dash. Auto. options no longer available in U.K. 1700 Transporter engine introduced. 'Super Bug' introduced in U.S. for 1972 model year. See 1303 spec (September 1972) for details. 1200 with 12-volt electrics introduced for 1972 model-year. 1300 and 1302S received 'safety' steering wheel with padded centre and padded surround on dash for following model year.

1972

July. 1302LS Cabriolet discontinued in U.K.

September. 1200 & 1300 front seats with extra contour. Gear lever and handbrake moved nearer driver's hand. Semi-auto. option no longer available on 1300 in U.K.

October. 1300A model introduced into U.K. similar to 1200 but with 1287cc engine. Cabriolet hood redesigned.

September. 1303 Beetle model introduced with 1285cc engine. Similar to 1302 but with curved screen and larger circular rear light. Padded black dash with instrument nacelle. Probably to special order at first. Reduced-noise softer engine mounts and softer clutch.

October. Saloon and Cabriolet 1303S model introduced, similar to 1302S but with curved screen and improvements similar to 1303. Sunroof and Cabriolet to special order only. Interiors for 1303 and 1303S completely redesigned with reference to U.S. safety regs. Rocker switches, non-reflective dash surfaces. New '84 position' adjustable front seats.

December. 'G.T. Beetle' introduced – special edition. As 1300 De-luxe but plus 1584cc engine, disc brakes, 1303-type rear lights, sports wheels, padded dash, cloth trimmed seats. Softer engine mountings on most models. 4½J wheels fitted to all Beetles plus paper element air cleaner and

modified handbrake. Transporter with larger brake callipers. 411 replaced by 412.

1973

July. Model 1300A withdrawn from U.K. Replaced by 1300. October. 1200 Beetle received 1303-type large rear lights. 'Europa'-style open-box-section bumpers in black and chrome trim deleted from window surrounds. October. New 1300 Beetle introduced in U.K., similar to 1200 but with 1285cc engine. 1200-type chrome bumpers with black inserts, chrome moulding on luggage lid, chrome instead of black handles, door pull armrests. Earlier model still theoretically available to special order until Oct. 74. 'Jeans Beetle' limited edition introduced. Based on 1200 Beetle, sports wheels, black bumpers, blue denim seats and black interior trim. 1500 (Type 3) ceased production. October. 1303 imported to UK as standard item. Self stabilising steering. Saloon and Cabriolet 1303S models with self stabilising steering. Still to special order only. 'Big Beetle' special edition introduced based on 1303S but with sports wheels, rubber bumper inserts, cord fabric seats and wood finish dash. 1200L introduced for 1974 model year with full headlining, still with 2-spoke steering wheel.

1974

July. Last Wolfsberg-produced Beetle left the factory. August. 1200, 1300 and 1303. Front indicators moved from wing/fender tops to bumpers. October. Rack-and-pinion steering introduced to 1303 Saloon and Cabriolet 1303S deleted in U.K. 412 (Type 4) ceased production. 1200 Beetle receives 'Europa' bumper bars in place of early-type narrow bars with over-riders, although matt black rather than chromed.

1975

LE fuel-injected Beetle available in U.S. only in attempt to meet stringent anti-pollution legislation. April. 'Sun Beetle' introduced, based on 1300. Sports road wheels, black interior trim and sunroof. Radial tyres. 'Campaign' 1303 special edition introduced with bamboo velour interior, agate brown metallic paint, sports road wheels, reversing lights and heated rear screen. September. 1200 De-luxe version replaces Basic version in U.K. with through-flow ventilation, 2-speed heater, heated rear window and reclining front seats. 1300 and 1303. Final vehicles imported into U.K. 1200A now without hub caps. 1200L reverts to pre-1972 spec. with chrome reintroduced to window surrounds and chromed bumpers with central black strip.

1976

1200 sole Beetle saloon sold by Volkswagen for this model year although 1600 engine still available, known as 1200S. Considerably improved interior trim. Padded version of 1958 dash. Extras fitted as standard. Optional high seat backs, to give head restraint. October. 1303LS Cabriolet reintroduced into U.K. with disc brakes, wide wheels and metallic paintwork. 914SC ('VW-Porsche') ceased production.

1977

LE fuel injected Beetle made available in Japan for 1977 and 1978. Beetle ceased to be available in U.S. market. Beetle in U.K. had smaller optional head restraints and seat backs reclined.

1978

January. Last Beetle (basic 1200 with matt-black trim) left Emden works. 1200: still with front torsion bars, swing-axle rear suspension and worm-and-roller steering in traditional Volkswagen form. Production continued in other countries.

Transporter

(This section kindly supplied by Audi-Volkswagen.)

The 'Volkswagen Transporter' project is unique in the history of van construction. During a production period of thirty years, this model became a world beater. 4.8 million personnel and load transporters were produced by VW and became a byword for economy, reliability and value all over the world. The inimitable concept of the van with engine at the rear with the comfort of a large car was brought to its optimum state by continuous development and maintenance of models. The 'bully', as the Transporter was commonly called in Germany had an attractiveness which did not change. The stages of development are a symbol of the technical improvement and progress in mass production of a van.

1949

Design and development of the VW Transporter based on the private car design created by Prof. Porsche with the engine at the rear and rear wheel drive. The economic recovery in the 1950's in West Germany started with the Volkswagen Transporter.

1950

The first VW Transporter was produced in February. Mass production started on March 8th with ten vehicles per day. Engine: four cylinder air cooled Boxer engine, swept volume 1131 cm^3, 25 HP at 3300 rpm, 7 mkp maximum torque at 2000 rpm. Four speed gearbox, crank axle at front, jointed cross shaft axle at rear. Tare weight 1050 kg, useful load 750 kg, permissible total weight 1820 kg. Tyres 5.50 x 16. Load space of box van 4.6 m^3, front steering design.

1954/55

The swept volume of the four cylinder engine was increased to 1192 cm^3 by a larger cylinder bore (75 to 77 mm bore). Increase in output from 25 to 30 HP at 3400 rpm. Maximum torque 7.7 mkp instead of 7.0 mkp at 2000 rpm. Introduction of

combined ignition-starter lock, improved seats and heating with better hot air distribution.

1955/56

The engine space cover was lowered by redesigning the fan, giving more load space over the engine. Introduction of stronger Duplex brakes at the front and Simplex brakes at the rear. Tyres 6.40 x 15, steel disc wheels.

1960/61

A total of 678,000 vehicles were produced in the first decade of the Transporter. These included:

Box vans	243,000 vehicles or 35.8%
Combi's	152,000 vehicles or 22.4%
Buses	148,000 vehicles or 21.8%
Trucks	129,000 vehicles or 19.0%

The remaining 1% were special models.

Numerous improvements were introduced for the 1961 models. The output of the 1192 cm^3 engine was raised from 30 to 34 HP and its torque increased from 8 to 8.4 mkp at 2000 rpm.

1961/62

A fully synchronous gearbox was introduced to make driving easier. The 1 millionth VW Transporter was manufactured.

1962/63

Vehicle exports were rising year by year. In order to comply with the requests of American customers for higher engine power, the VW designers provided a more powerful 1.5 litre engine as well as the 1.2 litre engine.

	1.2 litre engine	1.5 litre engine
Swept volume	1192 cm^3	1493 cm^3
Bore/stroke	77 x 64 mm	83 x 69 mm
Output	34 HP/3600 rpm	42 HP/3800 rpm
Max. torque	8.4 mkp/2000 rpm	9.7 mkp/2200 rpm
Max. speed	95 km/hour	105 km/hour

Apart from the improved heating, additional Eberspach heating was available on request. The tall box van with taller loading door and 6 m^3 transport volume was introduced.

1963/64

The VW Transporter models for 1964 were provided with many improvements. In addition to the types of 0.8 tonne load, the new 1 ton van joined it in various models.

Other modifications:
Crankcase ventilation with water separator as for the Beetle.
Large brakes with 1028 cm^2 braking surface and longer life as standard.
Larger boot lid and larger rear window (previously 900 x 730 mm now 1230 x 730 mm).

Side sliding door as an extra.
Larger front winker lamps.
Tyres 7.00 x 14.

1966/67

The single key system was introduced and the locks on the doors were made stronger. Fixings for safety belts in the driver's cab were fitted as extras.

1967/68

After 17 years of production and 1.7 million VW Transporters being built, a much modified and improved Type 2 was introduced to the market.

New design with greatly rounded windscreen, air inlet grill at the front, air nozzles in driver's cab and passenger area

and Bowden cable air control. Vehicle made 100 mm longer at the front and at the rear. Windscreen wiper system with compressed air operation. Sliding door to passenger space/load space standard for all models.
Large box van with plastic roof and higher sliding door.
New double joint rear axle with triangular longitudinal members. Greatly improved road position, better springing and comfort. Front axle bearings requiring little maintenance.
Two circuit braking system.
1.6 litre engine with output of 47 HP at 4000 rpm.
The production of the 2 millionth Transporter was celebrated.

1969/70

The modifications for the 1970 models come under the heading of 'greater safety, greater comfort'. Stronger doors, stiffer frame, steering column with safety break position.

1970/71

Cylinder heads with two inlet ducts and forked suction pipes were introduced to increase the output of the 1.6 litre engine. The engine gave an output of 50 HP at 4000 rpm and a torque of 10.8 mkp at 2800 rpm. Disc brakes with greater deceleration and longer life were introduced instead of drum brakes at the front.

The third million of Transporters was reached.

1971/72

A new 1.7 litre flat engine was added to the 1.6 litre Boxer engine with vertical fan. Its fan was situated on the crankshaft to save space.

	1.6 litre engine	1.7 litre engine
Swept volume	1584 cm^3	1679 cm^3
Bore/stroke	85.5 x 69 mm	90 x 66 mm
Output	50 HP/4000 rpm	66 HP/4800 rpm
Max. torque	10.8 mkp/2800 rpm	11.6 mkp/3200 rpm

Both engines complied with the exhaust gas regulations for the USA.

The 1.7 litre engine was equipped with a brake force amplifier corresponding to its output. All models received larger rear lights.

1972/73

An automatic gearbox for the 1.7 litre engine was a new item in the programme. In order to match the torque characteristic of the engine to the hydraulic torque converter, its output for automatic use was throttled to 62 HP. The carburettor engine in vehicles with manual engine still developed 66 HP.

In order to improve vehicle safety, the floor of the front of the vehicle was redesigned and equipped with a deformation part. The bumper bars at the front and back received a new profile and were made more stable. Steps were provided inside the driver's cab.

The vehicles with the flat engines were provided with a hinged engine cover to improve accessibility.

1973/74

The 3.5 millionth VW Transporter was manufactured at the Hanover Works. Daily production reached a record level of 1200 vehicles.

The 1.7 litre engine was replaced by a 1.8 litre version with an output of 68 HP at 4200 rpm and a torque of 13.2 mkp at 3000 rpm to increase the power for long journeys. Petrol was supplied to the engine by a double carburettor, as before.

1975/76

The Hanover Works reported the manufacture of the 4 millionth Volkswagen Transporter. The 1.8 litre engine with increased swept volume now had a volume of 1970 cm^3 and developed 70 HP at 4200 rpm.

The two circuit braking system with saddle disc brakes at the front and drum brakes at the rear was equipped with a brake force regulator to increase its safety. The transporter had a load capacity of 1200 kg in a total

permissible weight of 2500 kg. The increase in tonnage was made safe by additional helical springs at the rear axle. The driving characteristics remained as good as ever.

1977

The 4.5 millionth VW Transporter was manufactured.

1978

A special series of Type 2 vehicles with 2 litre engines, silver paintwork and comfortable equipment was started. A

prototype of the standard Type 2 model with four wheel drive was produced in the Experimental Department. The response of the market to a type 2/4 x 4 is to be tested by these five Landrover Transporters.

1979

After thirty years of manufacture, a new Volkswagen Transporter was introduced to the market on May 7th as a successor to the Type 2 — modern, with a revised design of bodywork, new axles and more of the character of a private car than its predecessor had.

Chassis Numbers

These are the year-end and major change-point chassis numbers of 1200 and 1300 models up to August 1972.

Year	Chassis	Year	Chassis
December 1947	1 - 072 743	July 1965	115 999 000
December 1948	1 - 091 921	August 1965	116 000 001
December 1949	1 - 138 554	December 1965	116 463 103
December 1950	1 - 220 133	July 1966	116 1021 300
December 1951	1 - 313 829	August 1966	117 000 001
October 1952	1 - 397 023	December 1966	117 442 503
December 1952	1 - 428 156	July 1967	117 999 000
March 1953	1 - 454 951	August 1967	118 000 001
January 1954	1 - 575 415	December 1967	118 431 603
December 1954	1 - 781 884	July 1968	118 1016 100
August 1955	1 - 929 746	August 1968	119 000 001
December 1955	1 060 929	December 1968	119 474 780
December 1956	1 394 119	July 1969	119 1200 000
August 1957	1 600 440	August 1969	110 2000 001
October 1957	1 673 411	December 1969	110 2473 153
December 1957	1 774 680	July 1970	110 3100 000
December 1958	2 226 206	August 1970	111 2000 001
August 1959	2 528 668	December 1970	111 2427 591
December 1959	2 801 613	July 1971	111 3200 000
August 1960	3 192 507	August 1971	112 2000 001
December 1960	3 551 044	December 1971	112 2427 792
August 1961	4 010 995	July 1972	112 3200 000
December 1961	4 400 051	August 1972	113 2000 001
August 1962	4 840 836		
December 1962	5 225 042		
August 1963	5 677 119		
December 1963	6 016 120		
July 1964	6 502 399		
August 1964	115 000 001		
December 1964	115 410 000		

5 Colour Schemes

Once again, we're up against the situation where there were so many thousands of different changes, it's just not possible to catalogue them all.

The first set of colour schemes shown here covers the 1200 saloon/sedan models from August 1958 to July 1964, from Chassis No. 2 060 332 up to 6 502 399.

The information is reproduced courtesy Volkswagen and was supplied via Rich Kimball of 'Bugs For You' in California.

	up to July 1963 up to Chassis No. 5 667 118	from February 1963 up to July 1963 from Chassis No. 5 315 042 up to 5 677 118	from August 1963 up to July 1964 from Chassis No. 5 677 119 up to 6 502 399
Car finish	L 225 Jupiter grey	L 390 gulf blue	L 456 (11) ruby red
Upholstery combination (cloth)	medium grey	medium grey	
Upholstery combination (leatherette)			70 grey cord pattern
Wheel disc	L 392 misty grey	L 393 king's blue	L 41 black
Rim	L 464 slate	L 392 misty grey	L 87 pearl white
Gearshift and hand brake lever	*) L 467 basalt grey	L 469 anthracite	LD 43 grey-black
Steering column tube	L 41 black	L 41 black	L 466 silver beige
Seat frame	L 466 silver beige	L 466 silver beige	L 466 silver beige
Bumper, hub cap, outer a handle	L226 silver grey	L 226 silver grey	L 328 steel grey

from August 1963 to July 1964
from Chassis No. 5 677 119 up to 6 502 399

Car finish	L 360 (12) sea blue	L 87 (13) pearl white	L 469 (18) anthracite
Upholstery combination (cloth)			
Upholstery combination (leatherette)	70 grey cord pattern	70 grey cord pattern	70 grey cord pattern
Wheel disc	L 41 black	L 41 black	L 41 black
Rim	L 289 blue-white	L 87 pearl white	L 87 pearl white
Gearshift and hand brake lever	LD 43 grey-black	LD 43 grey-black	LD 43 grey-black
Steering column tube	L 466 silver beige	L 466 silver beige	L 466 silver beige
Seat frame	L 466 silver beige	L 466 silver beige	L 466 silver beige
Bumper, hub cap, outer a handle	L 328 steel grey	L 328 steel grey	L 328 steel grey

Remark: *)   up to Chassis No. 4 010 994 L 467 basalt grey
from Chassis No. 4 010 995 O 469 anthracite

August 1964 up to July 1965, from Chassis No. 115 000 001 up to 115 999 000

Car finish	L 595 (09) fontana grey	L 456 (11) ruby red	L 360 (12) sea blue
Upholstery combination (cloth)	57 derby grey	57 derby grey	57 derby grey
Upholstery combination (leatherette)	83 mesh grey	83 mesh grey	83 mesh grey
Rim	L 87 pearl white	L 87 pearl white	L 289 blue-white

Car finish	L 87 (13) pearl white
Upholstery combination (cloth)	57 derby grey
Upholstery combination (leatherette)	83 mesh grey
Rim	L 87 pearly white

Wheel disc L 41 black; Gearshift and hand brake lever LD 43 grey-black;
Steering column tube and seat frame L 466 silver beige, Bumper, hub cap and outer a handle L 328 steel grey

August 1965 up to July 1966, from Chassis No. 116 000 001 up to 116 1021 300

Car finish	L 595 (09) fontana grey	L 456 (11) ruby red	L 87 (13) pearl white
Upholstery combination (cloth)	55 platinum grid	55 platinum grid	55 platinum grid
Upholstery combination (leatherette)	83 mesh grey/platinum	83 mesh grey/platinum	83 mesh grey/platinum
Upholstery combination (leatherette) M86	86 platinum	86 platinum	86 platinum
Rim	L 87 pearl white	L 87 pearl white	L 87 pearl white

Wheel disc L 41 black; Gearshift and hand brake lever, seat frame LD43 grey-black;
Steering column tube L 466 silver beige, Bumper, hub cap and outer a handle L 328 steel grey

Model 111, 112

August 1965 up to July 1966, from Chassis No. 116 000 001 up to 116 1021 300

	up to Chassis No. 116 1021 300	from Chassis No. 117 000 001
Car finish	L 360 (12) sea blue	L 633 (14) VW blue
Upholstery combination (cloth)	55 platinum grid	55 platinum grid
Upholstery combination (leatherette)	83 mesh grey/platinum	83 mesh grey/platinum
Upholstery combination (leatherette) M86		86 platinum
Rim	L 289 blue-white	

Wheel disc L 41 black; Gearshift and hand brake lever, seat frame LD43 grey-black;
Steering column tube L 466 silver beige, Bumper, hub cap and outer a handle L 328 steel grey

August 1966 up to July 1967, from Chassis No. 117 000 001 up to 117 999 000 and M 86

Car finish	L 595 (09) fontana grey	L 456 (11) ruby red	L 87 (13) pearl white
Upholstery combination (cloth)	55 platinum grid	55 platinum grid	55 platinum grid
Upholstery combination (leatherette)	83 mesh grey/platinum	83 mesh grey/platinum	83 mesh grey/platinum
Upholstery combination (leatherette) M86	86 platinum	86 platinum	86 platinum
*) Rim	*) L 680 cumulus white	*) L 282 lotus white	*) L 282 lotus white

Car finish	L 633 (13) VW blue
Upholstery combination (cloth)	55 platinum grid
Upholstery combination (leatherette)	83 mesh grey/platinum
Upholstery combination (leatherette) M86	86 platinum
*) Rim	*) L 680 cumulus white

Remark:

*) also for M 86

*) Wheel disc, gearshift and hand brake lever, steering column tube and seat frame LD 43 grey-black
Bumper, hub cap and outer a handle L 328 steel grey

August 1967 up to July 1968, from Chassis No. 118 000 001 up to 118 1016 100

Car finish	L 30 A (17) royal red	L282 (42) lotus white	L633 (14) VW blue
Upholstery combination (cloth)	09 platinum pattern	09 platinum pattern	09 platinum pattern
Upholstery combination (leatherette)	38 platinuim	38 platinum	38 platinum
Rim	L 282 lotus white	L282 lotus white	L 680 cumulus white
Car finish	L 70 (f (19) chinchilla		
Upholstery combination (cloth)	09 platinum pattern		
Upholstery combination (leatherette)	38 platinum		
Rim	L 680 cumuls white		

Wheel disc, gearshift and hand brake lever, steering column tube and seat frame LD 43 grey-black

August 1968 up to July 1969, from Chassis No. 119 000 001 up to 119 1200 000

Car finish	L 30 A (17) royal red	L70 (F) (19) chinchilla	L 90 C (63) toga white
Upholstery combination (cloth)	23 grey pattern 69	23 grey pattern 69	23 grey pattern 69
Upholstery combination (leatherette)	50 platinum 69	50 platinum 69	50 platinum 69
Car finish	L 630 (07) cobalt blue		
Upholstery combination (cloth)	23 grey pattern 69		
Upholstery combination (leatherette)	50 platinum 69		

Wheel disc, gearshift and hand brake lever, steering column tube, seat frame LD 43 grey-black; Rim L 581 cloud white

Model 111, 112

August 1969 up to July 1970, from Chassis No. 110 2000 001 up to 110 3100 000

Car finish	L 90 (D) (06) pastel white	L 630 (07) cobalt blue	L 30 (A) (17) royal red
Upholstery combination (cloth)	23 grey pattern 69	23 grey pattern 69	23 grey pattern 69
Upholstery combination (leatherette)	50 platinum 69	50 platinum 69	50 platinum 69
Car finish	L 70 (F) 19 chinchilla		
Upholstery combination (cloth)	23 grey pattern 69		
Upholstery combination (leatherette)	50 platinum 69		

Wheel disc, rim L 91 chrome colored; gearshift and hand brake lever, steering column tube and seat frame LD 43 grey-black

April 1956 up to July 1957, from Chassis No. 1 173 573 up to 1 600 439

Car finish	L 41 black	L 324 Polar silver	L 331 horizon blue
Upholstery combination (cloth)	53 light grey	53 light grey	52 blue
Upholstery combination (leatherette)	70 light beige	70 light beige	70 light beige
Upholstery combination (leatherette)	72a red	72a red	71 blue
Car finish	L 351 coral red	L 412 diamond green	L 378 Prairie beige
Upholstery combination (cloth)	50 light beige	50 light beige	55 copper red
Upholstery combination (leatherette)	70a light beige	70a light beige	70a light beige
Upholstery combination (leatherette)	74 light grey	75 green	72 red
Car finish	L 240 agave		
Upholstery combination (cloth)	50 light beige		Remarks:
Upholstery combination (leatherette)	70a light beige		Index a for carpet material only
Upholstery combination (leatherette)	72 red		

Model 113, 114

August 1957 up to July 1958, from Chassis No. 1 600 440 up to 2 060 331

Car finish	L 41 black	L 351 coral red	L 240 agave
Upholstery combination (cloth)	50 blue-grey/blue	51 brown-grey/red-brown	52 green-grey/grey-green
Upholstery combination (leatherette)	70 blue-grey	74 brown-grey	75 green-grey
Upholstery combination leatherette)	72 red		

Car finish	L 245 light bronze	L 334 glacier blue	L 243 diamond grey
Upholstery combination (cloth)	52 green-grey/grey-green	50 blue-grey/blue	51 brown-grey/red-brown
Upholstery combination (leatherette)	75 green-grey	70 blue-grey	74 brown-grey
Upholstery combination leatherette)			

Car finish	L 335 capri		
Upholstery combination (cloth)	50 blue-grey/blue		
Upholstery combination (leatherette)	70 blue-grey		
Upholstery combination leatherette)			

August 1958 up to July 1959, from Chassis No. 2 060 332 up to 2 528 667

Car finish	L 41 black	L 434 fjord blue	L 243 diamond grey
Upholstery combination (cloth)	50 blue-grey/blue	50 blue-grey/blue	52 green-grey/grey-green
Upholstery combination (leatherette)	70 blue-grey	70 blue-grey	75 green-grey
Upholstery combination leatherette)	72 red		

Car finish	L 335 capri	L 358 garnet red	L 14 mignonette
Upholstery combination (cloth)	50 blue-grey/blue	51 brown-grey/red-brown	52 green-grey/grey-green
Upholstery combination (leatherette)	70 blue-grey	74 brown-grey	75 green-grey
Upholstery combination leatherette)			

Car finish	L 343 Kalahari beige		
Upholstery combination (cloth)	51 brown-grey/red-brown		
Upholstery combination (leatherette)	74 brown-grey		
Upholstery combination leatherette)			

August 1959 up to July 1960, from Chassis No. 2 528 668 up to 3 192 506

Car finish	L 41 black	L 451 indian red	L 363 arctis
Upholstery combination (cloth)	53 fur grey/fur grey	53 fur grey/fur grey	50 water blue/water blue
Upholstery combination (leatherette)	76 stone beige	76 stone beige	70 steel grey
Upholstery combination (leatherette)	78 true red		

Car finish	L 440 flint grey	L 436 indigo blue	L 349 jade green
Upholstery combination (cloth)	50 water blue/water blue	50 water blue/water blue	52 dust green/dust green
Upholstery combination (leatherette)	70 steel grey	70 steel grey	75 light green
Upholstery combination (leatherette)			

Car finish	L 346 Mango green	L 419 Ceramic green	
Upholstery combination (cloth)	52 dust green/dust green	52 dust green	
Upholstery combination (leatherette)	75 light green	75 light green	
Upholstery combination (leatherette)	40 black 68		

August 1970 up to July 1971, from Chassis No. 111 2000 001 up to 111 3200 000

Car finish	L90 D (06) pastel white	L 20 D (12) clementine	L 54 D (21) marina blue
Upholstery combination (cloth)	09 grey pattern	09 grey pattern	09 grey pattern
Upholstery combination (leatherette)	52 alabaster 71	52 alabaster 71	52 alabaster 71
Upholstery combination (leatherette)	40 black 68	40 black 68	40 black 68

Car finish	L 91 D (65) kansas beige
Upholstery combination (cloth)	09 grey pattern
Upholstery combination (leatherette)	52 alabaster 71
Upholstery combination (leatherette)	40 black 68

Wheel disc, rim L 91 chrome colored; gearshift and hand brake lever, steering column tube and seat frame LD 43 grey-black

August 1971 up to July 1972, from Chassis No. 112 2000 001 up to 112 3200 000

Car finish	L 90 D (06) pastel white	L 20 B (07) brilliant orange	L 10 B (08) texas yellow
Upholstery combination (cloth)	08 dog tooth grey	08 dog tooth grey	08 dog tooth grey
Upholstery combination (leatherette)	50 black	50 black	50 black
Upholstery combination (leatherette)	52 alabaster	52 alabaster	52 alabaster

Car finish	L 54 D (21) marina blue
Upholstery combination (cloth)	08 dog tooth grey
Upholstery combination (leatherette)	50 biack
Upholstery combination (leatherette)	52 alabaster

Wheel disc, rim L 91 chrome colored; gearshift and hand brake lever, steering column tube and seat frame LD 43 grey-black

August 1972, from Chassis No. 113 2000 001

Car finish	L 90 D (06) pastel white	L 20 B (07) brilliant orange	L 10 B (08) texas yellow
Upholstery combination (cloth)	29 dog tooth grey	29 dog tooth grey	29 dog tooth grey
Upholstery combination (leatherette)	50 black 68	50 black 68	50 black 68
Upholstery combination (leatherette)	63 silver grey 73	63 silver grey 73	63 silver grey 73

Car finish	L 54 D (21) marina blue
Upholstery combination (cloth)	29 dog tooth grey
Upholstery combination (leatherette)	50 black 68
Upholstery combination (leatherette)	63 silver grey 73

Wheel disc, rim L 91 chrome colored; gearshift and hand brake lever and steering column tube LD 43; seat frame L 41 black

Model 151, 152

August 1959 up to July 1960, from Chassis No. 2 528 668 up to 3 192 506

Car finish	L 473 alabaster	L 361 slate blue	L 264 rock grey
Upholstery combination (cloth)	51 fur grey/true red	50 water blue/water blue	54 dust green/grey-green
Upholstery combination (leatherette)	78 true red	71 water blue	72 grey-green

Car finish	L 349 jade green	L 445 sargasso green	L452 paprika red
Upholstery combination (cloth)	52 dust green/dust green	52 dust green/dust green	53 fur grey/fur grey
Upholstery combination (leatherette)	73 dust green	73 dust green	74 fur grey
Car finish	L 41 black		
Upholstery combination (cloth)	51 fur grey/true red		
Upholstery combination (leatherette)	78 true red		

Model 113, 114

January 1954 up to February 1955, from Chassis No. 1 575 415 up to 1 823 604

Car finish	L 41 black	L 213 Iceland green	L 271 Texas brown
Upholstery combination (cloth)	50 beige	51 green	50 beige
Car finish	L 275 light beige	L 278 ultramaroon	L 227 strato silver
Upholstery combination (cloth)	50 beige	50 beige	52 slate blue

March 1955 up to March 1956, from Chassis No. 1 823 605 up to 1 173 572

Car finish	L 41 black	L 370 Nile beige	L 227 strato silver
Upholstery combination (cloth)	53 grey	50 rust red	52 blue
Upholstery combination (leatherette)	70 light beige	70a light beige	70 light beige
Upholstery combination (leatherette)	72 red	72 red	71 blue
Car finish	L 324 Polar silver	L 313 reed green	L 315 jungle green
Upholstery combination (cloth)	54 green	54 green	54 green
Upholstery combination (leatherette)	70b light beige	70b light beige	70b light beige
Upholstery combination (leatherette)	73 dark green	73 dark green	73 dark green

Remarks: Index a and b for carpet material only

Model 113, 114, 151, 152

August 1960 up to July 1961, from Chassis No. 3 192 507 up to 4 010 994

Car finish	L 41 black	L 456 ruby red	L 390 gulf blue
Upholstery combination (cloth)	59 silver/silver beige	59 silver/silver beige	59 silver/silver beige
Upholstery combination (leatherette)	75 silver beige	75 silver beige	75 silver beige
Upholstery combination (leatherette)	78 true red		
Wheel disc	L 464 slate	*) cadmium red	L 393 king's blue
Rim (Model 113, 114)	L 471 stone beige	L 471 stone beige	L 392 misty grey
Rim (Model 151, 152)	L 41 black	L 41 black	L 41 black
Steering column tube, gearshift and hand brake lever	L 467 basalt grey	L 467 basalt grey	L 467 basalt grey
Seat frame	L 466 silver beige	L 466 silver beige	L 466 silver beige
		up to 28.2.1961 up to Chassis No. 3 691 301	
Car finish	L 87 pearl white	L 380 turquoise	L 391 pastel blue
Upholstery combination (cloth)	58 silver/silver beige	61 turquoise/ice blue	61 turquoise/ice blue
Upholstery combination (leatherette)	74 silver beige	76 ice blue	76 ice blue
Upholstery combination (leatherette)			
Wheel disc	*) clay beige	L 381 sea green	*) night blue
Rim (Model 113, 114)	L 87 pearl white	L 286 turquoise white	L 286 turquoise white
Rim (Model 151, 152)	L 41 black	L 41 black	L 41 black
Steering column tube, gearshift and hand brake lever	*) sand stone	*) hydrate green	*) hydrate green
Seat frame	L 466 silver beige	*) ice blue	*) ice blue
		from 1.3.1961 from Chassis No. 3 691 302	
Car finish	L 380 turquoise	L 391 pastel blue	L 478 beryl green
Upholstery combination (cloth)	59 silver/silver beige	59 silver/silver beige	60 olive/soft beige

Upholstery combination (leatherette)	75 silver beige	75 silver beige	77 soft beige
Upholstery combination (leatherette)			
Wheel disc	L 381 sea green	*) night blue	L 382 olive
Rim (Model 113, 114)	L 286 turquoise white	L 286 turquoise white	*) opal white
Rim (Model 151, 152)	L 41 black	L 41 black	L 41 black
Steering column tube, gearshift and hand brake lever	L 467 basalt grey	L 467 basalt grey	*) nepal green
Seat frame	L 466 silver beige	L 466 silver beige	L 466 silver beige

Remark: *) no longer available

Model 113, 114, 151, 152

August 1961 up to July 1963, from Chassis No. 4 010 995 up to 5 677 118

Car finish	L 41 black	L 469 anthracite	L 456 ruby red
Upholstery combination (cloth)	59 derby grey	59 Derby grey	59 derby grey
Upholstery combination (leatherette)	78 true red	75 silver beige	75 silver beige
Upholstery combination (leatherette)		78 true red	
Wheel disc	L 464 slate	L 464 slate	*) cadmium red
Rim (Model 113, 114)	L 471 stone beige	L 471 stone beige	L 471 stone beige
Gearshift and hand brake lever	L 469 anthracite	L 469 anthracite	L 469 anthracite
Car finish	L 390 gulf blue	L 380 turquoise	L 87 pearl white
Upholstery combination (cloth)	59 derby grey	59 debry grey	59 derby grey
Upholstery combination (leatherette)	75 silver beige	75 silver beige	78 true red
Upholstery combination (leatherette)			
Wheel disc	L 383 king's blue	L 381 sea green	*) clay beige
Rim (Model 113, 114)	L 392 misty grey	L 286 turquoise white	L 87 pearl white
Gearshift and hand brake lever	L 469 anthracite	L 469 anthracite	L 469 anthracite

		Model 151, 152 only	
Car finish	L 478 beryl green	L 398 pacific	
Upholstery combination (cloth)	60 derby olive	59 derby grey	Remark:
Upholstery combination (leatherette)	77 soft beige	75 silver beige	*) no longer available
Upholstery combination (leatherette)			
Wheel disc	L 382 olive	L 289 blue-white	
Rim (Model 113, 114)	*) opal white		
Gearshift and hand brake lever	*) nepal green	L 469 anthracite	

Rim (Model 151, 152) L 41 black; Steering columb tube and seat frame L 466 silver beige

August 1963 up to July 1964, from Chassis No. 5 677 119 up to 6 502 399

Car finish	L 41 (10) black	L 456 (11) ruby red	L 360 (12) sea blue
Upholstery combination (cloth)	54 steel grey	54 steel grey	54 steel grey
Upholstery combination (leatherette)	70 grey cord pattern	70 grey cord pattern	70 grey cord pattern
Upholstery combination (leatherette)	73 red cord pattern		
Rim (Model 113, 114)	L 87 pearl white	L 87 pearl white	L 289 blue-white
Car finish	L 87 (13) pearl white	L 469 (18) anthracite	L 572 (19) Panama beige
Upholstery combination (cloth)	55 beaver brown	54 steel grey	55 beaver brown
Upholstery combination (leatherette)	71 brown cord pattern	70 grey cord pattern	71 brown cord pattern
Upholstery combination (leatherette)	73 red cord pattern	73 red cord pattern	
Rim (Model 113, 114)	L 87 pearl white	L 87 pearl white	L 87 pearl white

Car finish	L 518 (20) Java green	L 519 (21) Bahama blue
Upholstery combination (cloth)	55 beaver brown	56 Windsor blue
Upholstery combination (leatherette)	71 brown cord pattern	75 blue cord pattern
Upholstery combination (leatherette)		
Rim (Model 113, 114)	L 87 pearl white	L 289 blue-white

Rim (Model 151, 152), Wheel disc L 41 black: Gearshift and hand brake lever LD 43 grey-black;
Steering column tube and seat frame L 466 silver beige

Model 113, 114, 151, 152

August 1964 up to July 1965, from Chassis No. 115 000 001 up to 115 999 000

Car finish	L 595 (09) fontana grey	L 41 (10) black	L 456 (11) ruby
Upholstery combination (cloth)	63 brown-grey	63 brown-grey	63 brown-grey
Upholstery combination (leatherette)	83 mesh grey	83 mesh grey	83 mesh grey
Upholstery combination (leatherette)	87 mesh red	87 mesh red	
Rim (Model 113, 114)	L 87 pearl white	L 87 pearl white	L 289 blue-white

Car finish	L 360 (12) sea blue	L 87 pearl white	L 572 (19) panama beige
Upholstery combination (cloth)	63 brown-grey	64 leather brown	64 leather brown
Upholstery combination (leatherette)	83 mesh grey	84 mesh brown	84 mesh brown
Upholstery combination (leatherette)			
Rim (Model 113, 114)	L 87 (13) pearl white	L 87 pearl white	L87 pearl white

Car finish	L 518 (20) java green	L 519 (21) Bahama blue
Upholstery combination (cloth)	63 brown-grey	56 windsor
Upholstery combination (leatherette)	83 mesh grey	83 mesh blue
Upholstery combination (leatherette)		
Rim (Model 113, 114)	L 87 pearl white	L 289 blue-white

Rim (Model 151, 152), Wheel disc L 41 black; gearshift and hand brake lever L 469 anthracite;
Steering column tube and seat frame L 466 silver beige

August 1965 up to July 1966, from Chassis No. 116 000 001 up to 116 1021 300

Car finish	L 595 (09) fontana grey	L 41 (10) black	L 456 (11) ruby red
Upholstery combination (cloth)	59 mosaic teak *)	58 mosaic platinum	58 mosaic platinum
Upholstery combination (cloth optional Model 151)	58 mosaic platinum		
Upholstery combination (leatherette)	76 black	75 pigalle	74 platinum
Upholstery combination (leatherette optional Model 151)	74 platinum	74 platinum	76 black
Upholstery combination (leatherette optional Model 151)	75 pigalle	77 Balearic beige	
Rim (Model 113, 114)	L 87 pearl white	L 87 pearl white	L 87 pearl white

Car finish	L 360 (12) sea blue	L 87 (13) pearl white	L 518 (20) java green
Upholstery combination (cloth)	58 mosaic platinum	59 mosaic teak	58 mosaic platinum
Upholstery combination (cloth optional Model 151)			
Upholstery combination (leatherette)	74 platinum	75 pigalle	77 Balaeric beige
Upholstery combination (leatherette optional Model 151)		76 black	74 platinum
Upholstery combination (leatherette optional Model 151)			76 black
Rim (Model 113, 114)	L 289 blue-white	L 87 pearl white	L 87 pearl white

Car finish	L 519 (21) bahama blue	L 568 (37) sea sand	Remarks:*) for fontana grey and sea sand combination 59 up to
Upholstery combination (cloth)	60 mosaic amazon	59 mosaic teak*)	
Upholstery combination (cloth optional Model 151)	Chassis No. 116 232 890	58 mosaic platinum .	combination 58 from Chassis No. 116 232 891 combination 58 from
Upholstery combination (leatherette)	76 black	76 black	
Upholstery combination (leatherette optional Model 151)			Remark: *) see combination
Upholstery combination (leatherette optional Model 151)			
Rim (Model 113, 114)	L 289 blue-white	L 87 pearl white	

Rim (Model 151, 152), Wheel disc L 41 black, steering column tube, gearshift and hand brake lever LD43 grey-black
*) Covering – Front seat frame SL 43 grey-black – 58, 60, 74, 76; 672 rust – 59; SL 652 scarlet – 75; SL 662 almond beige – 77

Model 113, 114, 151, 152

August 1966 up to July 1967, from Chassis No. 117 000 001 up to 117 999 000

Car finish	L 620 (02) savanna beige	L 639 (08) zenith blue	L 595 (09) fontana grey
Upholstery combination (cloth) (Model 113, 114)	59 mosaic teak	69 water blue	69 water blue
Upholstery combination (leatherette)	87 gazelle	88 black	88 black
Upholstery combination (leatherette)	88 black		89 indian red
Rim (Model 113, 114)	L 282 lotus white	L 680 cumulus white	L 680 cumulus white
Car finish	L 41 (10) black	L 456 (11) ruby red	L 633 (14) VW blue
Upholstery combination (cloth) Model 113, 114)	64 platinum pattern	64 platinum pattern	65 platinum pattern
Upholstery combination (leatherette)	89 indian red	86 platinum	86 platinum
Upholstery combination (leatherette)	86 platinum	88 black	
Upholstery combination (leatherette)	87 gazelle		
Rim (Model 113, 114)	L 282 lotus white	L 282 lotus white	L 680 cumulus white
Car finish	L 518 (20) java green	L282 (42) lotus white	
Upholstery combination (cloth) Model 113, 114)	64 platinum pattern	61 gazelle pattern	Rremark: *) see combination
Upholstery combination (leatherette)	86 platinum	88 black	
Upholstery combination (leatherette)	87 gazelle	89 indian red	
Upholstery combination (leatherette)		87 gazelle	
Rim (Model 113, 114)	L 282 lotus white	L 282 lotus white	

Rim (Model 151, 152), Wheel disc, steering column tube, gearshift and hand brake lever LD 43 grey-black
*) Covering – Front seat frame SL 43 grey-black – 59, 64, 86, 89; SL 770 moro brown – 61, 87; SL 742 clematic – 69

August 1967 up to July 1968, from Chassis No. 118 000 001 up to 118 1016 000

Car finish	L 30A (17) royal red	L 41 (10) black	L 70 F (19) chinchilla
Upholstery combination (cloth) (Model 113, 114)	09 platinum pattern	09 platinum pattern	06 red pattern 68
Upholstery combination (leatherette)	38 platinum	41 Indian red 68	40 black 68
Upholstery combination (leatherette)	40 black 68	30 platinum	41 indian red 68
Upholstery combination (leatherette)		39 gazelle 68	
Rim (Model 113, 114)	L 282 lotus white	L 282 lotus white	L 680 cumulus white
Car finish	282 (42) lotus white	L 610 (22) Delta green	L 620 (02) savanna beige
Upholstery combination (cloth) (Model 113, 114)	06 red pattern 68	09 platinum pattern	06 red pattern 68

Upholstery combination (leatherette)	40 black 68	38 platinum	39 gazelle 68
Upholstery combination (leatherette)	39 gazelle 68	39 gazelle 68	40 black 68
Upholstery combination (leatherette)	41 indian red 68		
Rim (Model 113, 114)	L 282 lotus white	L 282 lotus white	L 282 lotus white
Car finish	633 (14) VW blue	L 639 (08) zenith blue	
Upholstery combination (cloth) (Model 113, 114)	09 platinum pattern	07 blue pattern 68	
Upholstery combination (leatherette)	38 platinum	40 black 68	
Upholstery combination (leatherette)			
Upholstery combination (leatherette)			
Rim (Model 113, 114)	L 680 cumulus white	L 680 cumulus white	

Rim (Model 151, 152), Wheel disc, steering column tube, gearshift and hand brake lever LD 43 grey-black;
Covering – Front seat frame SL 43 grey-black

Model 113, 114, 151, 152

August 1968 up to July 1969, from Chassis No. 119 000 001 up to 119 1200 000

Car finish	L 30 A (17) royal red	L 50 B (48) diamond blue	L 60 B (28) Peru green
Upholstery combination (cloth)	19 platinum pattern 69	21 blue pattern 69	19 platinum pattern 69
Upholstery combination (leatherette)	40 black 68	40 black 68	46 cream white 69
Upholstery combination (leatherette)	46 cream white 69		48 nut brown 69
Car finish	L 70 F (19) chinchilla	L90 C (63) toga white	L 620 (02) savanna beige
Upholstery combination (cloth)	20 red pattern 69	20 red pattern 69	20 red pattern 69
Upholstery combination (leatherette)	40 black 68	40 black 68	40 black 68
Upholstery combination (leatherette)	47 gala red 69	47 gala red 69	48 nut brown 69
Car finish	L 630 (07) cobalt blue	L 41 (10) black	
Upholstery combination (cloth)	19 platinum pattern 69	19 platinum pattern 69	
Upholstery combination (leatherette)	46 cream white 69	46 cream white 69	
Upholstery combination (leatherette)	47 gala red 69	47 gala red 69	

only for Models 151, 152

Car finish	L 19 K (35) Yukon yellow	L 54 (33) poppy red	
Upholstery combination (cloth)			
Upholstery combination (leatherette)	40 black 68	40 black 68	
Upholstery combination (leatherette)			

Wheel disc, gearshift and hand brake lever, steering column tube, seat frame LD 43 grey-black;
Rim L 581 cloud white Model 113, 114; LD 43 grey-black Model 151, 152;
Covering – Front seat frame SL 43 grey-black

August 1969 up to July 1970, from Chassis No. 110 2000 001 up to 110 3100 000

Car finish	L 620 (02) savanna beige	L 90 (06) pastel white	L 630 (07) cobalt blue
Upholstery combination (cloth)	20 red pattern 69	20 red pattern 69	19 platinum pattern 69
Upholstery combination (leatherette)	40 black 68	40 black 68	46 cream white 69
Upholstery combination (leatherette)	48 nut brown 69	47 gala red 69	47 gala red 69
Upholstery combination (leatherette)			
Car finish	L 30 A (17) royal red	L 60 D (09) elm green	L 41 (10) black
Upholstery combination (cloth)	19 platinum pattern 69	19 platinum pattern 69	19 platinum pattern 69
Upholstery combination (leatherette)	40 black 68	40 black 68	46 cream white 69
Upholstery combination (leatherette)	48 cream white 69	46 cream white 69	47 gala red 69
Upholstery combination (leatherette)		48 nut brown 69	

Car finish	L 20 D (12) clementine	L 70 F (19) chinchilla	L 50 B (48) diamond blue
Upholstery combination (cloth)	19 platinum pattern 69	20 red pattern 69	21 blue pattern 69
Upholstery combination (leatherette)	40 black 68	40 black 68	40 black 68
Upholstery combination (leatherette)	48 cream white 69	47 gala red 69	
Upholstery combination (leatherette)			

only for Models 151, 152

Car finish	L 19 K (35) Yukon yellow	L 54 (33) poppy red	L 66 B (60) deep sea green
Upholstery combination (cloth)			19 platinum pattern 69
Upholstery combination (leatherette)	40 black 68	40 black 68	46 cream white 69
Upholstery combination (leatherette)			48 nut brown 69
Upholstery combination (leatherette)			

Wheel disc, rim L 91 chrome colored; gearshift and hand brake lever, steering column tube, seat frame LD 43 grey-black;
Covering – Front seat frame SL 43 grey-black

Model 113, 114

August 1970 up to July 1971, from Chassis No. 111 2000 001 up to 111 3200 000

Car finish	L 50 D (01) sapphire blue	L 90 D (06) pastel white	L 60 (D) elm green
Upholstery combination (cloth)	17 dogtooth grey 71/ alabaster 71	08 dogtooth grey 71/ black 68	08 dogtooth grey 71/ black 68
Upholstery combination (cloth)	18 dogtooth red 71	16 dogtooth blue 71	17 dogtooth grey 71/ alabaster 71
Upholstery combination (cloth)		17 dogtooth grey 71/ alabaster 71	22 dogtooth cork 71
Upholstery combination (cloth)		18 dogtooth red 71	
Upholstery combination (cloth)		22 dogtooth cork 71	
Upholstery combination (leatherette)	47 gala red 69	40 black 68	40 black 68
Upholstery combination (leatherette)	52 alabaster 71	47 gala red 69	52 alabaster 71
Upholstery combination (leatherette)		52 alabaster 71	53 cork 71
Upholstery combination (leatherette)		53 cork 71	

Car finish	L 41 (10) black	L 20 D (12) clementine	L 31 F (28) iberian red
Upholstery combination (cloth)	17 dogtooth grey 71/ alabaster 71	08 dogtooth grey 71/ black 68	08 dogtooth grey 71/ black 68
Upholstery combination (cloth)	18 dogtooth red 71	16 dogtooth grey 71 alabaster 71	17 dogtooth grey 71 alabaster 71
Upholstery combination (cloth)		22 dogtooth cork 71	22 dogtooth cork 71
Upholstery combination (leatherette)	52 alabaster 71	40 black 68	40 black 68
Upholstery combination (leatherette)		52 alabaster 71	52 alabaster 71
Upholstery combination (leatherette)		53 cork 71	53 cork 71

Car finish	L 54 D (21) marine blue	L 68 B (60) deep sea green	L 12 D (64) shantung yellow
Upholstery combination (cloth)	08 dogtooth grey 71/ black 68	22 dogtooth cork 71	08 dogtooth grey 71/ black 68
Upholstery combination (cloth)	18 dogtooth blue 71		22 dogtooth cork 71
Upholstery combination (cloth)	17 dogtooth grey 71 alabaster 71		
Upholstery combination (leatherette)	40 black 68	52 alabaster 71	40 black 68
Upholstery combination (leatherette)	52 alabaster 71	53 cork 71	53 cork 71

Car finish	L 91 (65) kansas beige	L 96 D (80) silver metallic	L 97 D (81) colarado metallic
Upholstery combination (cloth)	08 dogtooth grey 71/ black 68	08 dogtooth grey 71/ black 68	08 dogtooth grey 71/ black 68
Upholstery combination (cloth)	18 dogtooth red 71	16 dogtooth blue 71	17 dogtooth grey 71 alabaster 71

Upholstery combination (cloth)	22 dogtooth cork 71/ alabaster 71	17 dogtooth grey 71/	
Upholstery combination (leatherette)	40 black 68	40 black 68	40 black 68
Upholstery combination (leatherette)	47 gala red 69	47 gala red 69	52 alabaster 71
Upholstery combination (leatherette)	53 cork 71		
Car finish	L 96 E (86) gemini metallic		
Upholstery combination (cloth)	08 dogtooth grey 71/ black 68		
Upholstery combination (cloth)	17 dogtooth grey 71/ alabaster 71		
Upholstery combination (leatherette)	40 black 68		
Upholstery combination (leatherette)	52 alabaster 71		

Wheel disc, rim L 91 chrome colored; gearshift and hand brake lever, steering column tube and seat frame LD 43 grey-black;
Covering – Front seat frame SL 43 grey-black

Model 113, 114

August 1971 up to July 1972, from Chassis No. 112 2000 001 up to 112 3200 000

Car finish	L 90 D (06) pastel white	L 96 D (80) silver metallic	L 96 E (86) gemini metallic
Upholstery combination (cloth)	03 alabaster	05 lapis blue	03 alabaster
Upholstery combination (cloth)	05 lapis blue	10 Bordeaux red	05 lapis blue
Upholstery combination (cloth)	10 Bordeaux red	37 black	37 black
Upholstery combination (cloth)	37 black	38 leather beige	38 leather beige
Upholstery combination (cloth)	38 leather beige		
Upholstery combination (leatherette)	50 black	50 black	50 black
Upholstery combination (leatherette)	52 alabaster	55 leather beige	52 alabaster
Upholstery combination (leatherette)	55 leather beige	56 lapis blue	55 leather beige
Upholstery combination (leatherette)	56 lapis blue	57 Bordeaux red	56 lapis blue
Upholstery combination (leatherette)	57 Bordeaux red		
Car finish	L 10 B (08) texas yellow	L 20 B (07) brilliant orange	L 30 B (02) kasan red
Upholstery combination (cloth)	05 lapis blue	03 alabaster	03 alabaster
Upholstery combination (cloth)	37 black	37 black	37 black
Upholstery combination (cloth)	38 leather beige	38 leather beige	38 leather beige
Upholstery combination (leatherette)	50 black	50 black	50 black
Upholstery combination (leatherette)	55 leather beige	52 alabaster	52 alabaster
Upholstery combination (leatherette)	56 lapis blue	55 leather beige	55 leather beige
Car finish	L 41 (10) black	L 51 B (18) gentian blue	L 54 D (21) marina blue
Upholstery combination (cloth)	03 alabaster	03 alabaster	03 alabaster
Upholstery combination (cloth)	10 Bordeux red	37 black	05 lapis blue
Upholstery combination (cloth)	38 leather beige	38 leather beige	37 black
Upholstery combination (leatherette)	52 alabaster	50 black	50 black
Upholstery combination (leatherette)	55 leather beige	52 alabaster	52 alabaster
Upholstery combination (leatherette)	57 Bordeaux red	55 leather beige	56 lapis blue
Car finish	L 61 B (17) sumatra green	L 91 D (65) Kansas beige	L 95 B (82) turquoise metallic
Upholstery combination (cloth)	03 alabaster	10 Bordeaux red	03 alabaster
Upholstery combination (cloth)	37 black	37 black	37 black
Upholstery combination (cloth)	38 leather beige	38 leather beige	38 leather beige
Upholstery combination (leatherette)	50 black	50 black	50 black
Upholstery combination (leatherette)	52 alabaster	55 leather beige	52 alabaster
Upholstery combination (leatherette)	55 leather beige	57 Bordeaux red	55 leather beige

Car finish	L 97 D (81) colorado metallic		
Upholstery combination (cloth)	03 alabaster		
Upholstery combination (cloth)	37 black		
Upholstery combination (cloth)	38 leather beige		
Upholstery combination (leatherette)	50 black		
Upholstery combination (leatherette)	52 alabaster		
Upholstery combination (leatherette)	55 leather beige		

Wheel disc, rim L 91 chrome colored; gearshift and hand brake lever, steering column tube and seat frame LD 43 grey-black;
Covering – Front seat frame SL 43 grey-black

Model 113, 114

August 1972, from Chassis No. 113 2000 001

Car finish	L 30 B (02) kasan red	L 20 B (07) brilliant orange	L 10 B (08) texas yellow
Upholstery combination (cloth)	26 silver grey	26 silver grey	05 lapis blue
Upholstery combination (cloth)	37 black	37 black	37 black
Upholstery combination (cloth)	38 leather beige	38 leather beige	38 leather beige
Upholstery combination (leatherette)	50 black	50 black	50 black
Upholstery combination (leatherette)	55 leather beige	55 leather beige	55 leather beige
Upholstery combination (leatherette)	63 silver grey	63 silver grey	56 lapis blue
Car finish	L 41 (10) black	L 61 B (17) sumatra green	L 54 D (21) marina blue
Upholstery combination (cloth)	10 bordeaux red	26 silver grey	05 lapis blue
Upholstery combination (cloth)	26 silver grey	37 black	26 silver grey
Upholstery combination (cloth)	38 leather beige	38 leather beige	37 black
Upholstery combination (leatherette)	55 leather beige	50 black	50 black
Upholstery combination (leatherette)	57 bordeaux red	55 leather beige	56 lapis blue
Upholstery combination (leatherette)	63 silver grey	63 silver grey	63 silver grey
Car finish	L 52 B (29) Biscay blue	L 91 D (65) kansas beige	L 96 A (71) Maya metallic
Upholstery combination (cloth)	26 silver grey	10 bordeaux red	05 lapis blue
Upholstery combination (cloth)	37 black	37 black	37 black
Upholstery combination (cloth)	38 leather beige	38 leather beige	38 leather beige
Upholstery combination (leatherette)	50 black	50 black	50 black
Upholstery combination (leatherette)	55 leather beige	55 leather beige	55 leather beige
Upholstery combination (leatherette)	63 silver grey	57 bordeaux red	56 lapis blue
Car finish	L 96 B (78) Alaska metallic	L 95 B (82) turquoise metallic	L 96 M (89) Marathon metallic
Upholstery combination (cloth)	26 silver grey	26 silver grey	05 lapis blue
Upholstery combination (cloth)	37 black	37 black	37 black
Upholstery combination (cloth)	38 leather beige	38 leather beige	38 leather beige
Upholstery combination (leatherette)	50 black	50 black	50 black
Upholstery combination (leatherette)	55 leather beige	55 leather beige	55 leather beige
Upholstery combination (leatherette)	63 silver grey	63 silver grey	56 lapis blue
Car finish	L 90 B (06) pastel white		
Upholstery combination (cloth)	05 lapis blue		
Upholstery combination (cloth)	10 bordeaux red		
Upholstery combination (cloth)	26 silver grey		
Upholstery combination (cloth)	37 black		
Upholstery combination (cloth)	38 leather beige		
Upholstery combination (leatherette)	50 black		

Upholstery combination (leatherette)	55 leather beige
Upholstery combination (leatherette)	56 lapis blue
Upholstery combination (leatherette)	57 bordeaux red
Upholstery combination (leatherette)	63 silver grey

Wheel disc, rim L 91 chrome colored; gearshift and hand brake lever LD 43; seat frame L 41 black

Additional Lacquer Numbers

1971 model year
Lacquer No
12D	Shantung Yellow
20D	Clementine (Red)
31F	Iberian Red
41	Black
50D	Sapphire Blue
54D	Marina Blue
60D	Elm Green
66B	Deep Sea Green
90D	Pastel White
91D	Kansas Beige
96D	Silver Metallic
96E	Gemini Metallic
97D	Colorado Metallic (Red)

1972 model year
Lacquer No
10B	Texas Yellow
20B	Brilliant Orange
30B	Kasan Red
41	Black
51B	Gentian Blue
54D	Marina Blue
61B	Sumatra Green
90D	Pastel White
91D	Kansas Beige
95B	Turquoise Metallic
96D	Silver Metallic
96E	Gemini Metallic
97D	Colorado Metallic (Red)

1973 model year
Lacquer No
10B	Texas Yellow
20B	Brilliant Orange
30B	Kasan Red
41	Black
52B	Biscay Blue
54D	Marina Blue
61B	Sumatra Green
90D	Pastel White
91D	Kansas Beige
95B	Turquoise Metallic
96B	Alaska Metallic (Blue)
96M	Marathon Metallic (Blue)
98A	Maya Metallic (Brown)

10B	Texas Yellow
21E	Tangerine
65K	Ravenna Green

1974 model year
Lacquer No
91Z	Atlas White
54D	Marina Blue
20B	Brilliant Orange
31A	Senegal Red
60A	Tropical Green
80Z	Sahara Beige
10A	Rally Yellow
61A	Cliff Green
41	Black
96M	Marathon Metallic (Blue)
96B	Alaska Metallic (Blue)
95C	Moss Metallic (Green)
98C	Hellas Metallic (Beige)

1974 model year (special campaign models)
Lacquer No
16M	Tunis Yellow
20A	Marino Yellow
32K	Phoenix Red
11C	Brilliant Yellow
61H	Lofoten Green
20A	Marino Yellow
32K	Phoenix Red
27N	Mandarin
32K	Phoenix Red
65K	Ravenna Green

1975 model year
Lacquer No
91Z	Atlas White
20A	Marino Yellow
13H	Ceylon Beige
51C	Miami Blue
61H	Lofoten Green
31A	Senegal Red
41	Black
10A	Rally Yellow
61A	Cliff Green
32K	Phoenix Red
96M	Marathon Metallic (Blue)
97B	Ancona Metallic (Blue)
98C	Hellas Metallic (Beige)
98B	Viper Green Metallic
28N	Orange

1976 model year
Lacquer No
91Z	Atlas White
20A	Marino Yellow
61H	Lofoten Green
57H	Ozeunic Blue
31A	Senegal Red
41	Black
10A	Rally Yellow
32K	Phoenix Red
97A	Diamond Silver Metallic
96N	Viper Green Metallic
99D	Topaz Metallic

1977 model year
Lacquer No
12A	Panama Brown
13A	Dakota Beige
32A	Brocade Red
04L	Black
51C	Miami Blue
63Y	Mantla Green
90A	Polar White
11A	Riyad Yellow
31B	Mars Red
62A	Bali Green
95D	Bronze Metallic
96N	Viper Green Metallic
97A	Diamond Silver Metallic
97P	Timor Brown Metallic
99F	Bahama Blue Metallic

1978 model year
Lacquer No
E9	Panama Brown
D5	Dakota Beige
A5	Malaga Red
A1	Black
K2	Miami Blue
M4	Manilla Green
P1	Alpine White
B4	Riyad Yellow
E6	Mars Red
M5	Bali Green
X4	Bronze Metallic
Y5	Viper Green Metallic
Z4	Diamond Silver Metallic
Y3	Bahama Blue Metallic
Z7	Colibri Green Metallic

⑥ Clubs and Specialists

Clubs

There are a large number of clubs catering specially for VW owners, most of them representing either a local area or a specific section of interest within the Volkswagen family of vehicles.

The national club, founded in 1953, is the Volkswagen Owners' Club of Great Britain, which operates via a central committee but has regional centres to which members may be affiliated. Apart from local and national events, the VWOC(GB) offers members a discounts scheme, 'mutual aid' service, and RAC affiliation (with its attendant advantages of insurance cover for competitive events).

Most of the general VW clubs are locally based and have been founded more on the special appeal of the Beetle or Transporter than on anything else. Beetles still figure strongly in club events and memberships, and owners of the model will therefore find themselves especially welcome if they turn up at a local club meeting. A full list of the many owners' clubs currently in existence, with contacts, is published most months in VW Motoring magazine.

Please send a stamped, return envelope (or International Reply Coupon for overseas) when writing to any club.

British Clubs

The Volkswagen Owners Club of Great Britain

This club was formed in 1953 by a group of VW enthusiasts in the London area and is now Britain's longest surviving and foremost VW Club. Since then, the club has aimed to provide opportunities for VW enthusiasts to meet at social functions, to enter competitions and to take advantage of the many other benefits of membership such as discounts, mutual aid and technical information.

VWOC(GB) is registered with the RAC Motor Sports Association for the promotion of motor sport and it is also a member of the Combined One Make Car Club which is an association of one make car clubs.

Apart from publishing its own quarterly club magazine and competition calender, VWOC(GB) has, since 1968, developed Centres around the country and currently these are flourishing in the West Midlands, Staffordshire, Scotland, Bedfordshire, Hertfordshire, Oxfordshire, Surrey and, of course, London and the Thames Valley.

The last-named Centre has recently made its mark by organising trips to Germany to see over the VW plants there and last October it embarked on a very successful and ambitious venture to Mexico for 14 days, during which it was a guest of VW de Mexico.

VWOC(GB) founded in 1976 an event called VW Action, which is now the largest gathering of enthusiasts of any one make of car in the world. This event is now held at the Royal Showground at Stoneleigh with the help of other VW Owners Clubs and a VW magazine. It also runs an event called Bug-In G.B. every year at the Three Counties Showground at Malvern, Worcs which takes place in July. London Centre too, runs an event for enthusiasts in southern England at Stonor Park, Henley, at the end of June.

Although the Club has centres, it follows that there are members living around the country who are too far away from any such organisation and for this reason, VWOC(GB) has two types of membership — Centre and non Centre. Both types of membership carry the same benefits.

Please send for further details to VWOC(GB), Dept N, 78, Benson Close, Luton, Beds. LU3 3QP.

Split Screen Van Club

Founded in 1983 by a small group of enthusiasts, the SSVC now has over 280 members nationwide. Although our growth has been rapid we are still a friendly club and anyone owning or interested in these vans is welcome. Members range from concours to

custom, restoration project to runabout and family camper.

We meet socially throughout the season (March to October) at our own club camping weekends up and down the country so there should be one at a convenient location for most members, as well as having a club stand and camping area at most major VW meets. We have our own 'Van of the Year' competition judged by members at our AGM and from 1986 will also be having an annual prize for the best restored van. Details of all club activities are contained in our bi-monthly magazine 'Split Screen News' along with technical advice, sales and wants and entertaining articles for the less mechanically minded. We are keen to see as many splits as possible kept on the road and members' mechanical problems can usually be solved through mutual aid. A lot of effort is made to track down elusive spares. (We are currently investigating the possibility of bulk buying king pins.) Finally, to show you are proud to belong, there is a wide range of club regalia — T-shirts, sweat shirts, badges, stickers and even tea towels!

We hope we are a club with something to offer everyone. Some words from a song by our own bard, George Thorman, sums it up:

We've info and rallies, good friendship and spares,

So come on and join us, the van club that cares.

For membership details contact Membership Secretary: Mike and Sue Mundy, 142, Junction Road, Burgess Hill, W. Sussex RH15 0PZ. Tel: 04446 41407.

General enquiries contact Secretary: Peter and Sheila Nicholson, 125, St. Albans Road, Lytham St. Annes, Lancs. FY8 1UZ. Tel: 0253 720927.

The VW Cabriolet Owners Club G.B.

This Club was founded in late 1978 by a handful of Cabriolet owners. At the time Cabriolets were rare in the U.K. to the extent that it took several years before membership reached 150. However, many Cabriolets have been imported since the early 1980's and present membership if nearly 320. For a small membership fee, one is entitled to a thick quarterly newsletter, dispensing anecdotes as well as useful advice. The Club has many contacts with Continental Cabrio Clubs which lead to interesting trips abroad to meet other Cabrio enthusiasts. At present, the Club is the only source of some no-longer-available parts. Still, it is hoped that saving money is not the only criterion for joining the Cabrio Club.

For more information please contact the secretariat: M & W Ritchie, 58, Bronwydd, Larksbrook, Birchgrove, Swansea SA7 9QJ.

Volkswagen Owners Caravan Club (G.B.)

This is the only Camping Club for Volkswagens, whether it be a Motorcaravan, Car and a Caravan or a car and a tent. It is a family Club and we hold weekend Rallies every weekend from March to December. The Rallies are held all over England with a holiday rally arranged to meet members requirements. Ferry crossings and insurance discounts are available to Club members.

We are a very friendly Club and members of all ages are welcomed. A newsletter is published every two to three months, with helpful hints, articles for sale, childrens page, rally reports, etc. The annual subscription is only £5.00. Application forms may be obtained from the Secretary — Mrs. Susan Songhurst, 41, David Avenue, Greenford, Middlesex UB6 8HG.

Historic Volkswagen Club:

Secretary (general enquiries) M K Johnson, 50, The Lane, Hauxton, Cambs. CB2 5HP. Membership Secretary S Parkinson, 15, Linnet Close, Bournville, Birmingham B30 1XB.

Mexican/Brazilian Beetle Register: Howard Cheese, Hoopits Greete, Ludlow, Shropshire or Johannes Feigl, 12, Rogers Walk, Woodside Park, London N12 7DA.

VW Hubmuller Registry: for owners of the two-seat Beetle convertible Type 14a. Details from Bob Shaill. (see below)

VW Split Window Club: for all owners and enthusiasts of Volkswagen Beetles 1938 —August 1960. Details from Bob Shaill, Hastings. Tel: 0424 52417.

VWOC of Northern Ireland: a club for every type of Volkswagen. Why not join a rapidly expanding club with members throughout N. Ireland. Technical help/advice, financial savings, plus regular meetings. Tel: Artie on 0232 772995 or Ronnie on 0232 611516.

Irish Club

VWOC of Ireland: hold monthly meetings and outings. All welcome — Contact David Moran, St Gerards, 32, Glasnamara Road, Glasnevin, Dublin 11, Ireland. Phone 01-342082.

United States Clubs

The Volkswagen Club of America: Produces a magazine known as 'The Autoist'. P.O. Box 963, Plainfield, New Jersey 07061 or P.O. Box 154, N. Aurora, IL 60542.

Vintage Volkswagen Club of America:
Eastern Region: Terry Shuler, 817, 5th Street, Cresson, Pennsylvania 16630.
Western Region: Michael Aceves, 323 1/2, Richmond Street, El Segundo, CA 90245.

Safari (Type 181) Club: Bob Hall, P.O. Box 1341, Morgan Hill, CA 95037.

Society of Transporter Owners: (Western Representative) Jeff

Walters, P.O. Box 17234, Irvine, CA 92713.

National Volkswagen Association: P.O. Box 2291, Irwindale, CA 91706.

Volkswagen Convertible Owners of America: P.O. Box 5848, Orange, CA 92667.

Split Window Club of America: 1675 Magnolia Blvd, W. Seattle, WA 98199.

Hebmuller Registry: 13279 Deron Ave., San Diego, CA 92129.

Rometsch Registry: 2510 N. Larchmont, Santa Ana, CA 92706.

Magazines

VW Motoring Readers of this book who are newcomers to the world of Volkswagen will be well advised to make the acquaintance of VW Motoring, the monthly magazine devoted to Volkswagen and its associated marque Audi.

Totally independent of the Volkswagen organisation, but enjoying close co-operation with it, the magazine was first launched (as Safer Motoring) in 1961, and for 25 years has kept owners and enthusiasts (the two quickly become synonymous!) in the know about the whole VW scene.

A typical 72-page issue includes a news round-up, road test, readers' technical problems answered, D-I-Y and/or tuning advice, special features, several pages of readers' letters, and a veritable goldmine of classified ads. Then there are the specialist trade advertisers, offering everything that's needed to keep your VW in good shape — and at sensible prices. The magazine even has its own insurance service for readers' cars.

VW Motoring is available nationally through WH Smith, Menzies and most main newsagents, while postal

subscription details can be obtained direct from the publishers at P.O. Box 4, Cirencester, Glos. GL7 1YQ, England.

Volkswagen/Audi Car Magazine Autometrix Publications, 28, High Street, Toddington, Dunstable, Beds., England.

VW Trends Magazine P.O. Box 2509, Santa Ana, CA 92707, USA.

Volkswagen & Porsche Magazine Argus Books, P.O. Box 49659, 12301 Wilshire Boulevard, Los Angeles, CA 90049, USA.

Dune Buggies & Hot VWs Magazine P.O. Box 2260, Costa Mesa, CA 92628, USA.

Specialists

House of Haselock. ('The independent company with a world-wide reputation'.) Without the help of proprietor Barry Haselock this book could never have been produced and House of Haselock appear in word or picture on just about every page for one simple reason — virtually all of the work featured here was carried out in the workshops.

Without a shred of doubt, they're the best independent supplier the author has come across and for depth of knowledge and experience and for helpful, friendly service from 'Baz' Haselock in person, they're the best. Haselocks' specialise in full restorations of both Beetles and Campers/Transporters (they'll collect vehicles from any part of the UK), they supply parts galore (detailed in their catalogue) and have long specialised in engine rebuilds. Contact House of Haselock at Slingsby Close, Attleborough Fields Industrial Estate, Nuneaton, Warwickshire, CV11 6RP, England. Tel: Nuneaton (0203) 328343.

Bugs for You, 'The Volkswagen Store'. Run by an extremely knowledgeable guy by the name of Rich Kimball, Bugs for You specialises in the supply of very high standard parts for older Bugs, detailed through this book and in high-class restorations. Rich writes articles on older Bugs for specialist journals, knows an enormous amount about older Bugs, and can supply just about everything you may need through his excellent mail order service. The Bugs for You catalogue details the excellent range of parts that Rich Kimball has available for these cars. Contact him at Bugs for You, 1460 N. Glassell, Orange, California 92667, USA.

There are of course independent Volkswagen specialists all over the place; some bad, some excellent and some indifferent. The author has no personal experience of any of them and so is unable to recommend them specifically here. If you wish to use your local specialist, try to find out what the company is like by talking to others who have used their service.

Volkswagen Inc. (in the United States) **Audi/Volkswagen** (in Great Britain) Volkswagen whose British importers V.A.G.(U.K.) Ltd have been enormously helpful in the production of this book, have a commendable degree of commitment to the Beetle and the air-cooled Transporter and many Audi/Volkswagen parts have been used on the vehicles shown under restoration at Haselock's.

In an age when major manufacturers shrug off their responsibilities towards models than just a few years old, Volkswagen still care! Volkswagen or Audi/Volkswagen dealerships still carry an excellent range of parts for the air-cooled vehicles although the first to dry up are always interior trim panels and sundry clips and small fittings, it seems. Volkswagen parts are

almost invariably more expensive than 'independent' parts but if you're not sure of the quality of your supplier, you know you can depend on the quality of your Volkswagen-made parts! Volkswagen (in the USA) and Audi/Volkswagen (in the UK) dealers can be found in all areas — consult your local traders directory.

Uro Autospares Ltd have also been tremendously helpful with the production of this book and many of their parts were used in the restoration of vehicles shown undergoing work at Haselock's. They boast the largest non-Volkswagen supply of Beetle and Transporter parts at very keen prices in the UK, carrying over 4,000 product lines. Their head office is at Unit 21, The Fort Industrial Park, Dunlop Way, Birmingham B35 7AR. Tel: 021-749 4700. There are also a number of agents for Uro parts (including Haselock) all around the country and a number of others selling Uro parts.

Cyclone Wheels manufacture very high quality chrome VW wheels based on original Californian designs. The author uses them on his Cabriolet. Contact Norman Head at 19-27, Railway Street, Braintree, Essex CM7 6JF. Tel: 0376 41853/41878.

Pirelli Ltd. produce the tyres currently most strongly recommended by the author for a combination of 'grip' and long-lasting qualities on a Beetle or Transporter. There are Pirelli tyres in everyday types, heavy-duty types for hard working Transporters with loads to carry and high performance, low-profile types, considered by many to be the best in the world. 'Pirellibility', they call it! Pirelli tyres are available from leading tyre sales dealers. Contact them at Derby Road, Burton-on-Trent, Staffs. in England.

UVA (The Unique Vehicle & Accessory Company Ltd.) stock a huge range of tuning and Beetle kit-car goodies, both from UK and US suppliers. Their knowledge of Beetle tuning, whether to improve handling, braking, performance and economy for road use, or taking a car to the ultimate VW engine or Rover/Buick V8 engine off-road spec. must be second to none. Argent's Mere High Technology Park, Hambridge Lane, Newbury, Berkshire RG14 5TU. Tel: 0635 33888.

Stadium Ltd. produce a wide range of car accessories including the superb Sparkrite car alarms, which are particularly recommended for restored or highly regarded cars because not only do they work extremely well, they can also be fitted without the need to drill holes in the bodywork, the alarm being activated by infra-red control. They also make high-quality electronic ignition systems which seem to suit the Beetle well. 82, Bath Street, Walsall, West Midlands, WS1 3DE. Products on sale in most motor accessory stores.

Mill Accessory Group Ltd. headed by one time leading rally driver Paddy Hopkirk market a range of accessory products including an impressive sound-deadening kit which is particularly effective for the Beetle. Again, they sell through accessory stores or contact them at Two Counties Mill, Eaton Bray, Beds. LU6 2JH. Tel: 0525 220671.

Kamei (and in the UK) **Kamei UK and Scotford Ltd**. Of all the accessory manufacturers anywhere in the world, Kamei have the longest established relationship with Volkswagen cars, having first marketed a Beetle front air dam or 'spoiler' in 1952! Nowadays, the range of these very high quality, largely German-built products is very large indeed. Kamei UK/Scotford Ltd can be found at Marriage Hill, Bidford-on-Avon, Warwickshire, England B50 4EP.

SIP (Industrial Products) Ltd. manufacture an impressive range of quality workshop equipment: MIG welders, spot and arc welders, spray guns and compressors in all shapes and sizes. Keen prices and highly recommended! SIP (Industrial Products) Ltd, Gelders Hall Road, Shepshed, Loughborough, Leics. LE12 9NH, England. Tel: 0509 503141 — ten lines.

Murex Welding Products Ltd. Manufacturers of Porta-Pack portable but professional quality welding kits. Used in combination with BOC mini-bottles and obtainable for private use. Regional sales office, P.O. Box 32, Oxford Street, Bilston, West Midlands WV14 7EQ, England. Tel: 0902 404811.

Clarkson Puckle West Midlands Ltd. One of the country's leading Lloyds brokers with a history dating back to 1852, Clarksons are the leaders in insurance for 'classic' vehicles, policies being arranged through Royal Insurance. Rates are surprisingly low even with agreed value and other everyday cars can be covered with a package deal. Limited mileage and 'storage only' policies are inexpensive but very thorough in their coverage. Clarkson Puckle West Midlands Ltd., P.O. Box 27, Falcon House, The Minories, Dudley, DY2 8PF. Tel: 0384 211011 — fifteen lines.

British Oxygen Company Ltd. BOC are the UK's largest suppliers of industrial gases. Their branches and depots can be found throughout the country. They now supply smaller cylinders of oxygen and acetylene (suitable for use with the Portapack, for instance) and argon-mix, suitable for use with MIG welders. See local telephone directory for nearest supplier.

Sykes Pickavant Ltd. Full range of excellent quality DIY and professional panel beating tools. See local DIY and accessory shops.

VW Books sell just about every book that has been written about the Beetle and that is still in print. Send a self-addressed, stamped envelope for their full list to 25, Cambridge Road, Cosby, Leicester, England.

ICI Automotive Paints are part of the giant Imperial Chemical Industries group, the people who make Dulux house paint among so very many other things. They make a full range of free product information sheets available at their dealer outlets, so there's no question of how to go about handling their paints. See your local telephone guide for supplier details, looking under 'Motor Factors' in the UK. ICI are suppliers of paint and paint shop products to Volkswagen themselves, by the way.

S.E.V. (UK) Ltd. Cibié Oscar H4 auxiliary lamps with integral dipping arrangement, are the best way to make the most of the Beetle and Transporters' only-just-adequate lighting. Internationally available, the UK address is: Stewkley Road, Soulbury, Leighton Buzzard, Beds. LU7 0EQ. Tel: 052 527 511.

Sandalloy Range Master. German built but internationally available, the Range Master back-up device which warns of out-of-sight obstructions is available in the UK through Sandalloy Ltd., Coventry Road, Narborough, Leicestershire, LE9 5GB, England. Tel: 0533 848199.

Metrinch Tools, socket sets to fit both metric and AF sizes are available on both sides of the Atlantic but in the UK are marketed by Richmond Tools, Titan (UK) Ltd., Hanworth Trading Estate, Hampton Road West, Feltham, Middlesex, TW13 6DH, England. Tel: 01 898 2428.

Cobra Superform manufacture Cobra seats. Find them at Unit D1, Halesfield 23, Telford, Shropshire, TF7 4EW. Tel: 0952 584020.

Comma Oils & Chemicals Ltd. produce the rust-proofing products shown here. Available in all leading auto-stores. Comma Works, Lower Range Road, Gravesend, Kent, DA12 2QX. Tel: 0474 64311.

SATA spraygun equipment. Their rust preventative fluid injector is recommended by Volkswagen. Internationally available through motor trade factors. Marketed through UK by Minden Industrial, Newmarket Road, Bury St. Edmunds, Suffolk, IP33 3TS. Tel: 0284 3418.

Graham Maurice Cars, Accident Repairs and Paint Specialists, East Goscote Industrial Estate, East Goscote, Leicester LE7 8XJ. Tel: 0533 601118.

K & N Filters are proven to boost an engine's efficiency while delivering clean air for longer than a paper element. In the UK and USA through motor accessory stores. K & N Engineering Ltd., 561 Iowa Ave., PO Box 1329, Riverside, CA 92502, USA. Tel: (714) 684-9762. Advanced Products, Wilderspool Causeway, Warrington, Cheshire, WA4 6QP, England. Tel: 0925 36950.

AutoVip cages for tipping a car on its side for easy, superb access to the underside. Autocradle (UK) Ltd., 8 Vicarage Road, Yardley Gobion, Northants, NN12 7UN. Tel: 0908 543218.

Autoprep high class respray to show standard if required. Autoprep, Maylite Trading Estate, Martley, Worcestershire. Tel: Wichenford 358.

7 British
and American Technical Terms

As this book has been written in England, it uses the appropriate English component names, phrases, and spelling. Some of these differ from those used in America. Normally, these cause no difficulty, but to make sure, a glossary is printed below. In ordering spare parts remember the parts list may use some of these words:

English	American	English	American
Accelerator	Gas pedal	Leading shoe (of brake)	Primary shoe
Aerial	Antenna	Locks	Latches
Anti-roll bar	Stabiliser or sway bar	Methylated spirit	Denatured alcohol
Big-end bearing	Rod bearing	Motorway	Freeway, turnpike etc
Bonnet (engine cover)	Hood	Number plate	License plate
Boot (luggage compartment)	Trunk	Paraffin	Kerosene
Bulkhead	Firewall	Petrol	Gasoline (gas)
Bush	Bushing	Petrol tank	Gas tank
Cam follower or tappet	Valve lifter or tappet	'Pinking'	'Pinging'
Carburettor	Carburetor	Prise (force apart)	Pry
Catch	Latch	Propeller shaft	Driveshaft
Choke/venturi	Barrel	Quarterlight	Quarter window
Circlip	Snap-ring	Retread	Recap
Clearance	Lash	Reverse	Back-up
Crownwheel	Ring gear (of differential)	Rocker cover	Valve cover
Damper	Shock absorber, shock	Saloon	Sedan
Disc (brake)	Rotor/disk	Seized	Frozen
Distance piece	Spacer	Sidelight	Parking light
Drop arm	Pitman arm	Silencer	Muffler
Drop head coupe	Convertible	Sill panel (beneath doors)	Rocker panel
Dynamo	Generator (DC)	Small end, little end	Piston pin or wrist pin
Earth (electrical)	Ground	Spanner	Wrench
Engineer's blue	Prussian blue	Split cotter (for valve spring cap)	Lock (for valve spring retainer)
Estate car	Station wagon	Split pin	Cotter pin
Exhaust manifold	Header	Steering arm	Spindle arm
Fault finding/diagnosis	Troubleshooting	Sump	Oil pan
Float chamber	Float bowl	Swarf	Metal chips or debris
Free-play	Lash	Tab washer	Tang or lock
Freewheel	Coast	Tappet	Valve lifter
Gearbox	Transmission	Thrust bearing	Throw-out bearing
Gearchange	Shift	Top gear	High
Grub screw	Setscrew, Allen screw	Trackrod (of steering)	Tie-rod (or connecting rod)
Gudgeon pin	Piston pin or wrist pin	Trailing shoe (of brake)	Secondary shoe
Halfshaft	Axleshaft	Transmission	Whole drive line
Handbrake	Parking brake	Tyre	Tire
Hood	Soft top	Van	Panel wagon/van
Hot spot	Heat riser	Vice	Vise
Indicator	Turn signal	Wheel nut	Lug nut
Interior light	Dome lamp	Windscreen	Windshield
Layshaft (of gearbox)	Countershaft	Wing/mudguard	Fender

Miscellaneous points

An oil seal is fitted to components lubricated by grease!

A 'damper' is a shock absorber, it damps out bouncing and absorbs shocks of bump impact. Both names are correct, and both are used haphazardly.

Note that British drum brakes are different from the Bendix type that is common in America, so different descriptive names result. The shoe end furthest from the hydraulic wheel cylinder is on a pivot, interconnection between the shoes as on Bendix brakes is most uncommon. Therefore the phrase 'Primary' or 'Secondary' shoe does not apply. A shoe is said to be 'Leading' or 'Trailing'. A 'Leading' shoe is one on which a point on the drum, as it rotates forward, reaches the shoe at the end worked by the hydraulic cylinder before the anchor end. The opposite is a 'Trailing' shoe and this one has no self-servo from the wrapping effect of the rotating drum.